Maynooth College ⬛⬛⬛⬛ able
and achievement ⬛⬛⬛⬛ ieve-
ment will be widely cel ⬛⬛⬛⬛ will
see the celebration of N ⬛⬛⬛⬛ d, the
CW01476652
training of priests for I⬛ ⬛⬛⬛⬛ of that
purpose over two centuries, eventually ⬛⬛⬛⬛ cation
of men and women in philosophy and theology, in the sciences, and in
the arts.

To honour in an appropriate way these two hundred years of teaching,
members of the college staff are publishing a series of books in a number of academic disciplines. Edited by members of the College Faculty,
these books will range from texts based on standard theology courses
to interdisciplinary studies with a theological or religious involvement.

The venture is undertaken with pride in the long Maynooth academic
tradition and in modest continuance of it.

Editorial Board:

Patrick Hannon
Ronan Drury
Gerard Watson

For Desmond Connell
in gratitude and respect

Thomas A. F. Kelly

Language, World, and God

An Essay in Ontology

the columba press

First published in 1996 by
the columba press
55A Spruce Avenue, Stillorgan Industrial Park,
Blackrock, Co Dublin

Cover by Bill Bolger
Origination by The Columba Press
Printed in Ireland by Colour Books, Dublin

ISBN 1 85607 181 2

Contents

Foreword   8

1   The Nature and Scope of Ontology   11
    1,1 Ontology   11
    1,2 Metaphysics: Onto-theology and Onto-anthropology   16
    1,3 The Source of Objections to Metaphysics   23
    1,4 ...ἐπιστήμη τις...   27
    1,5 The Design of this Essay   30

2   The Logic of Existence   36
    2,1 Introduction   36
    2,2 The Starting point of the Enquiry   37
    2,3 Scepticism as Starting-point   38
    2,4 Categorial Framework and Reality   40
    2,5 *Esse*, Property and Predicate   53

3   Analogy   60
    3,1 Introduction   60
    3,2 Extrinsic Attribution   61
    3,3 Intrinsic Attribution   63
    3,4 Ontological Applications of Intrinsic Attribution   64
    3,5 Proportion   69
    3,6 Metaphor   79

4   The Structure of Entity   85
    4,1 Introduction   85
    4,2 Entity: Identity and Difference   85
    4,3 Identity and Accident   88
    4,4 Identity and Essence   94

5   Coexistence I: Matter, Form and Telos   105
    5,1 Introduction   105
    5,2 Monism and Pluralism   106
    5,3 Materialism   107
    5,4 The Meanings of 'Material'   110
    5,5 Lot and Whole   111

	5,6 Coexistence	114
	5,7 Material and Formal Causality	116
	5,8 Final Causality	118
	5,9 Determinability: the Essence of Matter as such	119
	5,10 Quantity and Spatiality	121
	5,11 Form and Function	122
	5,12 Form and *esse*	124
6	Coexistence II: Causality	127
	6,1 Introduction	127
	6,2 Hume's Account of Causality	128
	6,3 Knowledge and Knowledge-claims	132
	6,4 Conscientiousness: the Intellectual Virtue	134
	6,5 The Ineluctability of Causal Interaction	136
	6,6 The Nature of Efficient Causality	137
	6,7 Transitive and Reflexive Causality	140
	6,8 Occasionalism and Participation	145
7	Time and Temporality	149
	7,1 Introduction	149
	7,2 Space and Time	150
	7,3 Temporality: Whole and Series	152
	7,4 Actuality, Possibility, and Potentiality	157
	7,5 Coming-to-be and Perishing	160
	7,6 Continuity	163
	7,7 Πάντα ῥεῖ ...	166
	7,8 Real Distinction and Participation	170
8	The Logic of Divinity	174
	8,1 Introduction	174
	8,2 ἔστι γὰρ εἶναι ...	177
	8,3 Creation and Omnipotence	181
	8,4 The Eminence of Divinity	183
	8,5 The Countenance of Divinity	184
	8,6 The Personhood of Divinity	189
	8,7 Personhood and Freedom	192
	8,8 ... a 'little thing' ...	194
	8,9 Univocity and Equivocity	195
	8,10 Language-games and Religious Utterance	199
	8,11 Analogy: the Dialectic of 'Divinity'	203
9	One and Many	211
	9,1 Introduction	211
	9,2 Ontological Unity and *esse*	213
	9,3 Diversity	214
	9,4 World: Unity and Plurality	215
	9,5 Worldhood	217
	9,6 Unity and Participation	222

10   Truth and Untruth   224
     10,1 Introduction   224
     10,2 The Meanings of 'true'   226
     10,3 Truth and Dis-closure   227
     10,4 Transcendence and Finitude   229
     10,5 Heidegger's Delineation of Finitude and Truth   233
     10,6 Transcendence-Finitude in Modern Philosophy   237
     10,7 Transcendence, Freedom, and Truth   238
     10,8 Freedom as Moral   240
     10,9 Value and Community   244
     10,10 Inter-Subjectivity, Community, and Language   247
     10,11 Divinity, Intelligibility, and Human Vocation   252

11   The Good   259
     11,1 Introduction   259
     11,2 The Emergence of the Good from Truth   260
     11,3 Knowing and Loving   261
     11,4 The Dimensions of 'ought'   262
     11,5 The Ineluctability of the Good   267
     11,6 Does Choice Create the Good?   268
     11,7 Culpable Wrongdoing and Tolerance   269
     11,8 Suffering and Sacrifice   271
     11,9 Good Will and Ill-doing   273
     11,10 The Universality of the Good   277
     11,11 *Bonum est diffusivum sui*   281
     11,12 Autonomy and the Vector of Freedom   283
     11,13 Divinity, Participation, and the Good   284

12   Beauty   287
     12,1 Introduction   287
     12,2 Art and Beauty   287
     12,3 Appreciation and Lust   288
     12,4 Will to Power and the Idolatry of Self   292
     12,5 The Ontology of the Artwork   293
     12,6 Beauty and the Real   295
     12,7 Beauty as Manifest Sustaining Presence   297
     12,8 The Icon   298
     12,9 The Three Kinds of Love   301

Bibliography   311

Foreword

This short personal foreword is at once a word of explanation and a word of thanks.

First, the word of explanation. I was invited to contribute this volume to the Maynooth Bicentenary Series by one of the editors, the late Thomas Marsh who was, for sixteen years, Professor of Dogmatic Theology in the Pontifical University at Maynooth. It was and is a great honour and privilege to be asked to add my voice to the scholarly polyphony which this Series represents. The invitation came about like this. Tom and I were sitting together before a meeting of the College Executive Council when Tom asked me if there was something I would like to contribute to the Series which could be prepared for publication relatively quickly. I was then working on a book-length study of Lévinas – which I have since shelved for the nonce – but it seemed that the course in Metaphysics which I give at Maynooth (and elsewhere) would answer. 'Well then, do it,' said Tom. And so I did. I am not sure whether the preparatory period was as short as either of us would have liked, for certain unforeseen circumstances intervened to lengthen it, not the least of which was the unexpected death of my dear friend and Head of Department, Flannan Markham. This was a great personal loss; it also meant a substantial increase in my teaching duties at Maynooth. Moreover, this was the last time I was ever to meet Tom Marsh, for he himself died unexpectedly a few weeks later. He was a man whom I would have liked to know better: a born raconteur, a man of elegant gesture and witty conversation, a kindly man of God; *This sweete preest, this goodly man*, Tom Marsh.

It would, however, be misleading to say that this essay is merely a transcription of my lectures. I have subtitled this work 'an essay in ontology', and I have used the word 'essay' deliberately. If my use of 'essay' echoes the use made of it by the early empiricists, let this be charitably reckoned as my emulation of their dauntless spirit of enquiry, if not of their actual positions or beliefs, and not at all as an attempt at grandiose comparison. This work, then, is my essay, my attempt, to think through the issue of ontology, and to do philosophy. The attempt, with all its flaws and imperfections, for which I am responsible, has grown out of some years' reflection on the matter of thinking, and as essay or attempt, is more a beginning than an end, more something offered for discussion, for elaboration and correction, than a final settling of accounts. But this is the case of all who take the task of thinking seriously: there is only truce in philosophy, never treaty.

I intend this book to be intelligible to anyone who is interested in its content, and not just to the scholar, even though it does presuppose some familiarity with the disciplines of philosophy and of logic. For this reason, I believe that it could act as an introductory text in ontology for undergraduate philosophy courses, although the lecturer would have to assign appropriate readings chosen from the history of philosophy, if full benefit were to be derived from using it. Throughout, this essay has a questioning – rather than a history – orientation. Although I believe it to be necessary and imperative to have an adequate grasp of the history of how thinkers have posed and tried to answer philosophical questions as a starting-point for reflection, of even greater importance are those questions themselves and the unremitting attempt to answer them ever more adequately; of greater importance, certainly, than the necessarily imperfect and more-or-less flawed doctrines and teachings which have been created in response to them.

Having said that, however, I am happy to say that the general orientation and origin of my thinking is Aristotelian-Thomist, though more, perhaps, in spirit than in letter. I believe that, though they are clearly not infallible, much is to be gained in the study of these particular *Maîtres penseurs*. This is why we are beholden to scholars in the Neo-Thomist tradition who, even in hostile climates, have kept alive the spirit of Thomistic thinking, and, more generally, an openness to, and appreciation of, metaphysics and ontology. The work of a Klubertanz or a De Raeymaeker is no mean patrimony.

In speaking of my own philosophical origin, I believe I should acknowledge here my debt to one to whom I owe much, namely, the man to whom this work is dedicated, Desmond Connell. I met him first when, as a shy school-leaver, I made my appearance at his office in University College, Dublin, where he held the Chair of

Metaphysics. I expressed the ambition, perhaps odd in one so young, to become a philosopher, along with the request that he tell me how I should go about it. Not a whit put out by my temerity, and with his characteristic kindness, humanity, and wisdom, he responded. By the time I left his office for the second time that summer, I had made, with his help, decisions which were to shape my subsequent personal and professional life, for they took me into philosophy, a country which I have never since been tempted to leave. Desmond Connell was to exercise a benevolent and shaping influence on this development in many ways, not least by introducing me, along with many others, to the tradition to which I have referred, and also by showing through example what it is to take seriously the vocation of philosopher, of seeker after wisdom.

My thanks are also due to many others. I would like to set down here how grateful I am to my mother, friends, colleagues and, not least, students, for their friendship, support, and intelligent questioning. In particular, I would like to thank the philosophy class, both day and evening, who graduated in 1995 from All Hallows College, where I also gave this course. These students were among the best I was ever lucky enough to teach. They have my thanks and best wishes for the future. I would like to express my gratitude to Professor Patrick Hannon for confirming the invitation originally issued by Professor Marsh to write this book, and for his support and gentlemanly forbearance despite my tardiness. I would like also to thank my colleagues, Professor James McEvoy, who read the manuscript, for his kindness and encouragement, and Dr. Keith Sidwell, for his generous help. I would like to say too how grateful I am to Patricia Pender of the Computer Centre at Maynooth, who is not only a good friend, but also knows at least as much about computers as I do about philosophy! Profound thanks are due also to my friend, colleague, and indefatigable and savante amanuensis, Caroline O'Kelly. And now, as the French are wont to say, *au boulot*!

CHAPTER ONE

The Nature and Scope of Ontology

1, 1 Ontology

Ἔστιν ἐπιστήμη τις ἣ θεωρεῖ τὸ ὂν ἣ ὄν, καὶ τὰ τούτῳ ὑπάρχοντα καθ' αὑτό … 'There is a science which regards being as being and those things which belong properly to it.' It is with these words that Aristotle begins the text later to be named the Fourth Book of the *Metaphysics*, giving a programmatic definition of what he himself called 'first philosophy'. The intention embodied in this essay is to follow the trail blazed by Aristotle. We should begin, therefore, by exploiting what this little map gives us, spiralling outward as we go to the why and wherefore of this type of enquiry, reaching the defining limit of the territory in the triad of our title: language, world and God.

We are told various things by Aristotle. We are told that there exists a science, ἐπιστήμη τις. Although it remains to be seen in what sense this enquiry is scientific, it is justly called ontology in that it directs its gaze – θεωρεῖ – at being; we meet in this rich verb the Greek identification of knowing and seeing when we are told of that of which this science is meant to be the account, the logos. The gaze which this 'science' is, is directed upon being as being, τὸ ὂν ἣ ὄν, and upon those things which, of necessity, accompany being as proper to it, τὰ τούτῳ ὑπάρχοντα καθ' αὑτό.The map discloses a nest of criss-crossing themes which we must explore and evaluate, but which we shall not take in the order given.

Let us begin with the phrase 'being as such', Aristotle's τὸ ὂν ἣ ὄν. As it stands, this Greek phrase is ambiguous, in that it can refer either to Being or to beings. τὸ ὄν can be the singular of τὰ ὄντα things. In this acceptation, the phrase refers to things, beings, as such. This would mean that what the science is to look at is that which is common to all things precisely as things, as it were, a common determination or structure which must qualify them in order for them to count as things. But, τὸ ὄν can also function as abstract,

11

like, say, ὁ ἵππος, which does not simply mean 'the horse' but 'horses' or what belongs to horses as such, and which all horses have precisely as horses. What is it that belongs to beings as such, and which all things have as beings? The answer must come, though hesitantly, 'Being'. Why should this answer be hesitant? Precisely because, even if it were licit to attempt the first kind of analysis, the second, the articulation of Being, seems either to be a pseudo-question or, by being posed in this way, to expect an answer of a definite kind, and from a definite direction. We shall return to this point.

However we may scruple with regard to the licitness of such an enquiry, the two-fold meaning of the phrase is clear. What is to be the subject of the enquiry is: in the first acceptation, the structure or determination which any and all things must exhibit to count as things, and in the second, that which is common to them all as beings, namely to be, which in Greek is τὸ εἶναι and in Latin *esse*. Thus it is one thing to ask what it is to be something, another what it is to be *tout court*, and correspondingly, Aristotle distinguishes τὸ εἶναι, 'to be', from τὸ τί ἦν εἶναι, *quod quid erat esse*, [1] or 'what it is to be an *x*'. Moreover, we have from the sentence in which the phrase τὸ ὂν ᾗ ὄν occurs evidence neither that one acceptation is to be preferred over the other, nor that the ambiguity is other than deliberate: this would suggest a close and necessary connection between is τὸ εἶναι and the structure which 'embodies' it in real things, a structure referred to as τὸ τί ἦν εἶναι.

Thus the phrase which is the continuation of τὸ ὂν ᾗ ὄν, namely, τὰ τούτῳ ὑπάρχοντα καθ᾽ αὐτό, will vary in meaning as a function of the meaning of the phrase which it qualifies. The impression is that this phrase, τὰ τούτῳ ὑπάρχοντα καθ᾽ αὐτό, 'what belongs to it – τὸ ὄν, in one of its acceptations – properly because necessarily' is merely an unpacking, an explication of what is involved in looking at τὸ ὂν ᾗ ὄν. To give an account of τὸ ὂν ᾗ ὄν is to disclose those things which are proper to it as necessary to it, for they are necessary to it as parts of what it is, of its meaning. Thus, the science is meant to disclose the coordinate parts which belong to the intelligibility either of beings as such or of τὸ εἶναι, *esse*, itself.

But this brings us round full circle, for we must further understand how all or any of this is to constitute an ἐπιστήμη, usually translated as 'science', although the Greek word only means 'knowledge', which as knowledge, is for the Greeks, certain, systematic, and exhaustive. Thus we come to the edge of our map, with questions leading over the horizon. Is there such a knowledge? Is it, and in what sense is it, scientific? How, if at all, is it related to 'other' sciences? What value does it have, and why should we cultivate it? Thus, we add these to the budget of questions already posed: is it possible, and how is it, to examine τὸ ὄν or τὸ εἶναι, or both?

It becomes immediately apparent that the latter questions intend the former in such a way that to answer them is to answer the others. To know how, and thus perforce that, it is possible to give an account of τὸ ὄν or τὸ εἶναι, or both, is to know what such knowledge counts as, and where it stands relative to other, and what other, forms of knowledge, and at least to suspect the value of such knowledge. Let us begin here.

Our first encounter is with the inextricability of the question of τὸ εἶναι from that of τὸ ὄν, which the ambiguity of Aristotle's statement might have led us to suspect, as well as with the concomitant primacy of the articulation of τὸ ὄν over that of τὸ εἶναι. We wallow and flounder in trying to answer in isolation a question like 'what is τὸ εἶναι, or *esse*, or existence'? This is not to say that the question is *prima facie* a pseudo-question, a *Scheinproblem*, but only that it cannot be got at in an immediate fashion. Moreover, how we can get at it (if we can) determines that it is an intelligible question, for the intelligibility of a question consists in there being some means to arrive at an answer. But, to ask what so-and-so is is to ask, 'what do you mean by 'so-and-so'?' *Prima facie*, to ask what existence is is therefore no more extraordinary than to ask what a kangaroo is, because 'existence' does have legitimate employment in our language. But, I can, if all else fails, under propitious circumstances say 'that's a kangaroo' or 'one of those things is what I mean by 'kangaroo'. Unfortunately, I cannot do the same for existence, but, I can see a way forward in that 'existence' is an abstract to which the use of the verb 'exists' is cognate. Thus, my question becomes 'how do I use the verb or verbs "to exist" or "to be"?'

Let us distinguish between these related verbs. The verb 'to be' absorbs the uses of the verb 'to exist' with room to spare, and, conversely, the latter makes explicit one meaning of the verb 'to be', whose uses are three: the predicational, the assertion (or denial) of identity, and the existential. Such is the commonplace of grammar and logic. It might well be possible to have a language which dispenses with the first of these. That 'is' is used for predication is an accident of a particular language or family of languages. We might imagine a language in which this function was fulfilled by all other verbs: *ambulo* means 'I am walking', ἡβάω means 'I am in the best of health' and so on. We might in a similar way eliminate the 'is' of identity. Thus it seems that the irreducible function of 'to be' is carried in 'to exist'.

Whatever else I may determine, I run up against the fact that 'exists' or some other tense of 'to exist', is woefully incomplete. If I say simply 'exists', my hearer will be motivated to ask 'what exists?', or, if the intention appears negative, 'what doesn't exist?'. Thus, 'exists' and its denial need a subject. In general, to determine the meaning of a verb is to know, at least in part, what it can be said of. To understand 'walks' is to know at least what subjects are suitable for it: 'Jane walks' passes, but 'September walks' does not, at least not in any usual sense. If that is so, then to know what 'exists' means is to know how to use it, which, in turn, involves knowing what to use it of. It is at this point that the interwovenness of τὸ εἶναι with τὸ τί ἦν εἶναι shows its use. To know what it is to be, is to know what it is for something or a whole series of somethings, to be, that is, at least, to qualify as subjects of the verb. Thus, the question becomes: what must be true of something if it qualifies to act as subject of 'exists'?

In posing this question, however, it is necessary to avoid a grave misunderstanding. The question means: if 'x exists' is true, what must be true for all and any x? It does not imply that, granted certain things must be true of x if 'x exists' is true, 'x exists' is *therefore* actually true; still less does it imply that 'x exists' must be true. The one or the other implication, namely, from the premise that x has to have certain features if it is to exist, to the conclusion either that x does or must exist, could only hold, precisely, if some feature of x implied that x existed. In this way the former conclusion, that x actually does exist is assimilable to the latter, that x must exist, in the sense that the implication to the actual existence of x holds only if x must exist, that is, if its existence is implied, i.e., made necessary, by some feature. Whether or not there is or can be such a feature, it is clear that the assertion 'x exists' is not a mere tautology, so that even if it were in some cases necessarily true, what makes the x capable of acting as a subject of 'exists' is distinct from what 'exists' connotes, and there is some relation, which need not be identity, between them.

This relation, between what qualifies x to exist and existence, may be called the mode of being, depending on the mode of the assertion which actually relates them. 'X exists' is contingently true if and only if 'x exists' is possible, and there is no feature of x as capable of existing, that is, as being a suitable subject of 'exists', which not only embodies this possibility but necessitates its fulfilment. On the other hand, if such a feature is possible, then it is possible that '"x exists" is necessary', is sometimes true.

Several conclusions follow from this. In the first place, the axes of ontology are thereby established. To examine what makes something suitable to act as subject of the verb 'exists' is, and is thus inseparable from, the examination of the relationship between the two. Ontology, in this sense, is irreducibly modal. This implies further that the determination of the meaning of 'exists' is possible, at least insofar as it is possible to determine those conditions which make something qualify as its possible subject, and which are therefore conditions necessary to existence: in general, to know under what conditions something can be said is to know what it means.

Secondly, the extent of ontology is also thereby given. The question of whether or not there is something which has to be is not a question contingent within ontology. All the modes of the relation between the subject of existence and existence itself must be explored. To say this is not to prejudice how this is to be done. We can only say at this stage that it may or may not be possible to articulate a condition which is not only a necessary one for the assertion of existence but also a sufficient one. Likewise, in the case that we cannot do so, unless the idea is logically impossible, this is not to say that there is nothing which has to exist. If there were something discovered in the articulation of the necessary conditions of existence which verified the assertion that something exists necessarily, then it would be possible to make this assertion without having to be able either to define any feature whatsoever from which existence might follow, or to claim to be able to articulate this feature in such a way that the necessary connection of existence to it were disclosed; under such circumstances it would only be possible to say that there must be such a feature but not what that feature must be. One might refer to it, without being able to define or articulate it.

It will be clear that such a feature would correspond to Divinity. One may be able to know that God exists, and if so that this must be in a non-contingent manner, without necessarily being able to define what Divinity, or its essential non-contingency, may be, apart from this and from what follows logically from this. Likewise, whatever any meaning the notion of Divinity has, it consists in this precisely, as well as in any feature which makes the inference to the existence of the Divine necessary. This is at least to say that a discussion of the existence and logic of Divinity is a part of ontology not contingently present in ontology. Thus, the supreme member of the triad named in the title of this essay is, of necessity, an object of ontological investigation. This is not to prejudge the issue of whether or not Divinity exists, though to construct an ontology is, in part, to have to raise this question.

1, 2 Metaphysics: Onto-theology and Onto-anthropology

If it is possible not only to raise this question but to answer it affirmatively, then it is necessary that ontology, precisely at that point, become metaphysics, at least in the sense that the object of investigation is μετὰ τὰ φυσικά, that is, beyond changing reality, logically prior to such contingent reality. Heidegger uses the word onto-theology to describe what he takes to be a trait of metaphysics. In maintaining this, Heidegger does not intend to compliment metaphysics. However, although we shall not enter into any explicit *Auseinandersetzung* with the great philosopher, we shall simply say that the word perfectly captures the inherently metaphysical capacity of ontology, to the extent that ontology naturally, and of necessity, becomes onto-theology.

Thus, the word as we use it is not meant to denote a form of deception, nor the rigged introduction of some favoured conclusion for reasons that cannot be justified philosophically, nor yet the betrayal of philosophy which distorts it by making it into a slave of religion. Ontology can, and we shall argue must, become metaphysics in the sense of onto-theology – although, as we shall also suggest, there is more in metaphysics than onto-theology – because it is possible and necessary to assert the existence of Divinity precisely as Creator and therefore as non-contingently existing, and because it is therefore equally possible and necessary to elaborate the dialectic proper to this concept. Thus there are, in fact, two sections of ontology, namely the analysis of the contingent relation between subjects and their existence, and, non-contingently on this basis, the elaboration of an onto-theology, the dialectic of the concept of the Divine. In this way ontology is intensively universal in that no possible mode of being escapes it.

But ontology is also extensively universal, in that no kind of non-Divine being, and therefore no being, escapes it. There can be, we note, nothing of 'kind' in relation to Divinity. God is not another kind of being, but as necessary, is related to the non-Divine as its Creator, just as, as standing to non-Divine being as Creator, Divinity is necessary: this is to be absolutely prior and unique, and in directing its gaze thither as well as towards the derived and many, ontology is intensively universal. Non-Divine being is essentially many, diverse in individuality and in terms of kind, and in being coextensive with such being, ontology is extensively universal. What is the justification of the claim that ontology is extensively universal? How can we be sure that the furthest reaches of ontology are those of the world? In this way, another member of what is becoming ever more clearly a necessarily related triad, comes explicitly into view.

Beings which relate only contingently to their own existence are essentially worldly in two ways. World is not another being but a way of things' being. The being of world is worldly being. To be in the world is to be necessarily and unavoidably connected in various ways with other entities, to coexist with them in various ways, and thereby to be obliged to form a complex plurality, a one out of many with them. Contingent beings rely upon others as in some cases existing in them, that is, as using them as matter, as requiring them as sufficient antecedent conditions, that is, as prematter,[2] and, precisely as contingent, as having a non-actual component which requires something other – and this often, though not invariably means another something – than that component itself, in order to actualise that capacity. Necessary coexistence in the various forms of causality is the consequence of contingency. But an equally necessary consequence of it is another, for many the most characteristic, of all worldly features, namely spatio-temporality. To be in space is to be in time, and things can only be in time, or be temporal, if the mode of being which is proper to them is contingent. Temporality is lived contingency, the event of contingency. But further, worldliness in this sense of contingent-temporal, is necessarily, in relation to its origin, creation, being-created. To discover this is to know that contingent entity cannot but posit its own Divine origin. This then is the three-fold notion of world as plurality, as spatio-temporal, and as creation. World in this way defines the extent of contingency, and to the extent that my ontology is adequate, it is worldly as coextensive with world, taken in these three interrelated senses: in other words, an adequate ontology can grasp and reveal the worldliness of individual things, which defines their necessary relation to world in these three senses. As extensive, ontology is coextensive with world; as intensive, ontology reveals the relation between God and world. Thus world and God define the territory of which ontology is the map. But this still does not explain how the map manages to be a map of this territory. To understand this, the third element of the triad, language, is necessary.

Language is not merely essential to ontology in the same way that it is to poetry, in that there could be no poetry where there is no language. Some poems use, but do not concern, language. Ontology of necessity both uses and concerns it. Emphasis must fall equally on both root elements of 'onto-logy': τὸ ὄν and ὁ λόγος. Viewed from the perspective of language, we must say that language is, and can only be, ontological. We may employ here another piece of Heideggerian terminology, again altered to suit our need, to catch respectively the use and necessary nature of language which founds and underlies the use, namely the ontic and the ontological.[3]

Language can be used ontically only because it is ontological(ly). The realm of the ontic is thus the actual linguistic dealings we have with the world and the people, including the people we ourselves are, the animals and things of the world, or, to speak in more terse Wittgensteinian terms, the ontic is the set of our actual language-games. But these dealings are not blind; they are carried on in a state of illumination-for-us of the world as extra-linguistic, and of its inhabitants, and are inconceivable without that world. This illuminatedness is the ontological essence of all language that bears on the world and consists in the necessary structure of such language. To be as language, the architecture of language must be that of reality. We may echo here Gadamer's principle, *Sein, das verstanden werden kann, ist Sprache,* [4] and even applaud it, but it may be better to recast it by saying, language, insofar as it carries understanding, is Being. For anything at all to be said, language must be capable of saying it, and it is only capable of this if it at least mirrors in its own structure the structure proper to reality.

This very firmly makes language the client of a reality which it neither gives rise to nor structures. Where does this leave Kant's Copernican revolution, or indeed, those attempts, such as that by Maréchal, to wed realism – which consists precisely in the belief that what is, is and is structured independently of human intending

– proximally represented by Aquinas, to the transcendental philosophy? We might reply using an intriguing text from Heidegger:

> *Doch was sollen wir dann an die Stelle der Ontologie setzen? Etwa die Transzendentalphilosophie Kants? Hier ist nur der Name geändert und die Ansprüche, aber sie selbst, die Idee, ist festgehalten. Auch die Transzendentalphilosophie muss fallen.* [5]

The transcendental philosophy itself must fall. For reasons which are not identical to ours, Heidegger calls for a new beginning in philosophy. We shall not discuss here what Heidegger intends by such a new beginning, but we concur, as will be apparent, with his call for the deconstruction of the Copernican revolution. Kant's critical philosophy arose to meet certain problems which grew out of the Cartesian problematic, whose essence was to reduce all to the inwardly-directed subject, and, therewith, as in the case also of Kant, to elaborate a conception of subjectivity itself along those lines.[6] If the Cartesian project is intrinsically flawed, both in its actual elaboration and even in its ambitions – that is, in the reduction and elaboration to which we have just referred – then the ground is removed which founds the transcendental philosophy, which, however ingenious it may be, becomes, at the least, an attempt to solve unreal problems.

Does this mean that we must simply ignore Kant's philosophy? Not at all. The task which philosophers have in hand, if our arguments here are correct, is to deconstruct modern thought – and contemporary thought too, including the thought of Heidegger (though this will be a quite different task) – to purge it, that is, of the empire of the subject, and to retain, in a newly liberated and unhindered form, those genuine insights which are to be found in it. This task is to be accomplished along the lines indicated by the very problematic whose investigation animates much contemporary thought, namely, that of language.

Any genuine articulation of the nature of language is rendered impossible in the Cartesian perspective, where a radically discarnate, always singular subjectivity, is, in principle, capable of articulating the world out of its own ideal resources, without attending, at least in any direct way, either to world itself or to other communicators.[7] Both Heidegger and Wittgenstein have shown up the insufficiency and inconsistency of such a project, the renunciation of which is thereby coterminous with the (re)instatement of language as genuinely and ineluctably intersubjective tissue. This, then, is one axis along which any genuine philosophy of language must proceed. The other relates to the function of language with regard to extra-linguistic reality. We shall not argue here that a linguistically transformed Kantianism is impossible. But it remains the case that such a philosophy must come to terms with the ineluctable necessity of talk about subjects and their linguistic interrelatedness, which perforce seems to presuppose the possibility of 'realistic' uses of language, in the sense we have given this term. Moreover, coming to terms with language means coming to terms with its own disclosure of its own place in relation to world, a disclosure embodied in such verbal forms as 'to be' and 'being', 'to exist' and 'existence', with their usage and 'grammar'. If this is so, then ontology is far from being an artificial construct, used as an excuse for distorting philosophy by means of some unphilosophically held dogma or other, but the ineluctably necessary kernel of any philosophy of language. It is at this point that we can see how, precisely, it is that the emphasis in 'onto-logy' falls equally on the two elements of that word: philosophy of language is and must ultimately be, philosophy of Being, while philosophy of Being must be carried on as philosophy of language.

Coterminous with these necessarily conjoined elements is a third. Language does not occur as network but as living speech, not as *langue*, which is an abstraction, but as *parole*, to which *'langue'* stands as explanatory abstract construction. Language happens as speech between real speakers, which are thus inseparable from it, such that its occurrence without them is unintelligible: speakers as speakers are as such in language, and language as such occurs only in their near or remote communicative acts. To fail to see this dimension of language is to fail to understand language, and to understand language requires that we understand what makes speakers speakers. Thus another axis of onto-logy is onto-anthropology, and it is this, precisely, which is the called-for replacement of the transcendental philosophy.

We must here crave the reader's indulgence for such a long-winded title, which is clearly modeled on 'onto-theology', but is meant to represent the other coordinate axis of ontology. Let us state this with the greatest accuracy we can: ontology can and must become metaphysics, this latter understood coevally as onto-theology and -anthropology. We must emphasise two claims if this is true, namely that the inclusion of onto-anthropology as one of the two coeval areas which constitute metaphysics is not merely arbitrary, and that it is the proper replacement of the transcendental philosophy.

In regard to the first of these, it is clear that since language is meant to extend in principle across the divide of Being into contingent and necessary, however intensively limited its application in each of these realms may be, it follows that that form of being to which language properly belongs is, at least, not another entity among entities, but a being which is genuinely open to Being as such. Entities which rest within the limits which define them we have elsewhere called immanent entities,[8] while what it is to be a being open to Being is what we have called transcendence.[9] If language covers Being in the way we have suggested, then it most properly embodies transcendence in such a way that being linguistic is transcendence. But if the attempts to formulate a philosophy of language and ontology are mutually implicative, then ontology must become an onto-anthropology, which answers to onto-theology as this latter deals with Being *par excellence,* precisely as defining the limits of that openness to Being which constitutes transcendence, and which is the proper province of onto-anthropology. In other words, Being as linguistically disclosed necessitates the articulation of certain items which, while remaining, on the one hand, truly ontological, are, on the other, the proper objects of an onto-anthropology, which is the articulation of transcendence as such. This in turn implies that such items are revealed as the necessary accompaniments of the (linguistic-transcendental) disclosure of Being, and even more that, although as ontological they are coterminous with Being, nevertheless their presence remains unrealised until that disclosure takes place, much as do the colours of the remote sea-floor, until the explorer's torch makes them seen and not just seeable. These items are the values without which no (linguistic) disclosure can take place, namely, truth, goodness and beauty. In sum, it is not the case that disclosure of Being as true, good and beautiful is ineluctable, but that Being is ineluctably true, good, and beautiful, or better, that Being is identical to truth, goodness and beauty.

These are, of course, the traditional, so-called 'transcendental properties' of Being. We take this expression 'transcendental properties' quite seriously. The ordinary justification for this expression is that these items are properties in that they are convertible with Being, and transcendental in that they are not confined to any one category, but transcend each. We, however hold that, although they are properties in the sense explained, they are transcendental in the sense that they are those meanings of Being which are properly only revealed by transcendence.

This brings us to our second point, namely that onto-anthropology is the proper replacement of the transcendental philosophy. In order to show this it would first be necessary to substantiate the claim we made above that the transcendental philosophy lacks any foundation as response to a misguided Cartesian problematic. We shall not attempt this at this moment, but the second element involved in such a justification would dovetail with the rejection of the subject as Kant conceived it, and its replacement with a pluralised, ontologically open, conception. It should be clear that transcendence opens the ground for such a view, in that as linguistic it is not confined to the isolated singular but is plural as a characteristic of the community of communicators, and in that it is precisely as openness to Being and disclosure of Being as ineluctably true, good and beautiful. It is precisely this – Being as ineluctably true, good and beautiful – as that towards which transcendence is, which is the core of onto-anthropology and which must replace the transcendental philosophy which Kant himself presents as a thinking-out of the implications of 'I think', but which turns out in essence, on the basis of its Cartesian foundation, to be an explanation of why and how it is that this thinking is unable to reach things as they are in themselves, which must therefore remain both unknown and unknowable.[10] It is, however, a nice reflection that, *pace* the style of thinking which belongs to transcendental Thomism, any correct elaboration of the nature of transcendence in onto-anthropology cannot but be the elaboration of certain ontological truths, if not of an actual ontology, given the directedness of transcendence towards Being, and the consequent bivalence of truth, goodness and beauty as ontological and onto-anthropological. One might think that any such replacement of the transcendental philosophy is a thinking which could well take as its emblem Augustine's *noli foras ire, in teipsum redi; in interiore homine habitat veritas*.[11] This saying, if we are correct, is true in a most literal sense. However, it is probably easier for a merely human intellect to start with ontology.

In relation to this point it might be worth making the following, perhaps not too far-fetched, observation, namely, that such an onto-anthropological analysis reveals the role which is peculiar to entities which have transcendence as their existence, for if what we have suggested is correct, it is only in transcendence, or, better, in beings for whom to be is to transcend, *in interiore homine*, that finite truth formally is. There is truth insofar as there is Divinity, but transcendence is that phase of creation itself in which all of creation becomes actually lit from within with the light of truth, goodness and beauty, and in which these are themselves formally articulated. We thereby become the voice of creation, the phase of finite Being in which finite Being becomes articulate. Some recent thinkers have discussed notions such as observership, have pointed out the fine attunement of the early events in the history of the universe which allows for the emergence of observers, and have thereby mounted a species of argument from design to the existence of God. Whatever may be the merits of such an argument, it does not remove contingency from those entities for whom to be is to transcend, and therefore does not ground any predictability or necessity in their coming to be from an examination of the pattern which events must follow or of the actual form which the world takes in accordance with that pattern. This means that no such examination of, say, the pattern of events we call evolution, or of the actual path which 'evolution' is meant to explain, can unambiguously ground the belief that our existence was somehow guaranteed by, or 'built into', this pattern. This would make of evolution a demiurge. But it is still true that a contingent and therefore unpredictable form of existence did emerge which stands to all else as what Heidegger would call a 'clearing', an event which can most probably be finally called only a happy accident if we look below it to those equally contingent patterns and events from which it emerges. But any attempt to explain human vocation must be ontological rather than ontic, and so must look upwards towards Being and God, not downwards in the forlorn hope of glimpsing a demiurge: even if there were, as it were, such an exotic being lurking in creation as a monster is believed by some to inhabit the depths of Loch Ness, its existence would be as much a puzzle as the existence of other, more homely and tame creatures.

1, 3 The Source of Objections to Metaphysics

It is now necessary for us to turn our attention to the unsubstantiated claim we made above, to the effect that the Kantian philosophy rests upon a misguided problematic. In what sense is the Cartesian project misguided? This question has a double relevance here, because it is precisely as a result of this project that the whole conception of ontology, except in a very truncated sense, has been rendered doubtful, and the word 'metaphysics' has, in the thinking of many philosophers, especially in the twentieth century, come to denote a kind of laughable *grotesquerie*, a species of 'woolly uplift' (Ayer), practised only by 'musicians without musical talent' (Carnap). We shall not attempt any systematic examination of such opinions but shall trace them back to their unwilling root in Descartes.

In the *Meditations*, Descartes uses the methodic doubt itself as a logical tool to gain ontological insight, particularly by means of what can, and cannot, be doubted. The strategy seems to be to distinguish things by means of the truth-conditions involved in their descriptions or notions. The general form of his argument seems to be, if A is notionally distinct from B then they are really distinct, and if one can be doubted while the other cannot, then they are notionally distinct. This in turn seems to be founded in the belief that a notion is in itself distinct, once clearly conceived (or stated), and so that of which it is the notion is possible precisely as instantiating it, and therefore distinctly. For this to carry, however, we must know that, if A and B are descriptions, they do in fact describe distinct things, as opposed to describing distinctly, that is, as notionally distinct. The doubt thus seems to disclose distinctly describing descriptions but, unless the things described differ, it does not *ipso facto* disclose distinct things described. This method of reasoning is applied by Descartes in two well-known arguments, namely for indirect realism and for the real distinction between mind and body.[12] These together are the arguments by which he supports his conception of discarnate, essentially inward-looking subjectivity, which, once deprived of his vision of that subject's epistemic self-sufficiency, becomes the touchstone of all modern thinking.

In relation to indirect realism, Descartes' procedure is to treat our perceptions as justified hallucinations. I cannot be in error unless I judge erroneously, for example that something is the case which is not. Thus, in order to be in error about a putative perception, I must have presented to me something which claims to be a perception. I cannot therefore doubt that this presentation takes place, for without it I cannot be in error. But I can doubt that anything real corresponding to it, which it mediates to me, exists. Thus the presentation and that which it appears to present are notionally distinct. It seems to follow that the presentation, which Descartes calls the idea, and the thing it mediates are distinct entities. I can always raise this doubt, hence every case of perception involves an idea's being presented which is a thing distinct from the thing it mediates.

Although perception is something other than the thing perceived, it does not follow that it is therefore another something than the thing perceived. Why should I think it was? The culprit here is the doubt: I cannot doubt that A exists but I can doubt that B exists, therefore A and B are really distinct things. I cannot doubt that the presentation exists but I can doubt that the thing it appears to mediate exists, thus idea and object are distinct things. However, perception is quite other than hallucination, (where 'hallucination' means something like 'believing that pink elephant is real') in such a way that the two are mutually exclusive. You either perceive or you don't, and it is nonsense to say that if John is hallucinating he is perceiving something. If I really can doubt that this is a dagger that I see before me, then I am, to that extent, failing to perceive. Perception is of (objective genitive) the thing perceived and is inconceivable without it: the logic of hallucination is that it never has a real object. Thus, in the case of perception, one cannot doubt that the object exists and is as it is perceived. Perceptions are not vindicated as such by showing that they are fundamentally the same as hallucinations while differing from them insofar as the illusory datum can be shown to picture something in the case of perceptions. 'What it is to perceive x' is not distinct from 'what and that x is', in that the latter is necessarily included in the former even though x can be, and be what it is, without its being perceived.

In general, to perceive something other than x is to fail to perceive x. Thus I cannot be said to perceive something if I perceive only the idea of it. Since, for Descartes, we always perceive only the idea of x, we must always fail to perceive x. Descartes' theory thus makes impossible the very thing it is designed to explain.

But what is this 'perceiving the idea of x'? If my perceiving x demands that I perceive something else, namely y, why does my perceiving y not require my perceiving a third something, z, and so on *ad infinitum*? This results from a fault in definition given in the explanation of the crucial term: 'perception of x' is defined as 'perception of the idea of x'; thus, since this is the case, replacing the word 'perception' in the phrase 'perception of the idea of x' with its *definiens*, which is 'perception of the idea of x', we get 'perception of the idea of the idea of x', and so on.

What we might call the Cartesian fallacy is perhaps more clearly effective in the establishment of the ego as discarnate. Again, I cannot doubt that A exists but I can doubt that B exists, therefore A and

B are really distinct things. I cannot doubt that I exist, but I seem to be able to doubt my body exists, therefore I and my body are distinct things. I doubt, affirm, deny, and the like, and so I can describe myself as that which does these things. This description is what I may mean by 'I' and its cognates. I may describe body, due to the thought-experiment of the piece of wax, as something which always involves extension. The two predicate-strings are notionally distinct. But unless I also happen to know that they are also really distinct, that mind is some other thing than body, my being able, if I am, alone to doubt the one but not the other is evidence only of this notional distinctness.

It is however more Descartes' indirect realism than his mind-body dualism which has done overt damage to ontology, in providing the scheme in terms of which the whole question of our knowledge of the world is posed. Descartes' ideas, suitably purged of any innate or universal content, become Locke's ideas, Hume's impressions, Kant's manifold of the senses and the sense-data so beloved of Russell and the modern empiricists and positivists. The question of our 'knowledge of the world' becomes that of our 'knowledge of the *external* world', that is, how do we get from these data to the real world, or, equivalently, what do these data reveal about the world outside the mind; the answer, however we may order the data, by synthesis, as in Kant, or by logical construction, as in Russell, is always 'nothing', precisely because I can apparently always raise the Cartesian qualm about the existence of what, if anything, may be said to be 'beyond' the data, or its correspondence with the data.

It is perhaps an interesting comment on philosophers that it seems to have occurred to very few (Neo-Scholastics are the notable exception) to challenge this Cartesian framework until the epoch of Heidegger and Wittgenstein. However that may be, it is very clear that this framework will disallow any talk of Being or reality, because it is precisely this which the framework occludes. Even the subject, in the interior of which these dubious data may be said to dwell, dissolves in the framework, insofar as any attempt to describe it takes us out of the ambit of the 'immediate given'. The occlusion of Being is at one with the occlusion of the categorial framework of language which reveals it, or at least, with the occlusion of the framework as revealing it, so that the framework acts, as it did for Kant, as a necessary, though undisclosive, organisational principle for synthesis. Yet, neither has anyone seemed to have noticed that the language used in talk about subjects and sensibilia is realist, and that therefore philosophers have had to defend a position which amounted to the belief that although there are no true statements about the world in itself, there can and must be true statements about sense-data, and thus about language and the subject, that is, although first-order statements cannot function in a realist way, second-order language can and must do so. In sum, it seems that the objections to ontology and metaphysics which became usual in much modern philosophy rested upon the Cartesian framework which we have outlined, one which, we further venture to suggest, is radically flawed.

1, 4 ...ἐπιστήμη τις...

We can now see that, and in what sense, ontology is an ἐπιστήμη. There is an analogy between how beings which transcend stand to all beings, or, better, to Being as such, on the one hand, and how ontology stands to the sciences, on the other. Ontology is not one of the sciences, where 'science' is understood as an ontic discipline which investigates some pattern of the way things happen in the world, and attempts in particular cases to trace the actual and contingent path which particular instantiations of the pattern have followed. Clearly, ontology cannot be on all fours with such projects, and is analogous to logic, which stands in the same relation to every discipline. Indeed, one might with some justification call ontology an existential logic, an articulation of that structure which all things as such instantiate, in the same way that all arguments as genuine and valid arguments instantiate logical principles. This means that all talk, in particular all descriptive talk, must utilise, or at least work (though perhaps unanalysedly) within the principles of the logic of existence which ontology discloses, and that ontology is therefore a kind of schema which all meaningful ontic discourse must embody if not explicitly refer to, and which that ontic discourse thereby particularises and makes concrete. Thus, for example, our account of causality is a schema according to which all causal explanation is to be constructed, outside, or apart from which, there is no such explanation. In general, logic is the theory of theory, the schema necessary to explanation and discourse in general, while ontology is what this schema dictates as the absolutely general structure that the things talked about must have if they are to be talked about.

It is in this way that we can understand precisely how ontological statements are informative: they are informative analogously to the way in which a logical law, such as CKCpqNqNp is informative. This statement is not informative in the way that the statements 'Aardvarks are long-eared' or 'There are three electrons in the element Lithium' are informative, for these disclose contingent truth, and are made true by what happens to be the case, while CKCpqNqNp is a tautology, and therefore a rule of meaning. While not all arguments instantiate it, its being true is a presupposition of there being any and all contingent meaning, any and all argument. This is the proper meaning of '*a priori*', which frees it of the 'psychologistic' or, better, subjectivistic interpretation that Kant gave it. In the same way, though we are not obliged to talk at any point of 'entity', say, or 'cause', when we use them we deploy a non-arbitrary and non-contingent meaning, which results from the structure which language must have if it is to be able to make any statement whatsoever. Again we encounter a non-subjectivist *a priori*, which inheres in the very fact of meaning. The coincidence of language as meaningful with its own metalanguage in the generation of such ontological expressions from its ontic uses, governing those uses' range and intelligibility – the category of 'entity' from names and analogous items, the category of relation from relational expressions, and so on – including more abstract ones such as 'existence' and 'truth' which intend the relation of language to what is beyond it, is the phenomenon which makes ontology both possible and necessary.

If this were all, it would be sufficient to make the construction of ontology (not an ontology, for there can be only one, just as there can be only one logic and for the same reason) rewarding, at least as the necessary completion of scientific discourse, where such discourse finds ultimate intelligibility and interpretation, and as the region in which all talk as talk about the world is explained. But we have suggested that ontology becomes metaphysics as onto-theology and onto-anthropology. This means, at least, that the enterprise is not possible without the adumbration of the ethical. No science is really value-free in that, although it may be conducted without mentioning anything at all about value, its subservience, at least to the value of truth, is enshrined in and as its methodology, without which it cannot be as truth-claim, and hence as science. But this is even more true in the case of ontology which, as necessarily onto-anthropological, occupies the territory in which the leading values of all forms of human life (the intellectual, the moral and the aesthetic) originate, since to be linguistic is to disclose these bivalent values. Ontology is thus the *episteme* of truth as such, the *episteme* of all intellectual activity as such, if we use the word 'intellectual' to capture our ability to generate and participate in truth. It stands in the same relation to the two other transcendentals, and so is the fundamental *episteme* of the moral and aesthetic forms of life as well. As the discipline which thereby discloses value as such it is a necessary concomitant of life under the behest of those values, that is, responsible and conscientious personal life. It is not a 'disinterestedly' interesting discipline, but a morally obligatory one. This is not to say that everyone must take on philosophical research, rather, that it be done and done well is the concern of all, though its actual practice be the duty of the few. Its moral force is thus akin to that of a discipline such as jurisprudence, which is a morally, and not just a logically, necessary accompaniment of the rule of law.

In this way, the logical relies on and discloses the moral, which in turn discloses further depths within itself, in real and universal relations which, though explored by ontology, are not generated by or peculiar to it, and form the territory inhabited by us, as linguistic and transcending beings, persons at once needing and capable of truth, goodness and beauty, and living freely and under their governance. This further depth is the truth which is proper to such personal life in its totality as the meaning of that life, and is the truth proper to onto-theology. The logical and moral relate as such to reality, and to Divinity therefore as reality *par excellence*, which emerges not only as explanation and instantiation of value, but as self-subsistent meaning and goal of personal life. In this way, although the word may excite incorrect resonances, the logical and the moral are founded in the religious, so that in this way the full, and thus in principle ontological, disclosure of personal life discloses it in and as the irrefrangible unity of logical, moral and religious. It would be silly to claim that everyone always is all three, or that their necessity in and for human life is self-evident, but to do ontology successfully is in fact to reveal them in their ethico-logical necessity. If all this is so, then ontology emerges not only as logically universal and morally necessary, but also as addressing the most intimate, urgent and important of human concerns, without which, not as discipline but as disclosure, the good life is not possible, nor is it possible for us to take in hand and employ freedom in a way which answers the dignity which belongs to that tragic and comic freedom. Ontology thus occupies the space disclosed in a vatic line of Goethe:

Es irrt der Mensch solang' er strebt. [13]

Striving and wandering, errant and erring, hope of finding and being found, held together as a single thing, which yet never fully is: such is the comedy and the tragedy of freedom. But the drama is played out not in absurdity or without hope. Something stirs within these *schwankende Gestalten* which opens another horizon. Augustine's words find echo in Goethe:

> *Ein guter Mensch in seinem dunklen Drange,*
> *Ist sich des rechten Weges wohl bewusst.* [14]

Transcendence is the intersection-point of the perishing which is not merely perishing, and the permanent which is more than the merely lasting.

1, 5 The Design of this Essay

The final task which awaits us in this introductory chapter is an outline of how the themes which have become manifest in the discussion of what ontology is are to be carried forward and treated. It is worth noting at this juncture that we have already been engaging in ontological investigation even thus far, and the questions of what ontology is and how to do it form an integral part of that very investigation. For this reason, our first chapter is not merely an introduction in an anodyne sense, but is the determination of the territory of ontology and a precursory enunciation of the themes necessary to it. We shall therefore now supply an overview of these, which will be announced in the particular introduction to each subsequent chapter, and will act as guide to the discussion contained there.

We shall lay the ground on which to construct our ontology, therefore, by means of a consideration of those aspects of language which make such an investigation possible. The two chapters immediately following this one will therefore in the main be concerned with such features, at a simple in the first, and at a more advanced level in the second. The simple level will be determined by examining the categorial structure of language, as this is revealed in logic, and how we talk about reality and make existential claims. A more nuanced view of the working of language is subsequently provided when, in the second of these two chapters, we mediate a Wittgensteinian perspective with an interpretation of the Thomistic theory of analogy. This mediation allows for an understanding of meaning as incarnate in and as diverse language-games, yet without allowing it to shatter into an intrinsically absurd diversity of unrelatable fragments. The saving factor here is the intended unity in real diversity, which is the hallmark of analogy.

Out of this grows our first characterisation of the real as such, in the form of that which is the proper subject of the verb 'exists', namely the category called 'entity'. In the fourth chapter of our essay, therefore, we delineate the structure proper to entity, and all the items involved in it, especially the notions of identity and essence, and their mutual relationship.

A theme of our ontology is that if entity is the proper subject of existence, existence, precisely as finite, is intrinsically plural, and opens that which is to others, in coexistence. Things do not simply exist, they necessarily coexist. There are, therefore, various relations, and precisely because of the finitude and contingency of entities, dependence-relations, which do and must obtain between entities. It turns out that these relations dovetail with the four causes distinguished by Aristotle. The material, formal and final causes are discussed in chapter five, and the efficient in chapter six.

If the finitude which belongs to entities emerges in and through this discussion, its nature is most clearly expressed in the spatial, and even more especially in the temporal, structure which it of necessity confers on things. To be finite and contingent is to be in time, or better, to be temporal. Chapter seven, therefore, is concerned with time. It is a pivotal chapter in our attempt to construct an ontology in that it most clearly reveals this nexus. It is in the following chapter, chapter eight, however, that the full significance of the analysis of temporality is revealed: the analysis of temporality makes it both possible and necessary to assert the existence of God, that is, the source of existence as such. This discovery of the existence of the Divine allows and necessitates at once the elaboration of the necessary meaning of 'God' based on the discovery of the source of existence as such, and an account of how language functions in relation to Divinity. To be able to talk philosophically about God is to be able to say how anything like God-talk is possible. It is at this point that our ontology becomes metaphysics as onto-theology.

The rest of our study does not claim to be a full-blown onto-anthropology, but is an attempt to outline those elements which are the conditions of possibility of the ontology which has thus far been constructed. These items are the transcendentals, unity, truth, goodness and beauty. Their presence here is, we maintain, neither arbitrary nor contingent, and this is so in various ways and for various reasons.

The presence of the transcendentals begins in truth as the absolute presupposition of the whole enterprise. Not only is no such thing as ontology possible unless there is truth, and it is possible only insofar as there is truth, but truth is the ground of language as such. This principle of the necessity of truth is enhanced by the bivalence of the transcendentals to which we have referred, though this bivalence only becomes evident in the course of our examination of the transcendentals. Truth, like the others, is at once interchangeable with Being, and a formal determination of transcendence as such. That this is the case is the real wonder of human existence: there is an entity whose being is to be what all Being is. The essence of the *anthropos* is Being, to be the realisation and disclosure of all that Being as such indeed is, but in an undisclosed fashion prior to the advent of *anthropos*. Disclosing this wonder is the heart of onto-anthropology, a word which now appears tautologous in that it means disclosure of what it is to be a being for Being, and coevally and reciprocally a disclosure of what it is to be. We might say, in a punning kind of way, that what is here in question is a kind of transcendental deduction, but not in any sense which Kant would have recognised. We do not deploy a system of categories whose very deployment is not only unconnected with what it is to be, the essence of Being, but masks that very essence. Nor do we deduce it from or within subjectivity, the solipsistically and discarnately conceived 'I think'. What we deduce is, rather, deduced as the condition of possibility, proximally, of language, and then of the transcendence whose medium and emblem language is, in a deduction, from what it is to be a being for Being, of what it is for Being to be. This, we suggest, is the replacement of the transcendental philosophy, and, if we wish to keep up the scientific metaphor used by Kant, we might say (perhaps with tongue in cheek) that we are not simply reneging on the Copernican Revolution in philosophy, but are doing for Kant something similar to what Einstein did for Newton.

Moreover, this 'transcendental deduction', if we may so call it, is not the haphazard throwing-together of a heterogeneous set of concepts, whose only justification is that they have been juxtaposed so often before. We hope to show, rather, that there is a logic of precedence and procession in the movement from truth through goodness to beauty, and this will be justified mainly in the introductions to the chapters which deal with them, namely, chapters ten to twelve. It is the case that there is a disanalogy between unity and all the rest, in that it occupies an intermediary stage between the ontology on the one hand, and the onto-anthropology, on the other. It is not a value as the other transcendentals are, but it is in some sense coterminous with Being and is presupposed in a special way by all talk about world as such, whose problematic is so much a part of the present essay. These issues will be further elaborated on in chapter nine.

This then is the structure of our essay. The members of the triad which forms our title are interlocked in such a way that to talk about one is to talk about the other two. It has not been possible to unpick them so as to discuss each in real isolation from the others, and thereby to structure our essay so as to have three easily distinguished, corresponding parts. Throughout, our concern has been to follow, like Socrates, the thread of argument wherever it leads, and to avoid foisting ready-made simplistic categories on what is in reality an organic and living process. Nevertheless, it is usually the case that one member predominates over the others at each point in the discussion. Moreover, the author hopes that the parallelism of logical structure between the various chapters will serve to bring out structural analogies in the matters discussed there, especially between and among the various transcendentals.

Finally, it is useful to add a rider to the effect that our approach here has been hermeneutic rather than maieutic, although we do mount some criticisms, in particular of the key modern thinkers, Descartes and Kant. We make no systematic attempt to examine or refute any thinker, although some, at least, of the assertions we make are contentious in relation to the work of some philosophers. It might also be said that the overall tone is inimical to that which obtains in these thinkers' works. This is not to say that such confrontation is unhealthy or unnecessary. But the essay would have to have been considerably longer than it is to contain such evaluations. What we have tried to do is to formulate a provisional position or discussion document which offers a set of alternative views to many currently espoused positions. The author has tried to follow the argument wherever it leads, and this, he believes, is what is essential to any philosophical endeavour. Since that work is, if not finished, at least begun, there is now something with which to confront those differing views, something which will be modified and expanded, altered and corrected by the clash of maieutic discussion, and this, the author believes, is as valid a way as any of doing philosophy.

Notes to Chapter One

1. See De Raeymaeker, *The Philosophy of Being*, translated by Edmund H. Ziegelmeyer, (St. Louis: Herder Book Co., 1966), p. 108, note 9.

2. This term will be introduced in chapter 5 below.

3. See the present author's previous work, *Language and Transcendence: A Study in the Philosophy of Martin Heidegger and Karl-Otto Apel*. (Berne: Peter Lang, 1994), henceforth abbreviated as 'LT'. For my discussion of the ontic-ontological distinction, see LT Part 1, subsection 30.

4. 'Being, that can be understood, is language.' H.-G. Gadamer, *Wahrheit und Methode*, (Tübingen: Mohr, 3., *erweiterte Auflage*, 1972), Dritter Teil, 3, c),'*Der Universale Aspekt der Hermeneutik*', p. 450.

5. 'But what should we put in the place of ontology? Something like Kant's transcendental philosophy? Here only the name is changed, but its claims, and it itself, the idea, is retained. Even the transcendental philosophy must fall.' LT p. 367, note 4, original emphasis here removed.

6. For our analysis of this historical movement, see LT, Introduction, subsections 3 and 4.

7. c.f. also LT Introduction, subsections 5 and 7.

8. LT Part 1, subsection 4.

9. LT Introduction, subsection 2.

10. LT pp. 11-12.

11. This remarkable and emblematic text is from Augustine's *De Vera Religione*, XXXIX, 72, Migne, *Patrologiae Cursus Completus, Sti. Augustini Opera Omnia, Tomus Tertius, Pars Prior*. Paris, 1861. *...et si tuam naturam mutabilem inveneris, transcende et teipsum. Sed memento cum te transcendis, ratiocinantem animam te transcendere. Illuc ergo tende, unde ipsum lumen rationis accenditur. Quo enim pervenit omnis bonus ratiocinator, nisi ad veritatem? cum ad seipsam veritas non utique ratiocinando perveniat, sed quod ratiocinantes appetunt, ipsa sit. Vide ibi convenientiam qua superior esse non possit, et ipse conveni cum ea. Confitere te non esse quod ipsa est: siquidem se ipsa non quaerit; tu autem ad ipsam quaerendo venisti, non locorum spatio, sed mentis affectu, ut ipse interior homo cum suo inhabitatore, non infima et carnali, sed summa et spirituali, voluptate conveniat.* I append here a slightly amended version of the translation given in *An Augustine Synthesis*, arranged by Erich Przywara, (London: Sheed and Ward, 1936), p. 19. 'Do not go outside yourself; return within: truth dwells in the inmost part of man. And if you find that your nature is mutable, rise above yourself. But when you transcend yourself, remember that you raise yourself above the rational soul; strive therefore to reach the place where the very light of reason is lit. For where does every good reasoner arrive, if not to truth? Since truth certainly does not attain to itself, but is that which reasoners strive to reach, recognise in it a harmony than which nothing can be superior, and bring yourself into accord with it. Confess that you are not what it is, since it does not seek itself, and you

have come towards it by seeking it, not by advancing in space but by an affection of the mind, to the end that the interior man may come into accord with that which dwells within him, in a joy that is not carnal and of a low order, but spiritual and of the highest.' Here we find finitude and transcendence expressed existentially, not merely as constitutive process but also as 'my' personal quest, whose destination is truth, the transcendental which, as the good of the journey, makes that journey both possible and necessary. Truth, however, is found interlocked with its implicitly indicated siblings, beauty - harmony - and goodness, that with which the searcher as searcher comes into accord. We could ask for no better emblem of transcendence, nor any better articulation of what, if anything, could replace the transcendental philosophy, than this.

12. The tripartite distinction of ideas is to be found at the beginning of *Meditation* III; God as guarantee of the reliability of ideas is found in *Meditations* V and VI; error is treated in *Meditation* IV. These are the essential elements of Descartes' indirect realism. The diversity of mind and body is disclosed in *Meditation* II, and confirmed in *Meditation* VI.

13. Goethe, *Faust. Herausgegeben und kommentiert von Erich Trunz.* (München: C. H. Beck, 1978). *Prolog im Himmel*, line 317: 'Man errs as long as he strives'.

14. *Faust, loc. cit.*, lines 328-9: 'A good man, in his dark striving, is *of himself* sure of the right way.' My emphasis.

CHAPTER TWO

The Logic of Existence

2, 1 Introduction

After our discussion of the nature and scope of ontology, we begin, in this chapter, to construct it. In the light of what we have decided about the nature of ontology, the requisite starting-point is not far to seek, and is at hand in language, more precisely in the 'depth grammar' of language, represented by its categorial framework. We rely here upon those structures which are universal in language as such and are not peculiar to particular tongues, and we look to logic, in particular to the predicate calculus, to reveal them. It is helpful at this point to contrast this starting-point to that which, since Descartes, has been customary, namely the determination of what can be known with certainty. As we have suggested, the problematic of certainty together with that of scepticism to which it is intended to respond, has influenced all modern thought, not necessarily to advantage, and has enjoyed this influence even when it remains in the wings and does not occupy centre stage.

The strictly onto-logical truth to which we appeal as our starting-point is the identity of the categorial framework of language with the structure of the real. The elucidation of this truth allows us to determine, at least in an initial sketchy way, what we mean when we use the verb 'to exist' and what qualifies best as subject of this verb, namely, that which belongs in the category 'entity', to which we give a provisional, non-Platonic or realist, definition. It is in this context that we can explain that realistic – both anti-sceptical and anti-Platonic – attitude which must accompany ontology. The chapter closes with a topography of the uses of 'existence' and of the relation between existence and that of which it is said, and of some of the terms which have been found necessary to this discussion.

2, 2 The Starting-point of the Enquiry

Philosophy is the passion for truth, not the search for certainty. The starting-point of philosophy, therefore, is not the essentially isolated and discarnate self, as Descartes, in accordance with the exigencies of the methodic doubt, discloses – or, perhaps better, constructs – it, needing nothing besides itself either to know or to be, but rather, the plurality of real, linguistic co-subjects, inhabiting the world. This is the ineluctable primary datum on which any and all philosophising rests, and inasmuch as Wittgenstein has demonstrated the impossibility of a private language, a language, that is, confined to the understanding of one speaker alone, even a Cartesian-inspired discourse must seek and find validation in that primary datum.

These considerations have their effect on what we attempt here. We take the first step on the road to constructing an ontology by noting the following two items: we, the linguistic community, are able to make sense of the world, and we are able to say how we do so. I use the phrase 'make sense of' here, rather than any narrower expression, because the linguistic community seems to exist as a kind of generator of meaning and significance, and this in very many ways. We talk incessantly, and in this talk bring into being all those significance-structures and forms of life which belong to us as community and individual; and if some of these, such as visual art, music, and dance, appear remote from talk, their interpretation and appreciation is, at least partly, carried out in and through talking.

But, in the narrower meaning, one of the ways we make sense of the world is by being able to enunciate true propositions about it. We shall not here embrace the once-popular, though mistaken, belief that all true propositions about the world are scientific ones. There is scientific – both natural and human – and artistic, religious[1] and philosophical truth, among others, variously called in virtue of the diverse canons whereby truth in each is arrived at, and none of these can be disqualified as significant by reference to some univocally conceived 'criterion of meaningfulness', which as univocal represents an attempt to give one canon of what is in reality an essentially analogical rationality hegemony over all others. The world is the whole of the things that are, and true propositions are such, in that they disclose what is. There is similarity and difference in the way in which propositions perform this task in the different reaches of rationality, and in the corresponding different provinces of reality, in which they are called into being. More simply, the mechanism of the proposition remains one and the same, despite the diversity of tasks it is called upon to perform, and the diversity of performative contexts in which that structure is at home. The analysis of this mechanism forms part of the discipline of logic. The very existence of this discipline, together with that of the other linguistic disciplines, is evidence for the second thesis mentioned above, namely that we can also make sense of how we make sense of the world: we can disclose how disclosure is possible. In this way, we refuse also to embrace another, this time more obviously Wittgensteinian, thesis, or perhaps better, dogma, namely that language cannot represent its own form of representation, or better, say how it says.[2]

The Cartesian habit, however, dies hard. Philosophers have been used for nearly four centuries to begin with the question of what can be known with certainty, or at least, to start from a position whose topography has been shaped by just this question. Are we simply to ignore the sceptical ghost which haunts the *Meditations*, and if we do so, will our treatment not lack the required philosophical rigour?

2, 3 Scepticism as Starting-point

Let us say that scepticism amounts to the following: there are no true propositions about the world; language is a systematic falsification of the world; there is evidence for both these theses. I add the third point here, because although we can worry about a great many things, fortunately, the number of things about which we ought to worry is rather smaller. We will not, therefore, waste time, which might be put to better use, on the analysis of a position for which there is and can be no evidence whatsoever. I take the first two theses to be equivalent. I have added the rider 'about the world' to the first, because the sceptical claim must intend the relation of language to the world; it is obviously nonsensical to try to deploy the very disclosive power of language to disclose that it has no such power. Thus, language cannot disclose the world, though, since there can be evidence for this claim, it can disclose itself and its relation to the world; language is a systematic falsification of reality – though it appears to disclose reality, it does nothing of the kind – but not of language itself.

It would, perhaps, be somewhat difficult to see why or how these strange beliefs could ever be true. But if we are to accept them, we must answer this 'why?' and 'how?' Any answer, however, would have to take the form 'because the relation between language and reality is such and such', which is the very relation the sceptic calls into question. The result of this, perhaps stilted, 'refutation' is that, although there can be the gravest objections to individual claims, there cannot be a coherent overall objection to the making of claims as such. The ability to judge claims competently on their merits is the epistemic virtue, which means not throwing up one's hands in despair at the objections which may be made to them, still less abandoning the learning process for the stubborn silence of the canny peasant, who fears nothing more than to be laughed at for his mistakes.

But can we not persist, and ask how we know that we do not falsify reality when we talk about it? It might be worth taking this extra step, for this is the very question raised by Kant in relation to the deployment of the categories,[3] and, as that case makes clear, there may well be many diverging paths from this point. Kant's answer is, in effect, to make the deployment of the categories a condition for the very being of the objects as objects known by means of them; there is no objectivity without subjectivity. This is to drive a wedge between what is and what appears, where this latter becomes object. In doing so, Kant was, of course, only granting a divorce in a relationship which had long since broken down, but this is to banish what is to the realm of the unknowable – Kant's actual move – and to reaffirm the disastrous doctrine that what I can know must be confined to my inward gaze, no matter how much this may be sculpted according to the immanent logic of that gaze. But Kant seems to leave unquestioned this Cartesian belief, one which rests upon the further belief that it is coherent to adopt the sceptical position: clearly, the methodic doubt amounts to entertaining a universal objection to the making of claims as such, even if only in order to secure results which are certain. But is there any good reason to tailor one's thinking to the gross contours of an absurdity?

If scepticism cannot be stated coherently, its opposite must be correct, an opposite expressed in these equivalent theses: we can enunciate true propositions about the world; language can disclose the world. And, if these theses are true, it must be possible for language to disclose its own disclosive power, for these theses are not about the world but about how language relates to world. But now we can raise the capital question, perhaps in a manner reminiscent of Kant: what must be the case in order that what we know to be true should actually be so? More precisely, what must be true of language if it is to be capable of doing these things? The answer comes as our first properly onto-logical discovery: if there are true propositions about what is, then the categorial framework of language must be equivalent to the ontological structure of what is. Let us now try to elucidate this claim.

2, 4 Categorial Framework and Reality

1. *Index, name, and predicate*

What is meant by the expression 'categorial framework of language'? The categories, crudely, are those classes of linguistic items which together constitute the totality of what can be said of something. The earliest and probably best-known attempt to delineate the categories is that of Aristotle, who distinguished these ten: substance, quantity, quality, relation, action, passion, when, where, position and possession.[4] Anything I say about something must fall into one or other of these overall classes of possible assertion. Kant seems to have found Aristotle's treatment unsystematic – and there is, indeed, clear overlap between the categories – but the approach has the advantage of looking to actual linguistic practice; the method seems to be to try to discover all possible questions one can ask about something as a guide to the possible assertions that can be made about it. Indeed, the names for the categories in Greek are sometimes simply the interrogative phrase or particle with the definite article before them. The great strength of this approach, namely its reliance on language, is at the same time its greatest weakness, for it is too attached to the peculiarities of Greek. We need to schematise the categories in a way coherent with all languages, and not in a way which is too closely bound to any one. Fortunately, we have such a schematisation already to hand in Predicate Logic.[5]

Predicate Logic distinguishes one- and many-place predicates, such as Fx (one-place); Fxy (two-place); $Fxyz$ (three-place), and so on, where the lower-case letters represent the gap in which some argument, a proper name, for example, may be placed. A one-place predicate ascribes a property, and may be read 'x has the property F', while anything more complicated ascribes a relation involving, usually, two or more distinct relata, although conceivably something may be related to itself, say, in the relation of identity. Thus we distinguish between two mutually exclusive and irreducible categories, namely properties and relations. We do not, however, distinguish between permanent and transient properties: 'x is human' and 'x is pale' are both properties because they are both one-place predicates, and the same goes for relations: 'x is the sister of y' or 'x is to the left of y' are, equally, relations.

Predicates alone are incomplete expressions, and require completion to be capable of 'saying' anything. The simplest way of achieving this is without quantification, namely, by filling in the x or y in the predicate with a name or names: if Fx is translated as ' - runs', then Ft, where 't' is a proper name translatable as 'Theaetetus', translates as 'Theaetetus runs'.[6] Two-place predicates work in the same way. Fmd translates, where Fxy is the predicate 'x is near y', and 'm' and 'd' represent 'Maynooth' and 'Dublin' respectively, as 'Maynooth is near Dublin'. Another logical entity, more primitive than a name, is an index, or index word,[7] such as 'this', 'here', 'now', 'I', etc. These, or at least some of them, can also act as arguments, as in the proposition 'this is a tree', 'I am running', and so on. These three kinds of logical entity, predicates, names and indices differ and are similar in the following ways. Predicates have both sense and reference, the Fregean *Sinn* and *Bedeutung*,[8] and, roughly, work by ranging over, by being true of, many; indices have what we may call a sliding reference, their work being to pick out anything for the application of one or more predicates; names have a fixed reference. Let us elaborate on this rough scheme.

To say of a (one-place) predicate that it has reference is to say that there is an indefinitely large number of entities t, such that Ft is true. The predicate ' - is human' can apply to a large number of entities, and these constitute its actual reference. The actual reference is that class or range of entities of which it is true that they are human. The predicate '- is a mammoth' has no actual reference. This is not to maintain that it refers to something like 'the empty class' or 'the class of potential referents' or something of the sort, merely that it can be, but is not actually, true of anything. We should observe here that to be meaningful, a predicate must have at least potential reference, where the phrase 'potential reference' is a feature of the mode of reference and not a range of referents. When we ask for the sense of a predicate – say, 'what does "Aardvark" mean?', or more simply, 'what's an Aardvark?' – we are asking to be given a predicate, or string of predicates, whose actual reference is exactly coterminous with that of the offending predicate. Working out such a string is the business of lexicographers. The sense of a predicate, then, is the range of its possible replacement-strings. The picture we are offered is, of course, that of the mathematical function, whose value differs according as the variables change, that is, whose meaning undergoes continuous variation, but on the basis of an invariant structure.

The grammar of an index, however, differs from this in that its use is to pick out something, though not necessarily the same thing, as a target for predication. A name, on the other hand, works like a specialised index, tagging one and only one thing for repeated identification. If a name is like a specialised index, an index is like a sliding name. Their meaning resides in their indexical or referential function, a function which is restricted, bearing not on a class of things, but on singles, either one only, or many in an exclusive series. Both are logically simple and incapable of reduction to more primitive items, having meaning only when there is a referent which they point out. Neither names nor indices say anything about anything: such is the function of predicates. In a sense, names as we have here described them are logical fictions, for if they work in the way that we suggest, each referent must have one and only one name, which is thus unique to it, and each name must have one and only one referent. It is as though we named referents by setting up a one-one correlation between them and an alphabetical or numerical series. In practice, the uniqueness of a name's designation is guaranteed not by the uniqueness of the name itself – there may be many women called 'Jane' – but by the intentional uniqueness secured in and by our communicative activity. It is not that we endow something with a name, uniquely its own, which belongs to it thereafter, but rather that the rules governing communicational practice see to it that this Jane rather than any other is picked out, and picked out again in and by talk about her, even if recourse must be had to description or other non-nominal resources. Indices function in the same way; it is what, in Wittgenstein's terms, could be called the immanent rules of the language-game which make possible the unambiguous use of indices; although ostension is carried in and by the use of the index, it is prepared for *a priori* by those rules: without them, pointing at a thing and saying either 'this, here', or saying its name while one points at it would be uncommunicative.

There are certain points here, of unequal importance, which we must recognise. The first of these is the Russellian one that many supposed names are covert descriptions.[9] The meaning of 'Socrates' is not this man, but a phrase like 'the teacher of Plato' or 'the philosopher who drank the hemlock', or the like. Names, unlike predicates or predicate-strings, must have referents to be meaningful. Nor are descriptions to be construed as names without paradox: if names are meaningful only when they have referents, and if 'the golden mountain' is a name, then the sentence 'the golden mountain does not exist' is a contradiction. But, not only is it not a contradiction, it is actually true. For these reasons, the phrase 'this doesn't exist' is also a contradiction, in that it has no direct revelatory use in language-games which purport to describe the world. But if that is so, the sentence 'this exists' is a tautology. Since 'I' is an index, the sentence 'I exist' is indeed necessarily true when the index is actually used, as presumably it is in talking about oneself; but this does not give this sentence so beloved of Descartes any deductive pre-eminence over other indexical sentences: its tautologous nature devolves upon it because of the grammar of indices. Moreover, like its denial, it has no direct revelatory function in the kind of language-game we have mentioned. What significance do these logical facts have for our inquiry?

In maintaining this tautologous and uninformative nature of the phrase 'this exists', it is not so much that the verb is idle, or that its logical credentials are suspect, for it can have a use and be informative, but rather that the behaviour of the index instantiates alone the, or a, meaning of the verb. What the verb means is already shown in the use of the index. This is what Aristotle seems to have meant when he said that substance is at least 'a this' or 'a this of some sort' τόδε τι, τόδε τοιόνδε[10] – where predicates explicate just what sort. The verb 'exists' here seems to mean something like 'being able to act as the referent of an index'. But, to be the referent of an index is to be distinguishably and discernably present relative to the speaker at some point in space and time, which would then be a, but not necessarily the, meaning of 'exists', unless we can show that this is all it ever means.

We ought to make at this juncture a Wittgensteinian point to the effect that although, like the controls of a locomotive,[11] indices may give the impression of uniformity and non-complexity, this impression is misleading, and what we have said applies to the grammar of 'this', alone or in combination with indices such as 'here' and 'now'. There is no discrete, spatio-temporally located referent for 'now', nor any obvious one for 'here' or 'there'. 'Here' is used to pick out the place where the speaker is, 'there', somewhere at some remove, 'now' the moment when the utterance is made, and so on. But, although they work in diverse ways there is a family resemblance, an analogy, between their uses. All of them serve to indicate relative distance to the speaker and the spoken in space and time, thereby allowing the speaker to address them in various ways.

Naming something makes this delicate process denser – we can indicate ripples on water, shadows, flashes of light, images in mirrors, sounds, odours, and the like, as well as less febrile and fugitive things, but it is the latter to which we give names. The purpose of naming is to be able to refer uniquely to such things, and to be able to find them again: in short, a name is a tag. Both names and indices are similar in that they require a referent to be meaningful, so that, in the case of a genuine name – say 'n' – as in that of a genuinely-used index, the sentence 'n exists' is a tautology, and the meaning of the verb is again instantiated by the working of the name. To say that n exists is to say that n is the sort of thing which it is sensible to name. What, in turn, does this mean? It means that n must be something, which entails being distinguishable from all others, and continuing to be the same thing through time. If one or other of these two conditions ceases to be true of n, n can no longer be said to exist. From now on, I shall use the word 'entity' to mean this sort of thing.

2. An Outline of the Nature of Entity

An objection can be raised to this: does my present whereabouts count as an entity? My whereabouts, as long as I stay where I am, remains the same through time, and it is tolerably distinguishable from everything else. It ought not to do so, for it is not the sort of thing which it is sensible to name. The reason for this is to be found in the qualification 'if I stay where I am'. Only if I stay where I am will my whereabouts not vary. There is nothing in my whereabouts, as such, which compels it to remain the same through time. For something to count as an entity, therefore, there must be something about it which compels it to remain the same through time: this is the same as saying that it must be unconditionally and of itself the same thing through time. Although it could be argued that this understanding is latent in our notion of what it is to be an entity, let us explicitly place it there. An entity is something, distinguishable from all others, which continues unconditionally and of itself to be the same thing through time.

In this way, Jane is an entity, because she is distinguishable from all others and remains the same person through time. For the entity to be in time is to say that it changes, at least in the sense that it exists at two distinct moments. Thus the entity may become other; this is not to say, however, that it becomes another.[12] If and when it does, since it is no longer the same thing, it ceases to be altogether. Thus becoming other and becoming another are the two kinds of change an entity is capable of undergoing, and by virtue of the notion we have now elaborated, it is continually undergoing one of these, namely becoming other, in at least the minimal sense of lasting through time. Of course, it is logically necessary that it should not become another insofar as it becomes other; insofar as something becomes other it must remain the same thing throughout, otherwise we are talking of the states of distinct entities, and not distinct states of the same entity. This is the foundation of the distinction between the essential and the accidental, and the kinds of change which they make possible.

The example with which we started the last paragraph would raise little counter-argument. Jane is something which counts as an entity. But there are other, potentially more contentious examples. Do Maynooth College and justice count as entities? I shall refer to such types of entity as 'conventional' and 'abstract' entities respectively. *Prima facie*, there would appear to be a difference between them, in that justice could appear to be something 'naturally' occurring – a standard of behaviour – while Maynooth College does not. The belief that there are or can be abstract entities I shall call Platonism.

But before we discuss the issue of the genuineness of conventional and abstract entities, there is another, perhaps more obvious, question to be settled, namely, could events, like the Battle of Waterloo or the birth of Christ, count as entities? In our definition of an entity as something, distinguishable from all others, which continues unconditionally and of itself to be the same thing through time, the word 'something' is to be taken in a narrow sense, that is, not as 'whatever may in some sense be said to be', but as 'some *thing*'. We must avoid circularity here. We do not wish to say that 'an entity is an entity … which continues unconditionally and of itself to be the same entity through time'. Moreover, as we shall see, (finite) entities have, of necessity, an event-ual or, better, processal character, so that it might not be amiss to assert that while not all events count as entities, all entities count as events, albeit of a special kind. But of what kind?

We note that phrases like 'the Battle of Waterloo' or 'the birth of Christ' are not names of these events but descriptions, which, as describing events, do not describe relative simples, but (usually relational) complexes which allow of more intrinsic plurality and diversity than entities could. This is particularly clear in the case of our first example. The Battle of Waterloo was not 'one thing', but a complex set of relations between many things. In that last sentence, the word 'thing' could well be replaced by 'entity' without loss or change of meaning. Knowing about the event in question means knowing how and what exchanges of various sorts, and other sorts of relation, obtained or came or ceased to be between various irreducible items – which is not to deny the inherent complexity of those items themselves – items which we call entities. Without some reference, either in general or with increasing degrees of particularity, to such items, any talk about the event or process is impossible. The event or process called 'the birth of Christ' is unintelligible without reference to Christ, as the subject of a certain kind (or kinds) of change. But the requirement for something to be a subject of a relation is that it be one and enjoy a certain ultimacy. It must be an *it*, and it must not be reducible to other items of the same categorial type. If it is either not one, or not ultimate in this sense, then there is no subject of the relation, and talk about it, or the event or process which contains it, is without end or definite meaning.

This would seem to suggest that the keynote in the notion of entity is one of ultimacy, and this is what is caught in notions like 'thing', 'something' in the narrow sense, 'subject', 'object' (though neither of these in any Cartesian sense) and the like. But what is it to be ultimate in this sense? Since a thing cannot be anything unless it is, the kind of ultimacy we are in search of is ontological ultimacy: what answers the description then, is something of which existence is said most properly. To be an entity is to be proper subject of existence, we insist. Entity is *being ultimate subject of existence in the way proper to, and determined by, what is, in the way that it is*. If we return to our rough definition we see that this is implicitly included in it. To say: 'an entity is something, distinguishable from all others, which continues unconditionally and of itself to be the same thing through time' is to say that it continues unconditionally and of itself to *be*, and *to be the same*, through time; it is the subject of the relations identity and difference, and, for the reasons given, is therefore one and ultimate, but is so precisely as existing, that is, as subject as such of existence. If it is not ultimate it cannot *properly be*, and something else *properly is*, otherwise, existence, *is*, has no subject. That existence must have a subject is the guarantee that there are entities: 'entity' therefore *means* 'ultimate subject of existence'. (To add 'finite' to this formula, so as to get 'ultimate finite subject of existence', is, analogously, to make the notion 'entity' internally complex as subject of identity, externally plural as subject of diversity, and necessarily temporal, as we shall see.) If all this is so, then entity as such is nonrelational, and must be diverse from property and relation, which are always properties and relations *of*. Entity is thus intrinsically nonrelational term of property and relation, of predication, and therefore also ultimate (logical) subject of discourse.

Let us now consider the issue of abstract and conventional entities; we shall look at conventional entities first. Maynooth College is indeed distinguishable from all others and has remained the same college throughout two hundred years (*felix faustumque sit!*). However, such entities only exist in and through human, and ultimately linguistic, conventions. Apart from such language-games, they do not exist. It is more convenient to talk of such entities-by-analogy as entities *tout court*, thereby fixing, under a common aspect which they are known to exhibit, the incorrigibly diverse and fugitive interlocking behaviours and behavioural habits, contexts, and regularities which such 'entities' are, and to which they can be reduced without residue, than to pick out and refer singly to those behaviours themselves. Such 'entities' therefore, belong in, and are supported by, the world of objective meaning generated by our communicative practice, which itself persists through time. Does this mean that that communicative practice itself is an entity? Clearly not, for communicative practice is many and diverse, which like Wittgenstein's thread,[13] is constituted by overlapping fibres, and is not run through by one continuous fibre.

Now let us turn to abstract entities. Probably the crucial difference between an Aristotelian and a Platonic approach in philosophy is the admission or refusal of the existence of abstract entities; the Aristotelian corpus is a mine of arguments intended to refute the position that there can be such entities, and Plato himself was not unaware of the difficulties of his own theory.[14] However, although this is a very large and difficult question, certain observations are apposite at this point in our study. In particular, it would seem that at least one reason for positing the existence of an abstract entity such as justice would be that when we speak of it we are speaking of something real and independent of us and of our intentions. This real something, we may feel, is a never-to-be adequately exemplified, unvarying standard, according to which particular instances may be judged as more or less just, which themselves are constituted as just by imitation of, or participation in, the standard. In a fully

Platonic perspective, that the standard has the hard edges – the non-arbitrary, whether-you-like-it-or-not quality associated with reality – and that it is unvarying and capable of being present in an indefinitely great number of particular instances, leads to the positing of it as a non-spatio-temporal entity. The seminal intuition present here, which is always to be respected, is that justice is something independent, not something arbitrary or merely at the behest of our conventions.

A crucial error consists in the disastrous inference that, since justice is independent and non-arbitrary, 'justice' is the name of something, and that therefore there is a corresponding, non-spatio-temporal something of which 'justice' is the name. 'Justice', however, need not be construed in that way, and can be read more elegantly as shorthand for the total range of the possible applications of the predicate '- is just', for the correct use, that is, of the predicate. Since this is so, the burden of proof lies upon the one who asserts that there are abstract entities. The matter is made more complex by the consideration that the totality in question is not, and may never be, completely available, which in turn is to say that we never have a full and complete definition of justice. Added to this is the more profound consideration that if justice means anything, if the applications of the predicate '- is just' are not merely haphazard and incoherent, the developments of and in its use must form an evolutionary development of ever greater complexity and adequacy, in the sense of being relevant to ever more cases and kinds of case, and though the logic of the development of our conception of justice must lead us to see this development as a gradual crescendo, this development need not, historically, occur serially, so that later is always better: concrete conceptual history will encompass decline as well as growth. Such a process may tend to be read spontaneously as a progressive unveiling of 'something' which is 'there' to be unveiled, or, in the event of decline, as the eclipse of 'something' which had earlier shone clear. The task of the thinker who denies the existence of the 'something' is two-fold: the evaluation of these intuitions and insights; and the construction of a theory which retains those evaluated as correct but which does not invoke abstract entities to explain them. In practice, of course, the one cannot be done without the other.

These reflections enable us to make a little more nuanced, and to confirm the adequacy of, the definition we have suggested for entity. Entities are always particular and concrete, never abstract. Moreover, since they last through time, the succession of their states forms a whole, where this term is to be understood as a plurality of parts or moments which intend a unity. We shall examine this point in more detail later,[15] but for now let us incorporate these items explicitly in our definition. An entity is a particular whole, distinguishable from all others, which continues, unconditionally and of itself, to be the same particular through time.

3. Realism

But more must be said in this context. If we had access only to indices or names we would only be able to point to things in one way or another, but would be unable to say anything about them. Predicates, as the name tells us, are the linguistic mechanism whereby we say something about something. Paraphrasing Kant, we might say that predicates without indices or names are empty, names and indices without predicates are blind, or better, mute. An unquantified statement which is capable of being true or false, is, of necessity, a totality of predicate, and index or name. If this is so, then for such a statement to be true it is necessary that the entity or entities referred to in the statement be disposed as the statement claims they are. In the case of the assignment of a property, 'Fj', it is necessary that the entity named 'j' really be as the predicate 'Fx' says, that is, it be F, while in the case of the assignment of a relation, 'Fjk', it is necessary that the relation Fxy really obtain between entities j and k, and so on for more complex structures. The minimal requirement for there to be such true statements seems to be that there be at least one entity with at least one property and at least one relation; in regard to this latter, the relation could be one of identity, whose terms are the same entity, perhaps at different times.

All this is the case when the statement in question is true, but such statements are contingent, which is to say, they are capable of being true, but are not true of necessity. We can, of course, qualify this in various ways; for example if Fx implies Gx, and Fj, then, of course, Gj is necessarily true – if being human implies being animal, and Jane is human, it follows necessarily that she is an animal. However, the point of supreme importance is that though what statements are true is a matter of contingency, that is, one cannot know on linguistic grounds alone what entities there are, what properties they have and what relations hold between them, it is necessary, if any statement about the world – contingent or otherwise – is to be true, there must be entities, of whatever sort, with properties and relations, whatever they may be: in other words, the categorial framework of language must be interchangeable with that of reality, otherwise true statements are impossible, and language is a systematic falsification of the world. It will be clear that by 'the categorial framework of language', which must be identical to the architecture of reality, we intend three elements: the category of entity, the category of property, and the category of relation, where entities are those real features which it is possible to name, while properties and relations are those features of entities taken singly or in combination which are disclosed by first-order predicates of the appropriate place number. What entities with what properties and with what relations there are is a matter of contingency, but, if language is to be capable of making true statements about the world, it is necessary that there be entities, with properties and relations. Moreover, the predicates which there are must be such that they articulate or describe – are capable of being true of – the actual features of the world, otherwise we can say nothing of those features. Truth occurs most primitively when real things, indicated or named, are as the predicate which is intended to disclose them says.

The position just outlined may be called 'realism', and is the necessary and sufficient foundation of any and all ontology. It is a necessary foundation in that if realism is false there can be no ontology, for the denial of realism is equivalent to the assertion that language need not mirror the critical features of the real in its logical structure, or that its actual range of predicates need not reflect any actual features. This amounts to the denial that language does or should mirror the real, a denial which is intelligible only if such a relation between language and world is meaningless. This, in turn, is the case only if another sort of relation can be said to obtain. The only other possible viewpoint seems to be the one which assimilates the real to language, in that either the real is in principle unknowable, in which case 'there is' only language, or the real is in itself unstructured, and is given structure either by my or our language. Both of these amount to the denial of the real as something independent of, or beyond, my or our language.

These points return us to our earlier considerations regarding scepticism. In the case of 'our language', there must be a real communication community, that is, a genuine plurality of distinct individuals who can talk to each other. Thus, the real turns up as this community, consisting of individuals who hang in some undefined space and who can only talk to each other about themselves and each other, and address each other in various ways, or, which amounts to the same thing, talk about and use language, though non-specious talk about anything beyond this is *ex hypothesi* impossible. But in order for such utterance to be true or appropriate, their language must reflect the structure of the communication community, and therefore must mirror the real plurality of (essentially communicative) entities and their properties. Thus the assertion of the anti-realist position is possible only on condition that the realist position be in some sense true. The anti-realist position thereby emerges as an arbitrary, and therefore unjustifiable, truncation of realism.

We may add as a rider that there are no private languages, and as we saw, the activities of the lone communicator must be assimilable to those of the community. Hence, the case of the denial of the real as something independent of or beyond my language collapses into the case we have just discussed. Thus any attempt to state an anti-realist position falls victim to these objections.

We also claimed that realism is the sufficient, as well as the necessary, foundation of any and all ontology. It is sufficient in that, given that the denial of realism is absurd, it follows that realism is true, and an examination of the necessary structure of language can and must yield an ontology, a theory of what categories of things there are, and what 'being real' means. We have already disclosed the necessary onto-logical framework, of entity, property and relation, and have ascribed some meaning to the verb '- exists'. We have now to investigate the relation between this pseudo verb and the categorial framework, for existence is not a member of any element of the categorial triad. We shall show, in particular, that '- exists' is not a predicate, which is equivalent to the denial that existence is a property.[16]

4. Existence

Existence as a verb has so far emerged as coterminous with the indicative function of name or index, and as adding nothing to this function in its actual employment; however, the tautologous nature of the coupling of name or index with the verb '- exists' does let us in on the meaning of the latter when it occurs in informative contexts. The use of the verb 'to exist' is not always tautologous; it is important to note that knowing something exists or does not is real knowledge: it comes as very real news to a child that the proposition 'Santa Claus does not exist' is, regrettably, a true one. Likewise to know that elephants exist is to know something about the contingent, as opposed to the necessary – i.e. categorial – structure of reality: there happen to be elephants. Now, the ascription or denial of existence must have a subject: we are obliged to say 'so and so exists' or 'so and so does not' – without this the assertion or denial could not be made. But this is not to say that Santa Claus is lacking something which we thought he had, and which real things possess, but rather, that there is simply no entity which fits the description 'Santa Claus'. To say that something exists, therefore, is to say of some predicate or string of predicates that it describes or is true of something, while to deny existence is to say that a given predicate string, not 'describes nothing', but rather, fails to describe anything.

By the term 'description', I mean simply a string of predicates, 'Fx & Gx & Hxy &...' which may be accompanied by a quantifier such as, 'is sometimes true', 'is never true', and so on. The denial of existence is tantamount to the denial that the predicate-string in question describes anything, that is, that there is anything which answers the description. We note, in saying so, that there is an onto-logical – being and language – relation disclosed in what we say, in that the denial or assertion of existence is also a denial or assertion about a description, a piece of discourse. The assertion 'y exists' is equivalent to the assertion ' "y" is sometimes true' or '"y" describes at least one thing', where 'y' is a description. The denial 'y does not exist' is equivalent to the denial '"y" describes nothing', '"y" is never true'. This, in its turn, is not information about nothing, but information about everything, namely that, if it is true that unicorns do not exist, take any entity, it is not a unicorn.

If, then, this broad equiparation between the assertion or denial of existence, on the one hand, and the second-order predicate '- is sometimes true' or ' - is never true', on the other, is correct, may we draw the conclusion that '- exists' is really a second-order predicate? By a first-order predicate, I mean one which can take names as its argument(s), by a second-order predicate, I mean one which takes first-order predicates as its argument(s), and so on, so that we have various levels of language – talk about the world, talk about talk about the world, talk about *that* talk, and so on. The predicates ' - is a (first-order) predicate', or ' - is tautologous', are examples of second-order predicates. A difference between '- exists', and its cognates such as '- is sometimes true', is immediately apparent: second- and higher-order predicates would seem to be applied on linguistic grounds alone, while existential assertions and denials are not. I can know, simply by inspecting some element of language, whether to apply or withhold such second-order predicates as are here exemplified, but, although I may, on purely logical grounds, be able to rule a given string of predicates a pseudo-description (which cannot describe, as opposed to merely happening not to describe), that is, in the case that the string contains a predicate and its negation (Fx & $-Fx$), no scrutiny of linguistic elements alone will oblige me to affirm or to deny existence. This is to say that statements regarding existence or non-existence are contingent.

In sum, to claim that a description is coherent is to assert that what it describes is possible. This is to say that, *prima facie*, it is possible that the description describes something, and equally, it is possible that it describes nothing. But which of the two in fact turns out to be the case is never a mere matter of language. From this we may draw a somewhat indirect two-fold ontological conclusion, namely that what exists is what makes contingent, existential propositions true or false, and this is irreducible to the working of language. Thus existence as such emerges as the contingent actualisation, in and as some entity, of the necessary categorial triad, the contingent truth that something of some sort is, namely, with whatever properties and relations which happen to belong to it. Let us now try to unpack some of the implications of this position.

2, 5 *Esse*, Property, and Predicate

The assertion or denial of existence is not just the addition of a predicate to the string, but is something, represented by the quantifier, which we do with the whole string. Since a one-place predicate is a property, this is equivalent to saying that in asserting or denying existence we are not either ascribing or withholding a property. Thus, existence is not a property.

A version of the ontological argument has it that by sheer inspection of the meaning or description associated with the term 'God', it is necessary to conclude that God exists. This is the version so devastatingly criticised by Kant, who seems to have been a precursor of the position that '- exists' is not a predicate, not the ascription of a property to something. Whether all versions of the ontological argument fail is something which we will not discuss here; nevertheless it must be noted that, however we may be obliged to accord unique status to Divinity, it is certainly true that there can be no 'ontological proof' for the existence of a non-Divine entity. This, in turn, is equivalent to the assertion that there is no property Px, which can figure in descriptions of non-divine entities such that, it is sufficient that if Py, where y is some entity, then y exists; if there were such, it would make the fact of y's existence a necessary and inseparable consequence of y's being P, and so, though not turning existence into a property, would make y's existence necessary. This further entails that any such property as 'Px' is itself equivalent to 'x is Divine'.

If we are to avoid going astray here, it is necessary to keep the following distinctions in mind. Although, as we say, in non-Divine entities there is no property P such that if Py, y must exist, there are many properties Rx, such that if 'not Ry', then y does not exist. Rx is thus a necessary condition for the existence of y. This is what is meant by an essential property, namely, one which must be true of y if y exists, so that the assertion of y's existence is tantamount to the assertion that all such necessary conditions are fulfilled, i.e. if y exists then it is necessarily the case that Ry, though, we insist, the converse does not hold. On this ground, that is, in relation to existence as such, we may make the strictly ontological distinction between essential and non-essential properties, though from the perspective of logic alone no such distinction holds, and both stand as determinations of y, equivalent to the 'how' of y.

It is important in the second place to note that ontological and epistemic necessity and sufficiency are not the same. It may well be sufficient for me to be able to conclude that, since Py, y exists, or, y exists because Py. If I see John lying unmoving and still on a hospital bed, I may be in doubt as to whether or not he is alive, but, on ascertaining that, say, he is displaying certain kinds of cerebral activity, I may conclude that he has not ceased to be. My reasoning is something like the following: since this kind of brain-activity is a necessary condition of John's being alive, and is therefore the necessary accompaniment of his being alive for as long as he is alive, the fact that it has not ceased is sufficient evidence for the belief that he has not died, though when it ceases, which it can do, this is equivalent to his having died. So, an assertion like 'he's alive because he's breathing' means something like 'I know he's alive, because he'd have stopped breathing if he weren't, since breathing as a necessary condition accompanies his being alive, for as long as he is alive.'

John must have the property since he exists, he does not have to exist since he has the property. This is to say, it is sufficient for me to know that a necessary condition of existence is being fulfilled to know that the thing in question (still) exists: this is not to say that the possession of the property is sufficient in reality for it to have to be the case that the thing exist. If it were sufficient in reality, then the thing's possession of the property would guarantee its existence, and, since the property is an essential one, the thing could not lack it. Thus it would always have the property, and perforce, always exist; its possession of the property would thus make its existence necessary, and its existence the fact that it had the property. In sum, the possession of the property and the thing's existing would necessary be mutually implicative and thus equivalent. Under such circumstances, the thing would be necessarily immune from ceasing to be, and thus would always be.

This gives a line on the ontologically sufficient characterisation of what it is to be a property. Properties are distinct from existence, and are subordinate to existence. In what sense, subordinate? They are subordinate in the sense that they do not guarantee or produce it, and so are completely receptive of it. But to say that y has a property P is to say that, given y exists, y is actually P or is determined as P; though this does not make y exist. This is reflected in the linguistic distinction between the 'is' of predication and the existential use of 'is'. In terms of predicates, 'that Px' is potentially true of many, as representation of a possible determination, though the predicate as such bears no further existential import than this. But, having a property is an actual determination of something which actually exists, and thus far presupposes actual existence. This seems to be the meaning of the Thomistic assertion that *esse* is the actuality of all acts or determinations, that is, whereby they count as actualities, i.e. as determinations of what is real.

From this, two more conclusions follow regarding properties. Firstly, a property is not without that whose property it is, for to be a property is to be a determination of something: to say y is P is to say simply that y is actually P, is determinately as P. This is badly understood if we invoke the metaphor of inhesion to picture it, because the property becomes a 'something', a kind of little entity, like one of the *tesserae* of a mosaic, stuck in an underlay (ὑποκείμενον) [17] which it inevitably therefore conceals. But a property is not 'some thing' – this is to commit a category mistake[18] – but the determination of something in some definite manner. It is true of y that it is P, y is P, y is actually P, y is determined as P; this is the way to speak, because then P is revealed as a determination, namely what *y* actually is, and not a concealment or an overlay veiling the real and internal constitution of *y*.

Secondly, since the denial of existence requires, as we saw, a subject, so also does its assertion. This means that it is a determinate something which exists. There is a necessary link between entity and property, such that there is no entity without property, just as there is no property without an entity whose property it is. Thus there is a reciprocity between *esse* and property, in that although *esse* is the act proper to entity as such, there is no *esse* without property, that is, which is not the *esse* of some thing (entity), determinate as something (property). It is this logical 'position' of entity which makes it the actuality of all actuality, and in this, precisely, consists the partnership of what is and *esse*: *esse* is the actuality, the final determination, the being real, of what is (determinate entity), which thereby is in and of itself an actuality, as really determined, in virtue therefore of *esse* as such, and not of any other determination. Things, properties, are actualities, each in its own way, only in virtue of participation in *esse*. A property as determination of the real is real with the reality of that whose property it is, not of itself, otherwise it would be an independent entity. Thus, the properly ontological characterisation of property is something of which '-exists' is said by extension, or, more precisely, by analogy of intrinsic attribution.[19]

But what of that to which the property belongs? It is, as we have seen, that which properly exists. It can only be so in virtue of its own *esse*, which is its being present as that which it is, with all its determinations. Thus, as many entities as there are, so many are the actualities of distinct existence, that is, *esse*. Without *esse*, there simply is no existing thing. Thus it is profoundly incorrect to attribute to 'what is' a kind of 'possible existence', an attenuated form of being, apart from *esse*, and which *esse* then actualises. This would seem to mark the difference between a properly existential philosophy and an essentialist one. Existence is not something which potential essents undergo; there is no 'world of the possible' apart from the world which is, some of which gets actualised in the history of the real universe. To take the opposite view is to make the possible somehow an actuality, however attenuated, for in some sense it exists prior to its incarnation in or by *esse*. There is also a suggestion that God's creative act could work only in relation to such possibility, and that God's act is therefore intrinsically dependent on it. Possibility, however, can be reduced to two meanings: what actually existing things can do or be, and what descriptions can or could have been true. These are the only subjects of the phrase 'it is possible that -', i.e. that y do or be x, that 'y' be or have been true. Language, in being able to describe the former, must be able to produce the latter.

We can further develop this issue by returning to the 'inhesion metaphysics' we mentioned above. We might, on the basis of such a picture, be led to ask, what is that in itself, which 'owns' the property? What would that something be like if we took away all its properties? Would we just have a particular spatio-temporal location, an indeterminate stuff like Aristotle's prime matter, or the like? A property as property is not simply identical to that whose property it is, otherwise it would be that thing, and not its property. But on the other hand, a thing is nothing apart from what it is, i.e., apart from its determinations. Likewise, I am Thomas, not humanity. Determinations are not abstract entities particularised in and as this individual in virtue of their encounter with matter: there is no such thing as humanity, but a predicate 'x is human' which is made true variously by various individuals, which is the meaning of universality, which is thereby revealed as a linguistic rather than a real feature. We shall return to this point, but we wish to announce the broad theme now that it is *esse* as such which confers individual existence, in and through which that which is, is. *Esse*, in short, is the proper realisation of individuality.

Notes to Chapter Two

1. An interesting discussion of this topic will be found in D. Z. Phillips, *Wittgenstein and Religion*, (London: Macmillan, 1993).

2. C.f. *Tractatus* 4.12 and 4.121.

3. LT pp. 10-12.

4. See *Categories*, 1 b 25. See also Ackrill's note on Chapter 4 of the *Categories* in his *Aristotle's Categories and De Interpretatione*, (Oxford: OUP, 1974), pp. 77-81

5. As background for this topic, see Mark Sainsbury, *Logical Forms. An Introduction to Philosophical Logic*, (Oxford: Blackwell, 1991), especially chapter 4. See also a more 'classical' presentation in A. N. Prior, *Formal Logic*, Second Edition, (Oxford: OUP, 1963), especially Chapter IV.

6. Prior, *op. cit.* p. 72. It is interesting to note that Plato would appear to have to some extent anticipated the modern name-predicate division, as opposed to Aristotle's term-copula division.

7. For the *locus classicus* of the presentation of index words see Ryle, *The Concept of Mind*, (Harmondsworth: Penguin, 1973), chapter VI, (6), pp. 179 and following.

8. See Anthony Kenny, *Frege*, (Harmondsworth: Penguin, 1995), chapter 6.

9. See, as background, Russell's paper 'On Denoting', published in *Mind*, vol. 14, 1905; also in the anthology of his essays (1901-1950), *Logic and Knowledge*, Robert C. Marsh (ed.) (London: George Allen and Unwin, 1977).

10. See David Wiggins 'Pourquoi la notion de substance paraît-elle si difficile?' in *Philosophie, Revue trimestrielle*, no. 30, printemps 1991, (Paris: Les Editions de Minuit), pp. 77-89.

11. 'It is like looking into the cabin of a locomotive. We see handles all looking more or less alike....But one is the handle of a crank which can be moved continuously...; another is the handle of a switch, which has only two effective positions, it is either off or on; a third is the handle of a brake-lever, the harder one pulls on it, the harder it brakes; a fourth, the handle of a pump: it has an effect only so long as it is moved to and fro.' *Philosophical Investigations* I, 12, p. 7e. On the previous page Wittgenstein writes (though using this time the metaphor of the functions of the objects in a tool-box), 'The functions of words are as diverse as the functions of these objects.'

12. 'To become other, without becoming another'; I owe this happy phrase to Desmond Connell.

13. See *Philosophical Investigations* I, 66-67, pp. 32 - 33e. Wittgenstein is referring to 'the complicated network of similarities overlapping and criss-crossing' between (language-) games: 'I can think of no better expression to characterise these similarities than "family resemblances"; for the various resemblances between members of a family: build, features, colour of eyes, gait, temperament, etc. etc. overlap and criss-cross in the same way. – And I shall say: "games" form a family.' Then he gives us the metaphor of the thread: 'And the strength of the thread does not reside in the fact that some one fibre runs through its whole length, but in the overlapping of many fibres. But if someone wished to say: "There is something common to all these constructions – namely the disjunction of all their common properties" – I should reply: Now you are only playing with words. One might as well say: "Something runs through the whole thread – namely the continuous overlapping of those fibres". '

14. See *Parmenides* 130b-135b.

15. In Chapter 7, below.

16. See G. E. Moore, 'Is Existence a Predicate?' originally published in *Proceedings of the Aristotelian Society*, Supplementary Volume XV, 1936. Also published in *The Ontological Argument*, Alvin Plantinga (ed.), with an introduction by Richard Taylor, (London: Macmillan, 1968).

17. ὑποκείμενον is a word used by Aristotle mainly in the logical and phys-

ical works for substance, as subject of predication and of change respectively; the word he prefers in the *Metaphysics* is οὐσία. ὑποκείμενον means 'that which under-lies', and is the term translated into Latin as *substantia*, 'that which stands under', meanings retained in the origin of the English 'sub-ject'. However, the underlay metaphor and the 'inhesion' that goes with it is at its clearest in Locke's *Essay*, II, XXIII, 1, 2, 3, and 6; also III, VI, 3.

18. Ryle, *op. cit.*, Chapter I, (2).

19. We shall explain this expression in the next chapter.

CHAPTER THREE

Analogy

3, 1 Introduction

The last chapter, as an attempt to delineate the broad parameters of our inquiry, revealed language as the clue to be followed in constructing our ontology. However, if we were to remain within the linguistic structures we have outlined, our understanding of the working of language would be less sophisticated than it should be. Language-use is usually neither simple nor univocal, but is an organically self-transformative matrix of the creation and extension of meaning. A proper and full delineation of this complexity would indeed be a daunting task, well beyond the scope of this essay. Fortunately, however, some of it is disclosed for us in a very subtle and nuanced theory or set of theories, originating with Aristotle and cultivated especially, though not exclusively, in the Middle Ages and in the Renaissance by such figures as Aquinas, Cajetan and Suarez. This theory is the theory of analogy.[1]

The theory of analogy amounts to an analysis of how meaning is generated and extended. It views language, not as static form, but as dynamic and changing medium, constantly growing out of itself in an organic process of development. Analogy is a dialectical theory in that it retains both unity and diversity, of the real and of how we talk about the real, in a single perspective, without doing violence to either. In virtue of analogy, meaning does not simply collapse into a sheer diversity of unreconciled, and perhaps irreconcilable, items, nor is the genuine diversity of meaning sacrificed on the altar of some false and simplistic unity. Unity is complex, diversity harmonised. That some such theory is required to understand how language works, and whose inclusion in the description of the working of language is not merely the foible of those who happen to be fond of ancient and medieval discourse, will be evident to anyone who has even a slight acquaintance with the work of the later Wittgenstein. In the later Wittgenstein, language-games are mutually exclusive, coevally linguistic- and behavioural-rule-horizons, diverse and disparate precisely in virtue of the incommensurability of their governing rules.[2] Though 'family resemblance'[3] may occur between them, they remain incorrigibly many, with no one invariant feature present in all, and, since there is no game-free meaning, meaning is therefore contextual, fragmentary and partial, neither needing nor intending any resolution in unity. Meaning in this perspective, in sum, is and can be, no more than the actual diversity of existing games, and there is no space even to ask for an overriding interpretation of world or language or self. A meaning thus trapped within a context is incapable of transmission, and incapable therefore of being an element in the historical growth and accretion of meaning which is tradition, and which makes up the essence of language.

Yet, in the very notion of the family resemblance, there lurks at the heart of Wittgenstein's discourse an adumbration of analogy, and if that is so, a need is apparent for an explicit theory of analogy. A family resemblance is not a univocal and unvarying something which appears now here and now there, but a range of at once diverse and similar features ramifying through a plurality of instances: not a single thing or an incorrigibly diverse lot, but an analogically united many-towards-one, a 'something' which systematically and organically transforms, and is transformed by, its context, dialectically harmonising real diversity in one space, really capable of accommodating it.

The following treatment is intended to be analytical rather than historical. Two main types of analogy are distinguished: attribution and proportion. These are further subdivided in two, giving us the analogies of extrinsic and intrinsic attribution, and those of proper and improper proportion. This last is an ugly expression normally replaced by 'metaphor', although it covers more than metaphor, and can be said to include maps and models also. We may dispense with the cumbersome terminology which normally accompanies the (Neo-) Scholastic presentations, but we shall retain these names in modified form.

3, 2 Extrinsic Attribution

The first analogy we shall examine is the analogy of extrinsic attribution. This analogy is meant to explain an extension of predicates beyond their apparently appropriate target, which takes place naturally in discourse. Thus, extrinsic attribution represents an extension of the meaning-complex connoted by the predicate to new, perhaps unexpected, contexts and cases. In this way, two inextricably linked events occur: the meaning is liberated from imprisonment in its home context, and the new cases are made to shine with enhanced significance by it, namely, as hitherto unrecognised examples of the now freed meaning. Yet the significance thus conferred is limited, for it is not possessed by the new examples as a function of what they properly are, but only in virtue of some relation they have with another. Their enhanced significance is merely borrowed, merely 'relative to'. Yet, what they receive does disclose what they are, does make bright an aspect of them which would otherwise have remained dull. Moreover, they do contribute reciprocally to the meaning, precisely as extending, and thereby liberating, it. It is not that the meaning is freed by being platonised into a contextless form, but rather that a context of application is gained for it both discontinuous with the home context and unpredictable from that perspective, in virtue of some contingent relation of the extensions to that context.

The standard example is 'healthy',[4] and how this can be applied to objects which can be in themselves neither healthy nor the opposite, such as diet, climate, and colour. The extension takes place in virtue of some relation which can be established between the objects of the extended application on the one hand, and the meaning of the predicate in what is taken to be its original range of application, on the other. Thus, while 'healthy' originally connotes the correct functioning of an animal's vital processes, diet and climate are said to be healthy or otherwise because they promote or retard animals' health, and to colour – complexion – because it discloses it. 'Healthy' is extended to these because there is a relation between them and the applicability of the meaning in the home context. We can now exemplify what we claimed above: the new contexts of application – diet, and the rest – are discontinuous with the home context because they simply happen to have some relation to the home context of the meaning 'healthy', the being healthy or otherwise of the animal body. Precisely as enjoying just such a contingent relation to them, the extensions are unpredictable from the perspective of the home context, although understanding the home context as well as the contingent relations which obtain, would seem necessary, not contingent, for understanding the extensions.

This form of analogy corresponds to the figure of·speech known as transferred epithet: the bird rose upon laborious wing. Wings are the embodiment of the bird's capacity for flight, so that their connection to the exercise of this capacity is non-contingent. But, in the case of this individual or species, or on this occasion, the exercise happens to be laborious. Here is the contingent line along which the epithet can be transferred. This, then, is the heart of this kind of analogy, namely, that the extension takes place in virtue of a contingent relation which obtains between the application in the original context and the new set of applications.

3, 3 Intrinsic Attribution

The analogy of intrinsic attribution differs from extrinsic in that no merely contingent relations play a part in the predicate's extension, since such extension moves along non-contingent lines, and is thereby, so to speak, built-in. This analogy therefore concerns the relation between primary and secondary meanings of one expression, and how these instantiate, or participate in, the one meaning, which is thereby diversified and pluralised. 'Living' has various related applications, but the primary, as characterising a formal property, is to animals, while a secondary application, in virtue of their participation in the life proper to the whole, is to bodily parts. For a heart to be alive is for it to be able to do what a heart does in the context of the living body, in which context alone it can be properly said to be actually alive, and thus a heart. This is even the case for organs already harvested and awaiting transplant, which are alive only insofar as they are still capable of playing – though now not actually playing – their characteristic role in a living being. The part participates in the life of the whole only in virtue of this relation which is constitutive, and therefore non-contingent, for it as part. Thus an account of what it is for the part to be alive is impossible without mention of this relation to the whole; to know what it is for the part to be alive is to know, at least insofar as the functioning of the part is really understood, what it is for the whole to be alive. Likewise, an exhaustive knowledge of what it is for the whole to be alive is a knowledge of how each part functions in the context of the whole, and how it participates in its living.

This is not to say either that we actually can say everything that can be said in the case of the primary application – that we in fact know exhaustively what it is for an animal to be alive, even if we have a very good idea of how the part is alive – or that what particular secondary applications, if any, there may be are all logically derivable from the primary application – knowing what it is for an animal to be alive does not entail knowing what all the particular vital functions are, or even that there are any, unless we know that a non-complex living being is an impossibility.

In the case of a living being we are faced with an entity whose being alive consists in its being able to function in certain ways, which it does in virtue of the structure proper to it as living being, as totality. Thus, to know that it is alive is to know that it is capable of functioning as a totality in certain ways. We observe that such entities are organised in that at least these functions, which are the necessary conditions for the entity's qualifying as alive, are embodied as the structures constitutive of the parts: 'if an eye were an animal, seeing would be its soul'. Thus there is a nice analogical proportion set up between part and function, on the one hand, and between organism and operation, on the other. The meaning-complex 'living' must, moreover, be permeable to new additions which may not be logically derivable from the central ones. It may turn out that all living things, or at least those of a given kind or set of kinds, must have functions and corresponding organs, which, though logically distinct from those delineated in the complex, are physically necessary for their life. In such a case, the extension of the concept over such unlooked-for instances, as well as over the predictable ones, is both necessary and possible, and in neither case is the extension contingent in the same way as in the previous kind of analogy.

This form of analogy is the analogy of participation *par excellence*, and has key applications in ontology. Probably the two most obvious are, firstly, the manner in which existence is to be asserted in the case of entities on the one hand, and of properties and relations on the other, and secondly, the discussion of the relation to *esse* in the case of Creator and created.

3, 4 Ontological Applications of Intrinsic Attribution

In the first of these, in which 'exists' is said of entities, their properties and relations, the full and proper meaning of the verb is deployed in the case of entities, and in a more restricted or '*secundum quid*' manner in the case of the latter. An entity is, precisely, that which formally exists, while the others exist only as belonging to an entity or entities, namely, in the manner of being called *inesse* in Scholastic philosophy, although this expression should not necessarily be thought to conjure up some kind of metaphysic of inhesion. The relation between something and its determinations is not the same as that between it and other things, though the relation between, say two, entities is a mutual determination, incompletely specified by reference only to one entity. A simpler way of saying the same thing is that what properly exists is entity, while the other categories participate in existence in virtue of the existence of entity: property and relation do not as such exist, but share in the *esse* of another. In this way the meaning of 'exists' and 'is an entity' dovetail, in that what is meant by 'exists' is best, though not exclusively – for then there could be no other uses – represented by what it is to be an entity as such. But any understanding of what it is for anything other than entity to be is intelligible only in relation to what it is for entity to be. The primary application of 'exists' is to entities, the secondary to the other categories.

Both properties and relations proper seem to have a kind of ineluctably relational nature, which the entity as such cannot be said to have. Properties are always 'determinations of' in themselves, and can only be realised, can only exist, in and through that whose determinations they actually are, and are thus analogous to the equation $x = 3y$, or to the incomplete locution 'beside the', which, as incomplete expressions, lack meaning until they receive some specification, either, as in the first case, by having a definite value assigned to y, or, as in the second, being placed in the context of a full proposition. Without that whose determinations they are, there are no properties.

The same goes, *mutatis mutandis,* for relations, except that more than one variable must be specified. Thus relations themselves share this quasi-relational character with properties, but represent a kind of shared determinacy, a mutual orientation, which is expressible only as: x is A in, and only in, relation to y's being B; x can be A only insofar as (some) y is B; x's being A requires (some) y's being B. Limiting cases of this would be where x and y are not distinct, that is, in a reflexive relation, or where A and B were not distinct, that is, where the relation is symmetrical. But, what in either case is in question is interlocking, or mutual, determination, which as 'determination of' is only realised, only is, in and as the determination of the terms which it relates.

This very incompleteness makes these terms secondary, by making them incapable of functioning as primary instantiations of the meaning of 'exists'. Any statement of what it is for them to exist necessarily refers to what it is for something of another category altogether to exist, and to which they necessarily refer, namely that whose determinations they are, which is entity. This is precisely what participated *esse* or participation in existence means: what it is for x to be is inseparable from what it is for y to be; x can only be insofar as y is. Thus what it is to be is best exemplified by what it is to be y. Moreover, though it may be impossible for y to be or to be y without some x, there is an area of being y which is quite independent of any relation to x, and, if this area can be talked about, there will be a range of sentences which talk about y without any express reference to x. We recall, in the case of the living being, talk about this latter cannot simply dissolve into talk about its parts, since talk about the parts is always talk about them in the context of the whole, so that, here too, there are assertions that are irreducible from whole to part, which is to say that there is an irreducible area of discourse proper to the living whole as such.

The area proper to entity consists precisely in its being other than in the manner that properties and relations are, namely, in not having the relational nature we have characterised. What does this mean? To have this relational character is to be 'determination of'; relative to this is to be that which is determined by this 'relation', to be the term which gives value and actuality to this relation, to be that of which the determination is the determination. In order to qualify as such, it is necessary that that which is determined display certain formal properties, that is, precisely as entity.

It is necessary, for example, that that which is determined be one, in the sense of not being an actual plurality, either simultaneously or serially, for as long as it has the determination. If it were an actual plurality, it would be possible to ask which elements actually held the determination; if some only, then the others do not, if some or all, then as holding it, the some or all are actually unified insofar as they hold it; if only one, then the one alone holds it. Thus, as being determined by some one determination, that which is determined is one. Likewise, being that which is determined cannot be one of its own determinations, for then it would simply be one more determination among many, of necessity irreconcilable, determinations. Distinct determinations are thus unified in being the determinations of one, which is perforce of a different categorial type to them. To confuse the two is, precisely, to make a category mistake.

All of this, however, throws light on how we intend 'exists', on the way we specify the meaning of *esse*. The verb 'exists' has, as we remarked, a relational, incomplete, character, always to be 'filled in' by some entity. To be is, in the first place, what it is for an entity to be, and secondarily what it is for a determination, of one or of more than one, to be. *Esse* is thus as many as there are entities; 'exists' means what it means for this or that to exist. More: being this or that, a one something, whatever that something is, which is thus ineluctably determined, is what it is, primarily, to exist, and secondarily, what it is to be the 'determination of' what exists in the primary instance. But since this is what occurs, and must occur, in each case of *esse*, of the true use of assertions of the form '*A* exists', it follows that the variety of the occurrence of what is, is a 'many towards one'. But the one is not an endlessly repeated entity or feature of an entity or entities, but the occurrence of these as such, and occurrence is not separable from that which occurs. But there is a family resemblance between all occurrence.

The family resemblance consists in the very notion of occurrence itself. Something that occurs can, equally, fail to occur, like a note in music which sometimes sounds and sometimes does not. The grammar of music does not dictate what notes shall occur, but only shows how one note coheres, or fails to, with another. The relation between music and its grammar is the same as the relation between *langue* and *parole*. What actually goes on is linguistic performance, though utterance which counts as utterance and not mere *flatus vocis* occurs as embodying rule. The meaning of *esse* is not so much what occurs but the mode in which what occurs does so. What must do so is entity and determination, but this is not to say that it must occur: the very notion of occurrence bespeaks the possibility of its opposite. Making this notion possible is the distinction between what is and can be, and what is and can not-be, therefore distinct from what must be.

In such a polarity, 'exists' is more perfectly exemplified by the latter, what must be, than by the former, what merely is. This is not to prejudge the question as to whether or not it is meaningful to talk about what must be, but if it is, then the relation between the two modes is the relation between Creator as what must be, and created, as what merely is. What merely is, is by virtue of another, and not because of anything it is, while what must be, if there is any such, therefore is, simply and solely, by virtue of itself, by being, as what must be, what cannot not-be. This means that existence is proper to what must be, and 'accidental' in what can not-be. Thus if 'exists' is to be characterised only in and through what is, what must be is the primary meaning of 'exists'.

In this way, the meaning of 'exists' deconstructs into 'what exists of necessity' and 'what exists contingently' standing in the relation we call creation. This relation is in turn specified as itself contingent in one direction, and necessary in another: to understand 'what exists contingently' is to understand it as what exists by virtue of another, so that the relation of creation is necessary to its existence, while to understand 'what exists of necessity' is to understand that it needs nothing other than itself in order to exist, so that the relation of creation is contingent to it. This is the point which distinguishes a metaphysics of creation from one of emanation, in which latter, precisely, the source of emanation is of necessity a source, and must yield that which emanates. This is not so in the metaphysics of creation, which thereby makes the source and exemplar of existence free in creating, labouring under no necessity whatsoever to do so. It is in this perspective, and, we may venture, only in this perspective that personhood can be attributed to Divinity, because freedom is the radical and constitutive determination of personhood. Thus, in such a perspective, the notion of person becomes the 'floor', the lower limit, of conception of the Divinity: God is personal and more than personal.

But it would be wrong to draw the conclusion that every time we use 'exists' this hierarchical relation is what we intend. A distinction has to made here reminiscent of that between inference, a psychological event, and implication, a logical relation, which, when it holds, does so independently of whether we like it or not, or whether we know it or not. Although this is not what we always intend in asserting existence, the meaning of 'exists' is only to be grasped ultimately in this context. If 'exists' means anything, and if the polarity we have discerned really holds, then 'exists' does intend Divinity as its primary instantiation, and contingency as necessarily secondary to It, in the manner suggested. Ultimately, the only way the existence as such of the contingent is intelligible is in these terms. Existence, in this perspective, is essentially participated: each contingent entity exists only within and in virtue of the necessary relation to Divinity, which Itself is what existence properly is.

But this, in turn, means that the possibility of any final or adequate enunciation of what the meaning of existence is must dovetail with that of any final or adequate articulation of Divinity. This is not to say that existence is absurd or that the word is a nonsense, but only that the full disclosure of what it is to be belongs properly to

Divinity; in simple terms, existence is necessarily mysterious, and we stand to it as one standing on the shore, looking out into the vastness of the sea. Existence, as Wittgenstein rightly believed, is the limit of my language, that which ultimately escapes articulation, but in some way marks and founds all articulation.[5] Certain things can be known to be true, things which at once orient us towards the ocean, and act as boundary between it and us, and mark the shore of our saying. It is the articulation of these things which makes metaphysics of ontology.

3, 5 Proportion

The next form of analogy is the analogy of proper proportionality, which we shall simply call 'proportion'. This is the kernel of analogy, because it is, as it were, the most analogical, and indeed the most interesting of all the analogies. To enter it, we may take the perhaps unexpected route already indicated, namely, the later-Wittgensteinian notion of the language-game.

Wittgenstein expressly forbids us to foist a counterfeit unity upon the essential diversity of language-games, and bids us look at and describe their truly radical diversity. The walls of each game are impermeable because the rules governing each, and the ontology consequent on these rules, are incommensurable. This may seem an unpromising starting-point, but in fact proportion benefits from being stated in these terms. There is no element univocally present in all the games, yet there is family resemblance. There is diversity, but no univocal unity. Yet, to understand something is to be able to describe it. This, in turn, implies that predications can be made about it. But there is no such thing as a predicate which can be used of one thing alone; predicates, of their nature, range over many. If two items are radically diverse, they have no common features. Hence, the same predicate can never be applied to both. But '- is a language-game' is a predicate. Thus, unless two language-games differ as hawk and hand-saw, the predicate they deserve precisely as language-games must capture this common feature, namely, that of being a language-game.

Wittgenstein holds that there is no unvarying feature univocally present in all language-games. Yet, at the same time, it must be possible to replace any predicate with another predicate or predicate-string exactly coterminous with the original: the expression 'language-game' must mean something. Such replacement is a condition of the meaningfulness of predicates, and if this replacement is not possible, it follows that the expression 'language-game' is meaning-less, and nothing can be described by it. This means that the non-univocal feature will then be revealed by replacing the predi-cate '- is a language-game' by an exactly coterminous substitute.

I submit that such a substitute might run: 'rule-governed, and therefore necessarily intersubjective and thus communicational performance'. While the point of a language-game is that, as rule-governed, it is not arbitrary behaviour, and so is open in prin-ciple to many players, it seems that it need not involve any actual utterance, and even if it does not, or is played by a *de facto* isolated player, it can and must retain its linguistic and communicational character. This character is indeed precisely what makes the verbal exchange possible, and not the reverse, and is founded in Wittgenstein's contention that there can be no private rule-follow-ing, and hence no private language, and thus no conceptual thought which is in principle private. Participation implies partici-pation in something definite, and this something is provided by the rules specific to each game, rules which can be learned by potential participants. To deny any of this is tantamount to the equivalent assertions that language-games are arbitrary forms of behaviour, that there are no rules, that there is no such thing as a correct, or indeed an incorrect, move, and so, if there is no linguistic activity apart from these games, that there is no language.

For something to qualify as a language-game, then, is for that some-thing to qualify as rule-governed activity. But this is clearly not a univocally present feature in all language-games, as we have antici-pated, and which becomes clear once we ask, in turn, what such activity involves. Not the same thing in every case, but something different according as the rules proper to specific games vary. What does being a rule-governed activity mean for, say, chess? Not the same thing that being a rule-governed activity means for tennis. Yet, the rules of chess stand to chess as the rules of tennis stand to tennis, and in this consists their analogy, their sameness-in-differ-ence, their family resemblance. 2 stands to 4 as 8 does to 16, yet 2 is not 8, nor is 4, 16: chess is not tennis, nor are their rules identical, but the role played by the rules is the same in each case.

In our numerical metaphor the relation is $y = 2x$. This phrase is uni-vocal, but it is quasi-analogical in that, though it can be stated in isolation from any of the couples which express it, it can be embod-ied in an infinity of such couples. Understanding the relation makes the couples intelligible; if we had no access to the relation we would see only random pairs of numbers. Understanding them as couples means understanding the structure which makes them so, and understanding that that structure has the same relation to other couples. In general, analogy renders intelligible the manner in which some apparently random or apparently radically diverse items are really unified, by disclosing the hidden harmony which unites them; if nothing of the sort can be found, then they really are random, really are radically diverse, and cannot be understood as moments in one continuum. In that case it would be wrong simply to bunch them together under some pseudo-denomination, and doing so would do violence to their diversity. But if such a harmony can be found, to neglect it would be to do violence to their unity for the sake of their diversity however real; it would be to absolutise this diversity, and correspondingly to randomise them and disjoint their real unity. The analogical perspective respects both, holds both together, and so emphasises neither at the other's expense.

The necessary and sufficient reason for holding that there is an unobvious unity in apparent diversity is that it is truly present. If an apparent diversity can be shown to be united convincingly, that is sufficient for holding that it is, and that we have insight here, and are not merely providing an intellectual equivalent of the rag-and-bone collector. Let us look at an example of this, namely, that of justice.

The meaning of a word is the job it does in a language-game. But 'justice', or words which apparently claim to be its equivalents, appear in many game contexts, diversified spatially, historically, and culturally. Often we can provide only an imperfect definition, or rubric, in which all cases of justice are united. We may say that certain individuals are just or the opposite, as are acts, laws, relations, states, societies, institutions, and we do so in a definite cultural context, at some definite moment in history. We may say what it is for any of these examples to be just and that this item is proper to it, and distinct from any and all the others. But we can try to put forward a rubric which will apply to more than one such example, a rubric which, if it succeeds, will in principle be open to extension over more examples. If this were not possible, then there would be nothing in which the various items could agree, and consequently no notion of justice, but only a random series of incorrigibly diverse, game-specific, communicational *praxeis*, the word 'justice' being a strictly equivocal term, a mere string of phonemes which by accident happen to be used for such radically diverse meanings, whose only connection is the sound.

Aristotle, for example, seems to maintain a notion of justice which is not inimical in principle to slavery,[6] and slavery has been a fact of life in many societies, not all of them ancient. It is however quite fundamental to contemporary conceptions of justice that persons can never be property, and that therefore slavery is a form of injustice. In short, in what we may call an equivocist perspective, the criteria for the use of 'just' and 'unjust' vary radically according to context and epoch, and to try to find some overriding, unifying perspective is to be misled by the accident that the same noise is used in these different contexts to do what the equivocist must think of as quite different jobs.

The opposed, as we call it, analogical perspective, is not, first of all, a simple, or simple-minded, assertion that there is one and only one set of criteria for the application of predicates like '- is just' and '- is unjust'. However, if such usages are not to be dismissed with a shrug as just different, then they are somehow united in a continuum, a spectrum of more or less; in short, one can be a more perfect – or less imperfect – representation of justice than another, and so counts as progress over that other. Progress here seems to mean something like getting closer to some ideal position, getting further into something, purging error. At first sight, such a position looks like Platonism, for it would seem to posit the reality of a 'something' called justice, a free-wheeling meaning or intelligibility, independent of any and all games, a meaning to which we gradually approximate.

However, the denial of Platonism is not the assertion of the equivocist view. What is crucial to the analogical perspective is not that there are free-wheeling meanings, but that actual concrete usage is capable of intending its own cancellation or superannuation in favour of a more advanced meaning, and indeed must do so if that actual concrete meaning is to be intelligible, is to count, that is, as a real meaning. This is to say that to count as a meaning, each actual usage must always and already intend a spectrum in which it finds a place, a spectrum which is at once progressive and climactic, and, at the same time, concretely historical as intending no 'discarnate' meanings.

Let us refer to current usages of such predicates as '- is just' as 'justice', and those current in, say, Aristotle's time, "justice". In the equivocist position, clearly 'justice' and "justice" have nothing in common, so that nothing of "justice" or its functioning can be predicted from 'justice', nor vice-versa, so that to users of 'justice', "justice" is unintelligible, and vice-versa. That this is not the case ought to be evident to anyone who reads Aristotle's ethics and politics. But, more profoundly, there is a general principle at work here, namely, that any game viewed from without must appear as an arbitrary set of behaviours, governed by arbitrary rules. But if this really is so, then the game can mediate no understanding even to its participants, and is simply stylised behaviour, a meaningless ritual, which the mere fact of being participated in by players cannot magically transform into meaning. The constitutive rules of the game must therefore mediate some meaning, and cannot be blind gestural prescriptions. But meaning is not properly incarnated by a set of mere behavioural prescriptions, but in and as a set of genuine principles which act as sources, as explanations of various and diverse examples of behaviour. Communication is not the deployment of a stereotypical vocabulary of concretely conceived moves, but an essentially plural and systematically varying real interaction between those who understand and seek to understand, on the basis of principles which cannot be cashed out in a series, however long, of univocal and unambiguous behavioural prescriptions. If this is so, then any and every concrete behavioural prescription which claims to be intelligible and to mediate meaning must, as part of its grammar, intend its own cancellation in favour of a more adequate incarnation of the meaning which it serves and which makes it intelligible.

If this reasoning is correct, then language-games are by no means well-defined, easily distinguishable behavioural units governed by unambiguous rules – we may call these rituals – but an ill-defined series of melding moments, only 'one' of which is ever visible, flowing and developing, merging and emerging. When a game becomes a ritual it dies, for it has lost the capacity for meaning. In a ritual there is only one path, or a limited number, from start to finish. In a more vital game, each move is actually a transformation of the situation, opening an indefinitely large number of possibilities of further resolution, many of which are unpredictable at the outset, and surprising: it is possible to surprise both one's partner(s) and oneself. The concrete disclosure of these is the understanding mediated by the game, their totality is its meaning. What govern such surprising interactions are not merely rules, but principles, which, though requiring some fixity, are irreducible to mere rules. Messiness is the price of meaning.

Something is messy when it is ill-defined, a little confused, lacking sharply-drawn lines, and language-games are always like this because they never 'are' fully, at any one moment; they are attempts at understanding, ready always for correction, a correction which takes place of necessity whenever they are played. To talk is to explore what it is to talk. Serious talk tries to improve on what has been said, and the rules of the game must be flexible enough to allow for this. 'Game' is after all, only a model or a metaphor; perhaps a better one might be an animal population, whose constituent species are unfixed, ever growing and evolving, sometimes interbreeding, and sometimes even becoming extinct.

If, therefore, meaning is not reducible to *de facto* rules, neither is it a 'something', fixed and given *a priori*, but is created and explored in and through the essentially progressive history of language-games. If this is so, there is no reason why the meaning animating one game should be insulated from that animating another. The *de facto* rules of the game may create a more or less well defined horizon for it, but what in Gadamerian terms is called the melding of horizons is both possible and necessary in the development of meaning. If this reasoning is correct, we should expect something of the kind to occur, and it does. This, of course, does not vindicate our view, but its non-occurrence would be fatal to it. Thus, it is to be expected that related -analogous - meanings, should arise, distinct yet similar, at one and the same time many, yet towards a one, either simple or complex, which is always both wholly promised and at least partially withheld. Such a melding, of course, need not mean the absorption or replacement of one game by another, which is a mastery and subservience relation, but the creation of a common space in which each (necessarily incomplete and partial) game or game-set, supplements and fills out the other in real partnership. This, one imagines, is the justification for the existence of the social and anthropological disciplines, which study the accrual of meaning in culture and tradition.

We ought to follow Plato's excellent advice and cut along the joints in discerning how this accrual occurs, which means following the actual paths indicated by usage. The melding of horizons, or the enterprise of translation, taken in the broadest sense, involves the discernment of proportions – analogies – between meanings deployed in different cultural-historical, or merely spatio-temporal, contexts. 'If a lion could speak, we would not understand him.' The substance of such an objection is that where the form of life incarnated in and as a given game or game-set is utterly different from ours, understanding, which thus emerges as the finding of analogues of the foreign games in our own, is blocked. But the attempt to square 'justice' and "justice" is not the attempt to square human- and lion-speak, but to find correspondences and differences between analogues, to discover how "justice" is or was to its home language-game as 'justice' is to ours.

Such games must fall within certain limits because of the ontological constitution of the entities which play them: common space is provided by the community of life-form incarnated in and as language-games. This community is strictly ontological rather than the result of mere biological consistency, the more-or-less-the-same-ness which the human 'model' has retained for perhaps a million years. There is a participation of all games in something which shapes, that is, gives form, and hence limit, to the possibilities of game, possibilities which are coterminous with meaning as such. This is not a simple something, the fibre which runs down the whole rope, but is proportionally diverse and analogically unified, the game which is played when any and all games are played, yet differently incarnated in each. We may call this the transcendental language-game, though this term need not have a Kantian sense. This game is transcendental in that it mediates transcendentals in and to our concrete communications, and is their formative condition of possibility. Every game is an engagement within – with and in – truth and goodness, at least. These transcendentals are the space which any game, which counts as meaningful, must occupy. This is not to say that they exist in some platonic fashion, as fully formed entities in themselves; but it is to say that human communication exists as functions of them, as with-in them, and as explorations of the territory they define.

Different concepts of justice, therefore, are explorations of the possibilities of being just. Justice does not consist in a heterogeneity of irreconcilable behaviour- and accompanying concept-clusters, but exists as a characterisation of ways of acting, themselves evolving in and as the diverse language-games which make up the body of tradition. It is thus incorrect to say that a given language-game defines justice, and that, therefore, the language-games played by, say, Nazis in the 1930s and 40s, are not open to criticism on the grounds of being unjust. Every moment of tradition, and every language-game, functions as part of the whole, and does and must, look forward to criticism and correction.

An interesting light is cast by the case of the relic unearthed by the archaeologist. Is the relic intelligible? We cannot understand the relic insofar as we have no access to the games which illuminated it; this is what it means to say that the relic is not actually understood. However, its intelligibility emerges from the language-games which can be played around it; it remains potentially intelligible – though perhaps never actually understood – for it incarnates meanings which fall within the purview of human forms of life. It would be possible that a society might eventually create analogues to allow the meaning incarnated in and as the relic to shine forth. But even if this does not happen – differing cultures and epochs produce diverse phenomena – the meaningfulness of the artefact lies in its ability to illuminate suggestively merely virtual features of current life-forms. The meaning thus arrived at is not the very meaning the artefact once had, but it is meaningful even in its home context only on condition that it function in this proportional-suggestive manner.

Something like this happens when we decipher an ancient script such as hieroglyphics or Linear B, or when, in general, we perform any act of translation. If some such meaning, which works by meshing with ongoing contemporary language-games, were not so incarnated, the relic would remain unintelligible, and there would be no difference between an Athanasius Kircher and a Champollion.[7]

This implies that once we use notions like justice and its opposite we are required, by a factor not distinct from the meaningfulness of the notion itself, to look forward to its fully-developed meaning, and to correct and improve its *de facto* situation in this light, to try to disclose that meaning where it is not given. This requirement is at once logical and ethical: logical, because to fail to do so is to renege on the development of the meaning in question without which there is no meaning, and ethical, because to fail to do so is to prefer the worse to the better. It is this meeting of the ethical and the logical which is the profound sense of rationality.

Furthermore, if justice is integral to the moral life, it follows that we must reach evaluations by using it. It would, of course, be absurd to blame Aristotle for tolerating slavery, but we recognise that such tolerance is finally unjust and is therefore to be superseded; but when someone tries – we recall the Nuremberg Laws for the Defence of German Blood and Honour – to create a situation which reverses gains already made, then ignorance, even where genuine, is culpable. Though Hitler and his cohorts would doubtless remain unmoved by such moral argument – we do it because we can – its presence means that the real undesirability of the situation they produce is disclosed, and the removal of the offending situation by more rational human beings, and its replacement by language-games more closely approximating to justice, are ethically and logically required.

In this way, there is a moral equivalent of the difference between Kircher and Champollion: namely, the difference between the reformer and the pervert, between Ghandi and Jack the Ripper. They have in common that they are unconventional, but the significance of this unconventional nature differs in each case. Ghandi is unconventional because he sees that present usages of the predicate 'just', and the patterns of behaviour interwoven with them, are inadequate to the fully developed meaning looked forward to in the use which is integral to their meaning, and are to be changed to approximate more closely to that meaning; the pervert, on the other hand, simply ignores the convention, and falls out of rationality.

Thus, our picture of the notion of justice, or of any proportionally analogical meaning, is not static one, but resembles the crescendo sign in music: '<' ; there is a definite inside and outside – not all usages of the predicate 'just' are correct, not all acts are just – and the incorrect is continually being hived off and the correct ever newly mediated by the intending of fulfilment inherent in the being-meaningful itself of the notion in question: this is the dialectic internal to the notion itself, which saves our exploration of it from becoming merely arbitrary, and hence not genuinely meaningful, or a genuine exploration, at all. Minimally, though we may not know at any given moment the full meaning of justice, we know that certain things are not, and never can be, compatible with it. The inside is the continual growth and development, which transcends *de facto* situations towards the 'final' unveiling of the meaning of justice. One meaning of justice can therefore be said to transcend another if the latter not only does the work of the former but extends its usages and removes anomalies. It is not possible to predict the latter from the former, but it is possible to retrodict the former from the latter: the principles essential to the former are thus more clearly served in the latter.

Our example will be helpful here. The principles underlying Aristotle's notion of justice, which was an explicitly proportional, or even analogical virtue, guarantee fair treatment for all; however, slaves as slaves have few entitlements. This is to say that slaves as slaves are debarred from a share in the common good. The question of the reformer, however he or she may come to think of it, is: why should there be slaves? The apologists' answer can be framed in terms of social need, custom and perhaps intrinsicist arguments. All these, apart perhaps from the last, rely on *de facto* language-games, which are, precisely, put into question by the reformer. The last type can be shown to be merely arbitrary limitations placed on the common good, and where they continue to be maintained, demonstrate the existence of vested interest rather than an attempt to cohere with the way reality is. In reality, however, the only argument which could justify slavery would be an intrinsicist argument: slavery might be justifiable if there were natural slaves, provided, of course, there were also natural masters. The other types of argument run aground on the consideration that, since no intrinsic grounds exist for slavery, there is no justification for it, except its sheer existence. When the reformer makes this truth accessible to all, or to a majority, he or she has succeeded as a reformer. The secret of reform is the strategy of the little boy in the fable of the emperor's new clothes, and the reformer is the wise fool who makes the irreversible proclamation.

Now, of course, this little story is not an attempt to sketch the actual course of history, which is at once more bloody and less simple, but it does represent the logical genealogy of concepts in a process which repeats itself throughout history, leading to a wider application of the concept of justice. Perhaps a vegetarian philosopher of the future will marvel at the barbarity of those who reared and killed our siblings, the animals, for meat, as we would in the same way look on those who still engage in, say, racism, and other forms of bigotry, as either fools or knaves or both. The point is that the idea of inhabiting a really higher vantage-point, and the disapprobation, which accompanies it, for those who ought therefore to know better, are genuine and justified, provided that language-games are not hermetically sealed off from each other, but form a continuum, at least along lines indicated by the inherently analogical and dialectical use of predicates.

But how does all this relate to existence? Existence surpasses our communicational intentions and is the ultimate context, norm and limit of those intentions, even of those which do not address it explicitly, since existence determines the real as real. However, the disclosure of anything in human terms has as its precondition the ethico-logical participation of individuals in language-games and groups, and hence has as its absolute precondition the reality of the transcendentals mediated in and through language. In disclosure that form of the good called truth is dominant. But the form of the transcendentals is receptivity, not projection. Like the light which is made to shine in the depths of the sea, they disclose, but do not create, the colours of things that were only potentially visible, and are now seen, a potentiality, that is, of those things themselves, not a property of the light which discloses them. This orientation of existence in and towards truth, or what is, and what is known, and actually intelligible as good and true, is the manifestation of existence and its resources as such. Being is the only adequate name for this totality. In this way, as the analogy of the transcendentals as such, proportion is the analogy of Being.

3, 6 Metaphor

The path which we have been following in this chapter debouches into ever wider plains of the deployment of meaning. In analogy, especially that of proportion, we see how meaning deploys itself by transcending its contexts, and by uniting those contexts often in new and unpredictable ways. This is the very essence of meaning. The imprisonment of meaning is its death. In metaphor, however, we see this unpredictable phenomenon at its clearest and most unpredictable, for in it we find things disclosively united which are apparently unconnected, and proportions established between things which are apparently disparate. In metaphor we find rationality at its most artistic pitch of deployment, and at its most human.

The key here is a kind of parallelism of relations, one of which is used to disclose the other. The most obvious example is a map, in which the spatial relations of a terrain are disclosed by the relations of the map's symbols. The map relies upon a one-to-one correlation to achieve its results, which is itself determined by the need which gives rise to it. A map, say, of the London Underground, or an Ordnance Survey map of County Donegal, answer different needs, though both work in the same way, by presenting a set of relations not immediately visible, in terms of something more immediately obvious. The same holds for models. The equations which describe the movement of fluids are used to describe the behaviour of electricity; electricity is treated like water which flows uphill. Algebraic equations are used to model figures in coordinate geometry. And so on. The point of modelling is that once the correspondence is set up, there is ongoing disclosure, for what is true of the more obvious domain reveals something of that being disclosed, thus allowing new truth to come to light. To create a model of something is, then, implicitly to have revealed it, and to allow for ever more of it to come to light. A map, then, is a specialised form of model, and illustrates the nature of modelling: disclosing one thing in terms of another; the correlation of two diverse sets of relations whose ultimate purpose is disclosure.

Beyond this stands metaphor. At first sight, the characterisation we have given of model is true also of metaphor. Something distant is revealed in and through something near. The all-pervasiveness of metaphor is disclosed in the readiness of the many ways in which language converts metaphor into literal description – 'style' from the Latin for a pointed writing-implement, 'exam' from the Latin word for a weighing-scales, 'psyche' and 'spirit' from the Greek and Latin for breath. Metaphor catches what it reveals in unexpected ways, perhaps suddenly and uniquely, or just as surprisingly, in a more extended way. Links are forged and held in metaphor between unobviously related realms. Metaphor is coined and passed on, a register of captured disclosure, to enlighten or perhaps become cliché: the story is told of someone who, on seeing *Hamlet* for the first time, was disappointed, because it was so full of quotes. What differentiates metaphor from modelling is its surprising nature. Once the correlation is set up in a model, what is required is ingenuity of exploitation, but there are as many rules for the creation of metaphor as there are rules for creating works of art, and both kinds of rule are equally successful. Metaphor begets metaphor and creates many ways of speaking and thinking in myth, art, religion, philosophy, and not least perhaps, in science, where equation-systems depict the world's pattern of working. Such capital metaphors cannot be simply reduced to the *A is to B as C is to D* model, which is the very proportion from which analogy takes its name, where even comparatively partial metaphors escape the net. Even the well-worn and apparently straightforward can surprise us:

Like as the waves make toward the pibled shore,
So do our minuites hasten to their end,
Each changing place with that which goes before,
In sequent toile all forwards do contend.[8]

An unimaginative, school 'translation' of this might well have us
believe that the poet wants us to understand the brevity of life by
comparing it to the swiftly moving waves. But neither waves nor
minutes toil forward, nor do they contend, they merely succeed one
another. These are the giveaway that the real comparison is unstated. Competitors in a race toil forward and contend, each against all,
to be first at the mark.

If this is so in the case of the momentary poetic metaphor, it will be
even more true in the case of the master-metaphors which govern
whole systems of thinking, totalities of shared experience, the
exploration and elaboration of which is coterminous with our
developing understanding of whole ranges of reality. Metaphor
tells us what it is to be this or that. And this 'what it is to be' is the
very marrow of metaphor. Yet, it discloses what it is to be something by revealing it in terms of what it most certainly is not. This is
neither to deny the principle touched upon in our first chapter, that
insofar as one perceives something other than x, one fails to perceive x, nor to rehabilitate anything like Cartesian ideas; but it is to
disclose the nature of metaphor as sign, whose function is always to
disclose something other than itself. Yet, metaphor is more than
sign in that the work of the sign is to be transparent for what it discloses, while the sign of metaphor boasts its diversity from what it
discloses.

It is precisely in boasting its lack of identity that the metaphor pro-
vokes commentary, interpretation and hence, understanding. 'God
is light in that...' This is how metaphor begets metaphor and thereby
fecundates understanding. To speak in metaphors is thus to create
an impacted focus which unrolls itself in and as understanding.
Metaphor, then, not only registers disclosure, but does so precisely
by holding together elements which are radically diverse. The wonder of metaphor is not so much that it is done well or badly, but that
it is done at all, for it may be that some things cannot be thought or
spoken about without it, and that it enters in some way into our
thinking and speaking about everything. Herein lies the surprise
and paradox of metaphor.

We may look at metaphor much as an Orthodox Christian looks at an icon.[9] Here is a depiction which is only wood and paint, yet which reveals and renders effectively present that which it represents. It would seem that here the metaphoric, the iconic and the intentional intersect, and do so of necessity. The intentional is intrinsically metaphorical and hence iconic, working by means of truth-bearing images. Knowing is always achieved by means of such icons, which are not the known, yet which reveal – rather than obscure – the known. Knowing works in a kind of outreaching spiral or magnetic field which energises and appropriates what comes into its ambit, that is, ever extending itself by progressive icon-creation, which then die as icons through being absorbed by what they disclose, however imperfectly, precisely because of their transparency for it: who now knows that the spirit does but 'mean' the breath, or realises the metaphorical origin of most of the language we use, however quotidian, literal, or dull it may seem? This iconic essence is what is proper to metaphor, then, not as mere 'figure of speech' or rhetorical device for entertainment or the enlivening of discourse, but as a way, the way, in which we appropriate the real. Symbol, simile, metaphor as applied simile, and all the appanage of the rhetorician, count as metaphorical in this iconic sense: disclosing and holding what is, in and by what it is not.

It is possible to regard an icon in two ways: namely looking through it and looking at it, being involved in it, and being involved with it. The two tend to exclude each other, and depend upon different perspectives. But it is the mark of the dialectic which belongs to philosophy, that perspectives which apparently exclude each other can be joined: it is a trait of the spirit that it is not confined to one alone. This 'looking at' posture would seem to be the invention of a third point, distinct from both the icon and that which it manifests; but this is not always the case, for the most fundamental occasion occurs when that which is given through the icon is at the same time given only in it. In such a case, there can be no verification of the aptness or otherwise of the metaphor. In any other case, we must seek more insight and judge the metaphor by means of its internal coherence, and its coherence with other things we can know. The case we mention here is the more fundamental, but it is the case in which, if the icon is no real icon, there are no icons.

Metaphor is what gives language its registral character. Metaphors can become fixed as meaning-complexes and thereby attain currency. In this way they are the memory of language, embodying a history.

To speak is to engage oneself in this history, and just as one does in living, at once to emerge from what has been, towards a new stage. But there is a dialectic of remembering and forgetting. The metaphor can sink into cliché, or it can be awoken and re-evoked. But such re-evocation is never simple, because the turns that meaning takes are unpredictable, and therefore allow for the existence of many, perhaps logically unrelated, stages. History, either that of language or that of communities, is never the simple unrolling of logical consequences. It is therefore possible to re-evoke quite distinct stages of meaning, just as it is possible to draw new and unexpected ones out of what is already present. An important element in all philosophy consists in awakening this linguistic memory.

Yet, at a more profound level, language itself is icon of Being. Language is only possible as such an icon, and if it were not, it could never function as saying something about something. Thus, language's capacity to say something about something (whatever the 'something' in each case may be) that is, its capacity for saying and being in truth, without which it is not language, is its iconic nature. Metaphors within language may fail, may die, but not the metaphor which language itself is.

To say that language is icon of Being – in the sense which we have earlier given to 'Being' – is to follow the Heideggerian *Leitwort* concerning the disclosure of language: *Die Sprache als die Sprache zur Sprache bringen*. The space which language occupies is the space of actual truth in which not merely beings but Being becomes, or can become, explicit. To look through language defines the ontic, looking at it defines the ontological. Yet the ontic is only as icon for what the ontological reveals, and the ontological is only as a making-explicit of the iconic nature of the ontic. It is this that constitutes their ineluctable mutual involvement, so that we could, in Heidegger's terms, speak of Being as destined for its clearing which we, as linguistic, are, and thereby understand that it is not *a* truth which is thereby destined to us, and which thereby shapes our life and history, but truth itself. This would then make us, not as some specific people, or as the hearers of some specific tongue, the place of the manifestation of Being, but as human, as dwellers within language. Likewise, it would not mean that this, though sent to us, is an inescapable fate, but a vocation which *asks* a response, an answer which involves looking at and through the icon which is language: to bring language as language to language. Onto-logy is done in the moment when 'through' and 'at' explicitly coincide.

Notes to Chapter Three

1. A good Neo-Thomist discussion of the doctrine of analogy is to be found in De Raeymaeker, where all the terms are distinguished; also useful is G. Klubertanz, *St Thomas Aquinas on Analogy*, (Chicago: Loyola University Press, 1960). More contemporary help will be found in *The Cambridge Companion to Aquinas*, Kretzman and Stump, (eds.) (CUP 1993). Cajetan (Thomas De Vio, Cardinal Cajetan) has been translated and annotated as *The Analogy of Names and the Concept of Being*, by Edward Bushinski, in collaboration with Henry J. Koren, volume 4, Duquesne Studies, Philosophical Series, (Pittsburgh: Duquesne University, 1959).

2. The seminal texts regarding the language-game, besides those quoted in the notes to the last chapter, are: *Philosophical Investigations* I, 2, p. 3e; *ibid.*, 23, pp. 11 - 12e; *ibid.*, 27, p. 13e. For our treatment of the language-game, see LT Part 3, chapter 2.

3. See footnote 13 to the last chapter.

4. *The Cambridge Companion to Aquinas*, p. 90.

5. *Tractatus* 6.44 and 6.45.

6. See the famous – or infamous – fifth and sixth chapters of the first book of the *Politics*.

7. Champollion's name is too well-known to require introduction; Kircher pretended to have translated hieroglyphics, but his efforts seem to have held more of the fantastic than the scholarly. See E. A. Wallis Budge, *The Mummy. A Handbook of Egyptian Funerary Archaeology*, (London: KPI, 1987), pp. 137-138 for an amusing account of Kircher's activities.

8. Sonnet 60. *Shakespeare's Sonnets*. Edited with an Introduction and Commentary by Martin Seymour-Smith. (London: Heinemann, 1973).

9. Leonid Ouspensky *Theology of the Icon*, vols. I and II, (Crestwood NY: St. Vladimir's Seminary Press, 1992).

CHAPTER FOUR

The Structure of Entity

4, 1 Introduction

In our last two chapters we tried to sketch something of the structure and working of language. Although what we have discovered is far from complete or exhaustive, we have seen something of the way language lives and behaves, and have attained to a view of language nearer the requisite sophistication. At bottom, language reveals Being, what is and existence. To investigate the first is to investigate the other two by looking at how we talk about them. Thus, the business of ontology is to talk about existence as such, which can only be done in terms of what is – for existence is the actuality of what is insofar as it is – in the hope of illuminating Being. We have discovered that what is, the real, insofar as we talk about it, is structured as entity, property and relation, the latter two being forms of determination of entity, which is the fundamental meaning of what it is to exist. It is therefore necessary for us to examine the ontological structure of entity as such.

Our examination falls into three parts. Firstly, we shall use the notions of identity and difference, which are foundational for the notion of entity, to elaborate the meaning of the initial characterisation we have given it. Secondly we shall investigate the notions thereby derived (which are contained in, and constitutive for it) their mutual relation, and their participative relation to *esse*. Thirdly, we shall investigate the relation of the chief of these, identity, as fundamental determination of that which something is, to the notion which traditionally does duty as an expression of this, namely essence.

4, 2 Entity: Identity and Difference

The minimal characterisation of entity we have developed is that of an independent self-standing something: distinct from all others and remaining of itself the same something through time. Identity and difference are two keynotes of this notion. We may elaborate it, therefore, by clarifying what we mean by identity and difference, which in turn may be done by turning to the Leibnizian principle of the Identity of Indiscernables.[1] In informal terms, if one thing is distinct from, i.e., is not identical with, another, some difference must exist between them, and, conversely, if no such difference exists, there are not two things in question, but one only. If everything that is true of A is true of B, then A is B, and if A is not identical to B then there must be at least one thing which is true of A and not of B or conversely. An entity is, firstly, distinct from all others then, in that some difference exists between it and any other and, secondly, remains the same something through time in that no difference exists between it as it is at one moment and as it is at another moment.

Let us examine the first of these points. An entity differs from something which is not an entity precisely in being an entity while that from which it differs is not, but it cannot differ from another entity in this way. As entities, A and B are identical, in that it is true of both that they are distinct from all others and remain the same something through time. But, unless there is only one entity, entities must be distinct. Thus, they differ from one another precisely in being the entities that they are. 'What it is to be this entity' must thus be unique in every case, and it is in virtue of this that any entity differs from any and every other. We shall refer to this unique feature henceforth as 'identity'. Clearly, identity is incommunicable, for if any two entities shared it they would be one and the same entity, and A's and B's not sharing the same identity is their real distinctness. Distinctness is thus reducible to the plurality of identity.

Let us examine the second point: an entity remains the same something through time in that no difference exists between it as it is at one moment and as it is at a later moment. Identity is necessarily seen from this angle as a reflexive relationship, i.e. as a relation whose form is Fxx, but extended in time. Entity e is I (where 'I' stands for the identity of e, everything necessary for anything to be e, where 'e' is a name) at a temporal point $t1$, and remains I at a later point, $t2$. It is identical to itself at both points in virtue of being I at both. Thus the 'relationship of identity' depends upon e's being I, which will, of course be different for each entity, in that e's being I is necessary for identity, but not sufficient for it, because being I at one point only is insufficient to secure the identity of something through time: e must not simply be I, it must remain I. Remaining I is, then, a reflexive, constitutive, and hence, internal, relation which unites the diverse states of e, where 'internal' means something without which the entity in question could not be. Such a constitutive internal relation is to be distinguished both from a non-constitutive reflexive relation ('I am my own worst critic') and from an external relation (x is the sister of y) which presupposes more than one entity, and hence a diversity of identities. Not everything which is true of an entity is part of its identity, and there is something which belongs to an entity which nesessarily falls outside its identity.

This is how this view can accommodate change which is non-destructive change. An entity can change by becoming other without becoming another. To say this is to say that an entity need not change as the entity it is through time, and this invariable feature or constellation of features, by virtue of which it is the entity it is, is what we have called identity. But this is not to say that an entity does not change through time, for it changes at least as persisting in two distinct moments, even though it need not thereby change as the entity it is. To say that something is destroyed is to say that there is some transformation of it which results in something not identical to it, as a corpse is not identical to the living person. The destruction of an entity thus consists in the alteration, and consequent loss, of identity as such. Change which is not destruction, on the other hand, is alteration in some manner or respect which is not of identity. If such change is to be possible, an entity must have at least one feature which is really distinct from its identity, that is, only contingently related to it. The features, if they are many, which constitute identity, must therefore be non-contingently related to one another precisely as forming the identity of some entity. We shall refer to the extra-identical features as 'accidents'. This usage is entirely in keeping with the Aristotelian notion of the συμβεβηκότα those things which 'go along with' substance. They are contingently related to the entity as accidental but not as temporal, if the entity is the sort of thing which is capable of undergoing accidental change, as all entities which are temporal and finite must be. Accidental difference can be the temporal diversity of one and the same entity, but simultaneous diversity is always distinction between different entities. This latter operates as a chief component of space. Thus, world is an incorrigible plurality of spatio-temporally diversified entities, each of which is unique by virtue of the distinctness from any and all others it enjoys by virtue of its proper identity.

4, 3 Identity and Accident

In this way, we have two distinct items which belong to entity as such, namely, identity and accident, and it is important to grasp the mutual relations of entity, identity and accident, and their relation to *esse*. Both identity and accident must qualify as properties, either simple or complex, in that they are as determinations of entity, determining it as the entity it is, or in some less radical manner. To be an entity, on the other hand, is to be that which exists, and exists as determined, radically and non-radically. Such determination is the necessary condition of the existence of entity as such. *Esse* is thus to be understood as the actuality as such of something with an identity as such, and, as the actuality of something necessarily changeable, and hence temporal and finite, as contingent actuality. As contingent actuality of something with an identity as such, *esse* belongs to identity in the first place, and to all else in virtue of their relation to identity, precisely as related to it. *Esse* is thus the actuality of individuality as such, so that, if it makes sense to speak of a Scotistic *haecceitas*, [2] this is coterminous with *esse*; in this way, '*esse*' is analogical and means something new each time it is used of some new entity. Identity, on the other hand, is that whereby *esse* is diversified and concretised. Let us explore some factors important in the characterisation of identity.

Identity as determination has a relational nature, but so too has the logical structure of identity. We say, for example, that John-Paul II is Karol Wojtyla. These two apparent proper names are, unless we can replace them with an index, shorthand for two incomplete descriptions, or strings of predicates. Who is John-Paul II? An answer would be, the currently reigning pontiff. Who is Karol Wojtyla? An answer: the author of the book *The Acting Person*. To know that John-Paul II is Karol Wojtyla is to know that one and the same entity is described by both predicate-strings. To know that the morning star is the evening star is to know that one and the same thing is picked out by the two expressions. A way to know that such an assertion of identity is correct is, presumably, to discover that a description of a property or properties or relation(s) which only one entity possesses or can possess is an element of both strings. The same is true of an assertion of identity which denotes the same entity at different times: to know that the author of *The Acting Person* is the currently reigning Pontiff is to know that it is one and the same entity which became the author of the work at a time $t1$, and became Pope at a different, presumably later, time, $t2$. Again, a way to know that such an assertion of identity is correct is to discover that a description of a property or properties or relations which only one entity possesses or can possess is an element of both strings.

Identity, in the sense we have given it, implies uniqueness, but let us explore what we mean by this expression in the light of what we have said in the previous paragraph. Is an entity unique because it is, or can be the *only* term of a given relation, or relations? Or, equivalently, is an entity unique in having a certain property, or a set of properties, be these accidents or otherwise? If Thomas and Mary have only one child, then any entity of which Thomas or Mary is a parent is *the* child of Thomas and Mary. This is uniqueness; by being so designated, the child of Thomas and Mary is distinct from all others, and since, even when Thomas and Mary cease to be, it remains true that this is the child of Thomas and Mary. In such a case it would appear, at least *prima facie*, that the fundamental conditions required for something to count as entity are met by this relation. Thus, to know of a putative entity $e1$ that it is the only child of Thomas and Mary, and to know the same thing about $e2$ is to know that $e1$ is the same entity as $e2$, to know that $e1$ is, or is identical to, $e2$. In sum, the designation 'x is the only child of Thomas and Mary' would function as well as a name in distinguishing the designated entity from all others in a consistent fashion, and the identity of the entity in question would be something like 'being the only child of Thomas and Mary'. Is this ontologically sufficient as a designation of identity?

It is certainly sufficient for practical purposes. But what is it for this picture to be ontologically sufficient? The only child of Thomas and Mary *happens* to be so, so the designation is external and accidental, not internal and necessary. Certainly the designation in question designates uniquely, but this is not the same as the designated entity's being in principle unique. We may imagine a set of entities which are indistinguishable save for spatio-temporal location – proverbial peas in a pod, or bees in a hive. Though they are, *ex hypothesi*, indistinguishable except in space and time, we could tag and number them. But though such tagging designates uniquely in that one and the same entity is consistently picked out, all the entities are, as it were, clones, and are only diversified by location.

But is such a picture coherent? Whether it is or not turns upon the meaning of the term 'clones' in the last sentence of the previous paragraph. We may take 'clones' to mean a set of identical siblings or set-elements. But 'identical' in this sense is not that which we have been exploring, and means, roughly, very similar, or difficult to distinguish. But if two putative entities were impossible in principle to distinguish, there would only be one entity, not more than one. Thus there being a set of entities presupposes their being, in Leibniz's terms, discernable. Entities must be discernable to be a plurality, and only a plurality can be numbered and tagged in the way we have suggested. We may conclude, therefore, that every entity differs precisely as the entity it is from all others, not merely in virtue of its relations or accidents, and conversely, its being related or accidentally disposed, presupposes that it have an identity. In sum, plurality presupposes diversity, so that diversity is logically prior to, and thus independent of, any non-reflexive relation or accident.

Before moving from this question, it would be useful to consider the notion of similarity, which, we have suggested, sometimes does duty for identity proper. Similarity is a kind of partial identity. If the relation of identity means 'being the same entity as', then similarity must mean something like 'being the same x as y' where y is some entity and x cannot be replaced by 'entity' or its equivalents, on pain of similarity lapsing into sheer identity. Thus, entity a is similar to entity b precisely in the case that for one, some, or many properties Fx, Fa and Fb. The more such properties Fx that a and b share, the greater their similarity, but identity does not admit of more and less: a is either identical, or not, to b. In this way, entities which are similar in every non-accidental property are identical.

We can make analogous points of relations. Here, similarity must mean that x is similar to y if it bears the same relation as y, which is possible in two ways: by mere identity of relation – Jane and Susan are both mothers, though not of the same people, and by identity of relation with identical terms – John and Susan are parents of the same people. It would appear that where entities are similar certainly in every, and, depending on the nature of the relation, even in some, instances of the second kind, they are identical, while not necessarily being so in the first kind: Georg and Martin are both authors, sons, fathers, citizens, and the like, similar in all relational respects, but not identical. We may conclude that relations are individuated by their terms: 'x is the mother of y' is always one and the same, but in this abstract fashion exists only in language. What actually occurs is Mary's way of being Susan's mother, and so on; since these terms are unique entities, so must the relation be which holds between them. In this way, relations are truly univocal only in language, but proportional in the real.

Is identity one item or many? It is impossible for anything to have more than one identity on pain of both being and not being what it is. Though identity may be complex rather than simple, and contain very many elements which are described by propositions, it is necessary that these be coordinated and conjoined in and as a whole, that is, as a totality of distinguishable parts which work as one, in the sense that any change in one of these elements represents a change in identity; if any item could vary without producing a concomitant change in identity, that item would *ipso facto* be an accident. Since uniqueness is distinction from all others relying upon coherence of self, it follows that the formal property of identity is uniqueness. Thus identity is not individuated, made unique, by anything other than itself. To be an individual is to be a really existent unique entity, to have identity realised in and by *esse*.

Is an entity its own identity? We must reply to this question with a resounding Scholastic *videtur quod non*. If we assume that an entity is its own identity, this means that it is identical to that which makes it itself. If e is identical to I, then there can be no difference between e and I, and everything that is true of e is true of I, and vice versa. This is clearly not the case because e contains accidents which I, as identity of e, does not. Likewise if e were identical to I, e would be incapable of any change which is not destruction, and such change must be at least possible if e is to last through time. Thirdly, if e is identical to I, *this* identity is the identity of e; thus I, as e's identity, is identical to 'e is identical to I', which gives: e is identical to, e is identical to I; which gives: e is identical to, e is identical to e is identical to I, and so on, *ad infinitum*. Nevertheless, it is true to say that e is I, so that the 'is' in question must be an 'is' of predication rather than of identity. But the 'is' of predication always ascribes a property. Hence, identity can only be a property, though the fundamental and defining property whose work is to make an entity the very entity it is.

The criterion of difference between identity and accident is variability. Identity is responsible for an entity's being the same entity through time, while accident is what can vary through time, allowing the entity to be other without becoming another. An entity which has this capacity is a temporal entity, an entity for which what it is to be is to be in time. However it does not seem necessary for an accident actually to vary through time for it to enjoy the status of accident; that it is capable of doing so without destroying the entity would seem to be sufficient. Thus what is necessary to accident is that it be a property or determination capable of change without change in identity, which is the determination of something as that which it is. I shall refer to the ensemble of identity and accidents as the state of an entity. All this allows us to specify more exactly the relation between the entity and its accidents. The actual states of any entity constitute a narrower field than its potential states, but the coming and going of its accidents are the actualisation of its capacity for change of state which is identical to accidental change. The entity, as identical to itself, is the constant factor in all its states, and accidents are *its* accidents precisely as actuations of its proper capacity for non-destructive change, i.e. change of state. Accidents are *its* accidents, then, in that what the entity can be or can become is determined by what it is to be that very entity, that is, by its identity.

Thus the relation between entity and accident is that between that which can be x, and either is or is not actually x, and the same thing actually being x. This relation is necessary to temporal entities, and constitutes the actuality of their being in time, though is not the root and cause of their temporality, a cause which must be sought in the relation they have to *esse*. The 'x' in each case is contingent, for it depends upon the existence of the entity in question, on its identity, which determines what it is capable of at the accidental level and how, and thus also upon whatever conditions there are which 'actually being x' imposes on the entity. In this way, accidents, like relations, are individuated by that whose accidents they are, at least in the sense that what it is for a to be green is not identical to what it is for b to be green; 'x is green' is a predicate, univocal only in abstraction.

Are activities and operations accidents or part of identity? Activities are more or less fleeting, though we can speak of some, rather old-fashionedly, as being operations, which, though not 'mere' activities, may or may not be 'on' all the time. A 'mere' activity is the contingent use of some operation: seeing is an operation, reading the newspaper an activity, to which the exercise of the operation is necessary. In both cases there is a determination which is more or less fleetingly attributable to the entity whose determination it is. The 'mere' aspect of mere activity seems to come from the contingency of the connection of an object to an operation, which may be more or less fleeting itself, like breathing or sleeping. However, it would seem that some such operations, however fleeting, are necessary for the entity's existing: does this make them part of identity?

Operation is a proper and characteristic activity of the entity as such. This means that because the entity is such as it is, it is open, as that which it is, towards the determination in question: because Jane is the (kind of) entity she is, she is capable of seeing, and for the same reason, she must breathe, and always be breathing, for as long as she lives. To say this is to say that her existing involves her always being capable of breathing and actually breathing. Death is not the cessation simply of breathing, but of her proper capacity to breathe, a capacity which is part of what it is for her to be. It is accidental to her capacity to breathe *as hers* that there be fluid in her environment which is breathable. There is a difference between 'Jane can't breathe because she's dead' and 'Jane can't breathe because the atmosphere is chlorine', namely, between Jane's ability to breathe on one hand, and the suitability, or otherwise, of chlorine, for breathing, on the other. The activity of breathing is founded on the capacity for it, which as capacity of and for, is a determination necessarily consequent on what the entity is, namely, on what it is for that, or that *kind* of, entity to be. This kind of determination cannot change without the destruction of the entity in question, and yet, it does not seem likely that the capacity to breathe should form part of something's identity, since identity as we have articulated it, is unique and vital to each entity.

We have suggested that an essential feature is one which is a necessary, but not a sufficient, condition for the existence of an entity, but, this requires qualification. An essential feature accrues to entity not precisely in virtue of the entity it is, but in virtue of the kind of entity it is. It is absolutely necessary to be able to group entities in non-arbitrary sets, otherwise predication is impossible, and for some of these sets to be based on the similarity which things share as the entities they are, as opposed to their accidental properties and relations.

But, 'the similarity which things share as the entities they are, as opposed to their accidental properties and relations' is their kind, or essence. We must distinguish therefore, between, 'what it is to be *n*', where *n* is the name of some entity (identity), as opposed to 'what it is to be *an n*', where *n* is a predicate representing some *kind* of entity (essence). An immediately obvious point of contrast between the two conceptions is that identity can belong to only one entity, such that to every distinct entity insofar as it is distinct, there corresponds a unique identity, while essence always bespeaks a participation of many in one shared nature. Here we have a question central to ontology: how is it possible to reconcile entities' being similar as regards kind, and their being diverse as individuals?

4, 4 Identity and Essence[3]

Clearly, any articulation of identity involves the use of predicates, some of which are essential, otherwise entities, precisely as distinct, could only be named and not described. Essence does not specify identity explicitly, but is inseparable from identity. It is clearly part of Jane's identity to be human, and all that being human necessarily entails, but her identity is more, and richer, than this. She is human in her way, according therefore, to her own identity, which always includes, but is always more than, just being human. So, even though it seems unlikely, determinations such as those we have been discussing, if inseparable from essence, are thereby inseparable from identity, and integral to it. Something is inseparable from the essence of entity *e* if *e* cannot be without this something; something is inseparable from the identity of *e* if *e* cannot be the individual entity it is without it; all else is accidental, either in relation to essence or to the individual as such. One can speak of what is essential to Jane as human, and what is inseparable from her as this human individual. Conceptually, the essential predicate comes first, to be further determined and tailored to reality, but really, the individual, with his, her, or its, identity, takes precedence. Our realist stance leads us to say that essence never exists except as a component of identity, and identity is a kind of further determination, a particularisation and individuation of what it is to be human.

In the Scholastic tradition, what diversifies the same nature among many particulars is 'demarcated material', *materia signata*, that is, matter 'as underlying certain defined dimensions', *sub determinatis dimensionibus*.[4] Hence the characterisation of matter as *principium individuationis*, source of individuation.[5] But, it is matter in general which enters the definition of human being, not demarcated material: not this flesh and these bones, but flesh and bones in general, though this would have to enter the definition of the individual if the individual were capable of definition. In this theory, all infra-specific differences are ascribable to matter. Aquinas tells us in *De Ente et Essentia*, that:

Socrates' essence differs from human essence only by being demarcated. *Socrates*, as Ibn Rushd says, *is nothing more than animality plus rationality; those are what he is.* [6]

Thus, it seems, my humanity differs from your humanity in that mine is the form of this quantified chunk of matter, here, yours the form of that, there, so that individual variation is only the result of material, that is, spatio-temporal, considerations. The contribution of matter to the composite is not formal determination but the facilitation of spatio-temporally diverse instantiations of one and the same structure. Spiritual entities, by definition lacking any material component, were in effect considered to be one-member classes; Gabriel differs from Raphael not as Jane differs from Joan, nor even as Jane differs from Peter, but as horse differs from cat. Hence the Scholastic 'axiom' that spiritual substances exhaust their species.[7] We may note in passing that, according to this view, only spiritual substances can have identity in anything like the sense we have given it, as exclusive to one entity alone. 'Nature', moreover, as 'source of motion and rest'[8] was characterisation of the individual as acting in the ways proper to members of the kind specified by essence. Thus, there is also an accidental quality even in action as attributable to individuals.

The position which this quotation may be taken to represent differs in more than one respect from the one we have presented. In the first place, our notion of demarcation is, as it were, qualitative rather than quantative. It is identity as such which demarcates entities as distinct and thus coevally as individuals, while *esse*, as actuality proper to entity through identity, is individuation. But this seems to be the difficulty: if identity is as such unique and unrepeatable, how is it possible for such distinct entities to be together non-contingently in one class, precisely as instantiating the predicate which generates the class, in a manner, that is, which is not artificial or merely arbitrary, and thus rendering the predicate itself really uninformative regarding the items which fall under it? I call 'nominalism' the view that all classes are merely arbitrary conjunctions of, in themselves irreconcilably diverse, particulars. If nominalism were true, it would make knowledge, precisely as dependent upon such classal conjunction's being really informative, impossible.

But, nominalism is self-refuting in that it presupposes what it denies, and does so by asserting that notions like 'class' are arbitrary thereby assuming the non-arbitrary and genuinely informative nature of, at least, predicates like 'x is a class' and 'x is arbitrary'. The truth which such a theory intends but does not reach is that universals as such are linguistic, and if essence is a shared nature, it is therefore present formally only in language, and, as a corollary of this, that the logical necessity which belongs to essence is grounded in what is intended by these two theses. It is at this point useful to underline that, in the view we defend, it is identity precisely as a totality which is inalienable and proper, though as complex it may consist of 'parts' which can be shared precisely as distinct. It is true of Bach and Mozart that each is musical, but each is musical as the existing individual he is.

In the second place, the relation of the individual to its nature seems to be done but little justice in the words of Ibn Rushd which Aquinas quotes with such apparent approval. It seems to make of Socrates not so much an individual as a kind of clone, identical in all important respects with every other member of the clone, in such a way as to devalue what belongs to him as the individual he is. The bravery, kindness, and piety which make Socrates – at least as Plato describes him – not merely so loveable and admirable, but which are intrinsic to his being Socrates, appear here to be demoted to the level of snubness in a nose: a quantitative eccentricity attributable to the disposition proper to demarcated matter.

The same account of individuation is reinforced in the context of cognitive theory.[9] Here the work of the intellect is to disengage the intelligible structure from its material situatedness. It is from this function or aspect that intellect is named: intellect is a seeing of the bright, hard lines of intelligibility and universality in the often inchoate flux of the particular and concrete. The metaphor of an x-ray leaps to the modern mind. The passive aspect of mind, the understanding, is passive precisely as receptive of the intelligibility disengaged by the light of the intellect. The understanding is made fecund by the active intellect, and expresses what it has received in and as the concept which it conceives, a universal which in principle ranges over many. Things are intelligible insofar as they fall under such shared concepts while the particular as such is not ultimately knowable. There is and can be no science, no conceptual knowledge, of the particular as such. If matter is the principle of the particular as such, then matter in itself is dense and dark, only to be grasped analogically and through form. The central and characteristic note of this theory is that it is the same item which appears, now as the structure instantiated in, and informing matter, now immaterially and conceptually in mind. This diversity of presence of the same allows for the mind's containing the actuality of what the real is, but without instantiating it.

My understanding, in knowing the real, knows what it is to be, say, stone(-in-general), and judges that this thing is a stone, thereby understanding the thing in correctly attributing the concept to it. My intellect, which is my cognitive capacity for the real, possesses the actuality of what it is to be stone without taking on the actuality of what stone is, that is, without becoming stone. This identity of actuality between the real and conceptual orders is meant to secure a firm foundation for knowledge, in that what I know is (identity) what there is: the actuality of what there is is (identity) what informs my understanding. In the pregnant phrase of Parmenides, one it is to think and to be.

The chief danger in such a theory is that, although it is not Platonism, and so does not treat such intelligibility as a complete or ontologically independent item – that is, an entity – it nonetheless may grant a certain priority to form, to which concepts are identical in the way suggested, relative to the individuals which are thus understood as instantiations of the prior item. Such a priority is characteristic of idealism, which often tends to go further and view the individual as a smudged copy of a crystalline original. The theory might seem to amount to the assertion that there is an unvarying feature, present at different spatio-temporal locations, its instantiations, but not existing apart from them. These instantiations would be discontinuous both spatially and temporally, could occur in different places at one time, perhaps at no place at some time, and so on. Yet there is an 'it', *ex hypothesi*, which, though only existing as instantiated, transcends spatio-temporality in that it remains itself despite the necessary discontinuity brought about by being occasionally instantiated, and at the same time, is not distinct from itself despite being on occasion simultaneously instantiated in different places. Interwoven with this platonising interpretation may be a tendency to see the concept as a kind of, albeit complex, name. To use the appropriate predicate, at least in the case of univocity, is to pick out an invariant, closed, 'something', which is present in all and each of its instances, the particular entities. Entities are thus simply spatio-temporal points at which universals are instantiated.

A keynote of modern existentialism, from Kierkegaard on, was a replacement of that tiresome eido-latry that has characterised much of Western thought with a more just appreciation of uniqueness, diversity, and individuality, even if it is impossible to grasp all the ramifications of this diversity. Moreover, we would claim, and we hope to show by using his principles to solve this nexus of problems, that the thought of Aquinas is existentialist in this way, and that, indeed, in an exemplary and pre-eminent fashion.[10] In particular, I take his *opusculum, De Ente et Essentia*, to which we explicitly refer in this chapter, to be a high-tide mark of philosophical speculation in regard to the issues treated here; I take the third chapter above all to be a kind of charter of realism, that is, as being a definitive statement of what realism is.

What is the relation between Jane and humanity, such that we can say truthfully of her that she is human? It cannot mean that there is a univocal aspect of her, cut off from all others, which the concept picks out, and which she exemplifies along with all other entities with whom she is of necessity formally identical, as member of the one species. It is this which is at the root of the platonising tendency in interpreting cognitive theory which we have been discussing.

The solution to the problem would seem to be that suggested by Aquinas himself in a capital text in the *De Ente et Essentia*:

> And because ... a thing's specific nature leaves undetermined which individual it is (just as its generic nature leaves undetermined what species it is), the species of an individual expresses – indistinctly – the whole essence of that individual (just as the genus of a species expresses implicitly but indistinctly the whole of what the species expresses determinately). And because this is the way the phrase 'human being' expresses the essence of his species, we may say Socrates is a human being.[11]

John, Mary and Philip are unique in their identities, but '- is human' must nonetheless be true of all three. Each is unique in virtue of identity, but are similar insofar as the same predicate applies to each. John, as the unique entity he is, makes the predicate true in his own way, and likewise for all such cases. Mozart's musical genius is proper to Mozart as the unique individual he is, but is coincident with his being human; the unique constellation which is identity is virtually, though not actually, contained in the predicate, which in turn is necessarily open to such further determination, for being human involves having unique identity, whatever this may be. To be able to range over many, the predicate must be abstract, meaning it cannot fit any one perfectly, and thus must draw back precisely from the uniqueness granted by identity; a predicate adequate to the identity of something would of necessity apply to that something alone, and would thereby cease to be a predicate. 'Being human' is not an unvarying 'something', but an expression, necessarily not fully determinate, of what it is to be an *individual* of a given kind, as it were, a sort of mean or average within which many individuals fall, not as instantiating merely, but as individuating it. Names always bespeak that uniqueness conferred by identity. Individuals as such can be named, though only imperfectly described. Only the complex is conceptualisable, and if identity were incomplex it would be only nameable and inexpressible; complexity in this sense is the presentation of diverse but united aspects which can be described, though indistinctly. To describe an entity is to approximate gradually to its nameable uniqueness, to deploy abstract nets to capture its concrete individuality, which thereby always slips through. 'Thou shalt make to thee no graven image' is good advice even in knowledge of the finite which, though knowable insofar as it is, is never in fact known insofar as it is, coterminously with all that it is.

Predicates intend universally, but do not intend universals. 'This is a giraffe', 'that is Mary', are answers elicited by 'what?' and 'who?'. It is incorrect to answer 'who?' by saying 'a human being'. Being human is all that Mary is but she is so in her own inalienable way. This would seem to grant a quasi-analogical nature to a predicate like '- is human'. The answer appropriate to 'what?' usually suffices outside the human, and perhaps part of the animal (it's Fido!), realm. But many things outside this realm are nameable, and will be named, or given a nominal equivalent, at need. The nameable and the named are not coterminous but where it is possible to name something, there is entity, there is identity.

Let us return again to Aquinas's text. Essence can be considered in two ways:

> Firstly, on its own, considering what properly defines it, so that only what belongs to it as such is true of it and everything else attributed to it false. Thus, being logical and animal and whatever else defines human beings belongs to them as human, but being white or black or anything else not included in humanness doesn't belong to human beings as human ... The second way of considering nature is as existing in this or that: and considered

in this way something can be attributed to it coincidentally by reason of what possesses the nature, as a human being can be called white since Socrates is white though white doesn't attach to human beings as human. Nature in this sense exists firstly in singulars and secondly in the mind: in both cases certain things are true of it coincidentally, and in singulars it also exists more than once in a diversity of singulars ... Clearly then human nature considered on its own abstracts from all these existences but cuts none out, and it is nature considered in this way that is predicated of all individuals.[12]

The hallmark of this text is realism as openness, precisely to individuality and diversity. Nature exists firstly as individualised as singulars, and secondly, abstractly, in the mind or in language, and the second way is parasitic on the first. This is realism. Likewise, nature as linguistically expressed abstracts from all these existences but cuts none out. This is openness to individuality.

Essence exists in the second sense as what individual humans are as humans and as individual humans. Socrates is brave and kind coincidentally because not all humans are brave and kind, though being brave and kind is a possibility for humans as the individuals they are. Aquinas gives a very definite priority here to the singulars over what is in the mind, or better, in language, where alone abstractions 'exist'. It would seem that what exists 'secondly in the mind' dovetails with the meaning of essence in the first sense, the formal concept of the essence in question, in relation to which conceptual or essential necessity and contingency are founded.

To ask what 'human' means is to ask what the conditions are for the correct application of the predicate. Such conditions are onto-logical in that firstly, they cannot be merely intra-linguistic, but must intend the real. Thus they cannot but involve perception of the world, and perceptions of the world are embedded in linguistic usage to the extent that a human perception of the world is impossible without language. My use of the predicate 'green' depends on my being able both to recognise examples of green, and to be able to employ notions such as 'identity' and 'similarity' in my judgement that this is yet another example of green. Though 'green' is univocal, univocity occurs only in language, while the real is genuinely proportional and analogical. There is not one thing at the further end of my or our perception, but a spectrum of individuals measured with an average embodied only in the predicate. This is not to say that one can be more or less human, but that reality is a range of cases both similar as 'cases of' and different as a range of individuals.

Most human beings have a linguistic capacity. But this is not to say that there is some exact or quantifiable level of linguistic competence that a speaker must have in order to count as having such a capacity. The competence of people will be a bell curve, a majority of instances clustering, with some falling above and below. Someone with the linguistic subtlety of a Joyce, and someone else who falls into childish onomatopoeia for want of a word, are, 'for a' that', united in having the predicate justly applied to them. That there are instances of mobility – one thinks of children or stroke victims – does not make classification any easier.

If this analysis is correct, then we are led to the conclusion that essence is linguistically mediated: where there is no language, there is, properly speaking, no essence. Let us be clear what this claim entails, and does not entail. It does not entail the nonsensical claims that the world is structureless, or, equivalently, that essence is entirely the product of convention. What the claim does entail is that what there is is identity, which, as such, makes the application of what we have called essential predicates appropriate or not. Only Divinity could know entities in their uniqueness and proper distinctness. Human finitude requires that we proceed by likeness and analogy. To say what a thing is by means of a predicate or set of predicates is to try to express its identity, and to fail to do so completely or adequately, as an unavoidable consequence of the way in which predicates must work. Essence is this necessarily imperfect, linguistic articulation of identity, in which many agree despite, or even because of, being the unique entities they are.

Although our predicates have a healthy indefiniteness about them, this is not to assert that that to which they of necessity, by a kind of happy fault, can only approximate, is itself indefinite or indeterminate. To say that we cannot define a pile as two hundred and fifty-three grains is not to imply that there are therefore no piles containing that exact number, or worse, that no pile has any exact number. We can and do come to know individuals by constantly refining our description of them, by adding ever more nuances to our picture of them, or, perhaps put more drily, by adding ever more predicates to our description. We might instructively compare the paltry definition of human being as rational animal with, say, the superbly detailed word-portrait of Pierre Bezukhov given by Tolstoy, or contemplate a painted portrait by Rembrandt in which we are shown, as it were in a flash, *this* man, *this* woman, even, what it is to be this man or this woman, an individual in his or her inalienable uniqueness. So, though for Aristotle and Thomas individuals as such were indefinable, individuals are, we might say infinitely, describable, in that we can keep tailoring our descriptions to them, to their individuality, which, mediated by identity as unique and by *esse* as uniquely existing, always escapes us. But all this presupposes that there is indeed a definite limit to which in each case our descriptions approximate; if that were not the case there would literally be nothing in particular to know. Thus we can say that that which answers to our descriptions is a real determination, the definite limit which our descriptive activity intends.

More profoundly, there is an ontological principle which is disclosed by these considerations, namely, nothing indeterminate can exist, or, more positively, all that is, is determinate. Indeterminacy occurs only at the level of human thinking and talking, when it is impossible, either in principle or contingently, to know some determination.

Let us summarise our findings, particularly in regard to *esse*.

Identity as complex confers similarity and difference with others on the entity whose structure it is. Identity functions as a whole in differentiating the entity which possesses it; the differentiating feature is identity, and uniqueness inheres in identity as such. Anything which is integral to it is *as integral* not shared, though sharable in abstraction, that is, as linguistically expressed. No two snowflakes, no two fingerprints, are identical, though the 'rules' which construct them are univocal and unvarying, and if there were a formula which adequately described each one, it would be a different formula in every case. This is what is meant by individuation. We may identify *haecceitas* with *esse*, because although it is identity which confers uniqueness, it is *esse* whereby things exist. An entity is as proper subject of existence, and can only be as individual, that is, as the entity it is, which it is in virtue of identity. Thus, it is through identity as such alone that *esse* is mediated to that of which it is said most properly: *esse* is the actuality proper to individuals, and as the realisation of individuals is *principium individuationis* and therefore qualifies as real *haecceitas*, if this notion means anything. Matter as such, then, is not cause of individuation, but it does have other functions. As we shall see, material causality seems to be reducible to the relation 'being matter for or in': something relies on something else as its matter because that something else is determinate in some relevant way, and so functions other than as conferring individuality.

Notes to Chapter Four

1. See Benson Mates, *The Philosophy of Leibniz, Metaphysics and Language*, (Oxford: OUP, 1986), pp. 10-11, and 132-136. Leibniz's own words are worth quoting here: 'Indeed, each Monad must be different from every other. For in nature there are never two beings which are perfectly alike and in which it is not possible to find an internal difference, or at least a difference founded upon an intrinsic quality.' *Monadology 9*, in *Leibniz, The Monadology and Other Philosophical Writings*, translated with introduction and notes by Robert Latta, (Oxford: OUP, 1971).

2. For a discussion of the Scotist approach, see Etienne Gilson, *Being and Some Philosophers*, (Toronto: Pontifical Institute of Medieval Studies, 1952), pp. 84-95.

3. There is a very interesting treatment of the topics of identity and essence in Baruch A. Brody's *Identity and Essence*, (Princeton, NJ: Princeton University Press, 1980).

4. *Le 'De Ente et Essentia' de S. Thomas D'Aquin*, M.-D. Roland-Gosselin, (ed.), Bibliotheque Thomiste VIII, (Paris: Vrin, 1948), *capitulum secundum*, p. 11. I use the elegant and 'politically correct' translation by Timothy McDermott, in *Thomas Aquinas, Selected Philosophical Writings*, (Oxford: The World's Classics, 1993). p. 94.

5. Joseph Bobik, 'Matter and Individuation' with comment and discussion following, in *The Concept of Matter in Greek and Medieval Philosophy*, Ernan McMullin (ed.), (Indiana: Notre Dame, 1965).

6. *De Ente, loc. cit.*

7. I owe my knowledge of this delightful axiom to my friend and colleague in the Department of Philosophy at Maynooth, Dr. Joseph McBride.

8. Aristotle, *Physics*, 192 b, 15-24.

9. The best treatment of Aquinas's cognitive theory known to the present author is that of Bernard Lonergan, namely, *Verbum, Word and Idea in Aquinas*, (Notre Dame: University of Notre Dame Press, 1967).

10. See Isaiah Berlin's essay, 'The Hedgehog and the Fox', in his *Russian Thinkers* (Harmondsworth: Penguin, 1978) p. 22. Aquinas, I suggest, like Aristotle whom Berlin mentions, is a 'fox', in that he too moves 'on many

levels, seizing upon the essence of a vast variety of experiences and objects for what they are in themselves, without, consciously or unconsciously, seeking to fit them into, or exclude them from, any one unchanging, all-embracing, sometimes self-contradictory and incomplete, at times fanatical, unitary inner vision.' From this perspective, I also suggest, idealists tend to be 'hedgehogs'.

11. *De Ente*, pp. 20 - 21; McDermott, pp. 97 -98.

12. *De Ente, capitulum tertium*, pp. 24 - 26; McDermott, pp. 99-100.

CHAPTER FIVE

Coexistence I:
Matter, Form, and Telos

5, 1 Introduction

The account which we have worked out so far has been fixed upon the structure of entity as such. Yet the very notion of entity we have explored, precisely as that which distinguishes itself from all others, contains implicit reference to those others. For this reason, it is necessary to amplify our account in order to make room for those relations which therefore must occur between the various entities, and which are necessary to world as the field of their possibility. The most obvious and fundamental worldly relations which occur are spatio-temporal and causal. Space and time are complex relational totalities intimately bound up with the existence of finite entities, along whose lines existence is mediated in identity and distinctness. Between these a third moment manifests itself, which we may call coexistence, whereby entites, for all their real distinctness, are held together in a kind of necessary nexus. Causality, as the production of change is a kind of coexistence, but this kind may rely upon a use-structure which is a more intimate kind of coexistence than the external relation which causality is. This use-structure is the structure *per se* of materiality, and so instantiates the spatio-temporality which is inseparable from the meanings of matter. Temporal entities are dis- or conjoined, in terms of identity or coexistence, spatio-temporally. Entities which coexist do so in the same space and share the same period; they are disjoined as occupying diverse spaces or by inhabiting non-overlapping periods.

It will appear that materiality itself can only be understood as member of that necessarily related triad of internal relations called by Aristotle material, formal and final causality.[1] This means that materiality can only be understood as intrinsically related to form and end, as its complements and completion. We shall, indeed, use a text of Aristotle to open and map this territory. We shall begin by exploiting the intrinsic pluralism, already referred to, involved in the notion of entity, to gain insight into the root-meaning of materiality as such, which yields the structure and items to which we have referred, which may be subsumed in what we call 'coexistence', and its opposite, to which we have given no special name. Things which coexist form wholes, things which do not may, given that appropriate relations – ultimately having a spatio-temporal character, of course – obtain between them, thereby form what we have called 'lots': aggregates defined by external relations between their participants. A striking and perhaps unexpected feature of this treatment is the place occupied by final causality, a place secured by the causality exercised by form, and which thereby emerges as a vital and ineluctable ontological structure, rather than as the instance of a more or less crude anthropomorphism as other treatments commonly portray it. We thus deconstruct coexistence in its primary instantiation into its coordinate parts, namely the triad of material, formal and final causality, with the items and features proper to each. The chapter ends with a consideration of the significance of all this for our understanding of *esse*, and with some extensions of this and of our notion of entity.

No general refutation of materialism, the belief that whatever is must be spatio-temporal, will be attempted in this chapter, though that transcendence of material causality, a transcendence which belongs to the entity as such, will be disclosed. Since the belief that all that is is in space and time amounts to a belief that all that is is finite, our assertion of the existence of Divinity in effect amounts to a radical criticism of any such belief, but since this is an essay on ontology rather than on philosophical anthropology, a proper treatment of the relation between personhood and materiality will not be attempted, though the lines that might be followed in such a treatment should be tolerably clear from the arguments that are to hand.

5, 2 Monism and Pluralism

The picture which has so far emerged is incorrigibly pluralist: the totality of beings as we have described it is an irreducibly diverse plethora of unique entities. In particular, there is no univocal principle or entity in whose favour these riches can be cancelled.

From this angle, as we have suggested, our ontology is radically existential and anti-idealistic, in that idealism in its various forms, or ontologies of idealistic provenance, tend to be suspicious of the concrete, the individual and the particular, and to do away with them in favour of the abstract, the universal and the general, items which tend to inhabit conceptual systems. The Marxist dialectic, though avowedly materialistic and scientific, is, at least in most of its versions, perfectly willing in theory and practice to sacrifice individuals to the abstract and systematic process of historical inevitability. One might be tempted to think that tyranny is often idealism turned into a political policy. Existentialism, on the other hand, both as an adverbial quality or value in the doing of philosophy and as historical movement, swims against this idealistic current. Though any approach which truly merits the title existentialist need not so discard unity as to turn diversity into irreconcilable isolation and ultimate exclusion, it must at least be tolerant of difference and multiplicity, and be respectful of the concrete and unique. Most profoundly, it must rest upon a respect for *esse* as source and analogical principle of individuality and difference on the one hand, and yet also, as we shall now see, of unity and community, on the other. We shall refer to the opposite of such healthy existentialism, namely the tendency to allow diversity to be swallowed up in some (specious) unity, as monism.

Monism has made its appearance frequently in the history of philosophy, often, though not exclusively, in the train of idealism. We recall that the very first explicit ontology, that of Parmenides, is a rejection of diversity as mere appearance in favour of the reality of an undifferentiated and static Being. However, it is neither necessary nor useful to refight battles whose outcome has long since been decided. Our task, rather, is to examine that form which monism wears for us, namely materialism.

5, 3 Materialism

The exploration and critique of materialism is of great importance for many branches of philosophical inquiry, not least for any form of philosophical anthropology. It comes into our purview, though, not for its intrinsic interest but because its refutation reveals issues that are of interest to ontology, namely, the nature of matter, and one of the meanings of coexistence, of community in *esse*.

What is the meaning of materialistic monism? If monism is the abolition of difference in favour of some univocal principle or entity, the principle or entity in question must be matter. Such an initial characterisation immediately gives rise to a nest of interwoven questions of unequal scope and importance: what is meant by the phrase 'univocal principle or entity'?; how can matter be said to qualify as such a principle or entity or, what argument requires that we assert it to be so?; what fallacy, if any, attends making matter out to be such? All these questions clearly hinge upon a cardinal question, namely, what exactly can we mean by 'matter'?

This last, at least, appears easily answered. As Joyce puts it, we encounter matter by beating our sconces against it. Matter is what I collide with, what I manipulate, what I touch and taste and see, what I am, or, at least, consist of. It is that, the investigation of whose structure, properties and origins constitutes the major part, if not all, of science, even of the life sciences, since what are living things but living matter?

Given this all-pervasiveness of matter, we begin to see what matter as univocal principle or entity in whose favour all diversity can and must be abolished, might mean. All the apparent diversity of the world is mere appearance, each apparent entity consists in a different, though, to matter, accidental, arrangement of the same thing; there is, at least now, no real coming-to-be or perishing, no genuine increase or decrease in the real sum of what is, according as 'entities', the accidents of matter, appear or disappear, but only the continued rearrangement of an internally invariant element or elements. This element is either one entity or many: if one, then it is an entity which can exist in a spatially dispersed fashion; if many, then 'matter' is a collective noun for entities which differ as to identity – and to say this, from our previous argumentation, is tautologous – but tend to some crucial average.

The necessary and sufficient condition, moreover, that matter must fulfil to qualify as such a principle is that it be necessarily the case that if anything exist it be material, or, equivalently, that nothing non-material can exist in principle, or, again equivalently, that the notion of a non-material entity is incoherent.

If matter is one entity, then it is an entity which can exist in a spatially dispersed fashion, that means, not that one piece of a continuous body is here and another there, but that the same thing can be in two discrete spaces. To call two spaces discrete implies that what fills the one is not continuous with the other, that there is some distance between the two spaces which is not filled with what fills them, and so what fills the one is numerically distinguishable from what fills the other. So if the same entity simultaneously occupies two discrete spaces then there is one entity which is simultaneously identical with itself and distinguishable from itself. Simultaneous distinguishability is the essence of space. Thus things can occupy discrete spaces only if they are different things.[2] In this way what should qualify as the purest form of materialistic monism, namely that matter is one entity, cannot in principle be true.

Thus 'matter' is a collective noun for entities which differ as to identity but tend to some crucial average, namely, being material. But this leads us to a curious conclusion: if there cannot be one entity called 'matter', it follows, quite literally, that there is no such entity as matter, but only material entities, just as there is no such entity as life, but only living things, no such entity as justice, but only just acts and the like, no such entity as language, but only speakers and what speakers do, and so on. Thus materialistic monism has in common with our ontology that what is is an irreducibly diverse plethora of unique entities, but that, in addition, these are, and must be, material, that is, fall into the spectrum of meaning signified by the predicate in question.

Let us recall for a moment the admittedly popular picture we painted above, namely, that each apparent entity consists in a different, though, to matter accidental, arrangement of the same thing, and that there is no real coming-to-be or perishing, only the continued rearrangement of an internally unchanging element or elements, and see how it now fares. Does each entity consist in such an accidental arrangement of the same thing, where 'accidental' means external to the identity of matter? Since there is no such entity as matter, there is no (one) thing of which anything else can be the accident. The entities which are, even if they are all material, are ontologically ultimate, that is, are not accidents or determinations of something other than themselves. Is there no real coming-to-be or perishing? If we rephrase the question in the light of these considerations we get: is there no real coming-to-be or passing away but only the persistence of (necessarily material) entities? The answer would seem to be that there is no coming to be or passing away of entities if the entities in question either do not or cannot come into existence or perish.

Is the notion of a non-material entity really incoherent? Could we say that, though no such entities happen to exist, or are not known to exist, they are, in principle, possible? In order to answer such a question, it is necessary to ask what is meant when we ascribe materiality to entities.

5, 4 The Meanings of 'Material'

The fundamental meaning of being material is being spatio-temporal, being located in space and lasting through time. But, if something occupies space it has dimension, and consequently is, in principle, divisible. It so happens that division can either be destructive, or at least disruptive, of something or fail to be so: dividing a living thing is the example of the former, cutting a piece of stone or pouring a liquid into different containers, of the latter. In this latter case, we seem to be dealing with 'stuff': something which has an identity – 'it's water' – but which is undifferentiated and homogenous, can exist as discrete chunks or lots, and also under different guises. Water on Mars, if there is any, is the same stuff as water closer to home, and water is the same stuff as ice and steam. Water is undifferentiated in that it is not a totality the way an entity, especially a living entity, of necessity is; water thus has no obvious differentiated parts and is therefore homogenous and divisible without harm. You can have *an* entity, but not *a* stuff, except in the sense that water is a stuff and carbon is also a stuff. Every measure of water is water, but not every part or quantity of an animal is an animal, and *a fortiori* not the (kind of) animal which the totality is. Moreover the decomposition of an entity which is a totality does not end up with the parts in the strict sense, of that entity – which can be as actual parts only within the totality of which they are the parts – but with stuff. This is probably the oldest notion of matter there is, it is the ὕλη of the Presocratics and Aristotle's τὸ ἐξ οὗ: the stuff of so and so, that from which something is shaped, that of which it consists, its raw material. Likewise, stuff as stuff looks, at first sight, impervious to all change except movement and decomposition. Carbon is carbon whether it is the stuff of diamond, coal or flesh, and for as long as it lasts it's just carbon. In this sense, stuff is mostly what we think of when we think of matter, and is what lurks behind the monistic picture which we have been discussing: is everything just differently shaped chunks or lots of the same ultimate stuff?

What are we to make of stuff? As we have characterised it, it is quite different from entity, and as such may appear problematic to us; above all, is it a rival to entity for the title of ultimate ontological category? The answer, briefly, which I take it to be necessary to give to this question is no, and the reason for this is that the notion of stuff is not independent of that of entity.

We may conveniently short-circuit much debate by noting that it is a commonplace of science that everything we encounter in the macro-world of our experience consists of atoms whirling in the void, and that things are mostly empty space. Wholeness is a matter of one's point of view. A stretch of sand, from far enough away, looks like one homogenous and undivided 'thing', which, on closer inspection, resolves itself into a vast plurality. To the physicist and chemist, everything is like this, consisting of particles within particles, like a nest of Russian dolls, albeit particles of an odd sort, perhaps ultimately coming down to electric fields or quanta of energy, or the like. However odd such 'particles' may be, they will still count as entities, even though our faculties of perception, however ingeniously refined and extended by technology, are, and always will be, too gross to allow us to appreciate them as the individuals they are and must be, if they are many, and so (spatially) distinct. In this way, we again return to the pluralist picture, into which 'stuff' collapses. Whether or not this collapse simply happens or is logically necessary, is a moot point; at least, we may say that what elementary particles – electrons, quarks or charms, or the like – into which material things in fact resolve themselves, cannot, of course, be known *a priori*.

5, 5 Lot and Whole

But, to say that what there is is simply a plethora of distinct entities is too simple. Entities can be related in ways other than causal interaction. To explore this claim let us turn to a cardinal passage in the *Metaphysics*:

> Now, since that which is composed of something in such a way that the whole is a unity; not as an aggregate (σωρός) is a unity, but as a syllable is - the syllable is not the letters, nor is BA the same as B and A; nor is flesh fire and earth [we would say carbon and nitrogen]; because after dissolution the compounds, e.g. flesh or the syllable, no longer exist; but the letters exist and so do [the carbon and nitrogen]. Therefore the syllable is some particular thing; not merely the letters, vowel and consonant, but something else besides. And flesh is not merely [carbon and nitrogen], but something else besides (καὶ ἕτερόν τι). ... It would seem, however, that this 'something else' is something that is not an element, but is the cause that *this* matter is flesh and *that* matter a syllable, and similarly in other cases. And this is the substance (οὐσία) of each thing, for it is the primary cause

of its existence (αἴτιον πρῶτον τοῦ ἐἶναι). And since ... all substances are constituted in accordance with and by, nature, substance would seem to be this 'nature', which is not an element
(στοιχεῖον) but a principle (ἀρχή). An element is that which is
present as matter in a thing, and into which the thing is divided;
e.g., A and B are the elements of the syllable. [3]

Let us enumerate and examine the themes laid out in this rich and
striking passage: a distinction is drawn between a whole, on the one
hand, and an aggregate, a lot, on the other, and the unity which is
proper to each is indicated; there are elements, and there is 'something else besides'; this something else is not an element but substance, οὐσία, a principle and source, the primary cause of existence,
of ἐἶναι, of *esse*.

Sand, to return to our previous example, is just such an aggregate or
lot. Imagine a load of sand being emptied from the back of a truck
as the bed of the truck rises. The movement of the lot *is* simply that,
the movement of all the grains together; there is nothing more to
what we see to be the movement of the lot than the sum total of all
the movements of the individual bits. The grains act together without acting as a whole; though they may bump and push each other,
and alter each other's motion as they fall, each operates as a distinct
entity. This, then, is the proper attribute of an aggregate: that there
is nothing intrinsic to, that is, constitutive of, the part which relates
it to the lot of which it is a part. This is what makes lots endlessly
(and to the endless delight of children!) divisible and (re)combin-
able, capable of being mixed to form greater, or parcelled out to
form lesser, lots. We may add in this context, then, to Aristotle's
definition of an element: it is not merely 'that which is present as
matter in a thing, and into which the thing is divided'; an element,
taken as one of the 'bits' involved in a lot, must have no such constitutive relation to the lot – what the element is must not be determined by its being in the lot, that is, its relation to the lot must be
external.

This is not the case, however, with a whole, or what stands to a
whole as an element stands to a lot, namely, a part.[4] The part, as
part, cannot exist except in the context of the whole of which it is the
part. This is what we mean when we say that the part has a constitutive and internal relation to the whole. Since to be for the part is to
be part of a whole, it follows that the part as part cannot act independently: it is the whole which acts, in and through its parts. In this

sense the whole is, must be, and only can be, present as a totality in each of its parts, precisely as the factor which shapes and determines the part as part. We may say that the whole informs the part, and is as the totality, but not the mere sum, of its parts, for although parts are that 'into which the thing is divided', we usually add together things which are independent. Parts are not independent, in that they immediately presuppose the whole to which they cannot but belong, and mediately, through the whole, one another. The relations which hold in a lot are at the level of accident relative to the entities whose relations they are, while the relations of the part to a whole *are* the identity of the part. In short, lots are accidental unities, while wholes are unities which are not accidental. The totality which is proper to the whole, then, is a complex unity of the necessary subordination of many *to* one. The apparent totality of the lot, by contrast, is the contingent coordination of many independents *in* one.[5] In this way, the whole is a kind of existing participational system, the primary instance and incarnation of the analogy of intrinsic attribution.

What of lots which remain the same through time and are named or described, chunks like the Koh-i-noor, dollops like the Atlantic Ocean, or what is denoted by the sentence, 'This is the very diamond I gave your Grandmother fifty years ago, when we became engaged'? A diamond is a chunk of stuff, not a whole but a lot, an arbitrarily limited quantity, composed of a finite number of bits of one kind or more, in this case the molecules of diamond. In cases of self-cohesive lots – chunks – it is the continuity and identity of the elements which guarantee the sameness of the chunk. It remains the same diamond as long as it retains the same 'bits' of which it is composed, something which also seems to hold in the case of artefacts. In the case of lots which are not self-cohesive – dollops like the Atlantic Ocean – continuity usually lies in the dollop's consisting of (an unspecified but perhaps rather large amount of) a particular kind of fluid, in this case sea-water, at a given location, and not in the sameness of the particular constituents. We might find some, perhaps quirky, exceptions to this like the blood of Saint Januarius or the contents of the sealed bottle venerated by Henry Ford as the last breath of Thomas Edison. Such cases are exact matches of that of the diamond, and one could find still more kinds of case. The decisive point however, is that the identity and properties of chunks and dollops depend upon their components, such that lots are not distinct from their components in the way wholes are. Does this mean that an entity is necessarily a whole? The answer to this, apparently, is no, if there can be non-complex entities. But an entity which is complex, insofar as it is *an* entity, and therefore one, must stand to its parts as the whole of those parts.

The whole is, at once, more than, and not more than, the totality of its parts: as Aristotle's text would suggest, the whole is always 'something else besides' either element or part. But it would be to commit a category mistake if we were to look for this something alongside its parts, as yet another part. It exists only as the whole incarnated in and through the parts, distinguishable as what makes them what they are, as the complex unity which they necessarily intend, and in which they are united, and as the context in which alone they are intelligible.

We note a vital distinction between part and element: elements can survive, except *per accidens*, the destruction of the whole, whereas parts, though they may be preserved as having an orientation to a whole or kind of whole, can not. In this way, parts are not present in a thing as its matter, because that from which a thing is shaped can survive the passing away of that whose matter it is. Therefore, the term 'matter' more properly applies to element rather than part, though it may be extended analogically to part, and it is more correct to say that something is 'decomposed into' or 'reduced to' its matter, rather than merely divided, inasmuch as decomposition requires the undoing of the totality, and the consequent release of its matter.

5, 6 Coexistence

In sum, we have so far distinguished four items: lot, whole, part, and element, and we understand something of the relation between part and whole, and of the similarity and difference between part and element. But what is the relation between whole and element? We have argued that the whole exists as incarnated in its parts, distinguishable as what makes them what they are, as the complex unity which they necessarily intend and in which they are united, and as the context in which alone they are intelligible. It may be true to say that at least some wholes are incarnated in elements, in that they consist of their elements, and even, perhaps cannot be without their elements, but there seems to be a kind of mutual indifference between whole and element. As we have seen, the whole does not make the element what it is, and, though the whole may unite a diversity of elements, they do not necessarily intend it, nor is the whole the sole context in which they are intelligible. Carbon is carbon whether it occurs in or as diamond, coal, or flesh, and is intelligible immediately, without reference to them.

On the other hand, wholes as such transcend their elements. Let us again recall our amended version of Aristotle's text: 'nor is flesh carbon and nitrogen; because after dissolution the compounds, e.g. flesh or the syllable, no longer exist; but the letters exist and so do the carbon and nitrogen. Therefore the syllable is some particular thing; not merely the letters, ... but something else besides'. Though there is of course, no such 'stuff' as flesh, but only living things and their organs, and though it is a nice point whether B and A may be accounted parts of the syllable or elements, it is clear that his most important assertion is that the whole is a something, most properly an entity, which is distinct from its elements, and is irreducible to them. This is clearest in the case of the living being. What are the reasons for this assertion? He tells us that the whole passes away, and by implication comes to be, distinctly from the elements. But this presupposes that it is something other than those elements: a circular argument? No, because implicit in the text is the realisation that 'flesh' is other than the constituent elements, since it can behave in a way which is not that of carbon or nitrogen out of the composite which 'being flesh' is. We know what a thing is, in general, by observing what it does; a whole is distinguishable from its elements because it does things that the elements as such are not capable of doing.

It may seem far-fetched to say that in this chair there is me, my body, over and above the atoms and molecules which compose it, but it is, equally, grotesque nonsense to say that a bunch of carbon atoms wrote Hamlet or that it was nitrogen which discovered relativity, because these elements are that from which Shakespeare's or Einstein's body was composed, or, rather, was that in which the wholes, which these entities were, were incarnated. This is partly what we mean by the term incarnation: the whole is *in* its elements, but is not *of* its elements. I shall call this relation between whole and element 'coexistence', and I wish to show that this is a non-symmetrical relation in the sense that the element is indifferent, in the way I have explained, to the whole, but the whole is what I shall call free, in relation to its elements. What does this freedom mean?

We note that there is a certain indifference on the part of the whole to its elements: though it may be necessary for the whole to use carbon, it need not be this, and only this, bit of carbon which it must use. This, of course, is not to say that the whole can get along quite well without *any* carbon. But it does mean that what the whole does is a function of the whole as such and not of its uncombined elements, and that therefore the whole exploits suitable properties of its elements, which it can use to do what it does. Carbon is suitable stuff for the processes that go on within living beings, though uranium, say, is not, and consequently there are no living beings made from it.

5, 7 Material and Formal Causality

An important aspect which we can discern emerging from these reflections is the subordination of the element in the whole. I say 'in the whole' rather than 'to the whole' to show the difference between the subordination of the part as opposed to that of the element. The element is used by, or in, the whole in such a way that what it does characteristically as the kind it is, or as the stuff it is, does not determine the outcome of actions or behaviour which are functions of the whole, nor of itself choose or actualise possibilities which belong as such to the whole. This is the meaning of 'subordination in', and it gives us access to both a, though perhaps not every, meaning of freedom, and to the nature of what Aristotle would call material, formal, and final causality.

Material causality is present in lots as well as in wholes. Material causality is the ability of something – the material – to produce change precisely as coordinate or subordinate in or to something else, lot or whole, that is, as having certain properties contributing to the behaviour of, or, in the case of a whole, usable by, that something else, and as a function of that something, rather than as a function of what it, the material, of itself is. The difference between lot and whole in this context is that though lots have properties and functions which belong only to the plethora, as opposed to components taken singly, this only means: to the singulars taken in sum, or working together, or the like. It is precisely the combined weights of the singular grains of sand which make the heap heavy and dangerous, but the elements of a totality do not singly have the, or some fraction (where any such thing makes sense) of, those characteristics which belong to the totality. This implies that formal causality is, at least, the capacity that something has to produce change as a function of its essence and therefore of its identity: as a function, in short, of what it is, rather than of some 'appropriate characteristic', in the sense we are discussing.

The hardness of some stuff might be the relevant factor in the case of its serving as material for, say, a hammer, rather than the stuff's being, let us suppose, metal as such, still less its being this or that bit of metal. An unshapen bit of metal, though having the relevant property, would still not be a hammer, for it would have to receive the shape, a whole, which would allow it to function in the way a hammer functions. Such functioning relies on, in the sense of being impossible without, the relevant property, the hardness, of its material: a glass hammer cannot function as a hammer; it has the μορφή, but not the εἶδος, of hammer, and it is the hammer as hammer, which functions, which as such is responsible for change. Thus, it is not the metal as such which produces change, but the hardness of the metal, in the form which allows or confers the capacity to function appropriately. This is even clearer in the case of an animal, whose functions, though relying in a complex, and perhaps ultimately mysterious way, on its elements, are quite different from those of its elements. It is not because they are carbon or nitrogen as such that human beings can feel depressed or write poetry, and these elements are not of themselves notable for such functioning.

The causality of the elements is, in sum, subsumed in the functioning proper to such entities. This is what differentiates the kind of causality proper to them. When something functions as the thing it is, and therefore in the manner proper to it, and characteristic of others of the same kind, we have formal causality: Jane is able to feel resentment and sight-sing, because she is Jane and because she is human. When something produces change in subordination to something exercising formal causality, then it acts in virtue of some characteristic which it has, and as the thing it is, or kind of thing it is only *per accidens*: this is material causality. Something may necessarily exercise formal causality in reliance on something which itself exercises material causality: living things have to function as living things, relying on, and utilising, a characteristic – we will call it 'x' – of some element y, which makes y amenable to their purposes, and y *happens* to be carbon if silicon were x, and were not unsuitable for some other reason, it would do just as well. Of course it may happen that being x is something only carbon can be, that is, to be carbon is to be x and conversely, so that being x is essential to carbon, but this does not take from the fact that it is being x, not being carbon as such, which is the core of material causality. In this way, we may characterise formal and material causality as we have elucidated them as the proper functioning of something and accidental functioning respectively. Use always intends some function, capacity or characteristic of something or, we may add the lugubrious reflection, someone, rather than that something or someone in and as itself: I may like oil paint for its 'butteriness' (which may, of course, belong to it and to no other paint), and want my workers for the labour I can extract from them, but I am not interested in them for their own sake or for what they are in themselves. Few artists bother with the chemical composition of their material, or heartless capitalists with the friendship which reveals individuals as the individuals they are, at least, not friendship with the workers they are exploiting.

5, 8 Final Causality: *omnis agens agit propter finem*

Final causality thereby enters the picture. Final causality is the causality exercised by a goal, (*finis*, τέλος) as conditioning the steps or actions which lead to it, Aristotle's τὸ οὗ ἕνεκα, 'the "for whose sake"'. Its inclusion here may seem, at first sight, obscurantist, in that it would appear to endow the brute and dead with volition and intention, and therefore to be that very anthropomorphism which (ought to have) died under the onslaught of science. Such a belief, however, would be mistaken. Final causality, as we understand it (and as Aristotle seems to have understood it) does not necessarily imply awareness or consciousness on the part of the subject in which it operates, nor that there is any planner or designer. Anything which appropriates and makes another its own by subordinating that other to itself as its material does so, whether consciously or not, in order to be what it is and in order to do what it does. It is this 'in order to', if we may use a Heideggerian locution, which is what we mean by final causality. Necessary to, and inseparable from, the absorption and use of something as matter by an agent whose behaviour as such is its own and proper, rather than that of the matter as such, is the fact of that user's existence and activity, which thereby *are* as goal, as that for and towards which, this process of absorption and use takes place. This I take to be the fundamental meaning of the old Scholastic 'axiom', *omnis agens agit propter finem*. Such a using *agens*, by virtue of its very existence subordinates and uses, thereby positing the *finis*, the τέλος, which is its own existence. One might conclude that this is a necessary self-positing of something as existing, and that this is the meaning of *esse*.

In general, the 'formula' of use is the triadic relation '*A* is subordinate to *B* for the sake of *x*'. To remove the third, and properly final element of the triad, the 'for the sake of', is to render the whole unintelligible, for use is always 'use for or in'. In the case of an inanimate user, this 'teleology' occurs only internally to the agent, while in living ones, the subordination can and does extend beyond the confines of the user itself, though what lies beyond can be appropriated other than as matter in the sense we have described, as when a bird builds a nest. The appropriation as matter by a living being of what is beyond it, is, of course, respiration and eating. In sum, to be this kind of using entity is, simply, to be an end, and therefore to have this unwilled teleology as ontological structure, for such an entity cannot be except as positing its existence, thus positing it as end, and the structure of something is what that something cannot help but be. It will be clear that the 'axiom', at least in the acceptation we have given it here, will fail in an entity in which the use we have described does not occur; but it is worth noting that every whole which we can encounter inhabiting the world is of necessity material, and therefore has the ontological structure we have described. A related point is also worth making, namely, that it seems to be possible to encounter what may be called, if only *analogice*, wholes which are not material, and do not inhabit the world as entities do. Examples of such wholes would be stories, pieces of music, works of art generally, deductive or axiomatic systems, and the like.

5, 9 Determinability: the Essence of Matter as such

Let us clarify some of the points which have emerged in our analysis thus far. To exercise material causality is to act in subordination to another, enabling that other to act as that which the other is. In one direction, the relation is enablement, in the other, reliance. The user relies in that it needs the used in order to be and do, though this doing and being are its own, not that of its elements; the used enables the user for the same reason. The relation, then, is not mutual. In order to be used, the used must have the appropriate characteristic – 'x-factor' – and must not disqualify itself by having characteristics which make its use incompatible with the being or activities of the user. To say this is to say that the used is suitable to function as matter in something because of what it is, and is therefore inherently determinable as the matter it is or can be. Determinability is the inherent orientation and capacity of something to act as matter for another. This notion of determinability is one of capacity, and was the leading notion in matter for Aristotle and the Scholastics. For them, the ultimate structure of matter was sheer capacity-for, sheer determinability-as, sheer openness to, form as determination, and thus the lack of all determination *per se*, which is conferred therefore by form alone. It is certainly true to say that to be matter is to be determinable and that therefore the 'stuff' of matter is determinability. But this is not to deny all determination and definiteness to matter – quite the reverse: if our analysis is correct, something is determinable as matter precisely because it possesses some feature, some determination, which qualifies it to do so. Something is material in this sense precisely as having a range of determinability-as because it is so-and-so. But this means that something is determinable as what it is, in relation to that in the context of which it can act as matter or exercise material causality. Thus, we agree with Aristotle and the Scholastics that matter is not a thing; what it is, however, is a relation: determinability, that is 'being determinable as'.

This gives us the line into the Aristotelian notion of matter as ulti-mate subject, underlay, as precisely that which persists throughout radical change, thus guaranteeing such change as transformation, and not as the annihilation of one thing and its replacement by another, newly created, thing. Clearly, this point is correct. But it is misleading to talk of matter as some indefinite principle, even if we do assert that it cannot exist independently, and can only be known by argumentation and abstraction. It is true to say that nothing indeterminate can exist, but what can it mean to say that something determinate has a relation to something in, or at least of, itself, inde-terminate? If something can exist only as determinate then it is, in fact, never indeterminate. And what, precisely, is 'it'? That which persists through change, and appears now as flesh, now as carbon. To explain how flesh is transformed into carbon in destruction, we need not invoke a third something which persists as an indetermi-nate underlay: in what sense can something, in itself indeterminate, be said to persist, which becomes flesh and then carbon, which therefore *is* now flesh, and *is* now carbon? This is to say that there is nothing which remains in itself indeterminate. Why should flesh always transform itself into carbon in dissolution; why not now into silicon and now into uranium? Since the form of flesh disap-pears in destruction, and since *materia prima* has nothing to con-tribute by way of determination to the process, what explains the invariable appearance of carbon in dissolution? The answer must be that the carbon is already present, and must be, because its being so is a condition of the possibility of the entity in question; the transformation of the entity which is its destruction is simply the release of the carbon from its subordination.

5, 10 Quantity and Spatiality

What we have said about destruction goes, *mutatis mutandis*, for coming-to-be. Indeed, genesis, as well as destruction, involves the transformation of something into something else not identical with it: the coming into being of one thing *is* the destruction of something else. In, say, conception, a new entity comes to be, not as such from parents but from sperm and ovum, whose essence is to fuse to form it, and which could therefore almost be said to be a kind of 'prematter', in that each exists in order to fuse with any of its opposite number to form something which is capable of behaviour of which neither of the two alone, or even in tandem, is capable. They perish in that, and when, they unite (not merely combine) to form something which is identical to neither. The being of such prematter as such is determinability as that entity which it is capable of originating. But again, elements are present as subordinate, now to the prematter, now to the entity whose prematter it was. What persists is carbon, now in subordination to the prematerial entities, and now to the entity formed by their union. Elements which are determinable are capable of becoming those things as which they are determinable, that is, as exercising material causality in subordination to them. In general, things come to be from those sources which are capable of giving rise to, and supporting them.

What is obviously common to flesh and carbon is that they are both spatial. This entity is transformed into something not identical with it. But more than this: this kind of stuff is transformed into that kind of stuff – flesh into carbon. But this is also insufficient as a description. The transformation does not take place at separate points in space. Fido does not, in perishing, disappear here, to be replaced by his chemical remains, over there. This would count as the annihilation of one thing, and its replacement by another or others in creation. Moreover, the quantities of stuff in transformation are related in a predictable way. It is as though there were a blank: 'being this amount of stuff here', which is itself no-thing, but filled in differently, now as flesh, now as carbon. This seems to be why matter is thought to be at once indeterminate and, at the same time, sheer particularity, as filling some place so as to exclude anything else, and thus as *principium individuationis*. The blank seems to take on a life of its own, to become a ghost, insubstantial but enjoying influence none the less. But there is no ghost: 'being this amount of stuff here' is not a blank something, or even a no-thing, variously filled, distinct from that which fills it in. 'Being this amount of stuff here' is a determination of the stuff, whole or lot, in question, a property of it.

Being material means having dimension, and therefore being quantifiable as, even if only notionally, divisible, or at least being localisable and quantifiable as capable of bringing about quantifiable change. Thus it is true that being material as such is not the cause or recipient of *esse*, because it is the property of something which exists, and is therefore secondary to that something. Moreover, something can contribute to, affect, or bring about something, in general, exercise causality, only insofar as it itself is definite and determined. This principle is an extension of the one we have already explored to the effect that anything which exists is determinate: things act insofar as they are, and to be is to be determined. Likewise, matter, in the Scholastic view, does not exercise causality precisely as indefinite, but as quantified.

5, 11   Form and Function

According to another Scholastic 'axiom', *forma dat esse et agere*: form confers being and proper functioning. We shall discuss the relation between *esse* and *forma* below, but we ought to say a word about form and function. Form we may take as identical to φύσις, nature, which is source of motion and rest, themselves the characteristic behaviour of a kind of entity. Things act insofar as they are, and as that which they are. What an entity is is constituted by its identity, so its identity is the formal cause of something's activity; things of the same kind act in the same kinds of ways, so that what it is to be this or that kind of thing determines what it is for this or that kind of thing to act. Nature, then, is what something is, considered as dynamic source of activity, as overflowing into activity, characteristic of this entity or of this kind. In this way there is a reciprocity, almost an identity, between form and function, between what a thing is and what it does. Form is incarnate function, function is form in action. We recall Aristotle's observations in the *De Anima* that if an eye were a complete living being, seeing would be its soul[6] – i.e., its form – and cutting would be the same to an axe, if an axe were a living being. What a thing does, *is* what it is, and vice versa.

Just as I do not merely speak English, but a dialect of English, and not just a dialect, but, identifiably, an idiolect, I do not act merely as belonging to a class but as the individual I am, and in the 'idiolectic' manner proper to me as the entity I am. Aristotle refers to form as first actuality, and to activity as second actuality. Yet, in a certain sense, an entity actualises itself, becomes ever more itself, in and through activity. A painter who never paints is not truly a painter, nor is a writer who has ceased to write any longer a writer; but an artist who practices confirms himself as artist in and through his working, while at the same time discovering what he, as artist, is capable of, a discovery which is impossible *a priori*. The positing of an entity in existence *is* the coeval positing of its activity, which is therefore the necessary expression and disclosure of the richness of that existence. This extends the meaning of the principle *omnis agens agit propter finem*, because the actualisation and disclosure which is activity subordinates an entity, as the entity it is, to itself. The structures which compose the entity are for action, for use, and, like the eye and the axe, their act-uation determines what they are. This is very clear in the case of artefacts and tools, whose function shapes their design. In this way, every entity is necessarily oriented towards action as the goal it posits for itself in and through the mere fact of its being. Once again, this inherent teleology is not necessarily or inherently conscious or deliberate, although it is all of these and more in the case of human beings who are, for the most part, responsible for what they do.

One might object that although we may allow a kind of teleology in the organ-structure to be found in living beings, it is sheer anthropomorphism to posit it in the case of the inanimate. How can the chemical properties of an element, which might be taken to be activities in its case, be the goal of that element's existence? How is an element subordinated to its behaviour? This is a useful objection, in that it enables us to make more explicit the structure of subordination. Being the element in question means behaving, when it does so, in the manner proper to it: formal causality is a thing's acting because, and because of what, it is. It deploys itself in and through its acting, on the basis that, and as what, it is. In temporal entities such deployment is not contingent; self-deployment is part of what it is to be such an entity. If this is so, then such deployment is the term of its being, to which that being is therefore oriented as its necessary completion. But to be oriented towards a necessary completion is to be subordinate to it, and, equivalently, to have it as an end. Something (temporal) which is, is and posits itself as existing and as behaving. Thus, in the case of temporal entites, the axiom of the end again holds, as between the entity as acting and its acting as end.

5, 12 Form and *esse*

But the principle we have been discussing asserts also that form grants *esse*, is, in Aristotle's words, αἴτιον πρῶτον τοῦ εἶναι. Let us now examine what this might mean.

Formal causality is exercised immediately by some thing or kind, while material causality always involves a second thing, which mediates and appropriates the effect of that which is being used. It is clear that the terms of this relationship of use, that is, the user and the used, are distinct, even if the user requires the used in order to exist. If the existence of *A* is a precondition of the existence of *B*, then *A* and *B* are distinct, because this only means that there can be *A*s without *B*s, but not vice-versa. Of course, where the existence of *A* and *B* are mutually implicative, then *A*, or the existence of *A*, is not distinct from that of *B*. It is along these lines that *esse* may be attributed, is one or many in accordance with such considerations. That a thing is, insofar as it is, is its *esse*; what it is, either as uniquely its own or as shared, as identity or essence, is the set of conditions necessary that it or its like have *esse* accrue to them.

This is not the case in that use-relationship where *B* uses *A*, because *B* needs *A* to exist: in such a relation, the used is a precondition of the accrual of *esse* to the user. Moreover, in such a use-relationship as we have called material causality, the kind of effect must be different for user and used. This simply means that the used is incapable of the kind of behaviour exhibited by the user, and this is demonstrated by the fact that the used outside the relationship simply does not behave as the user does. Thus the used is not a sufficient condition for the accrual of *esse* to the user. *Esse* accrues to the user insofar as the user is that which it is, which is what determines for it the range of being a user, and what and how it uses. The used, moreover, is used according to what it is, which is the principle of its determinability. In this way, in all cases, *esse* accrues to what is according to what it is, to identity and essence. This is the meaning of the axiom *forma dat esse*, or, in Aristotle's words is the first cause of being. Identity is thus οὐσία in Aristotle's sense. But what does αἴτιον mean? The adjective αἴτιος in Greek means 'responsible for'. This statement therefore means that identity as such is that which is responsible for the fact that something is, is the primary intrinsic factor responsible for the accrual of *esse* to what is. To say all this, however, is not to prejudge the mode of the accrual of *esse*, as necessarily or contingently accruing.

Insofar as effects are formally to be ascribed to something, without reference to some other which uses and mediates those effects, then this is equivalent to the proposition that the relation of subordination necessary to material causality has been abrogated: this sets what had been exercising material causality, necessarily under the sway of another, free from that other. This is precisely what happens when something ceases to be. If, for example, we talk about some complex chemical process going on in him, we have ceased to talk about John, except, in a general way, as the host or locus of such processes. If, further, we were successful in explaining John's behaviour in these terms, we would find that the behaviour in question was no longer John's, but that of the elements. Thus, to be, *esse* is to be capable of formal causality, and to say that something is incapable of formal causality is to say that that something does not exist.

In sum, then, this is what freedom as 'freedom from' means in the context of formal and material causality: A is free from B if, firstly, A is distinct from B, even if A uses B and requires B in order to exist; if, secondly, A is indifferent to B, in the sense that, if B is a stuff, it is indifferent which lot of stuff A uses; and, thirdly, if A has its own proper causality. Certainly, it is sufficient that A have proper causality to be distinct from B. In ontological terms, *esse* accrues to things to the extent that they are free. In a sense, *esse* is this very freedom.

All this leads us to an extended definition of entity. Since an entity is that to which *esse* properly and ultimately accrues, it follows that entities as such are necessarily free, capable of formal and final causality, and therefore contingently capable of exercising material causality as used. Corresponding to this, *esse* is necessarily free self-positing. This is a far cry from the simple picture of the world as plethora with which we started. The world is, at least, the totality of possible coexistence in the sense that these relations, namely of subordination and coordination, are possible within it.

Notes to Chapter Five

1. As background for this and the next chapter, see Jacques Follon, 'Réflexions sur la théorie aristotélicienne des quatre causes', in the *Revue Philosophique de Louvain*, tome 86, no. 71, Août, 1988.

2. See Leibniz, *The Monadology and Other Philosophical Writings*, translated with introduction and notes by Robert Latta, (Oxford: OUP, 1971), p. 377, note 96.

3. *Metaphysics*, Book VII, 1041 b 10, and following; Loeb edition, vol. XVII, translated by Hugh Tredennick.

4. Iris Murdoch, *Metaphysics as a Guide to Morals*, (London: Chatto and Windus, 1992), p. 1-2.

5. Many of these issues, such as whole and part, coordination and subordination are handled by Kant in Section I of his *Inaugural Dissertation*, precisely in the context of the problematic of world. This is a most interesting though relatively untreated little work. The English version is in *Kant, Selected Precritical Writings*, translated and introduced by Kerferd and Walford, (Manchester: Manchester University Press, 1968).

6. *De Anima*, 412 b, 10-24.

CHAPTER SIX

Coexistence II: Causality

6, 1 Introduction

In our last chapter, we discussed the relations which determine coexistence as internal to entities. In this chapter, we shall examine that form of coexistence which is, at least for the most part, an external relation, namely, efficient causality. Entities are not Leibnizian monads, which windowlessly mirror each other's changes and alterations in a dance choreographed by God from all eternity. The notion of coexistence, especially in the form of efficient causality, is a corrective of any such view of entity, conceived after the model of the solipsistic Cartesian subject. Entities are not simply existent but coexistent, sharing existence not only by participation but in that self-communication, that working of others in likeness to oneself, which is the characteristic of this kind of causality.

However, at least in the English-speaking world, no discussion of causality can take place without reference to the sceptical and reductionist treatment given it by David Hume. Our first task, therefore, must be to lay the ghost of Hume. We shall suggest that Hume's treatment is flawed by an unclarity regarding what it is precisely that we mean to achieve when we talk in terms of cause and effect. Our suggestion is that the flaw consists in his not having given sufficient weight to the explanatory intent of such talk. The necessary connection is logical, not psychological; the paradigm of causality is not to be discovered in the well-foundedness or otherwise of a prediction that the next flip of the coin will be 'heads' as opposed to 'tails' based on previous trials, but in the logical relation of the application of some universal proposition to a particular case to explain the case.

But this in turn raises the question of the legitimacy of the universals required by such a model. The answer to this problem seems to lie in the permanently provisional character of knowledge, or better still, in its asymptotic relation to reality. Knowledge is real – this is our anti-sceptical stance again – but it is finite and always in process. But the asymptotic process of continual approach to the point at infinity where curve and line cut is one which depends upon the epistemic activities and hence upon the ethical commitments of the community of communicators and researchers wherein and whereby alone, truth is to be attained. Thus there emerges in our discussion the necessity of a specifically truth-directed virtue which we, following a hint from John Henry Newman, one of its clearest and most resolute champions, call 'conscientiousness'. In this way, the present chapter looks forward to our discussion of truth and its relation to the good, and foreshadows some of the conclusions we shall draw there.

This leads us to a kind of second beginning in this chapter. We have so far cleared the ground, but we have as yet erected no edifice. The laying of the foundation takes place as the disclosure of the ineluctable necessity of causal interaction, or of its assumption, if there is to be anything like real knowledge of the world. A theory of causality such as we wish to construct, moreover, is simply a general account of those principles necessarily invoked in the construction of causal explanations. Such a theory, therefore, is nothing more than a logic of such explanation, an explanation of the terms which all such explanation presupposes and uses. There is no 'principle of causality' independent of the logic of explanation, but there is a principle which expresses what it is to frame such an explanation. This principle is the 'axiom' *omnis agens agit sibi simile*, and its application demands that we talk of causality in two senses: transitive and reflexive.

The final movement in this discussion is one which does not follow immediately from the foregoing discussion, because it presupposes conclusions which will not be reached until a later chapter, but it is convenient to treat the issue here. The issue in question is the problem of reconciling Divine with finite causality, without falling into the trap of occasionalism.

6, 2 Hume's Account of Causality

Our treatment of causality will begin with Hume. For Hume, for one event to be considered the cause of another, three conditions must be fulfilled, namely, that what is considered the cause be temporally prior to, and spatially contiguous with, the event which is to be considered its effect (these are necessary conditions if we are to attribute causality to a given event) and that the putative effect is the necessary outcome of the cause, this being a sufficient condition to assert a causal relation between the two events.[1] Hume ascribes this necessary connection between the cause and effect to habit.[2] Because we have seen a great many examples of a certain kind of event followed every time by examples of another, we become persuaded that there is some necessary connection between them. If billiard-ball B moves when billiard-ball A strikes it, the motion of A is the cause of the motion of B, that is, B's movement cannot happen without A's, and cannot but happen given A's motion. Given B's motion, then, there must have been A's motion, or something rather like it, and we have become convinced of this through our having seen other examples of the same thing countless times, and our never having seen such a sequence to fail to happen.

The effect of Hume's treatment is to move the connection of events out of the ontological, and into the psychological, sphere. The connection between events is not actual production but expectation.[3] Expectation can either be fulfilled or not, and there is no illogicality in either case. Even if a coin is tossed a great number of times, granted that it is not biased, and happens to come up 'heads' for most, if not all of those trials, this does not determine the next outcome, which is independent of all previous. If, on the basis of my past experience, I expect yet another 'heads', and if my expectation is disappointed, all I can infer from that is that it is disappointed. Even if the sun has always risen, that is no guarantee that it will rise tomorrow, so tomorrow's sunrise becomes as unconnected to its predecessors as the previous tosses of the coin are to the next. The same goes, *mutatis mutandis*, for any succession of events. No (necessarily) finite number of previous observations justifies our absolute confidence that the same thing must always happen.

But surely we can appeal to the fact that we know why the sun rises? It is at this point that we see how Hume's treatment of causality is at one with his deconstruction of the notions of substance and personal identity. In effect, Hume is the first consistent empiricist, in that he deconstructs Locke's attenuated metaphysics, itself the outcome of the Cartesian project. Since we can, according to both Locke and Hume, know only those immediate data immanent to consciousness which the former calls ideas and the latter impressions – this is the unexamined Cartesian premise of all their speculations – it follows that what Locke calls the internal real constitution of things[4] must remain unknown. This, for Locke, is substance and its existence must be inferred. But, as untranslatable into the language of impressions, it becomes, for Hume, strictly meaning-less.[5] For Hume, all we have access to is the necessarily heterogen-eous and arbitrary flow of sense-data, heterogeneous and arbitrary precisely because it is devoid of any underlying ontological struct-ure to unite it. There is no question of knowledge of the real constit-ution of things, and hence no knowledge of their interrelatedness in and through causality.

However, on closer examination, it will be discovered that Hume's conditions lack cogency. Is it true that a cause always precedes its effect in time? The heating and being-heated which goes on when a heat source is applied to water occur at the same time. The same goes for the cutting and being-cut which occurs when I slice an orange. An analogous difficulty appears to arise in regard to Hume's second condition. Certainly, physical proximity and con-tact are required if our model for causality is change brought about by impact, but we may find examples of change being brought about where no obvious physical contact need be invoked. The aural simulacrum of applause which I hear on my radio at the end of a concert broadcast from the Sydney Opera House is doubtless caused by the real applause produced in the Opera House, but there is no physical proximity or mechanical link between the two events. We can multiply such examples. A vital clue is given us here if we ask, if not proximity, then what is 'between' the two events? If I seriously needed to explain to someone who had never heard of such a thing how the broadcast from the Sydney Opera House was possible, how the sound there could be reproduced here, my explanation would involve telling them how, say, electro-magnetic waves could be employed to produce just this connection.

This brings us to the very heart of the difficulty in Hume's approach. What Hume seems to neglect is that the cause is meant to *explain* the effect. Indeed, Hume's approach seems to do away with any possibility of the cause's explaining its effect. We look for causes to explain how and why change occurs, and for no other reason; to be a cause is to be a source of change. It is no explanation of event B to say that an event A always precedes it and that the two are locked together in necessary conjunction. The next question to ask is 'why?'. Why does A provoke a B, why, if there is an A, must a B always follow? 'Because they always do' is no answer. Any answer to such a question will take the form: 'because…', and an appeal will be made to some such picture as we have in our example: 'because electro-magnetic waves are propagated thus, and because they can be made to …'. In general, appeal is made to some theory of how the world works, where 'theory' is understood in the broadest possible sense. The theory may be *wissenschaftlich*, that is, strictly formulated according to the standards of some intellectual discipline, or it may be of the 'folk' variety. It need not be confined to explanations of how the physical world works. Since we try to explain things in other realms, it may be theological or historical, or even magical. It may be wholly or partially inaccurate, and fail to fit how the world is at all, as do magical explanations. This is a point to which we shall presently return, but what is now to be noted is that the theory is some picture of how the world works, and it relates cause *A* to event *B* so that *A* explains *B*. 'Why did *B* happen? Because *A* happened, and in general …' Without such a mediating picture no logical connection can be arrived at to connect *A* and *B* in this manner. Noting that two kinds of event occur, or seem to, in constant conjunction is at best only the first step in building the logical bridge, and it need not be present if we are dealing with a unique set of circumstances: 'why did the dinosaurs become extinct? Because an asteroid struck the earth. So? Well, it caused a huge explosion, so that …'[6]

Clearly, the explanation which connects cause to effect is a general one, in that it invokes general principles. Explanation, as Aristotle rightly recognised, must rest upon at least one universal premise, and there is no such thing as a particular principle. To say that *A* is the cause of *B* is to say that, given premises (general principles) derived from at least one theory *T*, and given the case that *A* is a premise, *that B is the case* follows as conclusion. This of course does not mean that we start off in possession of universally explanatory axioms from which all possible cases can be subsequently deduced, as some of the classical rationalists seem to have believed. This brings us to the nub of Hume's difficulty, and brings us back to the question we postponed a moment ago. If our theory does not match the way the world works, provided it is coherent, it will be capable of attempting to explain a given event in the manner we have indicated. In this case we will have *an* explanation of the event. In the case that our theory matches the way the world works and that there is an event *A* such as we have described, we will have *the* explanation of *B*. Thus the true explanatory power of our account is a function both of there being an appropriate (diagnosed correctly, on the basis of the theory) cause and a correct theory. If we have such a theory we can, if we have the ingenuity, diagnose the cause, but do we ever have such a theory, and if the answer is in the negative, how does that sit with our attempt to understand the world?

6, 3 Knowledge and Knowledge-claims

The answer, we suspect, is sometimes in the affirmative, often in the negative. However, this Humean objection does not make it licit for us to pass from the obvious truths that we do not know everything and are often mistaken, to the disastrous conclusion that therefore, we do not, or even cannot, know anything. This would leave us in thrall to that absolute scepticism which can flourish only in the classroom. Doubtless at any moment in history people and peoples entertain many beliefs which are incompatible with each other and with the way the universe really is. It is better, then, to talk of knowledge-claims rather than knowledge, for the notion of knowledge is inseparable from the procedures used to obtain it. To make such a claim is, implicitly or explicitly, to call upon the community of communication and investigation to make this claim the object of research. The various intellectual disciplines exist for, and consist in, the progressive removal of error and misconception, and the fostering of positive truth. All our pictures of the world are, to some extent, false and inaccurate; this is not to say that they cannot be corrected. In this consists the finitude of knowledge; but finite knowledge is still knowledge. Part of the process of tradition, understood as the transmission of meaning, must consist in the process, at once rational and ethical, of investigation and correction. That reality can be known, and that apparent epistemic states are not mere projections onto something inherently structureless, means that we can bring our claims to the test of that reality, which is now understood as the arbiter of truth, in an ongoing and possibly endless, though never goalless, process of tailoring our beliefs to match reality. We approach 'what is in itself' as a curve asymptotically approaches a line. Reality is not the unattainable, but is the ever more attainable. The image of the asymptote affords us the nice reflection that as line and curve meet only at infinity, only at infinity, that is, only in the Divine, are knowledge and 'what is' coterminous.

This does seem to give our knowledge-claims a permanently provisional character. If this is so, it must be faced, but it seems, perhaps, downright wrong-headed to say that it is in any sense doubtful that water is an oxide of hydrogen or that the earth orbits the sun. But this allows us to see something of the complexity inherent in any knowledge-claim: to say that I know that *x is the case* is to rely implicitly on a whole host of other factors. My belief that a squirrel has paused on the path outside is justified as true if, for example, I can be relied upon to distinguish squirrels from other small animals, if I am not hallucinating, if my senses are working properly, and so on. To be able to make claims I must and can, if scepticism is incoherent, make this implicit reliance. Each of these items can be challenged, can become the object of scrutiny, but we can and must rely on them unless and until reason is given for not doing so – 'he wouldn't know the difference between a squirrel and a hare; her sight isn't what it was, and it was towards evening, and squirrels aren't common here, so maybe …'.

Every landscape changes in response to climatic and geological conditions and to human intervention, but even here certain things remain constant. In the changing landscape of knowledge, there are certain landmarks which seem to remain fixed and impervious to change. It is true that water is an oxide of hydrogen, granted that certain propositions in the realm of chemistry can also be asserted, the ones, namely, that give meaning to the phrase 'oxide of hydrogen'; despite the changes which take place as a result of the corrective and investigative historical process which we call the science of chemistry, this proposition remains untouched and is unlikely to be overturned in the foreseeable future, ensconced comfortably as it is in atomic theory, which seems to be the best and most elegant explanation for the nature and working of the physical universe. The permanently provisional stigma which marks such old warhorse propositions amounts to the ever-diminishing possibility, the decreasing probability, that they will ever be shown to be false, an eventuality that recedes to a mere point on the horizon. But it must be admitted that this is not absolute certainty. The transition from Newtonian to Einsteinian physics shows both that the securest intellectual empires have known *coups d'état*, and that scientific revolutions do not necessarily merely jettison all that has gone before as useless and false. New theories explain what the old theories did and more, and do so more elegantly.

But all this points to certain features which are of greater interest to the philosopher than the actual mechanics of what Popper[7] would call conjecture and refutation. That such a process of explanation really can and does take place despite scepticism, or such worries as the problem of induction, stakes certain claims which are equivalent to the foundational moments of a non-sceptical, i.e. realist cognitive theory. To know involves being able to deploy language, so as to be able to enunciate true propositions about things. Thus, a necessary precondition of the process is the existence and validity of logic: there can be neither proof nor refutation outside logic or in its despite, for proof and refutation are merely the particular deployment and application to a given subject-matter of the super-science of dialectic whose principles 'fall under no particular discipline'. A wider version of the same point is the proposition whose ultimate implications we are here engaged in tracing, namely, that it is possible for language to make sense of the world, for each language is a particularised instantiation of logic. Likewise, *we*, and in particular *I*, must be able to deploy logic and use language. For me to be able to display the (contingent) truth-value of a given proposition, I must be able to mount something in the nature, say, of a *Modus Tollendo* argument – CKCpqNqNp. This involves being able to assert that some propositions are (contingently) true or false; i.e. I must at least be capable of knowing their truth value. This, it seems, is what understanding a proposition involves. Some contingent propositions, moreover, represent beliefs impossible for me to have save through normally functioning senses.

All of this implies that causal interactions do in fact take place, otherwise both those mechanisms internal to language-users which make them capable of language use, together with those sensory processes upon which any apprehension of the world by these users depends, would be impossible. Such considerations form part of the logic of the project which is knowledge, which is simply the deployment of logic as such. But logic itself is not the motive force of knowledge, no more than the rules of chess constitute the playing of actual games. The motive force is the engagement of individuals, who investigate, who communicate, who deploy logic and language here and now. As we have intimated, rationality is coevally ethical and logical. What ethical items, then, are required by this process of the realisation of logic in and as knowledge?

6, 4 Conscientiousness: the Intellectual Virtue

Clearly, there is an intellectual excellence – a virtue – which each and every participant of the process must have, as participant, if the process is to be possible. Newman calls it the 'illative sense', and discloses what it means very well:

> We have arrived at these conclusions – not *ex opere operato*, by a scientific necessity independent of ourselves – but by the action

of our own minds, by our own individual perception of the truth in question, under a sense of duty to those conclusions and with an intellectual conscientiousness.[8]

Newman does not, at least not in this context, spurn the systematic or the scientific, but he does point out that these do not discover truth: people do. Human beings as knowers and speakers are agents, coevally rational and moral, who act in reliance on what has already been achieved, but who look forward, in their necessarily finite contributions to the process of knowledge-tradition, to what has yet to be achieved. They are conscientious knowers in that they take responsibility for their actions; freedom, which is the formal character of the person, is the ability to do so. This banishes the shoddy, and, even more, the arbitrary. A visual perception implies having a perspective, and it is in the nature of perspective for the observer to hold a station-point, from which, of necessity, some things are revealed and others hidden, some things loom, others recede. To that extent, it is always partial, and must be complemented by other perspectives. But, perception, though mine, is in and of the common world of the wakeful[9]: to perceive is to know that something is the case, and if I 'perceive' something which is not so, then I have not perceived and am in error. This prevents the pernicious attachment of possessive pronouns to perception and to that which is perceived – 'my reality', 'your perception', 'her world' – as though these were private and unrelated realms, at the disposal of those whose 'reality' they are; they are in truth merely the twilit half-world into which sleepers turn, where what is, is lost. This is not to deny that what is perceived, is so incompletely as from a particular station-point, nor that what is is, in some sense, translated into something other than what is, namely the linguistic and intentional complex of factors whereby speakers can apprehend and say what is. This is the meaning of the 'axiom', *quidquid recipitur ad modum recipientis recipitur*. But it is to assert that the translation remains faithful to the original, that truth is the revealedness of what is, that therefore it is this, and not I, which is the measure of perception and knowledge, and that this 'I', or the 'we' to which the I necessarily belongs as speaker, or any phase or factor of these, cannot get in the way so as to block truth.

Truth is therefore the pole to which our swinging needle must eventually point, and this pole's magnetism is ethical as well as logical, in that, that a proposition is true is a necessary and sufficient logical and moral ground for asserting it; if it is true I ought to accept it, and I ought to accept it only if it is true: if it is false I ought to reject it, and ought to reject it only if it is false. The responsibility for differentiating between the two is shared among all investigators. Truth is formally value and can to that extent be only in the realm of the linguistic and intentional. But although truth is revelation of what is, it adds value to what is, and thereby that appeal to free but finite rationality which is the characteristic of 'ought'. This is the heartbeat of the intellectual virtue which is conscientiousness.

6, 5 The Ineluctability of Causal Interaction

Let us draw together, in summary, the issues relevant to causal interaction which have emerged in our discussion so far. What emerges from this consideration of the nature of knowing is that it is founded on the necessity of there being genuine causal interaction, unless scepticism or the Cartesian picture of the inward-looking, discarnate self, which requires neither sensory input nor brain-process in order to know, is correct. We have said enough already in our first chapter regarding the misguidedness of the Cartesian project. Likewise, we have suggested that there is and can be no proof that language can grasp what is, in the sense that there can in principle be true propositions, for any such proof would be an argument, a piece of discourse, which would by the same token assume what it was intended to prove. For the same reason, there can be no argument to the contrary; an argument designed to show that there can be no assertions is evidence that the conclusion it is intended to support is false. Scepticism cannot be stated coherently, and there can be no evidence for it. There may, as we said, be radical difficulties about the truth of some claims, or even at some time about any claim, but there cannot be any overall worry to the effect that there are no claims. Intellectual conscientiousness, as we have outlined it, is the very virtue whose subject this is: bravery stands to danger as conscientiousness does to doubt. Thus we must choose between scepticism, on the one hand, and the possibility and actuality of truth on the other, and the anti-Cartesian, 'incarnationist' assumption this latter rests on – at least in the case of finite knowing – of the genuineness of causal interaction. This is no real alternative, because scepticism melts before even this brief analysis. Thus we come to the question which dominates this part of our discussion: what is the nature of what Aristotle called efficient causality?

6, 6 The Nature of Efficient Causality: *omnis agens agit sibi simile*

The other types of causality which we have so far encountered are the factors necessary to coexistence, as these occur within entities in virtue of the relationship of use. Efficient causality, however, is the production of change as such, and thus can, and usually does, represent the coordination of distinct entities with one another as opposed to the subordination of one thing to another. In this way, it is both what is meant by causality *par excellence*, and is the actuality of coexistence as interaction.

It will not do simply to represent this relation of coordination merely by saying 'A causes B' or the like, for this would be too vague. Efficient causality is not creation, the production of *esse* as such. To say this is to say that if something is to qualify as cause, in the sense of the production of novelty, it must be so in subordination to certain factors which as cause it does not determine or produce, and which are thus logically, if not temporally, prior to it. In particular, the novelty which it produces must be possible. But this is not enough to make its production real. Unless a cause is omnipotent, it cannot simply produce a new state of affairs merely because that state of affairs is internally coherent; if it did, this would count as creation, the exercise of omnipotence. Thus the possibility of novelty must be anchored in the real, must be a real possibility of what is, a potentiality. Potentiality is real, though as yet unfulfilled, possibility: that is, most fundamentally, what real things are actually capable of being or becoming. Thus for novelty to occur, it is necessary that there be such real potential for it. This is to say that there must be something which is capable of becoming something other than it now is in such a way that the novelty in question comes to be. This something may be called the potential subject, the subject that is, which is actually capable of taking on the novelty in question.

Actual capacity for novelty is a necessary condition but not a sufficient one for the novelty actually to come to be. If it were, the potential subject's being actually capable would guarantee the novelty's appearance. But at any moment any entity is capable of many states whose actualistion would be mutually incompatible. This is necessarily the case because an entity capable of change can either continue being x or can fail to do so. The realisation of both such states is inconsistent. It is possible to be capable of x and of not-x simultaneously, but not to be actually x and not-x simultaneously. In general, many mutually inconsistent states are simultaneously or disjunctively possible, which is to say that they cannot be simultaneously actual. This is why the modal proposition to the effect that possibility as such is distinct from (as not necessitating) actuality is necessarily true. Thus, actual capacity for novelty is a necessary condition but not a sufficient one for the novelty actually to come to be.

But if this is so, what is necessary for the subject which is potentially something to be that something actually? It is necessary that there be some factor which makes an actuality of the potentiality in question, a factor which is, at least, necessarily distinct from the potentiality itself. But to be distinct from a 'potentiality for x' is either to be actually x or to be really incapable of being x, and hence really not to be x. If something which is really not x actualises A's capacity to be x, this means that any factor which is not x is sufficient for A to be really x. Thus there is no connection between the factor and A's actually becoming x, which is as much as to say that A can become x without the intervention of any factor, and thus that A's potentiality for x is sufficient for A to be x actually, which, as we have seen is impossible. Thus, it is necessary that this factor itself must be actually, and not just potentially, what it actualises in the potential subject. This is what is meant by the word 'cause', a factor which, in virtue of being actual in some respect, makes actual the capacity of a potential subject to be actual in a related respect, while its correlative 'effect' means the change in the potential subject which is the realisation of that capacity. Thus, in any causal interaction, there must be these three terms: cause, potential subject, and effect, that is, something which is actual in some respect, something which has potential to be actual in like respect, and the novelty itself.

But what is the meaning of 'makes actual' in our attempt to define 'cause'? It cannot mean that it simply produces the 'missing' actuality in that which lacks it, for this would be tantamount to creation. We might say that it calls forth the actuality by virtue of its own being actual in that respect, in something which is capable of it. But, again, what does this mean? It means simply that the subject will become actual in the relevant respect granted that certain conditions are fulfilled, the sufficient one among them being this factor which, precisely as cause, is the factor already actual in the required respect. To say this is to say that things as actual are to be credited with the production of actuality to the extent that such changes are impossible in their absence. Potentiality, on the other hand, is openness to change on the part of a subject and hence receptivity to the appropriate cause. Things therefore precisely as actual tend to communicate their likeness, their actuality, to those things capable of that likeness: *omnis agens agit sibi simile*. The agent itself must, as agent, be actual in respect of what it communicates, although variation in degree within actuality is possible.

We ought to give due weight to '*simile*'. The agent works similar to itself, not identically to itself. This makes of the causal principle an analogical, not a univocal one. We capture this by saying that the actuality which qualifies the cause as cause must be such that an account of what it is must show it suitable to actualise the potentiality which it actualises. One does not boil an egg in potentially hot water, but the actuality of the water's being hot is such as to be at once the fact of the way the water is and the power to do what hot water does to eggs: the water turns to vapour while the egg solidifies. 'What hot water does to eggs' is the general statement which is, or is part of, a folk- (or more scientific) -theory of the actual working of the world, which must also include a statement of what conditions must be fulfilled if *this* water is to do what hot water does to eggs. Likewise, if it is true that smoking causes cancer, a successful causal explanation of this will disclose how smoking brings this about, namely how the chemicals released in smoking – which are themselves complex molecules, and thus ultimately entities – as a function of what they actually are, are such as to produce certain kinds of change in organ-totalities, which, because of what they in turn are, are capable of the changes in question. It is because something happens to be disposed in a certain way as a function of what it is that it is capable of being changed in some way by something else in virtue of what that something else properly is. This does not mean that it is the proper activity of chemical x to produce cancer, but that this power is necessarily accredited to it by virtue of what it properly is.

In sum, a causal explanation is a statement of how something is or comes to be as a function of something else's being actually thus or thus. 'Power', on the other hand, refers to that actuality's so functioning, though not necessarily 'now'. Power is distinct from potentiality which is a capacity to become, while power is capacity to do or to work change: both, though ontologically distinct, are 'forms' of possibility. All this brings out the empirical element in causal exchange, in terms of which these ontological principles are incarnated. The empirical pattern of change and causality is precisely what science investigates, and is the actual content of the theory necessary to causal explanation.

Causal exchanges, moreover, are more complex than the 'one way' system we have here suggested, though modification of this account adequate to this complexity merely applies these same principles more widely. Many, if not all, causal exchanges are reciprocal, in that a heat source, say, may lose heat in communicating the actuality of heat to another: each approaches opposite ends of a spectrum which is the actuality, in a proportional and mutual manner. But to remain a cause, the agent must retain the actuality to the extent necessary, an extent dictated by the kind of change, and therefore by the kind of entity, involved in the exchange. Causality and change do not occur except as individuated as this kind of entity changing in this or that respect under the influence of this or that kind of cause.

6, 7 Transitive and Reflexive Causality

Is this account sufficient for all kinds of causality? If potentiality as such is insufficient alone for change, then for change to take place there must be an appropriate cause. Thus the kinds and numbers of possible changes dictate the kinds and numbers of cause. How many kinds of change are there? There is accidental change and transformation. In the former, something becomes other without becoming another – which, of course, includes relational change, one type of which is motion – while in the latter, something becomes something else, something comes to be in that another perishes. The account we have given so far seems adequate *mutatis mutandis* for transformation, in that the potentiality realised is the coming-to-be or perishing of something, and in that the potentiality in question is precisely that which things have, alone or in groups, to become other things. Each of these changes requires an appropriate cause to the extent that capacity for change as such is not sufficient to produce it. But is it not possible for some causality to be reflexive? This means, do some things not change themselves? A boy, all things being equal, will become a man; something similar is the case with all vital processes and all cases of self- (including local) motion. It would appear, at least at first sight, that the account we have given so far would apply more to transitive causality, that is, precisely, where something communicates its likeness to another.

It is appropriate here to speak of reflexive causality to the extent that no change, as actualisation of potential, can occur simply on the basis of potential as such alone. The actual factor which explains Baby Jane's transformation into Adult Jane is her being the (kind of)

entity she is. It is necessary, if she is to change in the manner characteristic of her kind, that she be of that kind, while, all other necessary conditions being fulfilled (e. g., that food in sufficient quality
and quantity be available) it would also appear to be a sufficient
condition. If this is so, how is the parity of actuality and potentiality
in cause and effect maintained? Causes, we have claimed, evoke
like actuality with which they, as causes, are determined. But how
can Jane the girl be said to have, much less to communicate, the
actuality of Jane the woman, into which Jane grows? Is Jane the girl
the efficient cause of Jane the woman? And to what subject does
Jane the girl communicate the actuality of Jane the woman? To a
future, and hence not yet real, one?

Being Jane the girl is distinct from being Jane the woman, but they
are, nonetheless related as diverse states of the same entity. What
necessarily remains static throughout the change is Jane's identity,
the structure which makes Jane Jane. Precisely as having this, Jane
changes accidentally. Accidental changes are not always slight, but
what is necessary to them is that they do not result in coming-to-be
or perishing. It is identity, as essence, which may be considered the
efficient cause, or the main part of the efficient cause, of the accidental change. (Things do indeed change as individuals and in ways
appropriate to their kind. Moreover, in a complex change like Jane's
growing, other efficient causes are at work, such as, say, climate or
diet, which modify the action of the main efficient cause.) It is the
entity as capable of growth which is the potential subject of its own
identity's action. Things are not causes and effects in the same
respect, for they are never potentially and in act in the same respect.

Various points are to be noted here. Identity, firstly, is the cause of
change, (only) at the level of accident. We shall see that, and why, it
cannot be its own efficient cause, i.e. the cause of its own existence.
But secondly, and more profoundly, the same question, which we
have already asked, reasserts itself. Granted that Jane's change
from a baby into a woman is the result of the efficient causality of
her identity on the entity which she is, and which is capable of these
changes. But since this identity is not actually her being a girl or a
woman – if it were identical to either she could never change in that
respect – how can it communicate that in respect of which it is not
actual? Again, how is parity of actuality and potentiality preserved?

To be Jane, though constant for as long as she exists, is to be qualified in various ways: there is no such item as an atemporal 'being the entity Jane'. To be Jane is to be successively in the states of 'Jane being a child' and 'Jane being mature', the proper cause of which is that which persists through all these states, Jane being Jane in all her various states. But, Jane the girl is potentially Jane the woman, and the capacity is that of the entity which Jane is, actualised by her continued identity, which does not change through time, but which itself is not simply identical with the entity whose identity it is. Such change is therefore a function of the entity as such, not of its identity. Given that the entity will continue to exist, it can do so only as the succession of its states which are therefore virtually present within it, though modified by actual factors around it. The capacity of the entity for these states is actualised by identity which contains actually, though not expressly, all that the entity as the entity it is, can be. There is no such thing as the capacity to write *Pride and Prejudice*, though there is the capacity which is the endowment which can be used to write this book, and do other things of like and lesser difficulty. Jane at five may not be actually capable of writing it, but simply because she is who she is, she is already the person who will one day be capable of it. Thus, her identity does not actualise itself, but serially actualises the capacities which it, from the very beginning, gives and has given her. In this sense, she can only become what she already is, but the capacity is hers as the entity she is, and precisely as this entity she can be 'merely capable' of something, as opposed to being actually, or actually capable. As endowed with the identity she has, by contrast, she is and always was actually, though unexpressedly, capable of doing all that Jane can do. It is entities, not identities, which have a history, and it is in the connection and real diversity of entity and identity that the temporality of things is expressed. Identity as all that something is, is already all that that something can be. Thus identity is not only the formal, but the efficient, cause of all those accidents which are functions of it and inseparable from it as its expressions, as the factor necessary and sufficient for their being, though identity, the entity whose identity it is, and the capacities for being acted upon which identity grants the entity, are merely the necessary conditions for the other, more remote, accidents.

This, then is what is involved in those transformations which are the developments of a thing, or the phases of its evolution. Does the same account hold for coming-to-be and equivalent perishing? To say that something comes to be or perishes is to say that something else is transformed into it or that it in its turn is transformed into something else. It is the hallmark of prematter that this transformation is its *per se* effect, while, in the case of decomposition, the *per acccidens* effect of destruction: the capacity to become the animal is what makes seed and ovum 'seminal' elements, though we do not think of the living animal as the seed of its own remains. In the former case, understanding the kind – that this is prematter – and perforce their identity if these things can be called entities, dovetails with knowledge of the thus in-built purpose. To be prematter is to have as identity and essence the purpose of transformation into another. The contingency of the entity in question dovetails with what the entity is. The mode of being, the relation between existence and what is, is realised similarly but differently in the latter case, namely of decomposition. There, the purpose of the entity is its being as the particular entity it is, as we have explained, but its contingency is realised in and as its identity and essence, though not in such a way that these are 'for' contingency, as looking forward structurally to the destruction of the entity to which they belong. In the case of seminal elements, then, the capacity to become another is the actual identity of the thing, so that this identity is thereby the efficient cause of the transformation characteristic of prematter as such. In other cases, these structural features embody contingency, and are the formal cause of the capacity for decomposition – Jane dies ultimately because she is who and what she is – but not the efficient cause – Jane dies not just because she is human, but because she had, say, a heart attack or a stroke. Identity is thus necessary but insufficient for destruction, as it is for existence. It is the characteristic of finite causes however, that they can destroy, that is, realise a potential situation incompatible with the continued existence of something, but not create, give something *esse* as such.

Novelty and predictability are balanced in these relations, for things come to be or undergo dissolution as a function of their origins' capacity for the transformation in question, but are not predictable from these capacities, neither in terms of when nor of what. That something new comes to be happens as a result of the capacities of its prior conditions to produce it, but these capacities do not happen to be simple or predictable in their operation. The embryo in its particularity – 'who' – is not predictable due to the unimaginably huge repertoire of possibilities available in reproduction, as incarnated in the elements, though the embryo as embryo is not surprising given the process *in se*, and its actually having taken place.

Local motion is also a kind of self-motion, but is very imperfect compared to those we have just considered. Nevertheless, it can be used for this reason as an analogy for them. Motion is continuous variation of spatial relation, in terms, if we wish to be complete, of time. Identity as such is not the efficient cause of such change. Spatiality, or more properly, spatio-temporality, is its formal cause. Things move because they are propelled, and the efficient cause of this is something, belonging either to that which moves or to another, whose *per se* effect it is, precisely as actually moving. This is not to say that there is 'something' that always moves, but only that movement is always a feature of the world. In a world where nothing moved, nothing would move. That there is movement is not the result of some unmoved mover's activity, but that movement is endemic in the spatio-temporal world, as a virtual formal feature in spatio-temporal entities. Energy is the power ultimately to shift, to cause motion, and energy and its transformations, under appropriate efficient causality, is embodied variously in spatio-temporal kinds, which, from this perspective, are simply energy-economies.

But what of those activities that are of most interest to us, which embody our transcendence, our *per se* vectorial orientation towards the transcendentals, perhaps more simply called, the power to know and love? These are powers proper to entities of a certain kind, and thus we have implicitly dealt with their relation to that which underlies them in dealing with use and material causality, though the account of efficient causality allows us to see all this in a more dynamic fashion. In particular, transcendence requires a being-affected, which relies on efficient causality. But in all kinds of causality, one general principle holds: things are insofar as they act, and act insofar as they are. This principle shows the positions of being and acting relative to one another. Not only does it represent a kind of 'test' of something's reality – does this thing ever exercise causality *per se* or does it act always as a function of another? – but shows that causality is integral to the being of that which (finitely) is. To be finitely is not only to be, where necessary, able to appropriate the proper causality of another as one's own, but also necessarily to be able to go beyond, and thereby communicate, oneself as actual to others in the quasi-transcendence which is efficient causality.

Thinking does not occur precisely as a function or proper effect of the causal exchanges which occur between chemical elements, however much it may depend upon their occurrence; thinking occurs as the proper activity of a certain kind of entity whose power to think is incarnated in and as the structure of the appropriate organ, whose being is final-ly to use such exchanges insofar as it is, and whose activity is contingent to, and accidental in, those used exchanges. And so on for all such activities. The being and state of the organ determines the what, and how far, of the capacity, indeed in a sense, *is* the capacity. If the eye were an animal seeing would be its soul, and mental activity is to brains what seeing is to eyes. Thus the transcendence which is causality is used and transformed in transcendence proper, which is our stretching forth to existence as true, good and lovely.

6, 8 Occasionalism and Participation

How does this analysis of causality relate to the Divine? Occasionalism is the belief that there are no other agents than God, that God is responsible for all change. It would seem that we run perilously close to this if we say that God is responsible for all that is. Such an assertion seems to crowd out finite causality. Such a belief, apart from its intrinsic implausibility, would tend to make God not merely a Creator but also a doer, that is, the one who is really responsible for everything done in the universe. Thus the view would seem to deprive us of agency, and in particular, of moral agency. But the proper effect of Divine causality is *esse* as such, not particular features of the universe. Causality is relation, and relation is *esse-ad*, just as determination is *in-esse*. This expresses that each of these in its own way participates, by intrinsic attribution, in the *esse* which belongs properly to entities as such.

Entities do modify one another, but they do not confer existence as such on one another, even when they transform themselves into one another in perishing and coming-to-be. This is precisely the polarity of (not-quite-paradoxically, though apparently opposed) perspectives which must be reconciled if occasionalism is to be avoided. It is vital here to grasp the relative position of *esse* with regard to transformation of all sorts: transformation presupposes *esse*, which is only ever held contingently by the finite real. There are here two relevant forms of transformation, namely, when one thing changes another and when one thing becomes another. Of these two, the latter is clearly more radical, so let us look first at it. Even in the case where what something is may be seen as the efficient cause of its becoming another, it only is contingently and thus is receptive, but not productive, of the fact that it is. Thus, although it is necessary, *as the thing it is* that it become another, and for that reason does so non-contingently, it does so *as existing contingently*, and as presupposing its existing contingently. Becoming is what is necessary for and in it, not the fact that it actually is. Thus the process of transformation is like a contingent entity itself, which is only contingently, though within or under that condition, having necessary or essential traits. Existence, *esse*, this 'fact that it actually is' englobes the process of becoming as it does beings (which become) and is their yes or no, beyond them as not identical to, or necessitated by, any feature they may display. The same goes, *mutatis mutandis*, for transformation in the first sense distinguished, where one thing 'does something to' another. Causality is within existence, existence is not within causality. The world is a pattern of events, of causal exchanges, of transformations, which are contingently. That they are is the proper effect of creation, but how they modify one another and become, is a function of what they are. Thus the question of the relation of Divine to finite causality is the wider question of how any actuality relates to the actuality which is *esse*, existence, the proper effect of the Divine, and thereby relation to the Divine.

Any actuality is such precisely insofar as it is. *Esse* is thus the 'being actual' of anything actual as such, and is thus not a 'something else' wedded or superadded to that actuality. More than this, it seems, would be difficult to say, except that 'exists' is said along the lines indicated by what is: in the first place of entities and then equally in second place, of their determinations and relations, which participate in existing, and exist by analogy. Transformations dovetail with this schema for they occur within these categories, precisely as 'of' them, and so can be said to be in the same way that the other inhabitants of the categories can. The only restriction on this is that entities as such cannot change except insofar as they cease or come to be, but that is a change in identity, whose ontological status is determination, so there is no transformation proper to entities as such, though all change is, as all else is, ultimately 'of' entities.

Notes to Chapter Six

1. *Treatise*, I, III, II. See also, *Treatise*, I, II, XV: where Hume gives 'rules by which to judge of causes and effects'; the most important of these are: '(1) The cause and effect must be contiguous in space and time. (2) the cause must be [temporally] prior to the effect. (3) There must be a constant union betwixt the cause and effect. 'Tis chiefly this quality that constitutes the relation.' These notions are embodied in Hume's two definitions of cause: 'An object precedent and contiguous to another, and where all the objects resembling the former are plac'd in like relations of precedency and contiguity to those objects, that resemble the latter'; 'an object precedent and contiguous to another, and so united with it, that the idea of the one determines the mind to form the idea of the other, and the impression of the one to form a more lively idea of the other.' *Treatise*, I, III, XIV.

2. 'This therefore is the essence of necessity. Upon the whole, necessity is something, that exists in the mind, not in objects; nor is it possible for us ever to form the most distant idea of it, consider'd as a quality in bodies. Either we have no idea of necessity, or necessity is nothing but that determination of the thought to pass from causes to effects and from effects to causes, according to their experienc'd union.' Thus what underlies necessity is merely 'that propensity, which custom produces, to pass from an object to the idea of its usual attendant.' *Treatise*, I, III, XIV.

3. 'According to the present doctrine, there are no objects which by the mere survey, without consulting experience, we can determine to be the causes of any other; and no objects, which we can certainly determine in the same manner not to be causes. Any thing may produce any thing. Creation, annihilation, motion, reason, volition; all these may arise from one another, or from any other object we can imagine ... The constant conjunction of objects determines their causation ...' *Treatise*, I, II, XV, emphasis removed.

4. *Essay* III, VI, 3.

5. *Treatise*, I, I, VI.

6. 'One of the most dramatic of these [very rapid environmental] changes was the sudden extinction of the dinosaurs almost exactly sixty-five million years ago. Evidence is now very strong that this was the result of the impact of a 10-kilometer-wide asteroid on what is now the Yucatán peninsula. That catastrophic event seems to have killed off most land animals more than a few kilograms in weight, along with much of the ocean's plankton. It abruptly and dramatically simplified the complex ecosystems of the time, causing many previously occupied ecological niches to be vacated and even opening up a number of brand-new niches. The subsequent adaptive radiation of the mammals to fill these empty niches, eventually resulting in the appearance of animals as different as whales and bats, was relatively swift in evolutionary terms...' Christopher Wills, *The Runaway Brain. The Evolution of Human Uniqueness*, (London: HarperCollins

Publishers, 1994) p. 9. In these few elegant sentences, Wills presents the complex network of events which made possible the evolution of humans. One might say that the notion 'causal explanation' is tautologous: without the notion of causality it would be impossible to make the interconnection of these unique events intelligible. What is happening here is that the process which includes them all and makes them intelligible is disclosed on condition that appeal can be made to theories of how things work, in general; this is what framing a causal explanation means.

7. Probably the most comprehensive statement by Popper of his own position is to be found in *The Logic of Scientific Discovery*, (London: Unwin Hyman, 1990).

8. John Henry Newman, *An Essay in Aid of a Grammar of Assent*, (London: Longmans, 1895), Chapter VIII, section 2, p. 318.

9. Heraclitus, Fragment 89 in *Heraclitus, Fragments, A Text and Translation with a Commentary* by T. M. Robinson, (Toronto: University of Toronto Press, 1991).

CHAPTER SEVEN

Time and Temporality

7, 1 Introduction

In our last chapters we have discussed the nature of entity in itself and the features belonging to it, together with the various forms of coexistence of which entities are capable, and the forms of causality essential to such coexistence. This has enabled us to discern, though imperfectly, that relation between entity and *esse* which is the focus of ontology. Our treatment remains imperfect, as we have just remarked, because the central feature of entity, which is the necessary expression of its relation to *esse*, has itself so far remained unanalysed. This feature is temporality. By temporality we do not simply mean time, which is adequately defined by Aristotle as measure, but that on which time, and temporal and tensual linguistic usage, depend, the 'time' which is constitutive of, and necessary to, finite entity. This locution, 'temporality' says more than 'time', which is abstract and notional, and remote from the temporal, contingent, mutable being proper to finite things, but even 'temporality' fails to capture their be-ing as event-ual, as flowing. For this reason we use the verbal form 'temporalising' to grasp it.

Moreover, the spatio-temporality which being material bespeaks, and without which world would be unintelligible, invokes both space and time, and as necessarily conjoined. We must therefore also explore this junction of space and time, and this, in fact, is the appropriate point of departure for the analysis of time we intend to give in this chapter. We shall see that the junction is such that space is a function of time in that it cannot be, or be intelligible, without time, or, more properly, temporality.

The structure of this chapter is non-linear, at least in its gross outlines, but is a spiral which tries to move ever closer to the truth of temporality. We embark on this spiral by looking at entities' temporalising as whole and series, a strategy which allows us an *entrée* to the structure proper to temporality, as function of actuality and of actuality-anchored possibility, which is potentiality. It is this temporal structure, the conjunction of actuality and potentiality, which is the necessary embodiment of contingency, which is itself the relation of the finite to *esse*. Within the ambit of such contingency fall coming-to-be and perishing and, in a special way, lasting, items which are the modes in which temporality is expressed, that is, that in which the contingency of the contingent is 'lived'. In sum, temporality is the living out of the relation between entity and *esse*, in coming-to-be and perishing, and in the continuity of something's lasting. It is this analysis which lets us see the truth of finitude, of the being-created of the contingent, as this is announced in the saying of Heraclitus, πάντα ῥεῖ. It is this truth which gives the one necessary and sufficient entry into the existence and nature of the Divine, which we explore in our next chapter, and by virtue of which our ontology becomes metaphysics, as onto-theology. Finally, this in turn enables us to substantiate the notion, already familiar from our previous investigations, that the world is a real, analogical participation in and of *esse*.

7, 2 Space and Time

If time allows the possibility of the serial differentiation of one and the same entity, the essence of space is to allow the possibility of simultaneous distinction between (temporal) entities, and thus coevally the possibility of their coexistence, of their encounter, that is, precisely as distinct, and hence as excluding each other, and as involved causally with each other on this basis. The same thing cannot be in two places simultaneously, and no two entities can occupy the same space simultaneously unless there is a relationship of use between them, in the way we have defined this, in which case their occupation of the same space is necessary. To deny the first of these axioms of common sense or of the Euclidean world is to assert that the same entity can be 'here' and 'there' simultaneously. This is to say that one and the same entity has mutually exclusive accidental qualifications simultaneously, or that the one entity is distinct from itself, or has more than one identity; all of which are impossible. Thus, spatial difference rests upon distinctness of entities. But entities, though perhaps in a relation of dependence, are free from each other insofar as they are, and exclude each other to that extent. In the case that the working of the one is subsumed and taken up in the working of the other, that which is subsumed is excluded to the extent that its own causality is excluded as proper to it in the working of the entity in which it is subsumed. In simple terms, things exclude each other insofar as they are. Since space is the possibility of simultaneous mutual differentiation, so that things which are distinct define different spaces, spatial coincidence implies a kind of identity – the molecules which make up my body *are* my body – and identity is not exclusion. Exclusion properly takes the form of spatial non-coincidence. Space as such cannot individuate, but presupposes the individuation proper to entities; space is the possibility of something's being as being-individual, as distinct and free.

There is no such 'thing' as space, which is defined and made actual by that which is or are 'in' it, which is done either as occupation or movement, between which there is an analogy, as the simultaneous or serial actuation of locations 'in' space, respectively. A location is where something is or can be. Locations cannot be actually discrete from each other, but only potentially so as diversely occupiable, otherwise the Zenonian paradoxes would be correct and all movement would require the traversing of an actual infinity of points, and so would be impossible. This is the source of the 'infinite divisibility' of space. Locations can be partially identical, and are thus not distinct from, and exclusive of, each other in the same way that entites are, save as actually occupied by entities. This is the continuity proper to space. Occupation is by the distinguishable parts or sections of the entity which occupies it, and so is the simultaneous actuation of those points by them. We repeat, movement is their serial actuation, hence the analogy with occupation. Space is the possibility of movement, of continuous serial actuation. The continuity in question here is precisely the opposite of something's ceasing to be absolutely and then coming to be again. Continuity is the lasting of something through time. The possibility of movement makes the identification of spatial points possible, whose difference is distance. Space is defined as distance, serial actualisability of locations, measured therefore by time. Edge and surface mark the border between the actually and the potentially filled, and thereby the limits of something's exclusivity. Edge and surface define shape, which is based on simultaneous distance. But shape also requires direction as well as distance. This is also to be understood in terms of time. Any two distinct points define a direction (in Euclidean space), provided their mutual relation does not vary relative to other static directions identical to theirs. Things are static when the relations between them do not vary. Invariance of course, means constancy through time. This in turn yields dimensionality which is as the possibility of direction, and of the totality of its diversity. Things retain their shape precisely as retaining the ability to actualise locations in an identical manner, as allowing point for point, directionally identical, correspondences between the filling of any two locations serially, or the same location over distinct time-points.

To say all this is only to dip under the surface of the vast problematic of space, one which extends far beyond ontology and into the sciences. But from what has been said it is clear that spatiality has an intrinsic relation to time, such that something can be in space only if it is in time; more exactly, being spatial implies being temporal. Is the reverse the case? Can there be anything which is temporal without being spatial? It would seem that the answer is yes if the notion of something which lacks dimension, and hence all the characteristics we have just outlined, is coherent. It would, unfortunately, take us well beyond the limits of this essay to try to settle this question. Whatever way it may finally be settled, all reality can be divided into spatio-temporal things, and merely temporal things, and hence finite and created things, on the one hand, and Divinity on the other, which as one and uncreated is neither temporal, nor, consequently, spatial, nor finite. But the materiality of material things consists in their spatiality, and not in their temporality as such, for use as we have defined it involves collocation, and all material entities either use or are, elements.

7, 3 Temporality: Whole and Series

It is more correct to speak of temporality than of time. The notion 'time' conjures up a medium, a kind of stream, in which things are immersed, or carried along. We may tend wrongly to think, if we follow this line, that there is an absolute distinction between time and the things which are in it. Temporality, on the other hand, is a fundamental and intrinsic characterisation of entities, a 'being temporal' which englobes and determines the entity as such, or, more properly, its structure as entity, and what it is, which therefore flow from the mode of relation it has to *esse*; it is in this relation that temporality properly consists. If the relation is other than identity, the mode of the relation is other than necessity, and vice versa: if the relation is identity, the mode of the relation is necessity, and vice versa. Such 'being temporal', as we shall see, is a mutability devolving from this bond, and thereby founds the spatio-temporality of world as a complex relation of coordination between things or situations which change, which is, precisely, the origin of our ordinary notion of time. In the case of a world whose contents did not happen to change there might still be time, but it would be meaningless to speak of it in one whose contents were in principle incapable of change. 'Time' is as much an abstraction as 'space', and, like space, it is not a thing or an entity. If we are correct, then the notion of time is intrinsically dependent on that of change. Let us examine this notion.

We have distinguished entities, properties and relations, and change is possible in all three, when an entity comes to be or passes away, or when its accidents or the relations between entities, alter. The first category of change is radical, or as Aristotle would say, substantial, change, while the others are non-radical, or what Aristotle would call accidental, change; change at the level of defining property, that is, at the level of identity, is change of the first kind: John ceases to be John, or to be human, precisely because, and insofar as, he has ceased to be. Local motion, we may add, is relational change, that is, change in dimensional relations between things.

Aristotle recognised that change is real and non-arbitrary. Change runs along very definite and, in some measure, predictable lines. If this were not so, we would be living in a nightmare or fairytale world, where anything could become anything, for any or no reason. Things change as the things they are, though not always merely because they are the things they are: they may, as it were, require a little help to change, and the factor which offers such help we call a cause. We refer to the totality of what an entity is at any moment, including its accidental and other, properties, as well as its relations, as the state of that entity. I shall refer to the ensemble of entities to which it is in any way related in any of its states as the situation of that entity. Situations also, it is clear, have states. Change as such concerns the situation or state of an entity or the state of a situation. We could say that the history of any entity is the temporally extended whole of its states, while its coming into being and passing away are states of the situation in which it will, or has ceased to, be. The history of a situation is the history, the states, of each of its constituent entities. We could compare this with the endlessly fluctuating situation in which any lot finds itself, which has no distinct history apart from the histories of the entities which participate in it, which changes into new configurations as they change, either in what they are, or in their mutual relations. By contrast, the history of an entity rather than that of a state, is at first sight at least, a temporally extended whole, a lasting unity through temporally based diversity. When we used the notion 'whole', and its correlative 'part' heretofore, we were mostly referring to simultaneous wholes.

In a temporally extended whole, however, the parts are the temporally diverse states of the one which is in each of them as that whose states they are, and without which they would be simply diverse, and mutually unrelated. Clearly, that which lasts, that is, that which persists in and unites the diversity of its states, is the identity of the temporally extended whole. Identity is not merely the synchronic principle of differentiation and uniqueness, but, present as the core of each successive diverse state, it is also the diachronic principle of sameness and constancy. For this to be so, it must be present as a changeless totality at every moment from genesis to destruction; change in it as already existing is destruction, change regarding it as not existing, genesis. All other change is contingent relative to it, and this is precisely what we mean by accident – something capable of this kind of change.

However, to speak of a temporally extended whole is to speak analogically, because, if we think of the history of entity as a mere series of states, we deprive those states of their properly temporal character. We make them 'present together' in a common horizon, rather than as temporally differentiated series. Such states are mutually exclusive: the water which was not hot a while ago is now hot. Such mutual exclusivity is necessarily a feature of change, since things cannot become what they (already) are, only what they are not. Two states of an entity are distinct because something is true of one which is not true of the other. Does this mean that the minimum difference between the current and any other state of an entity is that something is true of it which is true of no other? Suppose that there are two identical states of the same entity – say of this particular quantity of water reaching the same temperature on two distinct occasions, all other factors remaining constant – is there any feature which is peculiar to one, which distinguishes them from each other? The answer is affirmative, because if they are in fact identical states occurring at different times, this means that each occupies a unique place in the series of states, relative to all others in that series. We will not be able to number the states, but it still remains true that this state occurred before or after some other state. Thus 'before' and 'after' establish relative priority and posteriority in the series of states which compose a thing's history. State A and state B may be identical in terms of content, but, if they are truly temporally distinct states of the same entity, they differ precisely in terms of before and after; to know that one event takes place before or after another is to know that they occupy distinct positions on the series which constitutes something's history.

But suppose that event *B* occurs immediately after event *A*, with which it is *ex hypothesi*, identical. In that case, there is no change from *A* to *B*, which means that there is a constant state from the beginning of *A* to the end of *B*, which is therefore *one* constant state, and not two. If there are to be two identical states, at least one state must intervene between them which is not identical to either. (If there were an intervening state not identical to only one, that is, identical to the other, there would be just two diverse states, and not two identical ones.) Thus states are differentiated serially by negation, by the lack of identity, by mutual logical exclusivity.

Now, supposing a given distinct state lasts for a while, this means that, as compared to some regularly occurring change, 'the busy beat of time', no change takes place. Likewise, we can only know that a pulse is regular in a situation in which movements are harmonised. If the system as a whole slows down or speeds up, this can not be discerned within it, unless we are able to make comparison with something outside it, which is *ex hypothesi* impossible. In this way, lasting is always relative to some situation, as a totality of inter-relative changes. This is well illustrated by one of the strange results arrived at in relativity: where a whole situation accelerates towards the speed of light, it slows down as a whole and relative to the situation which is the ongoing history of earth, though no point for point comparison is possible; the desynchronisation is only discovered to have happened when the errant situation rejoins the macro-situation called, for brevity, earth. The rightness of our clocks depends not upon what they do themselves alone, still less upon their relation to the totality of all beings and situations, but on their harmonisation with the distinct situation in which they exist.

But this does not tell us how the 'historical' view of events is insufficient, nor what the alternative is. If events in history were present together, there would be no history, but simply a series of, perforce contemporaneous, events. This is impossible, because each state differs from the one which follows and the one which precedes it by not being identical to them, and so by being logically incompatible with them; although there may be states in the series as a whole which are mutually compatible, the totality of states cannot *be* together. This is not to say that the series as such is impossible, but only that it is impossible simultaneously. Each state is present alone, incompatible with that which goes before and comes after it. Thus the privileged moment is 'now', the moment of what is, what is present, and each other moment has a quality distinct from that enjoyed by the now. The now is what is present, what is present is present now. Does the now move along an entity's history like a spotlight, disclosing one state after another?

Clearly not, for this again is to place the totality in one horizon, even if each element in the horizon is serially disclosed. The quality of presence must therefore be a feature of the states themselves, not of how we perceive them. They must not *be* (present) together: moments other than the present simply are not, otherwise contradiction will result.

But there is change: mutually incompatible states become present serially, a new state comes to be, incompatible with the previous one, which has by that fact, ceased to be, and is therefore, as such, a previous state relative to the one which has replaced it. While the old state was present, another, and incompatible, state was possible, namely, the one which has now replaced it, and is subsequent relative to it. This is the structure and meaning of change, all change, radical or non-radical. This, then, is the temporal structure of change: there is a moment, now, at which a given state exists; there is an immediately previous state, incompatible with it, which has ceased to be and given place to it; and at least one other, equally incompatible state, which is possible, that is, which can replace the state which now is; and both of these can be interpreted as a function of what now is.

In this way, change always involves three moments which are unsymmetrical about the now: what is, what is not but can be, and what is not but has been. What can be is, as such, distinct from what has been; though both are incompatible with what is, they may not be incompatible in content with each other. What has been is what is not as perished, what can be is what it is possible for what now is to become. The now is openness towards possibility, towards what 'what is' is capable of being, precisely as capable of it; nothing is capable of becoming that which has perished, precisely as perished and as non-existing. This is what makes the future orientation, the direction, of change, which is defined by what something is capable of, as capable of it. Has the past then, no life in the present? The past as past only has present life in things capable of memory; in things precisely as unremembering, past states are present only as the explanation of what now is, insofar as it is. The past, precisely as past, has perished.

7, 4 Actuality, Possibility, and Potentiality

This gives us, in every moment of change, a triad of past, present and possibility. We shall refer to that which is present as the actual, actuality. In this way actuality and possibility are modes of being temporal; the past as such is not – its actuality is just actuality, what now is, and it has no being distinct from that. To talk of actuality, then, is to talk in inherently temporal terms, inherently opposed to what was, and what 'can and will be'. Actuality is what is or has been realised of what once only could be. What can be, in the full sense and absolutely, is a function of something which is. But even this itself cannot be realised as a totality, for, just as successive states are incompatible, possibilities differ not as possibilities but by virtue of the incompatibility of those states which are possible. In this way we might define change as the necessarily serial realisation of only part of what can be.

In change, to say that something is capable of becoming x is to say that it is necessary for it to do all that is required for x to come about, and to pass through all the intermediate stages if there are any. The realisation of any possibility facing an entity excludes the realisation of many others and all that would have then been possible had they been realised. What a thing is at any moment, in its identity, accidents and relations, determines the range of possibilities open to it in the next; in one sense change is like music, in that every moment is open to resolution in a host of ways, though not necessarily in any one way. It is only when the resolution is reached that it appears as resolution of what went before it, thereby turning this history, of which only the current moment exists, into a significant whole.

This in turn leads to an important distinction. We can talk about possibility, in a general sense, as what can be. In general, something is logically possible if it contains no contradictions. But it is something else again to say what something is really or actually capable of. To be sure, this is possibility, but, as it were, anchored possibility, and it is this which we intended above, namely, the possibility which belongs to something as a function of what it is: this we will call potential(ity) or potency. Potential is real or actual possibility, because it depends not on the mere absence of contradiction, but on what is actually the case. Because A, an entity or situation, is actually x, it is capable of being y, where y is some state; the potential of A is the totality of such really possible states. When A is an entity, any y, as what A can be or do, based on what it now is, depends on the continued existence of A, the realisation of its potential to exist in the future, and, equivalently, on the non-realisation of its potential to cease to be, as necessary condition of possibility. When A is a situation, y may include the coming-to-be or perishing, not of a state as such, but of an entity. Though a situation may arise which is incompatible with the continued existence of something, the perishing of an entity is the proper potential of that entity, because if it were not really capable of perishing, no such situation could arise, but its coming to be is properly a potential of the situation, of the entities which compose that situation as cooperating to produce the new entity, rather than on some abstract 'realm' of possibilities. Potentiality in both cases depends on what the entities actually are which are involved, and thus on their actuality as such. Thus every current moment of change is a moment of past (as present), and future as, not just any possibility, but real possibility, potentiality.

Actuality, we infer, is what has been and still is realised (and thus present, as opposed to merely perished), namely of the potential of some entity or situation. Potentiality, on the other hand, is what is actually realisable, that is, given some actual entity or situation, in the way that it is actual. This is their reciprocity, namely, that actuality is always the realisation of some potential, whether that of an entity or of a situation, and that potency is the potency of and for some actuality. This 'of and for' is the specification of potency by actuality, without which there can be no potency, but actuality is always the realisation of some prior potency. This, in turn, is the limit of actuality by potency.

To say that x is actual is to say that x is possible, but to be x potentially is to fail to be x actually. Insofar as something has the potential to be something, it is really, actually or currently capable of becoming it, and therefore, is not (actually) it. Nothing, therefore, is potentially something insofar as it is actually that something, and vice versa: this is the principle of change, for change, as actualisation, would be impossible if it were false. Conversely, if something has no potency to become something, this is to say it is incapable of becoming it, and cannot change in that way: for x to become y, it has to have the (necessarily prior) potential to do so. Being actually

something is thus equivalent to being something really. Actual
being is being in the full sense, and therefore is what we mean primarily by 'Being', 'existence', and *esse*, and is what 'is' and 'exist'
signify most properly. Though being potentially x is not an absolute
nothing, it is essentially relative to actuality, as 'of and for' it.
Although actuality is always the realisation of some prior potency,
that potency is the potency of some prior actuality, without which it
is not. Likewise, if potency represents what a thing is capable of
becoming, this is equivalent to what it is now capable of becoming;
this is what it means to have a real, and therefore actual, potential.
All this is true even in the case of generation, which always entails
some thing's or things' becoming another kind of thing. Potency is
thus a function of actuality as such, of what something now is, not
what it was, insofar as it is what it is, not what it was. 'What it was'
is just what a thing is not, as realisation of the potential of that very
state. Moreover, what a thing was necessarily had different capacities from those possessed by what it actually is, at least insofar as
what it (actually) is, is the realisation, and cancellation, of one of
those past capacities.

This allows us to specify the differentiation and relation of the temporal moments even more. What is, is what *now* is, actuality. This is
intrinsically oriented, as the actuality it is, towards what it can be,
but actually is not: because A is x it can be y, and in this way its
potential is an actual feature of what it now is.

In some cases, because A is x, it can and will be y, so that its being x
is the actual cause of its becoming y, is necessary and sufficient for
its becoming y, and is the efficient cause of its becoming y, provided
A continues to exist, and equivalently, all conditions of this are fulfilled. This means also that A's being x is its potential to become y.
This does not violate the principle that possibility as such does not
guarantee its realisation, and that therefore the realisation of possibility requires an actual factor not identical to the possibility as
such. This is so because real potential is not mere possibility, but
capacity based on what a thing actually is, though that capacity, as
capacity for y, is not simply identical to actually being x.

In other cases, A 'merely can' become y, and its being x is a necessary but not a sufficient condition for its becoming y; this is the case
where it requires an actual cause distinct both from its being x and
having the potential to become y. The realisation of some capacities
is incompatible with the realisation of others, though having the

potential for such mutually exclusive actualities is not impossible. Thus, if having a capacity implied its realisation, situations containing mutually incompatible elements would result. Clearly A's being x, and being the efficient cause of its being y, means that any state y must be coherent and compossible with other states that A will have.

The lack of identity of the present state with any and all subsequent states is the difference between what is actually and what is only potentially, as what something now is and is actually capable, either immediately or more remotely, of becoming. Future states are not merely strung on to what now is like beads along a thread; they are precisely as the as-yet-unrealised capacities of what now is, and hence as intrinsically related to actuality, as possibility of its future. The future is always some thing's (or things') future. Actuality is realised potential, which, as realised, is potential no more, but actuality. The past as past is actual in and as the actuality which is the present, as the actualised potential retained in the present. A thing is what it is, not what it was, which is distant from it as the actuality which owned the potential which has been realised as the actuality it is.

When a given potential is actualised by an efficient cause, the proper effect of the cause as such is to realise a new state of an entity or situation. This means that a new state comes into being, which, as we saw, contains that actuality which accrued to previous states, and which is carried over into this present one. It is possible for an actuality not to have an effect in any future state of entity or of situation. I shall refer to actuality which does carry over as a transitive actuality, and to actuality which does not, as an intransitive actuality. The question thus is, in what sense is identity to count as transitive actuality which it must be if a given entity can be said to continue to exist through time? Let us therefore situate this question in terms of a consideration of generation and perishing.

7, 5 Coming-to-be and Perishing

In order for something to come into being, it must be possible for it to do so; in order that it will come into being there must be a real possibility of producing it, that is, the potentiality of some actual situation to produce it. Situations as an association of entities in terms of various relations do not as such produce anything, but provide the circumstances propitious to the outcome. It is because entities can come together, or at least behave in certain co-ordinate ways that other, new entities come to be. Something is produced, in general, either by something transforming itself, either alone or with another, or something other than itself, into the new something. Anything else would be creation. The latter case – something transforming something other than itself – falls under efficient causality in the proper sense. The former case, or perhaps better, cases – something transforming itself, either alone or with another, into something new – are of interest here. Under this might fall a cell splitting to form two daughter cells, sperm and ovum – which are the real agents of change, not the parents – uniting to form one living being, which would be the clearest examples. But we must not exclude some stuff's or stuffs' becoming another kind of stuff, but this is reducible to the former case. Likewise the case of efficient causality is also reducible to this, for when something transforms something else, it relies on that something else's capacity to become the something new. Such transformation, as the beginning of a new entity, is the coming-to-be of something as having a new identity which is thus not that of what is transformed. Such transformation may or may not involve a change in kind of being.

I use the word 'prematter' to mean the kind of entity whose identity makes it capable of becoming, alone or with others, a new entity or kind of entity, where 'new' means distinct from the prematter in terms of identity. In, say, animal generation, the elements underlying such changes remain themselves throughout, but the prematter, cell which divides, sperm and ovum, are as such destroyed in the process: their destruction *is* the coming into being of the new entity, in that something is which is not identical to them separately or to them together but distinct.

The entity to come into being is, we might say, exercising the characteristically backward causality of the final cause, whose matter is 'pre-' as existing before it, with it as the proper potential of the pre-matter as such. The prematter is certainly the formal cause of the change, but is it also the efficient cause? The answer is affirmative, because the actuality of the prematter as such is sufficient, once conditions relevant to the exercise of this capacity are fulfilled, to bring about the change. What an efficient cause does is to actualise a capacity with which it is not simply identical as actual, and thereby bring about a new state, of entity or situation. The prematter as actually prematter, realises that capacity, not identical to its actuality, as precisely for the new situation, namely of its own destruction, as the coming-to-be of another to which it is not identical. We say 'situation' here rather than state, because the destruction of an entity is not a state of it; for it to have any states, it must be. Thus we may call the prematter the (proper) agent of change, of its own transformation.

The event is slightly more complex where there is of necessity more than one prematerial agent. In that case it is the entities, necessarily distinct, though joined in some relation, which are properly the efficient cause. But, here again, it is their actuality as prematter, though this time working together, which brings about the change, and realises the potentiality which is tantamount to their destruction.

One may add here a small note about the difference between working in common and fusion. Entities fuse when they behave in the manner described, namely when they combine so as to form a new something, and perish individually in so doing. Entities may be said merely to work in common when they do not perish, even when they form an ensemble whose activities and effects are distinct from those of its constituents, which are therefore elements rather than strict parts. Hydrogen and oxygen are the elements of water rather than its parts, for although water has properties which they do not have alone, they do not lose their identities as the elements they are in the water molecule, and are not destroyed to form it. As elements, they retain the identity they had prior to such combination, during its existence and certainly if it is destroyed. So, although a water molecule has an identity, properties and effects which are over and above those of its constituents taken in isolation, these are explicable entirely in terms of the properties and effects of the elements precisely as associated, though unfused. Water, the fluid, has the properties it has because the water molecules which compose it are and have what they are and have, but these in turn are and have what they are and have because the atoms of hydrogen and oxygen are what they are, and have what they have. Water is thus not a distinct entity from these elements, because it does not exercise a causality which is really distinct from that of the elements. Water is not a something using its elements in material causality, it is merely hydrogen and oxygen working in combination.

A consideration of perishing as such adds little that is new to these considerations. We are not considering here that perishing proper to prematter as such, where the coming to be of a new being is the final cause of the event. The perishing we have in mind is not absolute annihilation either, but decomposition, in that something which was involved in what perishes emerges in its own right, namely the elements of the thing in question. This means that a circumstance, internal or external to the entity, arises, which is incompatible with its continued existence. This is only possible because the entity is capable of ceasing to be. This is an important point to which we shall return, but we shall only mark it now in passing. The efficient cause of perishing as such is the actual circumstance or circumstances which are incompatible with the entity's continued existence, and thereby realise its potential to cease to be. What of the formal cause of perishing?

In the case of each entity, identity is the formal cause of continuity and perishing, but not of coming-to-be, but at most the final cause of it, the final and efficient cause of coming-to-be is the prematter. But, entities are transformed and are according to what they are, and therefore according to their kind, so that it follows that essence specifies those conditions under which the entity comes or continues to be, as it does those conditions under which it perishes. Essence, in sum, is the specification of the needs, including those relative to generation, and the vulnerabilities of the kind of entity whose essence it is. But this presupposes that entities are capable of perishing, and this is so, in its turn, because of their total ontological structure as temporal and contingent. Essence thus is the specification of how a particular kind is finite, temporal and contingent, while identity is the same in the case of the individual. The fundamental actuality of entities is an incarnation of this contingency, itself real distinction, and all such conditions descend from it; essence, and most properly identity, are as limit of *esse*. Identity and essence are shaped by this difference in which contingency consists. Such being-limited need not, and cannot, therefore, be intrinsic to *esse* as such, which is contingent actuality only as actuality as such of that which is contingent.

7, 6 Continuity

In this analysis we have seen something of how the other kinds of causality are necessarily involved in these contexts, but we have yet to answer the question we posed regarding the role of efficient causality in the lasting and continuity of entities. In answering this question, our analysis will disclose the most essential element of temporality and will deepen the understanding of finitude which we have gained thus far.

That which lasts must do so as that which it is, so that lasting is continuity of suchness. This belongs to entities as such, since an entity retains its identity through time, and other things participate in it by virtue of relation to entity. The moments necessary to this process – entity as such, identity, and state of entity – are the moments necessary to temporality. Entities are contingent insofar as they are temporal, for the flow of time is the entity's living its contingency. Entities are temporal insofar as they are contingent, for being contingent projects being as possibility of continuity for that which already is, now is. Thus, temporality and contingency are coeval and coterminous. It would therefore be correct to express temporality as temporalising, a being(-contingent) in the flow of time.

We have so far treated states as undivided temporal totalities; we must now analyse the nature of their continuity: what does it mean for a state to last? To answer this question, we need to put the relation of the state to temporality as such, in question. To last is to have temporal duration. But what is the relation between this duration and change? For as long as a state lasts, change clearly, to that extent, does not occur, and the same holds for a total situation; if time is based on change, does this mean that for as long as a situation remains without change, time is to that extent, and within that situation, arrested?

Clearly, the answer to this question is no. A situation which remains constant does so contingently. It would therefore be possible to introduce into it, even if *de facto* there is not in it, a regular pulse, a clock, allowing us to measure the duration of the state's lasting, as we might its changing, within the state itself, without reference to any pulse outside it. If it were the case that the situation were in principle immutable, then change would be excluded from it; if time, or, more precisely temporality, is intrinsically dependent on the possibility of change then, in the case of such an immutable situation, there could be no temporal modality present in it and, since duration is such a modality, there could be no duration in it, and it would be impossible to introduce a clock into it, or measure it from without. Thus, if duration is to be possible even within a static situation, there must be a temporal 'space' which the lasting occupies, which, as such, is a flow or movement of before and after, within it, and against which it lasts. What could this be?

Again we must look to the temporality of entities, not to some extra-situational medium, called time, in order to answer this question. Our analysis of the temporality of entities has shown that this temporality consists in a triadic relation about the now which is actuality, what has been and (still) is, which is the foundation of the future as what can and will be. If time as duration rests upon this structure, then it must be present within the static situation. This is to say that the potency offered in the static state is not offered merely as the change which marks the end of its lasting, but throughout that lasting, and that consequently, the actuality of the situation is not given as a temporal chunk, but as a continuum. To say that something lasts is to say that it remains the same only contingently, and that every moment of its lasting is the realisation of its capacity to be different or to remain the same.

Let us examine this notion in more detail. When we use the expression 'moment', we do not intend an actually discrete temporal point, still less a fixed duration. Just as a spatial interval is potentially, but not actually – on pain of the Zenonian paradoxes – divided into an indefinitely great number of points, so is any temporal duration divisible into a like number of distinguishable moments. This is not to say that time comes in discrete packages, so that its flowing resembles the jerky motion of the early films. This would make change into an instantaneous jump, or set of such jumps, as each new state succeeded. The continuous nature of change means that between any two moments of continuous change a moment can be found which represents a mid-point between them. If this were not so, there would be no continuity in time, for there would be a ceasing to be and a coming to be of the same thing as between subsequent moments. Obviously, such moments are only distinguishable and not distinct, because time, like space, is infinitely divisible, and the sum of an infinite number of actual moments would be infinite, so that no finite movements would be possible. But in the series of moments, only the present is actual, and all future moments stretch away from it as increasingly remote possibilities of what is now actual: possibilities which are not those of actuality are possibilities of some actuality, itself possible, but not so remotely future as they, and consequently contingent upon the realisation of that actuality.

The same points may be brought out in a different way: imagine the case of a superficial change in some entity, for example, Jane shaking her head. Such a change is accidental and fleeting, but the same will go, *mutatis mutandis*, for less fleeting accidents. That Jane is capable of undergoing such a fleeting change is made possible by her being a temporal entity. The happening of the change takes place, as it were, on the surface of the flow which is Jane's temporal track. This temporal track is her continuity, her leaving the past and entering the future, continuously: her leaving the past is her entering the future, now is the durationless moment in which possibility becomes actuality, in which future and past intersect, and this in such a way that for the flow to cease is for Jane to cease to be. For each current moment of the fleeting change Jane is, for each perished moment, retained in the now only as the current position of her head, Jane was, a being retained in the current moment as her being now; for the next moment of the change to be able to take place from now, Jane must continue to be, and enter that next moment as now, as the cessation of her being in the moment now designated as 'now', thus actualising that which is a potential of her current now.

7,7 Πάντα ῥεῖ ...

The picture we seem to have arrived at is that, at any moment, the possibility of remaining as it is or of being different is offered to any entity or situation; every present moment is the actualisation of one or the other of these two, which are always offered in and as the next, and immediately future, moment. πάντα ῥεῖ, καὶ οὐδὲν μένει: everything flows, nothing stays.[1] Everything flows in that its being as temporal consists, for as long as it is, in the ongoing realisation of one of these two incompatible possibilities. Nothing stays, even when the possibility which constitutes lasting is actualised.

The past, as past, has perished, and is only insofar as it has conditioned the present, itself the realisation of a possibility offered to the actuality which was in and as the moment immediately past. The present is, equally, perishing in that it consists in the realising of its own future, which is the becoming-past of what is now actual. In this way, the present is actualisation and perishing at once. Nothing stays in that everything is being evicted from the present moment, its actual state, into its own possibilities which are being realised. Lasting is the continuation of the temporal process, not its cessation; consequently, nothing stays if staying means being immune to change. 'Perishing existences' was the name given by Hume to those data with which alone knowledge and perception were concerned.[2] We might with equal, or even more, justification use it to describe the real, temporal and processal nature of entities, since, if our analysis is correct, entities are not solid and permanently existing through time as stones in a stream; entities are temporal processes of which we only perceive that cross-section which is current and actual.

There is an oxymoronic or paradoxical feel to the expression 'perishing existences', yet it is one which captures the inherent division, distinction and tension belonging to contingent temporality. Things, insofar as they are, intend *esse*, and are as in it, yet fail to hold it as perishing, intend yet do not achieve it as perfectly incarnating it and achieving an identity with it. To be lasting is to be, yet to fail to be, to fail of being, to fall away, to be falling away, to be wasting. Lasting is saving and wasting in one, indeed, as one. Their conjunction in the identity which is contingent temporalising, is the disjunction which holds between *esse* and entity, between what is and that it is. Temporalising is contingent be-ing, not simply a being in the flow of time, but a be-ing *as* this flow of time: a being-towards the immortality of *esse*, which as such in itself is not contingent; as contingent failing mortally to reach it, entities live their death, die their life.[3]

Changing, it rests.[4] Change is continuous, both as always present and as flow. Change is not absolute in the sense that each state or moment is utterly unrelated to previous or subsequent moments. Thus the entity, as the entity it is, persists throughout those changes of state which are not the realisation of some circumstance incompatible with its existence, and so tantamount to its destruction. Continuity in the case of destruction consists at least in the lasting of something's elements, which emerge free from the subjection proper to material causality, as that which they are, both during and after the process which is the destroyed entity's history. The same is true, but in reverse, of coming-to-be, except the persisting elements take the form of those things which are capable of becoming the entity which comes into being, a change, which, as we saw, amounts to those things' destruction. In this way, continuity is the continuity of entities, which is itself their continuing to be the entities they are: throughout the process which is its history, as remarked, the entity continually becomes other without becoming another. Thus, identity is that in an entity which is always actual, that is, for as long as the entity exists. Accidents are precisely those actualities whose coming and going constitute the entity's change of state, its becoming other without becoming another. In order for this to be so, they must belong to the entity while remaining distinct from its identity. To call them secondary actualities, and identity primary actuality, catches this adequately.

In sum, from moment to moment, as secondary actualities come and go, changing the state of the entity, identity remains as the entity's being the same entity as it was before the change of accident. This means that at one moment the entity exists in state $s1$, and in the next moment, the same entity exists, again in $s1$, or in some other state $s2$, that is, *not* $s1$, which presupposes that the entity is capable of both these states, even though they are, as rival states of the same entity, mutually incompatible. This in turn implies that the fundamental actuality which is identity is realised from moment to moment, as the entity passes from state to state, or continues in the same state, otherwise there is no continuity. This is what lasting through time must mean. To say that something 'just is' through time is correct, but it is to fail to address the inherently temporal function which lasting connotes. Now, realisation means the actuation of some capacity. In this fundamental realisation, we therefore ask, what capacity of the entity is realised? The answer is, the capacity to exist, as such. If some entity is, it is clearly possible for it to be, and therefore it is possible for it to continue to be.

What is the necessary and sufficient condition for the realisation of this capacity to continue to be? For an entity to exist at moment m, and to continue to be at some subsequent moment n, it is necessary that there be an entity e with identity I both at moment m and at moment n, that is, for there to be an e which is I at both. It is thus also necessary that no circumstance be realised at n which is inconsistent with this being the case, since this would make n the moment at which e ceases to be. These are the necessary conditions for the realisation of this capacity to continue to be; are they, equally, sufficient conditions? Clearly, the answer is no, because if they were, the mere fact of e's existence at m, which necessarily involves its being I, would require its existence at n, and thereby prevent the realisation of any circumstance incompatible with the existence of e and its being I. That is, no circumstance could arise incompatible with the existence of e, that is, of e precisely as I. This would mean that for the duration of m and n, e was incapable of ceasing to be, and was indestructible, and that its existence would be compatible with any and all possible circumstances. But if something exists necessarily, then it is incapable of ceasing to be. Likewise, something exists necessarily only if its existence is compatible with any and all circumstances. Thus, something's existence being so compatible is for that something necessarily to exist. Thus if the existence of e at m is a sufficient condition for the existence of e at n, it follows that *e* exists necessarily, is thus incapable of coming to be or passing away, and so never has come into being and never will cease to be. Since this is not the case with *e*, it follows that *e*'s being at *m* is merely a necessary, and not a sufficient, condition for its being at *n*. Since *e*'s being involves its being *I*, it follows that neither does its being *I* as such qualify as a sufficient condition.

Before we ask what does qualify as such a sufficient condition, we must advert to another point: if something is unconditionally, it is incapable of any change, not just coming-to-be or passing away, so that if anything changes, it cannot exist unconditionally. Why is this the case?

If something cannot but exist, then, that it exists at one moment is a guarantee that it exists at any and every other moment. Where this is not the case, the existence of something at one moment makes it only possible in the next. Unless this requires its existence – and in that which is not necessary, we have seen that it cannot – in the next moment, it follows that its possibility of existing in that next moment is equally a possibility of its ceasing to be in that moment: the two possibilities are thus mutually implicative. But in the case of something which has to be, once it is, there is no possibility of its ceasing to be, and hence no unactualised possibility of its being. Thus, to be for it at any time is for it to be at all times: if it is, it is 'all at once', without before or after, with no difference between its past and future; its present is all it is and ever was, its past the same, its future no mere possibility but actuality. This form of being therefore does not have the actual-possible structure of temporality, and therefore is not temporal. But temporality is made possible in and through change. Thus if something is non-temporal, it is not 'in' time and has no capacity for change whatever. Conversely, if anything is capable of change, it is temporal and therefore not necessary. We may also conclude that its being *I*, which is its identity, and thus the necessary condition of its existence, is a sufficient condition for its timeless, Being-all-at-once. Moreover, it also follows that such a thing is incapable of being brought into being by another, precisely because its identity is the sufficient condition of its Being, so it either exists or does not.

(It is vitally important to remark here, to avoid misunderstanding, that I am not therefore claiming that there is such an entity, but am now merely examining the logic of temporal existence. In short, I am not arguing from the logic or concept of necessity to its real existence. This is not a species of the ontological argument, and the real existence of something which has to be must, and indeed can and will, be established on other grounds.)

This allows us in turn to give a definite interpretation to Aristotle's αἴτιον πρῶτον τοῦ εἶναι, which is something's fundamental actuality, what it is, its identity. In the case of something which must be, identity is αἴτιον πρῶτον as both necessary and sufficient condition for being, while in any other kind of being, which, namely, is not necessary, and therefore capable of being generated and perishing, identity is αἴτιον πρῶτον as necessary, but not sufficient, condition for existing, where 'existing' means being temporal in the way suggested.

7, 8 Real Distinction and Participation

This, of course, is equivalent to the assertion of the real distinction between *esse* and essence (and identity) in contingent beings, and their real identity in and as necessary being, two ways of relating to *esse* which have been intended throughout this chapter, and on which a good deal of our argument rests. Much is made of this Thomistic distinction by Thomists, who contend that Aquinas's metaphysics is existentialist because it is a metaphysics of *esse*. [5] We recall here that, for Aquinas, *esse* in contingent being is a really distinct actuality or determination, to which essence is the corresponding potency, the actuality in and of all actuality. To say that *esse* and essence are distinct is at least to say that being x does not necessitate being *tout court*, which is precisely what we have concluded. But is *esse* truly a distinct act or determination? Since so much depends upon an affirmative answer to this question, it is worthwhile going to the trouble of answering it explicitly, even if we at first give the appearance of reiteration in so doing. Moreover, doing so leads us to see something of how participation in being can and must be applied to contingent temporalising.

In an entity which is capable of not being, its future existence is an actualisable possibility. A thing's capacity to be anything is contingent on its capacity to be: for it to be possible that x be y, it is necessary that x be, and if x is not, then it is not y. Thus, the congeries of possibilities which represents any number of distinct and mutually exclusive possible futures of x, depends upon the actualisation of this one and identical underlying possibility, from which they are therefore really distinct. Since potency is a potency for some actuality, it follows that for every potency there is a corresponding act.

Likewise, potency is an openness for some actual determination, and actuality is as determination, that is, of potency. But, the possibility of x's being is a possibility distinct from all others: therefore the actuality of its being is a determination distinct from all others.

Moreover, every moment of a thing's being is the actuation of its capacity to be: it can be and is, though it might not have been. In this way, the mutuality of potency and act is retained at every moment of a thing's existence. The actuality of the existence of something which need not be, is as fulfilled capacity, as determination, precisely of the capacity to be, which in turn makes possible all other capacities and determinations which the thing may have. But all these, as determinations and capacities of something, are only insofar as that something is, insofar as its capacity to be is realised, that is, they participate in being as qualifying that which is, and not on their own account. It is this, precisely, which mediates the ontological unity of the entity, that is, as existing as one.

It is worth noting at this point what is being claimed and what is not. It is not being claimed that *esse* is an accident, attribute or property of that which is, which would then be 'in itself' a kind of 'potential being', to which *esse* 'happens'. We would then be able to view this possibility as a kind of appetite for being, as indeed, Descartes seems to have done. This, in turn, would be to set up a kind of ghostly ontology in opposition to the real ontology, a lush world of possibles, which the Divine can choose, or not choose, to actualise. This would produce many absurdities, not least of which would be the reduction of the Divine to the status of demiurge as actualiser of possibilities. Likewise, it would be to attribute some kind of being to something, other than that which has *esse*, namely, to the possible as possible, which would lead to paradoxical conclusions. A merely possible entity is not an entity, but a description which only potentially describes. Thirdly, it would give substance to silly kinds of question, and to an absurdly prolix world-view. I shall not pursue these questions here, but we are not saying that *esse* is a property, and when we call it actuality and determination, we must be understood to be speaking analogically of something which is not otherwise intelligible.

To each thing that is, insofar as it is, belongs its own act of existing, its *esse*, unique to it, and therefore, since everything that is is unique insofar as it is, it is the actuality which confers the uniqueness of *haecceitas* which is inseparable from existing. Yet to be in any sense is to be actual, which is not identical to any feature or features which make up what is actual. Identity and essence are the conditions under which a given entity can be actual and are thus necessary but not sufficient, conditions for this actuality. *Esse* is measured and limited by the identity which gives this inherently conditional quality to contingency, which is thus the temporally 'lived' disjunction of identity and *esse*. *Esse* is the measure of ontological independence, a Being-free, as being oneself, from all else. This freedom, though uniquely granted in each case in and through *esse*, is that common field of unity which proportional terms confer. Things which are so present are present together, as in one way or another, coexistent. It is in this way that *esse* is one and coevally many. To be is either to be as subject of *esse*, or as qualification of that which is the subject of *esse*. A relation is insofar as it is qualification of more than one subject of *esse* and so is the actuality of the coexistence of the real.

Esse is always the proper act of a distinct and unique something which is, free in and as being, while, at the same time, each thing as temporal and finite is receptive of its own being and is thereby brought into the one community of beings, is illuminated as the entity it is by esse. This makes room for a whole ontology of existential participation, which is identical to the real analogy of Being, for, we can put this in terms of participation as follows: each thing participates in Being precisely insofar as it is a recipient of being, rather than as a sufficient condition of it. Finitude is the real, analogical participation in and of *esse*.

The notion of participation is notoriously difficult, as Plato points out: we must not conceive of it as a crude 'getting a chunk of'.[6] Participation involves an improper relation to Being of that which participates in Being, as receptive of *esse*. Something which has something *per se*, does not participate in what it has, but has it, precisely, *per se*. Participation involves being or having something in virtue of something other than oneself, which is or has that something properly. That which participates has what it participates in as its own, but not exclusively, at least in principle, otherwise participation as such would be impossible. Thus, that in which the participant participates is somehow common, but, insofar as it is manifest only in participants, cannot occur otherwise than as being in those, in principle plural, participants. Genuine participation is distinct from the mere plurality of instantiations, of appearances of one and the same form, diversely exemplified. *Esse* is not one invariant 'something' which appears unchanged in each being: the work of participated *esse* is diversity and coexistence, as being 'present' together. *'Esse'* as such is abstraction: its particularity is identity, its commonalty, plurality and consequent coexistence. We shall show that the source of both at once is that which is as being *esse* and more-than-*esse*, to which *esse* is, in its ultimate participatory form, as relation. The freedom which is *esse* is transcendence as necessary relation to (and *ipso facto*, necessary distinction from) the more-than-*esse*.

This diversified sameness of analogical participation is well caught in a verse from the ancient Easter hymn, the *Exultet*:

> *ignis... qui licet sit divisus in partes, mutuati tamen luminis detrimenta non novit.*[7]

These are themes that run throughout our treatment, and through all ontology. But now we must face the supreme questions of ontology: is it possible and necessary to posit this source? What can we say about it? How can we say what we can say about it? It is to these questions that we now turn.

Notes to Chapter Seven

1. This is not one of the fragments, but Plato attributes it to Heraclitus, *Cratylus*, 402 a.

2. *Treatise*, I, IV, 2.

3. Heraclitus, fragment 62, in T. M. Robinson, *Heraclitus, Fragments*, (Toronto: University of Toronto Press, 1991).

4. Heraclitus, fragment 84 a, in Robinson, *op. cit.*

5. See, in particular, Etienne Gilson, *Le Thomisme*, (Paris: Vrin, 1989), p. 455.

6. As a sail is spread over many people: *Parmenides*, 131 b, and following.

7. 'The fire ... though divided, suffers no diminution from the borrowing of its light.'

CHAPTER EIGHT

The Logic of Divinity

8, 1 Introduction

Certain issues were left outstanding at the end of our last chapter. We have ascertained something of the ontological structure proper to finitude, contingency and temporality, and have discovered that, in the case of entities whose ontological structure is temporality, identity, as αἴτιον πρῶτον τοῦ εἶναι, is the necessary, but not the sufficient, condition of their existence, and that the consequent receptivity of 'what is' to 'being realised' is finitude. This poses the question of that sufficient condition, the factor which actuates this receptivity. Does it exist? What is it? These questions are not independent in that to answer the first is implicitly, at least, to answer the second.

It is clear that this set of questions is a simple continuation of the problematic we have been engaged in thus far; these questions are implied by the understanding we have so far gained, and the issues they raise are not merely gratuitous insertions into an ontology which would be as well off or better without them. These questions and their resolution are thus necessary to ontology, and since we need employ only the same logical tools and methods we have used from the outset in resolving them, their resolution is possible for ontology. As will become clear, the issue which now confronts our ontology is the very source and foundation of finitude as such, which is itself not finite precisely as not merely receptive of existence, and therefore not temporal. It is for this reason, and at this precise point, that our ontology becomes a metaphysics *sensu stricto*, as an ontology of that which is essentially beyond, and foundational of, τὰ φυσικά, temporal entities. For precisely the same reason, namely, the object of our ontological investigation's being that which, as source of *esse*, exists of itself and not by another, and so is what we mean primarily by *esse*, our metaphysics is ontology. Because what is of itself, and so is what is meant by 'is', *esse*, τὸ εἶναι, is what we mean by Divinity, it follows that our ontology-metaphysics is at the same time an onto-theology. Thus, in this chapter, the triad of terms from which our essay takes its name are found in the highest mutual involvedness which is possible for them: existence is what Divinity is, and talk of the one of necessity requires talk of the other. There is no onto-logy that is not ultimately theo-logy, no theo-logy that is not at the same time an onto-logy. Put another way, language about being is only possible if God-talk is, and vice versa, and ontology is thus also a philosophy of the logos of both ontology itself and theology, and proceeds, and must proceed, as an investigation of language.

For these reasons, this chapter will contain three interrelated movements. The first of these is quite short and consists in drawing the conclusion, warranted by our previous analysis, that there exists a source of *esse* as such, which is what we mean by Divinity. Underlying this assertion is the principle of the equivalence of temporality and contingency: if anything is temporal it is contingent, and if anything is contingent it is temporal. To be temporal means to exist now and to have one's future existence as a real possibility, a potentiality of one's existence now. If one's future existence were more than this, it would not be a potentiality but either an actuality, which as 'being now' is impossible for future existence, or a necessity. But if anything is necessary it cannot not be, is invulnerably, and simply is, and fails thereby to be temporal. What is of necessity is as having to be, and this invulnerable Being has been orbited by European ontology since its dawn in the poem of Parmenides, from whom we borrow the headline for this phase of our argument, ἔστι γὰρ εἶναι, a compelling embodiment of its author's most profound insight.[1]

It is of vital importance to note that here our ontology parts company with a whole tradition or manner of thinking in Western philosophy, which might first appear friendly towards it. This manner of thinking is one which characterises Divinity as demiurge, and has been with us since the Nous of Anaxagoras. It has appeared in various guises since, such as the finite, changing god of process theology, as the 'evolution' which features in the thinking of Bergson or de Chardin, as the 'Great Architect' of Hume's Cleanthes, or as Paley's celestial watchmaker, together with the 'gods' of sundry other, doubtless well-intentioned, but metaphysically inept, minor thinkers. What seems to be common to such conceptions is the belief that the model of the relation between Divinity and world is one of making. But making is not creation. Such a 'god' (as opposed to God) is not responsible for existence as such but for some feature – motion, order, or the like – of what is. This is to say that such a god is not the absolute origin of all that is insofar as it is, and that there is therefore something which is independently of the demiurge. This is quite clear in the earliest example of that kind of thinking which we have mentioned: the Nous of Anaxagoras orders, but does not create, matter.

To assert that Divinity is Creator is to assert that Divinity is the absolute origin of all that is insofar as it is, and therefore that God requires nothing other than the Divinity which God is in order to create, and depends on or can depend on, nothing other than Divinity in creating or in being. But to say this is also to say that Divinity neither needs to nor can 'engineer' what it creates nor 'contrive' it, organising means to suit Its purposes and ends. Thus, Divinity is either Creator or demiurge, but not both. The failure of the 'argument from design', that from motion or causality is thus not surprising, since these could lead only to *a* god but not to God, whose existence as Creator, not demiurge, can be demonstrated, as we attempt to show here. Such arguments, in short, are neither necessary nor possible since the notion they posit – *a* god as opposed to God – is defective.

The notion of God – Creator – however, is gained in the necessary continuation of the analysis which shows that the being of the finite and temporal is intelligible in and through the necessary dependence it can and must be discerned to have on a, or the, source of *esse*, which is what we mean by 'God'. Thus, the first movement turns naturally into the second, in which the nature of this source is delineated. To be the source of existence as such, Divinity must have certain formal properties, namely omnipotence, necessity, immutability, absolute uniqueness and unity, unsurpassability or eminence, freedom and personhood. These formal properties are not gratuitous but are mutually implicative (such that to deny any one is to be guilty of incoherence) and are themselves as a whole implied by the notion of source of existence as such, that is, of Creator, which our analysis of the finite things themselves has made it necessary to posit. The second movement of this chapter is a disclosure of, and of the necessary coherence of, this cluster of formal properties of Divinity, in short of the logic of 'Divinity': not of Divinity, which is incomplex and immutable, but of our notion 'Divinity'.

The third and final movement of this chapter regards the nature and working of talk about the Divine, the logic, or better, the dialectic, at work in 'Divinity'. Here we look at how our language intends, or can intend, the Divine. Here, too, we do not depart from what we have already accomplished, for talk about the Divine is merely a special application of the logic we have been using all along. This discussion takes the form of an elimination of two equal and opposite accounts of how language can relate to Divinity, or rather, in one way or another, can fail to do so. This very elimination suggests a third way, the way of analogy, which presents language as demonstrably intending the Divine, while allowing that there is a realm of the in principle unsayable (the mystical in the early Wittgenstein's sense) to which language can point but can never express: what we cannot speak about we must pass over in silence.[2]

8, 2 ἔστι γὰρ εἶναι ...

Let us begin by stating clearly the picture which has emerged in the course of our analysis. To be material is to be spatial, temporal, and therefore contingent, because being spatial implies being temporal, and temporality in turn implies being contingent. The necessary condition for the lasting, the continued existence, of any contingent entity is its identity, that is, its remaining the same entity, retaining the one identity, for as long as it lasts. However, remaining the same entity is not a sufficient condition for its continuing to be; if it were, then simply because the entity is what it is now, it would have to exist at some point subsequent to the present. Its mere existence now would thus actuate the possibility of its later existence, which, precisely as not so actualised is (futural) potentiality, not necessity. Thus what a thing is does not guarantee its existence at any other time than now. This is to say that there is no feature of an entity which as such realises the possibility that it will exist at any moment subsequent to now. More formally, there is no feature Fx, at least of any non-Divine entity a, such that if Fa, then: a must exist (at some future time, and if at that point, then also now); a denial which means, [the conjunction 'Fa at moment n' and 'a ceases to be at moment $n + m$' ' is inconsistent], or ['Fa at n, implies a cannot cease to be'] are both always false, which in turn implies that even if Fa, and while Fa, a is still capable of not being. These stricken propositions would amount to a kind of 'ontological proof' for the existence of a. The 'property' 'Fx' would be equivalent to 'x is Divine'. There are, of course, many features Gx, such that if *not Ga*, a does not exist: these are, precisely, the necessary and essential conditions of the existence of *a*. It may not be idle to add, moreover, that once a thing is actualised at the moment subsequent to now, that moment becomes now, and the same question may be posed again. Let us analyse the implications of this.

Firstly, that, and what, an entity is now makes its existence, at any later moment, possible but not necessary. We advert to the axiom, a thesis of the modal calculus, that what is possible is not, *ipso facto*, actual. Thus we must invoke a factor which accounts for the realisation of the possibility in question, beyond the existence or the identity of that whose possibility it is. Now, since the proper action of a cause is precisely the realisation of possibility, we may call this factor, namely the necessary and sufficient condition of a thing's future existence, the cause of its existence. What, then, is the cause of existence? Let us refer to this question as 'question one'.

We must add here that the cause of existence is not a demiurge. The cause of existence relies on a 'pregiven' possibility only to the extent that it continues the existence of that which *already* is, i.e., continues to communicate *esse* to what is, which is, of course, only insofar as *esse* is granted it. This is not to say that the cause of being, save in this sense, requires anything outside its own capacity to grant *esse*; if it did, it would be a demiurge.

Secondly, we have made a more profound discovery. Just because a thing is, does not mean that it is necessary. To say the same thing another way, when a thing (now) is, its (present) existence is contingent. Which in turn implies that there is no feature belonging to something, be this its identity or anything else, which is sufficient of itself to account for the thing's *present* existence, for if there were, the thing would be necessary and not contingent. If this were the case, the thing in question would not be temporal and (which is equivalent) would be changeless. Thus, even the present state of a contingent entity is always a 'being actualised' in the limited sense we have given this, that is, receptive of *esse*, and never a self-actualisation in that sense, which would be the prerogative of necessary being. In other words, being necessary is never equivalent to being possible-and-actual. Again, the question must be posed: since possibility is of itself insufficient to account for actuality, and so for the final actuality of *esse*, even in present actuality, what is the cause of existence? Let us refer to this question as 'question two'.

What is the cause of existence? Could there conceivably be more than one such cause?

It will become clear that there will not be two distinct answers to our two questions: the cause of a thing's present existence is one and the same as the factor which is responsible for its subsequent realisation. To be clear, we underline that the subsequent existence of something is a potential, which like any possibility is insufficient to guarantee its own realisation, and that in the case of present existence, though that which is now exists, its existence is not necessary, but only possible and actual, that is contingent, and, invoking the same modal axiom, the possibility of the existence of something now actually existing is insufficient to explain that it actually exist, otherwise its existence would not be merely possible and actual, but necessary, and so would always be, and even subsequent existence would thus be guaranteed. In order to find the answer, let us ask what, exactly, causing existence, in the sense which we have given this expression, actually involves.

It will be immediately clear at least, that such causality is similar to, but distinct from, ordinary efficient causality. The two forms of causality are similar in that they both involve the realisation of some possibility; they differ in that efficient causality requires a recipient, a potential subject, which persists throughout the change which it works, in other words, something other than the cause as such itself, otherwise the efficient cause would produce actuality of itself alone. But to do this is to create, to bring something into being *tout court*, rather than to transform something which already is. The cause of existence on the other hand, means just that, namely, that which needs nothing other than itself to confer the actuality which is *esse*. Now, the only candidates for such a cause, since the existing entity and any feature of it have been ruled out, are its producers or some other entity or entities. We can rule out its producers, for these, as that which become the entity, cease to be as soon as it comes to be, and so cannot continue to realise it. Thus the cause of existence must be some entity or entities, which is or are distinct at once from the prematter of the entity, and from the entity itself and any feature of it. What might such an entity or entities be?

In the case that something already is, what is to be explained is precisely that it is actual, that it exists as such and as a whole at all, and not some feature of it. In the case of something which continues to be, it is again the existence or actuality of the entity as a whole

which is to be explained: as we have seen, its previous actuality is
not sufficient to explain its current actuality; in any case this current
actuality is that which it (now) is, all past actuality being just that,
that is, having ceased to be (actual), and it would be a curious
causality indeed which is currently exercised from the past by
something which has, as past, ceased to be. In sum, then, we require
a factor which produces *esse* as such, which therefore does not
transform, but relying only on itself, grants reality, actuality and
existence as such, that is, which creates. If, on the contrary, we do
not invoke such a factor, we shall be obliged to say that possibility
as such is sufficient for the actuality of that which is possible, and if
this, in turn, were true, all possibilities would be actualised and an
infinite number of incoherent, inconsistent and hence impossible
situations would result. It is precisely on this principle that our
argument rests, and not on any general and vague act of faith in
something like 'the intelligibility of the universe'. More simply, our
assertion of the existence of the cause of existence is unavoidable,
otherwise we would have to assert that something is because it is
possible, a position which is nonsensical, because the axiom we
have borrowed from the modal calculus is necessarily true.
Likewise, unless there is some fallacy or hidden inconsistency in
our argument, the conclusion it is meant to support must be possible.

(That there is no such hidden flaw will be the subject of further discussion; but it may be helpful to point out that this argument and
indeed the whole enterprise of this essay, is possible only if what
we might call a realist epistemology is true. If, on the other hand, a
Cartesian-inspired or Kantian epistemology is true, realism is not.
However, there are good grounds for supposing modern, that is
Cartesian-style, epistemology to be radically misguided. That our
argument or position, in part or in total, may be unfashionable is of
no importance whatever. Russell once pointed out that all notions
which constitute progress – and a valid argument based on true
premises constitutes progress, much as knowledge does over ignorance – were once new-fangled, and therefore unfashionable. More
profoundly, once we believe a conclusion to be both possible and
necessary, it is intellectually dishonest to ignore or deny it for any
reason: we are required, as persons of conscience, and as practising
the virtue at one with mature and responsible research, to say with
Luther: *ich kann nicht anders.*)

Such a factor, then, *in fine*, namely, the cause of existence as such, the Creator, implied by the being-created of contingent and finite reality, is what everyone would agree to call God, and it is from this datum alone that all that we know philosophically of God can and must be inferred.

8, 3 Creation and Omnipotence

Thus our argument demonstrates that the assertion of the existence of the Divine, as Creator, that is, of the cause of contingent reality precisely insofar as it is, as such, is both possible and necessary on pain of incoherence. By the term 'creation' we understand the emergence of contingent, non-Divine *esse* as such, of and from the Divine alone and of Itself. Although some of this has yet to be clarified, it is clear that the Divine is the sufficient cause of the existence as such of contingent reality, that is, as we shall soon make explicit, of all reality which is not Divine. Divinity is the proper source of temporal and thus contingent actuality, that is, of all present being, which includes the accumulated determinations which are the realisation in the present of the possibility of past, that is properly speaking, recently or more remotely perished, actuality, a present which is necessary condition of all future actuality, which comes into being precisely as a realisation of the potency of what now is (actual), due to the creative effect of the Divine.

This is to say that the Divine is the adequate source of actuality as such, and through it, to all that belongs to actuality. The prior existence of something is not the efficient cause of its being now, this is the proper function of the Divine. The past existence of the thing which now is, is just that, namely gone and perished; previous existence is merely the condition of the temporal continuation of that which is. In this way, all that is contributed by any such previous existence to present existence is continuity, namely the having-existed of this thing in the recent and ever more remote past, a past which as 'memory' in the present partly determines *what* now is, but not *that* what now is is, since the past only is as determination accumulated in what now is, and is, like all actuality, receptive and patient of realisation, and is not its own origin. This means that the effectiveness proper to the Divine is adequate of itself for such realisation, since the past or present existence of what is makes no effective contribution to the fact *that* what now is is.

In sum, the Divine alone must be adequate for the realisation of any possible state or situation, without need of what is, except as necessary patient and term of this absolute effectiveness, because it is logically impossible to realise without realising something. Therefore what has-been-and-is is only a condition of continuity, not of creation as such. Thus, to be Divine is to be omnipotent, in the sense of being able to realise any coherent, that is any possible, that is any, situation, for an incoherent situation is not a reality but an artefact consequent upon the structure necessary to language.

In this way the phrase 'All-powerful God' and its equivalents are tautologous, because the Divine is what creates, and to create is to be omnipotent in the sense described. Things simply and absolutely are not if the Divine ceases to create them, and all that is is as the effect of the Divine's adequately effective causality. Thus, destruction is not the proper work of the Divine, whose work as such is entirely positive, namely, to hold in being the perishing existences of which the world is composed, which cannot but perish except as recipients of that Divine creativity.

If the Divine is all-powerful, moreover, it is sufficient both of and for itself, and so cannot be given something which it needs by non-Divine entities. The Divine is absolutely independent therefore of anything other than the Divine. In the case of a conscious such entity, the combination of its being and its awareness would, as the Hindus say, be uninterrupted serenity, bliss. The bliss proper to Divinity, however, is the unimaginable beatitude proper to the more-than-awareness of the Divine. Likewise, if the Divine is independent in this way, it cannot be obliged to create by any need; its creation is therefore completely free and gratuitous. This implies that it is not obliged by anything other than itself to continue what already is.

Thus the Divine cannot exploit the non-Divine for, as all-powerful, it can have no needs which the non-Divine can supply, nor can it need to dominate the non-Divine, because domination betrays some manner in which the master needs, and needs to exploit, the one he enslaves. This view would seem to be coherent with certain religious intuitions. Firstly, the notion or feeling, the arrogance, in the most literal sense, that we can become Godlike through the capacity to construct weapons of mass destruction, through mastery, or, by extension, through any scientific or technological progress, betrays a serious misunderstanding of the nature of the causality proper to the Divine, and does the Divine that injustice of reduction to the status of demiurge, which, if it were consciously done, would be called blasphemy. Secondly and more profoundly, the recognition of what the Divine causality is, is at one with a fundamental, and fundamentally eucharistic, attitude, a consciously receptive, and therefore thankful one, which is inseparable from any and all, at least monotheistic, religion. Servile fear of the Divine is as little to be desired as arrogance, and for the same reason: both diminish the Divine, though not in Itself, but in our eyes. To be created is ultimately to be safe.

8, 4 The Eminence of Divinity: *id quo maius cogitari nequit*

Clearly, the Divine is a reality, but not just another entity. What meaning, then, are we to attribute to Divinity in itself? Our answer to this question must be on the basis of what we have so far discovered; we shall see that our argument implies that the notion of Divinity dovetails with that of supreme excellence. Divinity is not merely different from all else, it excels all else. How is this verified?

Anything which receives its being from another is to that extent dependent on that other, and is absolutely dependent on it if without that other it would simply cease to be. To be Divine, as that to which the non-Divine owes everything, and Which to the non-Divine owes nothing, is necessarily to surpass the non-Divine: it is not merely to be other than, but better than. Yet, the Divine as thus different from all else, does not surpass all else merely by being the best there is; it is unsurpassable in principle by the non-Divine. What is this unsurpassability?

To be non-Divine is to be in principle inferior to the Divine, but not as a weak man is inferior to a stronger man, lower on some standard of excellence which embraces both greatest and least in terms of some determination of the same or similar things. The Divine does not surpass by being superior on a scale which runs through Divine and non-Divine alike, thereby placing both in the same league, but by being unassignable to any definite point on any such scale which measures the non-Divine, *and that precisely as excelling it*. Being the best, even the best possible, example of something means excelling the worst by some finite amount, and thus also being of the same kind as the worst, limited ultimately by the same bounds which constrain the worst. To be the best swimmer in the world is to be subject, say, to tiring, though not as quickly or as often as the worst swimmer in the world. In sum, the Divine is not of the same kind as the non-Divine, and so is beyond any scale or limit which measures the non-Divine. It is not merely that the Divine excels in some, or even in all, respects, but is such that nothing can excel, or even approach, It in any respect. This is the meaning of the infinitude, the unlimitedness of the Divine, the immeasurability which belongs to it as Divine and unsurpassable. Nothing the non-Divine can do (or have done to it) can bridge this gap.

This seems to be the meaning of Anselm's subtle *id quo maius cogitari nequit*, subtle precisely because it points into the unsayable by simultaneously concerning, defining the extent of, and transcending, what it is possible for us to say, or, to use Hartshorne's more dense formulation of the same Anselmian notion, the Divine is 'the Unsurpassable'.[3] To be Divine is not to be either the greatest thing, or even unsurpassable, but to be *the* Unsurpassable. The rest of our logic of 'Divinity' will be a thinking-out of the implications of this Anselmian insight.

8, 5 The Countenance of Divinity: *ipsum Esse per se subsistens*

As we have shown, the Divine is source of existence as such, but, as Divine, the Divine must excel the non-Divine *as the Being It is*; the Divine must exist more perfectly than the finite. This is to say that the Divine cannot be dependently or contingently; Divinity cannot 'just happen' to be, otherwise It is just another (contingent) being, and does not *in principle* excel the finite. To say 'it is possible that *x*' is to say 'it is also possible that *not-x*'. This implies that the Divine is not merely possible, nor possible-and-actual, but necessary. But this necessity in turn can only be the identity of Divinity with its own *esse*, such that to be God is to be. Divinity is therefore *ipsum Esse per se subsistens*. This necessity proper to Divinity, as we shall see, is also entailed by the omnipotence which we have found to be necessary to It as Creator. This is not to say that 'God exists' is anything but contingent for us, but this itself does not mean that God exists contingently.

The Godhead, as necessary, has no unrealised possibility of being, and so just is: God is of necessity everything that God can be. It is thus not the case that God is realised, even by Divinity, for a necessarily fulfilled possibility is never a passive 'being realised' or 'being actualised' or 'being made present': insofar as the Godhead is, it is fulfilled. To be passive, on the other hand, is to be receptive of determination, to have some capacity which can be actualised only by an efficient cause; this would bespeak dependency on such a cause, even were the cause identical, in some manner, with oneself. But, since God is all that God can be, God has no mere possibilities, and, equivalently, there can be no passivity or receptivity in God. Receptivity is the essence of the finite. This is to say that there is no potency in God; but since change is impossible without potency, it follows that God is incapable of change. To say that Divinity is the simultaneous enjoyment of all that the Divine can be is to do it less than justice on two counts, for no talk of simultaneity and capacity can be adequate to the Divine, yet it is to point in the direction in which the Godhead lies. This seems to mean that God is therefore incapable of suffering, for the essence of suffering is passivity and loss.

To be of necessity means that there can be no circumstance which is incompatible with the existence of that which is of necessity. God cannot perish because perishing means having such a circumstance realised. A need is a possibility which, if left unfulfilled, brings about a situation incompatible with the continued existence of that whose need it is. God has no needs, not just of anything created being can supply, but absolutely: this is to be without the vulnerabilities and needs which are one with the mode of non-Divine being. We see then, what they mean who deny that God has any essence, for, in the case of the non-Divine as we saw, essence, as the form of such vulnerabilities and needs, is the defining limit of existence, the necessary expression of contingency, the meaning of finitude. Analogous points may be made about identity. God therefore has no identity in anything but a highly analogous sense. As necessary, God is ὑπερούσιος [4] in that there is no limit internal or external, on the existence of God, who is therefore just existence.

In finding that Divine being is necessary being we have found the source of the Divine omnipotence which is the power to create. To be necessary is to be simply in virtue of one's identity, which in the case of the Godhead, is (by analogy) Divinity. What God is (equivalent to that God is) makes it impossible that God is not. But this tells us, precisely, that what Divinity is, is, as such, to be source of being, and thus to be all-powerful. What makes God God – i.e., incapable of not being – is what makes God Creator – i.e., able to grant existence as such to the finite. Being Divine, being all-powerful and being Creator are thus necessarily equivalent and mutually implicative. God is that which most properly is, and is properly of itself, unlike created being, which is only of itself receptive of existence, thus requiring the Divine to be.

It is of vital importance however, on pain of seeming to fall prey to

Kant's objection,[5] to be clear regarding the order of argument. We begin with the fact of contingency, and on this basis discover that the assertion of the existence of Divinity is both necessary and possible if we are to explain the actuality of the real, and subsequently we discover that all-powerful Divinity cannot but instantiate the notion of ontological necessity. Since Divinity does instantiate the notion of ontological necessity, it follows, of course, that this notion is coherent, otherwise it would be impossible for it to be instantiated. None of this amounts to a dependence on the ontological argument: our argument's philosophical ancestry is to be found in Thomas Aquinas.[6] Some versions of the ontological argument seem to require us to say that, since the notion of Divinity or of ontological necessity is coherent, there must exist a God, or an ontologically necessary entity. But, this is to turn what we argue upside-down. That there is a source of *esse* as such is required by the fact of contingency, and this is a conclusion not a premise. That this source cannot but instantiate the notion of ontological necessity which is *therefore* coherent is likewise a conclusion. In short, we do not infer the existence of the Divine from the nature of the Divine, rather, the nature of the Divine from the structure of contingency.

We must now add that not only does Divinity instantiate the notion of ontological necessity, Divinity uniquely instantiates it. To be Divine is to be absolutely unique, not simply as individual or even as class: this means at least that there cannot be more than one Divinity. It means also that Divinity is not merely one, but is unity. To be Divine is to be necessary, all-powerful, thus all-perfect, since all that Divinity can be it therefore is, and is therefore the Unsurpassable. There clearly cannot be more than one Unsurpassable, for if there were, they would have to differ from one another. But to differ from unsurpassability is to be surpassed by it: thus if there are two distinct unsurpassables at least one would be actually surpassed, which is incoherent.[7]

It is worth noting here that, although the Third Way may be accounted a philosophical progenitor of our argument, we shall make explicit a consideration which is not apparent in the famous argument. To be Divine is to *be* of necessity and of oneself, and therefore to be incapable of being created: to be created is neither necessary nor possible for Divinity. The Divine can create because all-power belongs to it, which belongs to it as being necessary, as we saw. Thus, not only does the Divine create, but only Divinity can create: to be Divine is to be creative, but also, to be creative is to be Divine. Thus, nothing that is created creates. That is, nothing contingent can create. In this way, creation is an immediate relation between Creator and created, and it is incoherent to talk of a series of subordinate creators. Indeed, one might add that the very idea of a subordinate creator, even apart from these considerations, is a monstrosity. Our argument need not raise the question of the possibility or otherwise of a real infinite series. Although we are not imputing to Aquinas any such assertion as that of a series of creators, it does appear that in the Third Way he fails to think through, in an adequate fashion, the implications of his own position.

In this connection it is necessary to say that finite *esse* is actually relation to the Divine. Thus it is not the case that 'something' called *esse* is present in different ways in God and creatures, with Divinity acting as highest instantiation, or the like, of this something. Rather, what God is is *Esse*, and *esse* is relation to *Esse*: this is the very structure of Being. This makes it impossible to say ultimately what *esse* is, which is to be conceived only analogically. However, to assert this is not to cut off *esse* from anything and everything we can know, but it is to make finite *esse* the limit beyond which is ineffable Divinity, unsayable *Esse*. We shall return to this point.

The premise on which these arguments rest does away with any idea of a God in process. Being all-powerful means being all one can be, having no unactualised possibilities, no potentialities. In this way Divinity can never surpass itself, and is all it can be insofar as it is. Thus the notion of the Divine surpassing the Divine is as incoherent as the notion of there being two unsurpassables, with which it is in fact identical. This is part of the 'temporality' of Divinity which we call 'eternity'. As we have seen, there is no temporal structure of possibility awaiting actualisation in the Divine, nor is there, as we have just seen, any prior or consequent nature in God – the two denials are logically equivalent. Nor is there process in God, nor passivity, assertions equivalent to the Divinity's being incapable of owing anything to anything, even to its (earlier) self. Thus, eternity is atemporal possession by Divinity of all the fully real resources of its own being, a 'temporality' which is not temporality at all but a being beyond time, and a condition of the possibility of temporal things. Although 'eternity' is often taken to be equivalent to 'everlasting', to assert any such equivalence is to do the Divine less than justice. 'Lasting' is the prerogative of the temporal, not of the eternity of the Divine: God does not last, God simply is, as the Utterly Unsurpassable, that is, as Unsurpassable even by the Divine.

This leads to another conclusion. Accidents make it possible for something to become other, while identity ensures it does not thereby become another. Thus if Divinity is eternal, excluding all change, it follows that Divinity has no accidents. Thus Divinity is internally one as well as externally or numerically one; that is, Divinity is incomplex.

This notion of incomplexity can be taken further. When we predicate x of y, we are asserting that y is an example of x. As the Unsurpassable, Divinity cannot just be another example of x; insofar as x is applicable to the Unsurpassable, the Unsurpassable must be, precisely, the unsurpassably excellent example of x, that is the *ne plus ultra* of x, the exemplar of x, which Divinity must have of itself, and which others have insofar as they participate in Being, through being created. Thus God must be what we ultimately mean by x, or, at least, all that we can mean by x is the floor for what God is. Thus, the 'is' that we use of God must be the 'is' of identity, not of predication. This is why we said above that God is unity and not just one. To say that God is just, is to say that God is more than the preeminently excellent example of all that justice is or could be, that is, that God is what we intend when we use the term. This is to say that God is not simply just, but justice itself, and more than justice. In this way, we can credit the Scholastic 'axiom', *quidquid in Deo sit, Deus est*. This, in turn, means that there is no differentiation in God, Who is thus not only incomplex, but utterly simple even in the merely apparent plurality of Divine attributes.

But would this not mean that there is incoherence in the Divinity, for surely justice must mean different things at different times and places, and if God is everything that justice is or could be, then are we not doomed to find Divinity impossible because of this incoherence? That Divinity exists is guarantee that Divinity can contain no inconsistency. Justice, as we saw, is both an analogical, one-intended-in-many, and a dialectical, concept whose history is therefore a resolution of *de facto* incoherence and shortcoming in an ever wider and more coherent unity. Divinity is not this process, nor simply identical to any putative resolution, representing some final state of the concept. As the Unsurpassable, Divinity is the Surpassing, and the non-Divine the surpassed, for nothing can surpass Divinity and only Divinity can equal it. If God is justice, this is not simply as we do or can understand it, but as it is in God, therefore excelling our power to say, and so ineffable, but pointed to, in and by all our saying, and so not utterly unrelated to that saying, which thus remains an inadequate and incomplete saying, falling short of What Is.

Thus, it should be clear that when we call God 'all-perfect', we do not and cannot mean that Divinity is the totality of all perfections, if we take 'perfection' to mean either determination, simply, or the fullest possible measure of an actuation which allows of more and less, particularly which allows more and less excellence. In regard to the latter case, we have just seen that the Divine is not just the best possible thing, but the infinitely excelling exemplar (not mere example), *the* Unsurpassable. God is not the best possible, but the ineffable ultimate which the best possible intends. Likewise, to say that God is everything that God can be is not to say that God is therefore everything, not only because of the excelling proper to Divinity, but because this would make Divinity incoherent, since such perfections are not all compatible. Thus, firstly, no predicate which implies contingency can be properly said of God; these can be attributed to God only insofar as Divinity is said to be able to create them. This, then, represents a kind of floor for our assertions, and since excelling is proper to Divinity, there is no ceiling: thus, secondly, no predicate which implies limitation to a particular point on a scale is directly applicable to God. In this way, it is nonsensical both to call God hot or green, for this would imply being physical and therefore temporal and contingent, though these bear witness as realities to the omnipotence of Divinity, and equally, it is nonsense to say God is this or this, and no more. Thus, nothing can be said adequately, still less exhaustively, of Divinity, but our sayings can bear witness to the direction in which Divinity lies.

8, 6 The Personhood of Divinity: I (AM), thou (art); God as Thou

God is not to be thought of as a platonic form, or set of forms. When we talk of God, we probably wish to underline the unity and simplicity of the Godhead or that the Godhead is a subject, not a set, a subject, at least, of Divinity. But, since God is utterly simple, God is Divinity, and no difference can be between the 'two'. But this raises a more profound question, in the following way: when we refer to God, we mean much more than the bearer of the 'Identity' which is Divinity, we mean to address the personhood of the Godhead. But, in philosophical terms, what can it mean to say such a thing of Divinity?

We might, in consideration of such a question, have recourse to the Boethean definition of person as an individual substance of rational nature.[8] But this, even if it were adequate, would be to reify the person, making person a substance, a thing, among substances, among things. Of course, a person is an entity of a special and unique kind, but the personhood of person, if we may so express it, is given in a more disclosive context, one which is presupposed by this reification, whether intentionally or not. Person as person is not, and indeed cannot, be disclosed in and by a relation which makes of the person an 'it', and therefore a 'something' which can be a term in a relation of ownership, of having. The necessary and sufficient disclosure of the person as person takes place when the person is addressed, namely as 'thou'.[9] A person is not a 'that' or a something, but is someone, equivalently, one capable of being addressed as 'thou', that is, one who is correctly and therefore adequately, addressed as who they are, as 'thou'.

It is notable that English, unlike most other European languages, has not retained its familiar form of address, so that to use the old form sounds and looks contrived. Nonetheless, we may use it to differentiate a kind of being which in practice is as real as it is in German or French, though differentiated from others by the context of utterance. To utter 'thou' is to surround ourselves with and in a relationship within which, precisely, the thou can be disclosed. To utter 'thou' is to do so as I, facing the other in mutuality and reciprocity, to evaluate the other as another I. If to utter 'thou' is to salute another as another I, then 'I' itself is uttered as 'thou' for the thou I address. I learn to say 'I' first only in the context of such a relationship, with a loving parent whose loving address allows the emergence of my I. It is from this that I learn that I stand out, emerge, stand forth, free and distinct from that which emerges therefore as my background, as able to do and be, an emergence which is my own ek-sistence, which finds voice as 'I am'.

This primitive 'I am' is no prereflexive *cogito*, no intellectual intuition of that 'subject' in which all experiences meet fanwise in a point which grants them the order of perspective without itself being disclosed, the always hither, lonely and unique spectator for whom all that happens happens, as object of its scrutiny. Rather, the 'I am' is a lived, engaged and relational matrix, which defines itself first, analytically and in time, by rapport with a thou, and is as one horizon of a two-way thou-calling. I am able to say 'I' because 'thou' was said to me first, and a human I in principle without a thou, and hence without language, is inconceivable. We want to picture this relation as face-to-face. Being face-to-face reminds us of parent and child, and of lovers, where uttering 'thou' is most vibrant. Friends stand side by side, their relationship a we. But 'we' is only possible where uttering 'thou' is a possibility. As Aristotle has it, a friend is another self; being friends means being thou for one another. Only in this matrix is uttering 'it' a possibility, and is never primary, either in time or in logic. Talking in this neutral third person is not reciprocity, but use, because I see the it as not being my equal, as not capable of being a thou, as letting or resisting, my handling, but never as accepting me, which consists in my being called and calling, 'thou'.

We shall not explore the relation to the animal, which, though not an it – animals cannot be property in the true sense, because one may not simply do with them as one likes – falls short of being a thou, precisely because full and mutual self-disclosure involves language. Now, so far, we have spoken of Divinity as It. Such a way of speaking does avoid a very literal anthropomorphism, for Divinity is not truly 'he' nor, by the same token 'she'. Nonetheless 'it' does scarce justice to Divinity. To refer to something as an it which cannot be a thou is not merely to mark it as different, but to mark it as inferior to one who can, for to be capable of being called 'thou' is to have greater ontological resource than a mere it. So although calling Divinity He or She is a literal falsification, dictated by tradition (or in reaction to or in that tradition) nevertheless, it is at least to recognise in Divinity a superiority to the mere it, even if we capitalise the initial letter. But there is one personal pronoun which, amazingly, is adequate to the Divinity and does not foist upon Divinity a character which is not intrinsic, and which is therefore inferior: this pronoun is 'Thou'.

This is not to disguise the essentially impersonal with the mask of the personal, as it would if we were to, say, entreat a natural force and try to befriend it. If we can find an example of an excellent thing, given the stricture we have seen that being limited cannot be a proper feature of Divinity, we can say that God is not simply other than it, but infinitely more excellent than it; it is a ceilingless floor above which God is. If being a person is such an excellent thing, then God is person and more than person. Being personal is not, but points in the direction, of what God is, and it is to persons we must turn if we would find some reflection of what God is. But to be a person is to be one whom it is possible to address as thou. To be a person is to be a thou who is 'I am'. Thus to be God is to be Thou and more than thou, it is to be I AM.

The eucharistic element of religion we have mentioned thus is at once a thanksgiving addressed to a thou, *the* Thou, a conscious and willed reception of a gift given by the Thou, and coterminous with the 'I am' which is rooted in this Giving. The 'I am' knows itself ultimately, though not immediately, only in and through the Thou, whose I AM is Giving, Giver and Gift. This is the meaning of the Divine I AM, known in and as these three, Who utters 'thou' as calling the one who is thus called into existence, thereby opening I AM to be called 'Thou' by the one who is called, who thereby receives, precisely, the 'I am' which allows of hearing, and is a hearing. The 'I am' can only finally know itself by rapport with the I AM, Who is as Giving. This saying of thou on the part of I AM makes possible, grants the actuality of, 'I am', without being capable of any gain from it. This originative 'Thou' is therefore adequate to all that the one who is addressed thereby is, a giving of a self which is a Giving of the Self. When we say that God is love, this then is what we mean, that 'I am' is given, called and held in being, by I AM, Who is as Giving and as Self-Giving.

8, 7 Personhood and Freedom

There is moreover another, less existential and more metaphysical, argument which tends in the same direction as that which we have just been discussing. The *Leitmotiv* of this argument is freedom, and the argument warrants more discussion than will be possible here. The Boethean definition of person recognises, at least implicitly, the essential connection which exists between person and freedom in characterising person as rational in nature, for there is no rationality which is not free. This connection has, perhaps, grown tired and strained in the history of philosophy, even to the extent that some deny it, and we would do well to try to refresh it.

We have seen that *esse* as such involves freedom. To be is to be free, not necessarily as being capable of exercising moral choice, but in the minimal sense of 'being free from' that which is used, precisely in using and thereby transcending what is used, and therefore, being the being one is is 'being free for', being free to be, the being one is. This continues into the realm of action: things are insofar as they are capable of acting as themselves and are thus capable of having acts attributed properly to them and not to their elements, or the like. An epileptic fit is something that happens to or in Jane, but is not something which can be properly attributed to her as such. That which can be so attributed are, preeminently, her actions. Even 'what she does' may only be attributable to her as representing a kind: she breathes, say, as all entities of that kind must. But her moral action is attributable to her as her own. The same is true, *mutatis mutandis*, of any entity, which is insofar as action is attributable to it precisely as the entity it is.

But it is also true, as we shall see, that the transcendental properties rest on freedom, insofar as formal truth is impossible without freedom, and truth is the transcendental which discloses all the others. This means that freedom itself is a transcendental property of Being, which in turn means that freedom and Being are coterminous: not only is freedom in some sense entities' mode of being, but, insofar as there is unity, truth, goodness and beauty, freedom must be, not only as entities' being but as absolute precondition of their disclosure, as well as that of the transcendentals. But if this is so, then since Divinity is *esse*, and must therefore be unity, truth, goodness and beauty, Divinity must also be freedom and more-than-freedom. But this freedom is manifested in a manner intelligible to us in and through the action we know to be that proper to Divinity, namely creation. Creation is and must be the manifestation to us of Divine freedom. Creation must be free. That it is free is easily established, for it is clear that Divinity has nothing to gain from creating, and that though the relation of creature to Creator is necessary to and absolutely constitutive for the creature, it is neither, but is utterly contingent, from the side of the Creator. Creation is the utterly free and gratuitous act of the absolutely self-sufficient.

But to say all this is to say that freedom of action in an exemplary and preeminent way is a characteristic of the Godhead. This in turn is to say that, since personhood is impossible without freedom, creation is a personal act, the personal act, in an absolutely exemplary and preeminent way. Thus, Divinity is personal and more-than-personal.

Moreover, the relation between person and freedom will bear a little more in the way of analysis, and may be revealed in a more primal way than in the implicit manner characteristic of Boethius's substance-and-essential-attribute definition. Persons are not simply free as all entities are, but are free for their own freedom as such. It is this involuted personal freedom which is essential to and instantiated in, all activities, including moral and intellectual, of which persons as persons are capable. Freedom is the person's way of being and is at the root of all that person as person can be or do. Involuted freedom means that a person as entity is free for their own being, and therefore that freedom is the apex, culmination, and goal of their being. Their essence is the being-free which is coeval with *esse*, and it is precisely in this that they are the image and likeness of the Godhead, for this links identity and *esse* in a more intimate way than in non-personal entity. This, in turn, means that freedom understood in this way makes a person a being for Being, a transcending subsistent relation to Being as such, *animale metaphysicum*, ζῷον λόγον ἔχον. In this way, Heidegger's programme announced in *Sein und Zeit*, never fully or adequately carried through by him there,[10] of approaching Being through human existence remains possible, still to be carried out, though such a carrying-out would necessitate an abandonment of the Cartesian and Kantian delineation of the person as 'subjectivity', as inward-looking 'self', as well as a transformation of some ideas dear to both the proto- and the deutero-Heidegger; that is, not so much a 'destruction of ontology' as this was intended in *Sein und Zeit*, as a deconstruction of most of the notions on which philosophy has been based at least since Descartes, and a radicalising of philosophical questioning such as has not often been seen in the history of philosophy. These remarks are more programmatic than substantive, but one thing is clear: ontology (or onto-theology) is ultimately coterminous with onto-anthropology. *Noli foras ire...*

8, 8 ...a 'little thing'...

What we have said thus far is expressed symbolically in the writing of the fourteenth century English mystic, Dame Julian of Norwich:

> And he showed me more, a little thing, the size of a hazel-nut, on the palm of my hand, round like a ball. I looked at it thoughtfully and wondered, 'What is this?' And the answer came, 'It is all that is made.' I marvelled that it continued to exist and did not suddenly disintegrate; it was so small. And again my mind supplied the answer, 'It exists, both now and forever, because God loves it.' In short, everything owes its existence to the love of God.

She continues:

> In this 'little thing' I saw three truths. The first is that God made it; the second is that God loves it; and the third is that God sustains it. [11]

For Dame Julian, there are three moments, creation, love and conservation. Love, however, is not, and cannot be, just another moment. Love is creation and conservation, which are themselves identical. Thus, ultimately, there is only love. The opposite of love is abandonment. Creative love is such that it does not abandon, or 'deposit' that which it loves, for that which is loved Divinely only is insofar as it is loved. Thus, creation must be redemption, where redemption is none other than a real and efficacious will to the ultimate, final and permanent (or eternal) good of that which is loved, for this is what love always does, or tries to do, and is the effect of the 'I (AM), thou (art)' relation which we have tried to delineate.

But a final question arises, one which will take us beyond the reaches of this chapter: how is it possible to reconcile the Divine self-sufficiency with love? Surely the foundation of all care is compassion. Can a Divinity incapable of suffering be really caring, and if Divinity really is Care, what are we to say to the reality of evil?

8, 9 Univocity and Equivocity

We come now to the third movement of this chapter, namely the task of discussing the relation of our finite saying to Divinity. As we have pointed out, to be able to talk of God philosophically is to be able to talk philosophically about how anything like God-talk is possible.

In giving an account of how language works in relation to the Divine, we must first disclose the general usage of language which is applicable in this case. Language is used here either univocally, equivocally, or analogically; used, that is, respectively, unvaryingly in making attributions to the Divine and the non-Divine, having distinct and unrelated meanings when used of the Divine and the non-Divine, and retaining something of the meaning of the non-Divine when expanded to take in the Divine. Let us examine each of these alternatives in turn.

When language is used univocally of the Divine and the non-Divine, the same attributions are made to both. Thus, if I say that God is good, although the goodness of God may excel human goodness, I mean that it is not of a different kind, but only a, perhaps more advanced, version of what we already know as goodness. As a dialectical, analogical, term, goodness is the totality of potentially correct usages of the predicate '- is good', and is, as such a continuously evolving open-ended term. The position we are now discussing in effect identifies the goodness of God with the end point of such a developmental process. In this way, the Divine is no less than the precursor and end-point of all our knowledge about the good, and is the ultimate instantiation of it. This means that God simply is, is no less than, everything the good is.

We have used the phrase 'is no less than' at two crucial points in the last paragraph. But, what is essential to this view is that the phrase 'is no more than' can and must replace 'is no less than' in the same places: God is no more than the precursor and end-point of all our knowledge about the good, and simply is, is no more than, everything the good is. This is because we are dealing here with the ultimate and final deployment of the notion of the good, the point, in other words, at which all its freight of potential meaning is deployed, and all the pseudo-uses of 'good' have been unmasked for the falsehoods they are. There is, as it were, at this ultimate point, no more ground to be covered, no territory of the good left unexplored, no variety of goodness left unexamined. At this point we have all and only what the good is in the concept 'good'. Although, we might argue, the distance which separates us from such a putative end-point may be infinite, and consequently, the full exploration of the good may be a never-ending task, it is entirely within the sense of Divinity that it should fall together with such a point. If, after all, the notion of God is to have any assignable content, it must involve the notion of superiority and excellence. We might well ask, what is wrong with this account? Is it not an eminently sensible way to talk about God, which makes God-talk free of gratuitous mystification?

Before offering objections to this account, it is well to note that it implies a fundamental religious attitude, which is to be found at some point in virtually all religious traditions. This is the attitude which stresses the immanence of God within the world. This attitude, which must form a part (though not necessarily the whole) of any genuine religion, can take many shapes, ranging from a recognition and celebration of the presence of God in creation, through a sense of creation, in its each and every diverse facet and part, as something holy. There are many examples of this attitude, and we can find some close to home in ancient Celtic forms of spirituality,[12] where an intense sensitivity to the beauty of the creation is coupled with an equally intense presentiment of, and longing for, the indwelling Creator. However, in isolation, it amounts to an identification of God with the creation, that is, to pantheism.

The reason why pantheism could be the religious side of the linguistic theory we are discussing is clear: if God is taken to be merely the indwelling spirit of creation, it is natural to see God-talk as a simple continuation of the talk we normally engage in, without any further refinement. In this way, the linguistic theory and the attitude which confines itself to the sense of God as indwelling, agree in drawing God into the creation, so that nothing is left over, beyond it.

However, an immediate difficulty arises for this view, or, these views, if one takes the religious attitude into account. This is the difficulty regarding compatibility. Although 'good' is an analogical term, so that it covers a host of interrelated significations, this does not mean that the same thing can instantiate all this diversity either at once or even serially. Certain phases of goodness, though in the same family, can never be compatible in the sense of being characteristics of one entity, for the entity would then have to have contradictory properties, or if any putative entity had them serially, it would have to change in the passage from having the one to having the other so radically, that it could never remain the same entity throughout. This should be fairly obvious; to be a good car one must be a car, to have a good – meaning here healthy – body, one must be an animal, and so on. If we are dealing with a 'Divinity' which is capable of adopting various distinct forms of goodness, then it is capable of change, and is something less than Divine.

Let us develop this criticism a little further. Suppose Divinity to be identified with the most excellent along a given line, as in this perspective it would seem to, as most good, most beautiful, and the like. Now, even if the full deployment of the associated meanings is taken to be infinitely diverse, it will be finite as applicable, for it will presuppose a finite subject: after all, the varieties of goodness arise in and from finite entities and, unless we are to adjust the theory radically, must be sayable of those entities, and only of them, or their like. This, indeed, is the distinguishing feature of the theory we are discussing. Thus, if these points are allowed, we have no guarantee that God is one, that is, that the most beautiful *is* the most good, and so on. In this way theism can be converted into a form of Platonism, and a quite primitive form of it at that, because in this version, the good is the best thing, the beautiful the most beautiful thing, and so on, which, we may presume, cause beauty and goodness in some way in things other than themselves. It is, moreover, unclear that something like this is not what disciples of Whitehead and Hartshorne actually contend.

Finally, it follows in general (and in particular from the conclusions just drawn) that if God does not transcend creation, then the 'God' in question is not God but a demiurge, a god. What is not Divine is contingent, and the totality of contingent things or some part of it, even a large part, is always contingent. If 'God' does not transcend the world, then this god is to be identified with either all or part of it. But that which is contingent cannot create. If god is a demiurge, there is or can be something outside the ambit of this god's activity, or something on which its exercise of causality must depend. Moreover, as contingent, such a 'god' might not have existed. Thus, the denial of transcendence to God, at one with the identification of god with contingency and with the theory of language which demands that this be so, requires that we abandon the notion of God altogether. In this way, the unavoidable assertion of the existence of God as source of *esse* as such is equivalent to the denial of any and all purely immanentist approaches, and the theory of language which carries them. Thus, God's transcendence of the world is inseparable from the relation between Creator and creature, and a non-immanentist approach to language is necessary. But what can 'non-immanentist' mean?

An answer to that question might lead us to the equal and opposite position, namely that the meanings of any terms applied to God are utterly discontinuous with their normal significations, and therefore are better denied than affirmed of God. Again, this position is coherent with a certain religious attitude, namely, one which emphasises the transcendence of God, who is affirmed to be utterly beyond creation, and not to be imprisoned by any of our affirmations. In such a view, even the fundamental assertion that God exists is taken to be misleading, for to assert it is to attribute spatio-temporality to God, as it is in the case of finite being. But if we take away spatio-temporality, what are we left with? Nothing, or at least nothing readily intelligible. The same is true of any assertion, because if any are true of God, they cut Divinity down to finite size. Better talk in negatives, then; better still, say nothing.

However, there are obvious difficulties with such a position. Clearly no theist can be satisfied with a position which rules even the very assertion of God's existence out of court, and will be forced to ask how a consistent application of this doctrine is to be distinguished from atheism. Atheism, we say, rather than agnosticism, because this latter position is the belief that we can never know whether or not God exists. But to hold this is to hold that at least some sense can be given to the word 'God'. However, if we hold an unrelenting cataphatic theology, we are obliged to hold that any sentence 'God is x', where '- is x' is some attribute, is strictly non-sensical, for the attribute, when applied to God can retain no meaning which is continuous with any other meaning it may hold in relation to non-Divine being. Thus the term 'God' is empty of any meaning, and any and all God-talk can only be got away with unless and until we realise that its subject is a dummy, and that, on that ground alone, there are no real attributions being made. In sum 'God' is a string of letters and no more, and might as well be replaced by any other random string in such 'discourse', and indeed, to unmask the futility of the 'discourse', and to show that no crypto-subject, even some shadowy psychological item in the speaker, can be somehow intended, we might insist that a new string be used each time a subject of attribution were called for.

In this perspective the nonsensical 'sentences' 'Phrag is gluph', or 'Thrink is not sclug' are as meaningful as 'God is good' or 'Divinity is not finite', though the latter two are better disguised. In sum, here the one word covers both the Divine and the non-Divine only equivocally, and given such absolute discontinuity, any extrapolation from ordinary usage is disallowed, and we are left unable to arrive at the Divine meaning. Moreover if assertions are to be rejected, so are negations, for negation is the logical operator which turns 'true' into 'false', and vice-versa. According to this cataphatic view, there is no truth in assertions about God, so neither can there be in denials. Thus, even the grammatical particles which signify these operations, the 'is' and 'is not' in the nonsense sentences we coined above, can be replaced by random letter-strings, for they signify no real logical moves. In this way, the truth of the unmixed cataphatic position is revealed: that religious language is no more than the mere *flatus vocis*, not beyond, but beneath, rational discussion, functioning exactly as does the inarticulate howl of disappointment or encouragement which comes from the crowd at a football match, supplying in individual cases, as Ayer would have said, fodder for the psychoanalyst.

8, 10 Language-games and Religious Utterance

We might integrate a Wittgensteinian objection to our line of thought here. Religious language, it will be objected, does not function as descriptive or assertive language does, and to think it does is to confuse the switch and the brake in the cabin of Wittgenstein's loco-

motive. Religious language, we will be told, makes sense in the context of the language-game called 'worship', and must not be judged
according to the criteria of a different game; it is foolish to criticise a
move in chess because it makes no sense in poker.[13] Religious language-games, in this view, provide us with the grammar of 'the
Divine' and its equivalents, a notion underwritten by the Wittgensteinian point that language-games are all right as they are, and are
the final court of appeal in regard to the use and therefore to the
meaning of any expression. The meaning of the word 'God' thus
has no free meaning, one given, that is, in independence of any
language-game.

This view or its analogues was in fact used to preserve religion from
verificationist objections. Unfortunately, it 'preserves' religion
much in the way that the work of the taxidermist preserves the car-
cass of an animal; it may look the same, but all life has departed.
This view coheres with the logic of the apophatic position, for if it is
correct, then religious activity as a self-contained game is meaningful, but says nothing – and 'nothing' here really means nothing –
about the world, but also about the other language-games which
are carried on there. In this understanding, we leave religion
behind when we pass out through the door of church, mosque or
synagogue. Yet surely we ought not to disregard the opinion of
many who frequent and have frequented such places that what
they do there has an intimate, and reciprocal, connection with all
their other activities? Further, is it not possible that this universal
quality is essential to religion?

It is, of course, possible to play any language-game without asking
what its ontological commitments are, but the self-understanding
of many, if not all, of the players of such games is that that which is
addressed in such games is something which transcends them, that
the game or games are expressive of a relationship with that
game-transcending reality – a relationship which is not confined to
the playing of specifically religious language-games – and, more
strictly, therefore, that if no such reality exists, the game itself is
futile, or, at best a matter of mere social convention, and, perhaps,
of moral reorientation. This is the understanding mediated by such
games, at least as they are traditionally understood in the three
great monotheistic faiths. Given that this is so, the game, whether
we like it or not, makes ontological claims, and to that extent does
attempt, minimally to 'describe the world'. If we believe that games
are all right as they are, it would be very hard to contradict this

claim. The question then becomes one of the probity of testing the inherent ontology.

Some versions of Christianity, and certainly some Christians, do not encourage such questioning, while others do, and even make, or have made it, mandatory. If it is true that some such testing is not discouraged and is even required by the understanding mediated by the games themselves, it is hard to see how it is possible to rule such questioning out of court, and to rule it so, however uncharitable it may appear to say it, smacks of insecurity, of an unvoiced or repressed suspicion that the ontology may be found wanting. This, in its turn, may become a rejection of philosophy or even of reason itself, perhaps an impassioned one, which sees reason as the Devil's strumpet. However, uncomfortable truth is to be preferred to comfortable falsehood; faith need not be bad faith. If all this is so, then there is no reason why such questions should not be posed. The 'ask not' approach might appear to have been justified in the epoch of verificationism, but if this belief is itself no more than mere dogma, then the apparent 'justification' it gave to the approach in question is not only specious, but quite obviously so.

Even if we want to say that what really happens in worship is a moral conversion and attitudinal change that has nothing to do with any religious ontology, this is already to modify the Wittgensteinian conception of hermetically sealed, mutually incommensurate language-games, in the direction of meaning-development and -cultivation in a common horizon. But from the point of view of religion, such a move would be to reduce religion to ethics, or at least to make of it an ethical training-ground. Doubtless, this is part of what the great monotheistic faiths are, but is it all of what they are? Kant, and with him, adherents of some versions of at least one of these faiths, would reply with a resounding 'yes' to this question. As far as they are concerned, the important thing is to become virtuous, and it matters little what story, if any, we contemplate to help us attain this end; if watching a film, looking at a picture, listening to music, or any activity, artistic or otherwise not vicious in itself, is helpful in the serious business of becoming good, then it is as religious as any overtly religious activity, and may even be more so if such overt activity fails to help us in our serious intent.

We ought to take seriously the contention that we do not preserve something by showing that it is really something else. If religion is really ethics, then there is only ethics and no religion. In what sense, then, are religious activities religious, and how are non-religious activities to be distinguished from them? In what sense is a morally good religious person different from a morally good non-religious person? The answer would seem to lie, minimally, in the presence of God-talk in the activities we call religious, if this word is taken in the context of the three faiths, traditionally understood. Ethical training is interwoven in these faiths with such talk, so that, although ethical training may be carried on without it, in that case, it will be of the non-religious kind. Likewise, the religious person's self-understanding and the account they would give of their activity, even of that part of their activity which is not explicitly religious, will be unintelligible and arbitrary without God-talk. Although there appears to be no moral obligation to which religious people owe allegiance that non-religious people do not, there will be some, at times considerable, behavioural divergence between them, a divergence which is unintelligible unless some appeal be made to God-talk. Now, if the cataphatic position is correct, there is no God-talk, and thus all conduct, understanding and speech which require God-talk in order to be intelligible are condemned to irrationality. Religious activities thus become irrational activities, comparable to the elaborate and sometimes 'clever', though ultimately absurd, fantasies worked out by those unfortunate enough to be suffering from one of the more serious forms of mental aberration. We cannot have it both ways: either religious activities are meaningless insofar as they transcend ethics, or they are ontologically weighted and make claims which can be evaluated by ontology. Religious activities are meaningful, therefore, insofar as they make claims which can be the object of philosophical inquiry.

Religious language-games, then, are not the final court of appeal in determining the meaning of 'God'; these games are – one might argue, notoriously, from an historical point of view – open to correction and reformation, as indeed are all games, otherwise we make the work of the social reformer strictly unintelligible. We can, and if we take them seriously, we must, submit religious games' ontological presuppositions to examination in the light of what we can determine philosophically about Divinity. This assertion clearly goes hand in hand with the assertion that there is knowledge of Divinity which is 'natural', that is, which need not be derived from any specifically religious language-game or tradition, and against which we might measure the ontological claims contained in them.

This considerably curtails the apparent profundity of the pseudo-mystical side of the unmixed apophatic approach. It is perfectly true that whereof one cannot speak, one must pass over in silence. It is probably also true that those who embrace the apophatic approach do so inconsistently, and, however implicitly or covertly, disregard it at certain convenient moments. The reason for this is that the mystic is not one who has dissolved all possibility of assertion regarding the Divine, and has thus consigned to absurdity any and all references to it, including the word itself – that is the atheist. The mystic is one who recognises that language, though finally inadequate, can point into the unsayable, and who therefore waits still upon God.

8, 11 Analogy: the Dialectic of 'Divinity'

What has emerged in our discussion thus far is that language cannot capture the Divine perfectly, and so cannot be used univocally of the Divine and the non-Divine, but, on the other hand, the assertion that it must be used equivocally is tantamount to the assertion that nothing at all can be said of the Divine, and that even the word itself is strictly meaningless. However, the question now is, how is it possible to justify analogy, when that which the analogy is meant to reveal escapes adequate expression in language? How is it possible to talk of the relation between God and creation, a relation absolutely unique and *sui generis*, in terms of any relation between things in the world, such as parent and child, craftworker and artefact, or the like, without being, at the very least, seriously misleading? Even more radically, do words like 'creation' not simply embody this misleading analogy, and so fail to be a genuine disclosure at all?

The answers to all of these questions, it would seem, must emerge, if at all, in the answer to what we have called the most radical question of the problematic: just what does 'creation' and its co-ordinate terms mean, and how does any such meaning accrue to them?

The answer to this has in a measure been given by us, in that the meaning of 'Divine' is what has emerged in our discussion of the being of entities. This should be legitimate unless there is a genuine objection to the possibility of ontology as such. It is part of the ontology of temporal entities that they be receptive of *esse*, not productive of it, on pain of the violation of the modal axiom that possibility as such does not entail actuality. 'God' is precisely the name given to the unapproachable and unsurpassable source of such entities' *esse*, a source, we have shown, which cannot be identical to them as temporal. The logic inherent in this assertion is that this source must be, minimally, all-powerful, unique, free and itself atemporal, features which are, we might say, the formal 'properties' of Divinity, 'being God', being this source of *esse*, in such a way that it is logically impossible to assert that anything which is source of *esse* fails to be so qualified. It is this complex of ontological factors which is and can be the only source of God-talk and in which alone all God-talk is verified and vindicated. This is the linguistic shore of the sea of Divinity: we can come to land's end and know that beyond it is no land but the shoreless seas of God.

Creation dovetails with contingency in such a way that the meaning of creation is derived from the meaning of contingency. It is not that the notion of creation adds something to that of contingency which was never found in it before, but is as the consequence that contingency imposes. The denial of creation, the positive assertion, therefore, that temporal entities are sufficient to account for their *esse*, is the violation of the principle to which we have referred, and the coeval assertion of a logical absurdity. Though far from completely understood, the hither side of the relation, temporal existence, itself demands the relation, which appears as included in it as its necessary and foundational feature. The delineation of the further term is thus neither wanton nor gratuitous, but an application of the everyday logic and conceptual apparatus we have already to hand. The assertion of Divinity is thus not the special pleading in which, we are told, believers are wont to engage. We do not say that talking of God requires a knowledge or, worse still, a logic, to which only the believer has access, and which is unrelated to that used by others or by believers in contexts other than the religious. The delineation of Divinity is thus of a piece with our delineation of the world, and something can be wrong with the former only if there is something wrong with the latter, in or with logic, or in fact.

The requirement that God be all-powerful simply is the requirement that the source of *esse* be precisely that, and the freedom of the source is consequent on that, for what is all-powerful can have no needs – and this is the meaning of what it is to be all-powerful. Uniqueness is likewise entailed, as we have seen: it is logically absurd to assert the existence of more than one such source. This is why we can speak of a logic of Divinity, which is no Divine logic, but logic applied to God, or, better, to 'God'. The peculiarity of language which engages our attention here is most manifest when we begin to touch on the eternity – only to be thought of as a-temporality – which must belong to the Divinity. The peculiarity is that Divinity must be said to be atemporal on logical grounds, while, at the same time, the assertion means that God is not temporal, whatever this may mean. It is in this phrase in particular, 'whatever this, namely "being not temporal", may mean' which discloses the oddness of this kind of discourse. Yet we assert, and hope to clarify, that this oddness is not a scandal, but to be expected on the basis of the implicit theory of meaning which is, and is in, ordinary linguistic usage.

'Whatever this, namely "being not temporal", may mean.' The oddness here is carried by more than one element, but perhaps most strikingly by the place of 'not'; we have the seemingly ungrammatical 'being not temporal' rather than 'not being temporal'. Likewise, we have the strange frame-phrase 'whatever this, namely x, may mean.' These two oddities are in fact one oddity, or at least, intersecting oddities. The point of intersection lies in a kind of incompleteness of meaning of the x in question, carried by the form of x, to be sure, in this case, in the shape of the oddly-placed 'not'. This incompleteness, we suggest, is the finger pointing into the infinite, the 'what cannot be said'. This is the point at which language, not so much annuls itself, as shores itself, draws the line between it and the mystical.

The frame-phrase, the 'whatever x may mean' conveys a partiality in the meaning of x: x means something, but that meaning is finally undisclosed. X does not finally say, but intends, and what it intends is somehow an extension of what it says, a pointer in a definite direction. The burthen of the frame-phrase is not to annul x, but to manifest its incompleteness. To annul x here would mean to assert that the content of x might well be other, and thus that the actual content is meaningless. This would be the equivocal approach again, and so is not what happens to x. What x says is asserted, but transcended, indeed, asserted as transcended in and by the frame-phrase. It is not simply equivalent to the phrase 'God is (simply) not like this', but to 'what God is is beyond what is like this'. 'Beyond' functions analogically. What God is, whatever that may be, is as the 'whatever' left undefined by x, and may never be known by us, but the feature which is named and negated is intended, as being precisely that which is negated as what it actually is, thereby intending what God is, from that starting-point. God is as beyond this, more than, superior to. But to be superior to, even by infinity, is not just other than, and different from. Like this, yet not like this, but in being more, in being superior to. This being superior is what is both not simply identical to our meanings and not simply divorced from them. To be God is not to be the world or any 'thing' in it, but to be related to it as that which surpasses it, surpassing precisely that which Divinity is 'not', as in being not-temporal, being something which is at least a positive surpassing of what it is to be temporal.

Implicit here is a rule of meaning, the very grammar of 'Divine' and of its cognates. God is that which surpasses, in that, whatever God is, is not what this is, precisely as surpassing it. Part of theology is the application of this grammar to each and every term and definition. To have finished this job is to have a complete theology, yet this is not to have caught up with the Divine. The grammar of the Divine as surpassing is the result of, on the one hand, the application of everyday logic as we saw, in the context of the ontology of entities, and on the other, the failure of the univocal and equivocal approaches. In this way, our position, as deconstructable into these features, is not mere mystery-mongering, and countenancing mystery for obscurantist reasons, but the very necessary application of the very logic and language which obtain elsewhere and everywhere. The Anselmian 'that than which ...' as that beyond which is nothing, yet not coterminous with the end of our saying, is the formulation of precisely this ineluctable grammar, which is both logical and existential - onto-logical.

An important element implicit in what we have said ought at this point to be highlighted. Surpassing implies a something surpassed. But also, that which surpasses does so in the manner proper to it. If God surpasses, then God does so as Divinity would do. The surpassing proper to the Divinity dovetails with the failure of univocity and equivocity as such, as being unexhausted by all we can say, yet pointed at by all we can say. God as God is not limited by anything or all that we can say, yet is the only thing that can be pointed to by affixing the transcending 'not' to anything we can say. This is precisely coterminous with the Anselmian phrase.

Someone might say, God is white. We 'verify' this in the only way possible, by checking its coherence with the grammar of 'God'. The results of the test will be one of two possible outcomes, coherence or incoherence, the latter in the sense that a logical contradiction or inconsistency will result. In such a case, the assertion is a pseudo-assertion. If the assertion is in fact coherent, it may turn out to be deducible within the framework of the grammar, or it may not. In this latter case, provided there is no hidden internal inconsistency in the assertion itself, or inconsistency of it with the grammar, the assertion is undecidable in respect to God, though believers of all three monotheisms lay claim to such assertions on other grounds than mere coherence, namely revelation, but on grounds which, they argue, are at least not at odds with this grammar. From the point of view of the grammar, such assertions, if they meet the stated criteria, are possible, but not imposed by the grammar.

Let us put 'God is white' through this filter. It is impossible to be coloured and not in space, and whatever is in space must be temporal. Thus, God, one of whose formal features is to 'be not temporal ' is temporal. Thus God is not white. But this denial is not simply that God is not white in the same way that something green is not white, but that God surpasses any such manner of being, in being not temporal, and by implication, not spatial. In this way, this, and other such silly assertions can be useful by providing grounds for denial, and so a valuable exercise and clarification for the grammar, exercise and definition which are the proper work of philosophical theology. Moreover, in this theory, room is left for the religious genius who can take the grammar a step or two further. The 'whatever this may mean' thereby leaves open the meaning in the sense that there may well be space for extension in the direction pointed out in the denial. The border between sea and shore is a fluctuating band and not the clean line we see only from a great way off.

Where is the analogy, the likeness, in all of this? Is not the proper form of analogy *a is to b as c is to d*? There are two answers to this. There is, in God-talk as in all talk, the possibility of, and the need for, metaphor. The aptness of the metaphor is judged in the light of its nearness to, or distance from, the grammar, as we have indicated. The grammar can suggest the metaphor, or be embodied in it. Thus, the grammar is the matrix of metaphor, a feature which it shares with many other elements of our experience. In this sense, it is analogical. But it is also analogical in a more profound, and dialectical, sense. It posits what is as negatived and as surpassed as shore for any assertion regarding what it is to be Divine. Shore is border. Border shapes. Not that the Divine is shaped by what is inferior to it, but in making that very denial – the 'not' which begins this sentence is the 'not' of surpassing – we assert the being-shaped of the finite by the Divine. This dialectical reversal is the very analogy, the

proportion between the Divine and the created. The created is analogy by virtue of the 'not', the analogy is always the disanalogy of
surpassing. The essential is always the surpassing, which is only
accomplished as surpassing of (objective genitive) something
which is surpassed, in the manner of surpassing proper to that
which surpasses. Ultimately what is surpassed is finite *esse*, so that
God most properly (for us) surpasses all that that *esse* is, precisely as
God would surpass it. But all that *esse* is is unity, truth, goodness,
beauty and freedom. Whatever is is one, true, good beautiful and
free insofar as it is. God is what surpasses this as more than these,
precisely as proper cause of *esse*, and as proper cause of these as
coterminous with *esse*. Thus it is proper to call God always all that
these are and more: this is what it is to be ὑπερούσιος, excelling substance, *esse*, as such. It is here we find the most profound unity of
our trinity of language, world and God. All language of the world is
implicitly capable of intending God, and God, in this way, is present in, and is beyond, all our meanings, so that, if language were
not so capable, it would not be deprived of a vocabulary or level of
discourse, but would cease to be altogether. God-talk is talk about
Being: talk about Being is God-talk.

Divinity in sum, is both near and far, palpable to mind yet not
explicable, a darkness, yet a close and holy darkness, a night which
is a thou:

> I too pass from the night;
> I stay awhile away O night, but I return to you again and love
> you;
> Why should I be afraid to trust myself to you?
> I am not afraid … I have been well brought forward by you;
> I love the rich running day, but I do not desert her in whom I lay
> so long: I know not how I came of you, and I know not where I
> go with you … but I know I came well and shall go well.[14]

Notes to Chapter Eight

1. I follow the presentation of the poem of Parmenides in Ritter and Preller, *Historia Philosophiae Graecae, Editio Septima*, Gothae 1888, p. 88 line 43.

2. *Tractatus*, 7.

3. Anselm's famous phrase occurs in chapter 2 of the *Proslogion*. The expression 'the Unsurpassable' occurs in Hartshorne's study of the ontological argument, *Anselm's Discovery*, (La Salle: Open Court, 1991). It would seem, however that he holds this to mean 'unsurpassable by anything except itself'. See also his study *The Logic of Perfection*, (La Salle: Open Court, 1991). Although we do not here espouse Hartshorne's position, it must be admitted that his understanding of ontology and of the problem of God is exceedingly profound.

4. The term ὑπερούσιος, 'beyond being or substance', and the approach to God which it expresses is a venerable one in the West. The word itself seems to be Neoplatonist in origin and is to be found in the writings of the pseudo-Dionysius, and has therefore enjoyed much influence on Christian mysticism as well as on theological speculation. We suggest that it expresses an attitude indispensable to both.

5. Kant's treatment of what he considers to be the only possible arguments for the existence of God are to be found in the Transcendental Dialectic, Book II, Chapter 3, sections 3 -7, *Immanuel Kant's Critique of Pure Reason*, translated by Norman Kemp Smith, (London: Macmillan, 1973), p. 495 and following. Although we cannot attempt here any systematic treatment of these objections, we allege, at least, that the collapse of the cosmological into the ontological argument – at least as Kant understands the ontological argument – is avoided by the way in which our argument is structured.

6. The argument here advanced for the existence of God is a more condensed version of the present author's article '*Ex possibili et necessario*: a Re-examination of Aquinas's Third Way' which, at the time of writing, has been accepted for publication by *The Thomist*. This article also touches other issues explored in the present essay.

7. The argument here rests upon the Identity of Indiscernibles; Boethius, who clearly had great influence on Aquinas's thinking in this context (see footnote 10 in our article cited in the previous footnote to this chapter) implicitly appeals to this principle: see *De Trinitate*, III, in *Boethius*, Loeb Classical Library, vol. 74.

8. Boethius's definition of person, *naturae rationabilis individua substantia*, is found in his *Contra Eutychen*, Loeb, vol. 74, p. 85, and following.

9. The best-known elaboration of the I - thou relation is to be found in Buber's *I and Thou*, translated by R. G. Smith, (Edinburgh: T & T Clark, 1994). Lévinas is also of great interest, where the other is disclosed in and through the face. It is a quite remarkable lack that although *Dasein* is coevally Being-with-others and Being-in-the-world, there is no mention of

friendship anywhere in *Sein und Zeit*: see LT Part 1, chapter 1, subsections 8 -10, also Intermediate Conclusion, especially subsection 2.

10. For Heidegger's programme, see LT Part 1, chapter 1, subsections 3 and 5, as well as the Intermediate Conclusion.

11. Julian of Norwich, *Revelations of Divine Love*. Translated and with an Introduction by Clifton Wolters (Harmondsworth: Penguin, 1966), chapter 5.

12. See 'St Patrick's Breastplate' by N. D. O'Donoghue in *An Introduction to Celtic Christianity*, James P. Mackey (ed.) (Edinburgh: T & T Clark, no date).

13. See D. Z. Phillips, *Wittgenstein and Religion*, (Swansea: Macmillan, 1993).

14. From 'The Sleepers', in *A Choice of Whitman's Verse*, Selected with an Introduction by Donald Hall, (London: Faber and Faber, 1974), pp. 92-93.

CHAPTER NINE

One and Many

9, 1 Introduction

We come now to a cardinal point in our study. We launch ourselves into that part of ontology which deals with what are traditionally called the transcendentals: these are four, namely, unity, truth, goodness, and beauty. We have suggested that these are best understood as intrinsically related to that way of being which is ours and which sets us up as open intensively and extensively to Being as such, that is, what we have called transcendence. However, it must strike us that the first of the transcendentals is somewhat out of step with the others, in that their axiological nature is clear, while unity as such can hardly be described as a value. This indeed is so, and unity as transcendental is *sui generis*. However, although it lacks any overt component of value, unity is nevertheless a transcendental, and constitutes a suitable point of departure for a discussion of them.

Unity is not to be considered alone. Insofar as something is, it is one, either as a simple and undivided unity, or as a complex, consisting of parts or divisions participating in and intending the unity, equivalent to existence, which belongs alone to the whole, that is, as unity. It is in this sense that we can say *ens et unum convertuntur*, so that the status of transcendental is conferred on unity. But, in that unity need not be simple, it allows division, and hence intends plurality. Unity implies identity, for things are one insofar as they are one and the same. Division implies both identity and diversity: the self-identity of things which are or can be distinct from one another. Hence, from unity, plurality, which in turn can only be understood as diversity among things, which, as self-identical, are one. Unity, which we have just discovered to be a formal characteristic of Divinity, moreover, excludes any sense of plurality, and is the exemplary cause of unity as coterminous with *esse*, which, as finite, is diversified and participational, so that unity is said in an appropriately analogical manner of God and world.

Precisely insofar as there is finite reality, there is plurality, both as
the unified and thus intensive plurality which is complexity, and as
the formal and hence extensive plurality which is manyness. This
means that the 'categories' of unity and plurality are absolutely necessary to, and necessarily used in, any sort of talk which is capable
of being true of the world. More, it is this dialectical opposition of
the two which is proper to talk about world as such, for world is the
greatest possible extensive unity of both intensive and extensive
plurality, for which the ground is finitude, understood as contingency and temporality. The proper field of application of this transcendental and its dialectical mate is world, and this chapter is simply an explication of this: the unity and plurality proper to world.
So, though it lacks axiological character, unity – and perforce plurality – is, understood as coextensive with finite being, the last stop
in the discussion of world, and for that reason, the first stop in the
discussion of those more colourful features which themselves are,
like unity and plurality, coextensive with Being and ineluctably
involved when language is deployed to address the real. It is precisely as having access to these – to unity as well as to the others –
that the truth of transcendence is disclosed, which is itself the manifestation of Being as such and those properties which belong to it
per se.

In this way, our treatment of the one and the many shows how this
structure is fleshed out in and as the finite temporality of things;
how unity is related to diversity and plurality in and as world; what
is proper to worldhood, the essence of world as such; the essence of
that participation which belongs necessarily to the many-towards-
one which is world.

We might add as a rider here that an adequate articulation of world
is both a task and benchmark of a successful attempt to construct
ontology, and the problematic of world has been a hidden, though
capital, topic of modern philosophy, from Kant's *Inaugural
Dissertation* [1] to Heidegger's *Sein und Zeit*. To do justice to Being is
to do justice, proximally, to finite being, which is in and as world,
and any failure to do justice to Being has been a failure to articulate
world in an adequate manner, making world tributary of subjectivity (the Kant of the critical philosophy, where the categories are
principles of the world as my world) or of a projection which is
always mine (the earlier Heidegger)[2] or making it an epoch and
function of language (the later Heidegger)[3] or, perhaps worst of all,
making, as Leibniz does, the ensemble of monads[4] a mere agglom-

eration of radically independent entities, which amounts to a denial of world as such.

9, 2 Ontological Unity and *esse*

Precisely insofar as something is, it is one, for if this were not so, the 'thing' in question would in fact be a plurality, and hence a diversity, and what would exist would not be the so-called thing, but the elements of the plurality, each of which would be in itself one, on pain of being resolved into yet more primitive units. We have seen that identity, moreover, is the principle of the persistence of the same thing as one and the same, through time: something can be itself only as one and the same. In this way identity guarantees both synchronic and diachronic unity although, in the latter case, only one state of the diachronic whole can exist at any time, its wholeness and unity being guaranteed by the self-sameness of identity which underlies the diversity and manyness of its states. This processal unity of the diachronic whole, more precisely, is guaranteed by the present's being all that remains of this one thing's previous states, while its future is that ensemble of possibilities presented to it as that ontological unit which it is. To have one's own identity, distinct from all others is, in sum, to be an ontological unit, which is what we mean by 'entity'. The unity of an entity is that of a whole, composed of those elements which constitute its identity, which with its accidents constitute its state. It is the characteristic of accidents to be determinations of something more ultimate, and to be only by participation, precisely as sharing the *esse* of that something. If to be is to be as a unity, it is the unity as such which exists, not its ontological parts, which are only as parts of the complex unity, the whole.

If something has its own *esse*, its own act of being, then it is an ultimately existing unity. If an accident were such, it would be an entity for that reason, not an accident. Identity by contrast, is determination, but not accidental determination. Both accident and identity are as determinations: determinations, namely, of something which they characterise, in a more or in a less fundamental way, according to the thing it is, distinct from all others or to some respect which can change without the entity's ceasing to be, whose determination it is. The structure proper to determination is '*A* is (determined as) *B*', where the 'is' in question is that of predication. Suppose the 'is' were that of identity. In that case, *A* would be *B*, its own determination. A determination can only change by ceasing to be the determination it is, and therefore, ceasing to be, as such. Thus *B* could not change without A's, to which it is *ex hypothesi* identical, ceasing to be. In such a case, there could be no continuity in change, only an actual, continuous infinity of mutually unrelatable states. The 'is' of predication posits a real distinction between A and B, as determined and determination respectively, and by the same token, a relation and not sheer difference. But this relation can only be that whereby the determination is *of* that which is determined, for if this were not so, there would indeed be a sheer diversity between them.

Thus the 'of' betokens in the case of each, a kind of incompleteness. The determination can be 'of' what it determines, only if it in itself has the structure 'x is determined as B', requiring the blank, 'x', to be some A which B determines, on pain of the determination's either not existing or of being an entity in itself. On the other hand, A without the determination is not determined as this or as that. To be determined is to be actually this or that: determination is actual being, which is what makes non-modal, indicative propositions either true or false. Although A can lack particular determinations, it cannot lack every determination, on pain of being a real nothing. Thus, determinations are absolutely necessary to something which is, though to be a something which is, is not to *be* a determination, but to *have* determination, as this or as that actual something. To be, it is necessary to be determinate; to be determinate is only possible as the way something which is is. This, then, expresses the proper incompleteness and consequent mutual orientation of entity and determination, and makes clearer the participatory nature of determinations' being. Although it is trivially true that everything that is, is, nonetheless it is entities which properly exist, subjects of *esse*, which itself belongs only by virtue of participation to anything other than entity.

9, 3 Diversity

To be an entity is to be an actually existing something, that is, to be uniquely subject of *esse*, which is possible, though, only as the entity one is, that is, as one and the same something in temporally diverse states, and thus capable of being secondarily, accidentally, determined on the basis of what one actually is. *Esse* is the actuality which is existence. Entity is that which actually is, the subject of *esse* and of all determinations which are only as determinations in or of entity. Identity is that determination without which that which is cannot be (that which it is), and is thus the necessary, though not the sufficient, condition of the existence of entity. But identity is not itself simply identical to entity; entity is what is, while identity is most properly what that which is is. To say that 'what is' is identical to 'whatever "what is" is', is not merely to say that a thing is what it is, but rather that something which is, is identical to what that something which is, is. But 'what that "something which is" is', is itself a determination, so that to assert their identity is to assert that an entity is a determination. But a determination is always a determination 'of'. Hence, an entity would have to be a determination of something, which, since it is *ex hypothesi* identical to its own identity, must in its turn be the determination of something else, and so on *ad infinitum*. Thus entity and identity are not identical, and so must differ. They differ precisely in that it is entity which is and not identity as such, save as fundamental determination of what is, and that entity is not as such determination of what is, but rather what is, *tout court*.

But is not Divinity identical to its own identity, and will therefore the same infinite regress not arise? Divinity is incomplex: there is no real distinction between what It is and that It is. The identity of Divinity is not a determination of Divinity, which as determination is necessarily distinct from that which it determines, but Divinity as such. Thus the overall feature of 'having determinations which are distinct as determinations "of", from that which they determine' is a hallmark of finitude. Being so determined is possible and necessary only if one is as distinct from what one is. Divinity is simple and irrefrangible unity in that there are no determinations of the Godhead in God, but only the Godhead: there is nothing in God which is not God.

9, 4 World: Unity and Plurality

In this way, there is an utterly simple and unitary principle of the plurality of the world as one world. But the questions which now require to be asked are: what is meant by 'one'? This can, in its turn, only be answered if we have some idea of what 'world' means. At first, this latter question seems to be utterly without mystery, perhaps even hardly worth the asking. Surely the world is just the totality, or even the mere sum, of all that is?

Clearly plurality is implied by the notion of world. A world consisting of one entity is not a world, even if that one thing is the only existing thing. World, therefore presupposes the existence of a real multiplicity. Since this is so, it follows that the world is not a whole or totality in any real sense. In the case of the whole, it is the whole which exists, and the parts exist only by participation, since the part, to be what it is, relies on what the whole is, while the whole is in the parts as determining their form and function, in subordination to its own, as we saw. A whole is an analogical, as opposed to a simple, unity of those parts which are only in the whole, as subordinate to the whole, and which have, therefore, no independent existence. The 'parts' of the world are not parts in this sense, subordinate in this way to a putative world-whole, but must be ontologically independent as distinct entities, not as parts are distinct from one another or from that whole whose parts they are; and however much they may need each other, even to stay in existence, this need is not the kind of need which parts have of their totality, without which they cannot be. The kind of relation of part to whole is subordination, while the relation between ontologically independent things, i.e., distinct entities, is coordination, apart from the relations associated with material causality.

Thus, the world is, at least, a real plurality of distinct but co-ordinated entities, not a totality consisting of subordinated parts. What do we mean when we use this phrase 'distinct but co-ordinated'? And when we say 'not a totality consisting of subordinated parts', what are we at pains to deny, or even, perhaps, to affirm?

Two things are distinct when there is a lack of identity between them. Entities are distinct in being what they are in such a way that no other can share in this identity. This is the uniqueness which founds diversity which itself is necessary to plurality, and as such is proper to plurality, since the one entity can never be diverse in this way: no matter how many its parts or diverse its states, entity as such must remain always one. Moreover, entity, as entity, is that which has identity, and is thus determined, never determination. To it belongs property and relation, though it itself belongs to nothing further in this way. Although properties and relations can themselves be the subjects of further properties and relations, their being presupposes that of the entity, which they determine. And though properties and relations can themselves be subjects of change, any change in them is a change in the entity or entities of which they are the determinations. This is the ontological ultimacy of entity, which makes it the unqualified subject of property, relation and change. Together, ultimacy, with the identity and uniqueness it presupposes, are the elements of the ontological independence enjoyed uniquely by entity. Where there is such independence, the finite relations of anything to the independent entity, causal or otherwise, are external, in the sense that they presuppose the existence of the entity, precisely as independent, while the relations of the independent entity to others occur as a function of itself, as independent: *omnis agens agit sibi simile*.

Ontological independence, however, must not be confused with necessity: to say that entities are ontologically independent is not to say that they have no needs or vulnerabilities, that they cannot be influenced by others, or have no need of others; it is to distinguish them in their relation to *esse*. To be independent means to be that most properly of which *esse* is said, while to be other than independent is to enjoy *esse* by participation. So, when we deny that the world is a totality consisting of subordinate parts, we are, more profoundly, asserting that it is a real plurality, that is, one which is genuinely diverse, consisting of independent entities, which act as functions of themselves, not as functions of, and therefore in subordination to, some other, namely world itself. Coordination can thus be nothing else than the possibility of relation of some sort between such ontologically independent entities. If this is so, then the world is the sum of all possible such relations, or better, the context within which alone such relations are made both possible and actual. In sum, then, the actual world is a real plurality of independent entities, and the unique context within which any and all relations of which such entities are capable, occur.

9, 5 Worldhood

Let us view this from the perspective of the worldly entity, where 'worldly' here means 'being in the world', rather than an opposite of 'spiritual'. For an entity to be called worldly, we conclude, is for it to be capable of relation to others, as well as to be, indeed, insofar as it is, independent in the context of other entities. To be a member of a plurality is to be capable of relation within it, and to have actual relations with other members. Thus the opposite of worldly is to be incapable of relation, therefore to be other than in the context provided by the plurality. An entity which is unworldly is necessarily isolated. But anything which is unworldly is incapable of being influenced or generated, since these would imply relations, and only necessary being could be so. Thus to be worldly is to be non-Divine, and therefore contingent and temporal.

But, is world itself contingent and temporal? Things come to be and pass away, change and alter, after all, without the world itself doing so. Since the world is a plurality, it is clearly not Divine, to which all plurality and difference are repugnant. 'Divinity', 'eternity' and 'ontological necessity' are equivalent concepts, so the world is therefore contingent and temporal. But is world distinct from worldly entities? This question aims at that which is at once most fundamental and most mysterious in the notion of world. The question makes of world an 'it', a 'something', which may, or may not, be said to have a time of 'its' own, distinct from that of its members. A plurality is not an 'it' or a 'something', but a plurality. Moreover, we know on scientific grounds that there is no universal time, that is, a time proper to the world as such, but only 'times' confined to situations, and therefore reducible to the temporality of those situations' members, just as in music there is no absolute time but the coordination of the different voices' rhythm.

What is a plurality? What is it that gives it its identity as plurality? What makes a plurality to be such is its manyness, its being the context which unifies many. The many become or are one in that they are capable of relation, and have actual relations with each other. In this way, the plurality is neither a simple unity nor a sheer heterogeneity, like a whole, an analogically unitary many-towards-one, but unlike the whole, where the 'towards' is incarnated in subordination, the 'towards' of the plurality depends on a coexistence which is not properly subordination. In co-existence there is equal emphasis on both 'co' and 'existence': the condition for the existence of a plurality is the co-existence of its members, an existence which is therefore necessarily both independent and mutually oriented, precisely as capable of mutual relations. It would appear, therefore, that the correct description for such a plurality, based upon independent existence and mutual orientation, is ontological community.

World, then, is that plurality which counts as ontological community. To be sure, there are other pluralities. Moreover, as we have used the word here, it is to be distinguished from both whole and lot, though each of these in its own way is many. A plurality is not a mere agglomeration of heterogeneous things, but a many which is a *co(mm)-unity*: a being-together in one of independents on some common basis, in which they participate, and one which has limits, defined, namely, by the extent of that in which the members participate. Clearly, the common basis of world as we have indicated is the all-common existence. The word 'community' is justly applied here since the hall-mark of community is equality and mutuality; all entities are equal as entities and in being, while their mutuality is their orientation towards each other, their own capacity for relation with one another. The limit of the world is the extent of existence, so that the world is not divided by it merely from other pluralities, but is opposed, as existing, and as community of the real, to nothing. Can there, therefore, be only one world? We must give an affirmative answer to this question in that the world is now revealed as the community of existence. World, in this way, is Being in one of 'Being's' (independent) acceptations.

(We note here the various acceptations of 'Being' as independent: existence, *esse* as such, and the transcendentals convertible with it – their being convertible with *esse* and with Being are mutually implicative – ; *esse-Esse*; identity-or-essence and existence; potency and act, particularly as incarnated as identity-or-essence and existence; world as we here delineate it; God. World is virtually identical with *esse-Esse*, though world usually intends the finite alone, while 'God', only notionally distinct from *Esse*, intends *what* God is, rather than *that* God is. These then are the, or the main, analogues of 'Being' which we have encountered.)

But, if we champion existence in this way, do we neglect co-existence? It is not simply existence which is necessary to world, since this is presence, but presence is not, at least immediately, relatedness; we therefore must require that co-presence be integral to it as well. Is this co-presence integral to, or based on, the existence which is or confers independent presence?

Clearly we can look to no other determinant than existence to find our answer. The question therefore becomes one of how co-presence is a mode of existence, whether it belongs to it necessarily or contingently. If we look to the Divine, we see that co-presence cannot belong to it of necessity, but only contingently. This, we hasten to add, is not to introduce contingency into the Divine, but merely to say that if contingent things receive existence from the Divine, since they are contingent, that they do receive it is contingent. Change and contingency are entirely on the finite side of the ontological-modal difference. The Divine is not intrinsically oriented towards them, so that if both modes, Divine and contingent, exist, they are not in a community in the sense elaborated: God is not just another (worldly) entity, but the principle of entity and the ground of world. This cannot be the case with contingent entity. To be contingent is to require Another in order to exist, so there is, in finitude, an intrinsic and necessary orientation towards the Godhead, coter-

minous with the existence of the finite and contingent. But to be
contingent is also to come to be, to continue to be and to cease to be,
in accordance with this contingency as this mode is expressed in
and as what the contingent being is. But this, in turn, bespeaks relatedness to other contingent beings. More precisely, contingent entities can come to be only if other contingent entities can become
them, can continue to be only if their requirements are satisfied by
others, can undergo certain kinds of changes only if there are virtual
others capable of acting as agents to bring about the changes in
question, can cease to be only if they can decompose into other
entities not identical to them. It is perhaps this point more than any
other which brings out the necessary, ineluctable and essential temporality of world, which may, and usually does, include spatiality.
World as community and plurality of possible relations devolving
from contingency *is* spatio-temporality.

Thus, contingency necessarily implies relatedness and hence
worldliness. The converse is also true, so that being worldly and
being contingent are mutually implicative and hence equivalent. If
this is so, then the true nature of worldliness is to be found not
merely in existence as such, but in existence as contingent: worldliness is contingency, and the final definition of world is the plurality
of contingent entities, the field of contingency and spatio-temporality, analogically one as existing, as community, and as, and on the
basis of, being created.

The relatedness which we have found to be necessary to world, and
which is a necessary concomitant of contingency, is, to use
Wittgenstein's metaphor, like the interwovenness of rope-fibres,
where there is no one thread which runs down the entire rope. Just
so, there is no one relationship (except that to the Divine) which
pervades the world; relatedness means the possibility of all this
web of relations' occurring on the basis of contingency, not only
those relations mentioned which are demanded by contingency,
but also those which they make possible, such as 'being bigger
than', or 'being to the right of', or the like. Now, the extent to which
this occurs may not, and indeed, probably is not, simply coterminous with the extent of existence. How beings are related depends
on the identity proper to each, and hence upon the essence of the
classes of beings in question. This might mean the extent of possible
relatedness could be limited, and fall far short of the extent of existence, and this either necessarily or contingently. A galaxy which
happens to be too distant for us ever to see or detect it is contingently

excluded from relatedness with us, while there may be regions of entity which in principle fail to be capable of relation to us or to our region. A non-relation can count as a kind of meta-relation, a differentiation proper not merely to entities but to regions of entity. Such failure, and in-principle inability to relate, is a function of the essences of the entities which compose such mutually exclusive regions. Thus, it could be said that different worlds are, after all, possible, insofar as there are, or can be, such incompatible regions of existence, though clearly such regions are not the 'possible worlds' dear to some logicians, in that such possible worlds are usually thought to be, not real possibilities but, in some respect counterfactual, alternatives of the actual world, or of our region of that actual world. There cannot *be* many possible worlds in this 'logical' sense, because they are only possible as non-actual, precisely as counterfactual and mutually inconsistent.

This then is our notion of world. It is clearly an ontological notion of world, as community of beings, distinct from the 'human world' or from that elaborated by Heidegger, certainly in his pre-*Kehre* period, though having something in common with that elaborated by the pre-critical Kant. Indeed, it is not unfair to say that world has been the hidden, though crucial, issue for all philosophy since Descartes, or, more precisely, since the Cartesian failure to be able to give a coherent account of how I can know anything beyond my own mind and its content. It is precisely world which is occluded in and by this Cartesian failure, which conditions the problematic faced by subsequent philosophy, up to the time of Heidegger and Wittgenstein, and this in two ways: as inwardly directed, the self fails systematically to transcend towards contingent things which can only be as worldly and intrinsically 'in the world', and in so failing, and, in general, as discarnate, the self fails itself to be in the world. Discarnation is falling outside of world, which if it is to be restored to the doubting subject, can only be so in an attenuated fashion as object, not as world. Incarnation is a full-blooded being in the world, being part of the world, inhabiting the world. But to affirm the world in this way is to affirm transcendence, not as constitutive of it, but as being part of it, and all that belongs to transcendence. This means affirming real and independent entities which can either only be known as 'it', or as worthy of being called 'thou'. It is also to affirm the intelligibility of Being which belongs especially to world as the total pattern of possible relations between things.

Even for the pre-*Kehre* Heidegger, world is simply the milieu in which *Dasein* resolves the issue of its being, and is therefore an affair of *Dasein*, occurring only within *Dasein*, as a function of *Dasein*'s necessarily projective understanding, whereby it projects its own possibilities in and as world, and thus devolving ultimately from *Dasein*'s essential concern with its own being. In the post-*Kehre* Heidegger, an attempt is made, probably for the first time since Kant, to put forward a notion of world which is not a function of one entity alone, but is that which is revealed in and through the Event which is the essentially intersubjective and historical coming to pass of language, though even here world is made to depend on something other than the community of beings as beings. In the debate with Heidegger, I suggest that the notion and status of world is crucial, and I submit that any realist alternative to the Heideggerian must be, or be very like, that elaborated here. Moreover, I use the word 'realist' advisedly, precisely because this picture of world is one presupposed by any view of knowledge that holds that we can know something other than ideal entities, and that this something is not a mere projection or convention.

9, 6 Unity and Participation

Let us now briefly examine the notion of ontological participation to which we have been making repeated reference in our treatment of unity and of world. The notion of participation denotes having a share in, as the Latin origin of the word, *partem capere*, shows, which appears to be a translation of the Greek μετέχω. Though participation is a wider notion, we emphasise that we are here referring to the participation in and of existence as such, which is what we mean by ontological participation. *A* participates in *B* when *A* is not *B* of itself but only by virtue of another: an entity participates in being or existence since it exists not of itself but by Another. In other words, *A* is contingently *B* because *C* is necessarily *B*: contingent entities are contingently because Something, necessarily one Something, is of necessity. The notion of sharing is apt here. That which is of necessity is of necessity one, while that which is contingently could be alone only contingently, and so many contingents are possible and actual, which thereby have a share in what Another properly owns. These contingents are united most fundamentally in that each is only in virtue of the fact that, and what, Another is, that is, only in virtue of sharing what belongs properly to Another. They are united less fundamentally in that, since each is worldly, it is necessarily related to others which also are contingently, that is, it is a necessary, though not a sufficient, condition of

the being of each that it be related to others in ways which are determined by its being worldly. In this way, each coexists as contingent
with others in community, participates as member along with others,
in virtue of One which is necessarily and therefore necessarily
alone. 'Being' is thus said properly only of the One which is of itself,
and contingently, by analogy of participation, of those that are by
virtue of that One. In this way, 'being' is said of contingents along
the lines of a many-One relation.

The truth of participation may also be expressed as a proportion in
each contingent thing between *esse* and what it is, in a one-many
relation: that A is and that B is, and so on, are each related in the
same way, by the same relation to what A is and what B is, and so
on, because what each is is only contingently related to *esse*.
Therefore there is One in which the proportion is identity, which
defines that One as origin. That the relation is one of contingency
means that what each is is variously determined, though in its
every determination, by its being only contingently. In each case,
'being' means contingency and all that goes with it, though at the
same time, the meaning of A's being is given in and as what it is to
be A. To specify what it is to be A, conversely, is to specify how A
(contingently) is, namely, what it means for A to be. In this way, in
general, what it means to be is always given as what it means for
this or that to be, which, in its turn, is always what it means to be
(variously) contingent, which in turn requires and allows us to infer
that something is of necessity. The one-many relation of proportionality thereby necessarily returns to the many-One relation of
participation; such is the unavoidable form, the ultimate 'hard fact'
of ontology.

Notes to Chapter Nine

1. The *Inaugural Dissertation* in *Kant, Selected Pre-Critical Writings*, Kerferd
and Walford (eds. and trans.) (Manchester: Manchester University Press,
1968).

2. LT Part 1, subsections 4, 6, 13 - 18, and 22 - 24.

3. LT Part 2, subsections 2 - 3, and all of chapter 4.

4. *The Monadology*, 7, in Leibniz, *The Monadology and Other Philosophical
Writings*, translated with introduction and notes, by R. Latta (Oxford: OUP,
1971), also, p. 50 of the same volume, including note 1.

CHAPTER TEN

Truth and Untruth

10, 1 Introduction

In our discussion of unity in the last chapter we have, as it were, placed the capstone on our consideration of the two realms of Being, the worldly as contingent and created on the one hand, and the Divine as creative and necessary, on the other. This constitutes an ontology inclusive of metaphysics as onto-theology. But, lying over against this as its condition of possibility, as it also is of all ontic uses of language which take place within, and in relation to, the territory revealed by ontology, is transcendence, without a consideration of which ontology would be truncated and incomplete. The true nature of the necessity which brings on this consideration which is onto-anthropology, can only at this juncture be suggested, for it is only in the course of its elaboration that the bivalence of the transcendentals, as at once ontological, belonging to Being, and properly transcendental, that is, as revealed in finitude only in and by transcendence, is disclosed.

There is a nexus here between finitude and transcendence, which indeed, we must explore, in that transcendence is only possible for finitude as falling short of that towards which it transcends, on the one hand, and, on the other, in that finitude is radically incapable of creating: as we shall see, transcendence does not give itself its goal, its towards-which. This makes of transcendence a receptivity and capacity rather than anything like a synthesis based on categories, as Kant would have it, or a projection, as it is represented in *Sein und Zeit*, accounts which would mask rather than disclose that which 'transcendence' actually intends.

In this way, transcendence must be, in the first place, capacity for truth, as disclosure of Being. This is the first moment in the ineluctable process which stretches between truth, goodness and beauty. Truth is, as it were, the closest transcendental to language, which is the emblem of transcendence. In the course of this chapter we shall discuss the issues we have just outlined, taking as our initial clue the quotidian uses of 'true' and its cognates. It is a remark-able fact that language is a self-illuminating medium which directs whoever would think about it in the way they should go, and if we cling to the advice which language itself gives us, our treatment will be neither one-sided nor arbitrary. Pursuing this leads into the transcendental notion of truth and its inherent connection with finitude. These issues are best brought to focus in a superb passage taken from Heidegger: we shall use this text in our exploration of the issue of truth, but we emphasise that this treatment is not meant to be an exegesis of Heidegger's thought nor an exposition and dis-cussion of his thinking. We merely use the text to grapple with the issues which have arisen in our own problematic, but it does allow us to detect in clear terms the fundamental failure of modern thought to come to grips with truth. This criticism is at one with, but not identical to, the criticism of the Cartesian-inspired problem-atic which we put forward in our first chapter.

Probably the most important item which will emerge in this discus-sion is the discovery that transcendence cannot be simply as clear-ing in Heidegger's sense alone,[1] but must be fully-fledged moral freedom. In this way there is an orientation internal to truth towards the good: openness to truth is openness to the good. Thus, the ontological treatment of truth anticipates that of the good as its completion.

The end of this discussion explores the non-contingent plurality of transcendence, such that openness to truth is not the prerogative of the essentially isolated singular thinker or speaker. This, then, is another item which counts against a deracinated subjectivity. To give an account of transcendence which approaches adequacy is to see it as essentially incarnated, an incarnation which has more dimensions than simple embodiment, but also bespeaks the neces-sary location of the singular thinker and speaker within the linguis-tic community.

The final movement of this treatment of truth accomplishes a kind of dialectical reversal. Transcendence relies upon an openness in that which is (beyond it) inherent in that which is, as necessarily coterminous with its being. This is intelligibility. This is the onto-logical axis of transcendental truth: truth as transcendental is onto-logical, inseparable from the being of that which is, and not merely a characteristic of transcendence as such. Here lies the bivalence of truth; so it is possible to change perspective and view truth not only from the vantage-point afforded by transcendence, but also from the universal perspective of that which is in general. We would suggest that it is this bivalence which is absent from modern philosophy, which contents itself with a reduction of truth to transcendence itself or, since this is impossible without vitiating transcendence, to something in such speculation which replaces transcendence. But the problematic of intelligibility as proper to Being as such, cannot therefore be discussed without reference to Divinity as Being, or in neglect of the true and final contour of the human project: in this way the coordinate nature of metaphysics as coevally onto-theological and -anthropological is shown, though not explicitly discussed, in this context.

10, 2 The Meanings of 'true'

We begin by noting that the notion of truth is an abstraction. Abstractions tend to be a kind of shorthand, giving the 'essence' of an array of uses and meanings. An inquiry which remains at such a level would lack that primitive character required by the kind of enterprise we now have in hand, as both Heidegger and Wittgenstein would be quick to point out. Rather than looking at the distillate represented by 'truth', we must return to the primitive usages. We must look to the point at which truth becomes an explicit phenomenon, as Heidegger would say, or, in Wittgensteinian terms, to the grammar of 'true'. So, how do we use the predicate 'true' and its equivalents?

When we use the word as an adjective, it seems to connote the genuine as opposed to the merely seeming; as a relation – being true (to) – it connotes faithfulness, in the sense of to be relied upon to be something, undeviatingly, again, to be genuinely that something, as opposed to merely seeming, or failing, to be, or being so only sporadically; as meta-predicate, 'true' indicates what is, as opposed to what is not, or may merely seem to be: 'it is true that x' or '"x" is true', means that what 'x' says is really the way things are. These, too, have their opposites. Related to such uses of every day are those of the verb 'to seem'. Things may be, or not be, what or as they seem: 'Jane seemed to be in the best of health when I saw her yesterday, but you tell me she died last night'; 'so it would seem that the real culprit is Smith'. There is what merely seems to be the case, and is not as it seems, and there is what 'now seems' to be the case over against what had 'merely seemed' to be so. Mere seeming is false appearance, while 'now seeming' is mere seeming's dissipation.

Each of these oppositions presents itself – it would seem! – as one between what is, and what is not.

These usages allow us to triangulate the geography of truth; it is a landscape which always brings with it an 'as opposed to', an opposite. It is impossible to discuss truth without discussing its opposite. The genuine opposes the merely apparent or bogus, the undeviating is opposed by the sporadic or the absent, the saying of what is, is set over against that of what is not, for being able to say what is, is equivalent to being able to say what is not, true. Recognising these oppositions places truth for us: truth can occur only where its opposite is possible, where it is meaningful to speak of what is not as well as what is. The locus of truth is not therefore, merely in what is, in Being, since there can *be* no such 'thing' as 'what is not'. Part of the ontological investigation of truth, an attempt to delineate the being of truth, must therefore be a delineation of this locus, and an explanation not only of how truth is possible but also of how and why its opposite is equally possible, and what exactly the relations are between them.

10, 3 Truth and Dis-closure: *ens et verum convertuntur*

Thus the terrain of truth begins to show itself, however misty it might at first seem. First there is what is. Secondly there is the, necessarily distinct, locus in which what is and what is not can be, and be related. Thirdly, there is what makes possible, and differentiates, the second above and beyond the first. Fourthly, there are the relations which occur within and between these two areas. Any ontology of truth must be an account of these elements.

In regard to the first, Heidegger's return to the Greek conception of truth as ἀλήθεια, which pervades *Sein und Zeit*, [2] is apt. ἀ-λήθεια, consisting of the privative α, and ληθ-, related to λανθάνω, 'I escape notice', is translated as 'unconcealedness', deliberately privative to show that truth must be won from its opposite, concealedness, which thereby gains a certain ascendency; Heidegger was and remained fascinated by this, and throughout his work, sees unconcealedness and concealedness to be constantly interwoven. This is the context in which the seminal metaphor of truth and Being (rather than beings) as light, and the opposite of truth as darkness, comes into play: beings are originally those things which come into the light, and are revealed in the light. We find this alignment of Being-truth and light in Greek thinking – there is a beautiful passage in the *Protagoras* where the parallelism seems gently to be hinted at.[3]

What such metaphors bespeak is fundamental. What is, if it is disclosed at all, is so, insofar as it is; nothing cannot be shown, and to show something as it is not is to fall short of what it is, which thereby leads in the showing. That something is, is the condition of its being shown as that which it is; it is in this sense that *esse* is the light which allows disclosure, while what that which is is, is that which is thereby illuminated. In short, to be is to be disclosed, and truth as revealedness is coterminous with what is. This means that truth, as coterminous with what is, is not simply identical to what is, but what is as (being-) disclosed. This is what is meant by truth as transcendental property of Being, expressed in the 'axiom' *ens et verum convertuntur*.

This, in turn, means that there is some orientation inherent in what is, insofar as it is, towards disclosure if it is to be disclosed; if this were not so, that which is would not be capable of being disclosed. This factor, at least in the pre-*Kehre* Heidegger, was accounted for with relative ease, because everything disclosed in and for *Dasein* was so as emanating from its projective understanding of its own possibilities of being: *Dasein* had no access to anything other than this, so that *Dasein* itself was disclosive, principle and source of disclosure. If, however, we take the kind of view explored in this essay, this access granted us by that which is to itself insofar as it is, becomes highly problematic: we are led to ask why and how should such access be given, since that which is revealed is independently of us to whom it is revealed? What is the principle of its and our coming together in such a disclosive relation? How are Being and truth coterminous? This is the problem of ontological truth as such, and it is at this point that all forms of scepticism and relativism interpose themselves between us and a coherent answer.

Such a consideration immediately throws us over to the opposite of light, to the darkness of opacity and coveredness. If there is ontological truth as disclosedness, is there also room for an untruth coterminous with the real? This does not mean that there could or need be a kind of 'negative essence' in reality, or a positive non-Being, or any such nonsense, but the question does touch the possibility of ontological opacity, a lack of access to what is insofar as it is. Put another way, does undisclosedness come in at the level of what is, or at the level of that in which disclosure takes place (or fails to)?

10, 4 Transcendence and Finitude

This brings us to the second item we mentioned above, namely, that in which disclosure takes place, in which falsity can formally be, and be related to truth. Before proceeding further, however, it is essential to note that, although we may well think these items *are* separately, they are ontologically interlinked, and any answer to a question regarding the one is echoed in what we say about the other, and conditions thereby what we say about the relations which unite them. Even the most rudimentary knowledge of the history of philosophy shows how difficult it is to bring this ensemble of items into the light, doing justice to all its parts.

Luckily we have already seen what appear to be two of the major landmarks of this second region necessary to truth: first, this region is that in which, and, we may add, for which, disclosure takes place; second this is the place where untruth, what is not, falsity in all its forms, can formally be. Together these two interwoven and inescapable principles give shape to this region. Let us now try to trace this shape.

This second region is not a mere entity among others, for it is not simply there, side by side with other worldly things; it is more worldly, we might say, than they are, precisely because, as that for and in which disclosure takes place, its work is to stretch beyond itself towards all things that are insofar as they are. All other things, rest, insofar as they are, within the limits which define them as the beings they are and insofar as they are. Something which is in this way can merely be 'beside' something else, that is, although such things relate to one another as the things they are, and insofar as they are, this is a condition of there being any relation between them, but is not the content of that relation. To be something in and for which something is disclosed as that which it is, insofar as it is, is to be something which does not remain within its constitutive limits, but which, necessarily, as that which it is, oversteps those limits, stretches itself beyond them in an impulse which is coterminous with all existence.

We use the word 'necessarily' advisedly here. Such a capacity cannot accrue to an entity as accident, but only as integral to, and culmination of, that which it is. Thus it is a necessary characteristic of such entity to be-stepping-over. The latin verb 'to step over' is *trans scandere*. For this reason, we may justly call 'transcendence' that ineluctable openness for disclosure which characterises the second

region necessary to truth, and precisely because the ineluctable culmination and essence of this region is transcendence, we may say
that it is transcendence: in this way we shall henceforth call the second region necessary to truth transcendence, and would thereby be
taken to mean that that for which to be is transcendence is to be that
which, as that which it is, relates to, as disclosing, all that is insofar
as it is. This is also a new addition to the notion of truth as
transcendental: truth as such *is* only in and as the relation *of* that
which oversteps itself towards existence *to* the existence towards
which it transcends, in virtue, namely, of a 'transcendental' relation
of that which transcends towards all that is insofar as it is, that is,
towards existence as such.

But if the gaze of our inquiry remains fixed on transcendence, we
shall find that we are neglecting another, and equally important co-
constituent in this second region of truth, one that finds voice in the
second structural principle we touched on above, namely, that this
place of truth is also the place where untruth, what is not, falsity in
all its forms, can formally be, and it is so, we may add, precisely
because it is the place where truth is. What sense are we to make of
this?

The very notion of transcendence itself bespeaks limitedness,
because it is not proper to something which is already coterminous
with all existence, and, indeed is only possible to something which
is not. Transcendence, as stepping beyond, is movement. If there is
to be movement, one cannot already be where the movement leads.
The fact of movement thus requires that there be a falling-short,
namely, in terms of where a real movement is to lead. Likewise, an
already-being coterminous with all that is would not be transcendence, but something more excellent, the characteristic of something which, as coterminous, has neither need nor capacity for transcendence. Thus, transcendence is the characteristic of the less
excellent, of that which falls short, but whose impulse is to cross the
gap, and which is therefore subject to the reality of the gap which it
seeks to cross. This being less excellent and being subject to the gap
across which the movement of transcendence stretches, are one, as
the limitedness which belongs of necessity to transcendence. This
limitedness is finitude, as failing to be coterminous, being subject to
the gap, and therefore having, as truth-ful, to stretch across it in
transcendence. Thus, transcendence and finitude are mutually
implicative, and therefore identical. Another name for transcendence is finitude.

We might add here that the linguistic expression of finite transcendence *par excellence* is the question. The question intends precisely what is unknown, as still concealed but only provisionally so, and it does so from its vantage point in truth, in unconcealedness. It is a bridge which bestrides the gap between the two – although not in any full or final sense – or a line cast out into the darkness. One might whimsically say that the most human of all symbols is the question-mark.[4]

It is finitude as such which is responsible for untruth, and allows untruth as formal possibility of transcendence. Finitude is the necessary falling-short which belongs to, and in, transcendence. But transcendence is the openness to disclosure, as that in and for which disclosure takes place; in this way, finitude is a falling-short of disclosure, the absence of full disclosure, in the sense of being final and complete or adequate. Thus, finitude as falling-short, is the possibility and necessity of untruth, of occlusion, namely, of what is insofar as it is. Insofar as transcendence is necessary to that whose culmination it is, disclosure, without which there is no transcendence, must occur, but as finite, this disclosure can and must fall short, allowing for the two forms of occlusion: ignorance where something is not disclosed, and, consequent on this, error, where something as not fully disclosed, is held to be other than it is. To be in error is to mis-take something, to take it for other than it is. These two, as forms of occlusion, are not unfortunate interludes in the march towards truth, but, as it were, an unavoidable state of transcendence, which always accompanies transcendence as finite, the concealment that truth as ἀ–λήθεια must rend and penetrate. Thus we have a kind of dialectical interwovenness of truth and untruth in the interlocking of transcendence and finitude.

This interwovenness, however, does not bespeak an equiparation of truth and falsity; truth is the dominant 'partner', because untruth is its failure, not a positive being or mode of Being, but unavoidably present due to the finitude which is transcendence.

But if occlusion is due, as such, to finitude, there is a more profound way in which finitude conditions truth. This lies, precisely, in the connection between the two regions of truth, transcendence and that towards which transcendence stretches. The most radical occlusion which can occur is the occlusion of existence as such: such an occlusion, dominant in philosophy since Descartes, is coterminous with the occlusion of the first region of truth by the second, which itself bespeaks a falsification, an occlusion, of this second region, so that its mutually implicative structural characteristics as finite transcendence are themselves lost.

As transcending and as finite, the second region of truth is unthinkable without the first, existence, and to deny or to ignore this intrinsic and necessary relation is to deny or ignore transcendence and finitude. Such a denial or occlusion of the first region is to take the second region as sufficient without the first; it is to reduce existence to the second region, and to deny its autonomy; and thus it is to delineate this second region as autonomous. In opposition to this, a true vision of the true must be to take the second region as *in*sufficient without the first; to assert the autonomy and ontological independence of the first; to delineate the second as dependent. The second region is autonomous only if there is no independent existence, only if, that is, all existence is a function of it and is dependent on it. But if this were so, then the second region is not correctly characterised as transcendence, for there is nothing toward which it stretches and fails to reach; that is, it does not stretch, and is therefore adequate to all that is disclosed in it. Thus there is and can be no falling-short, no occlusion, therefore no ignorance and no error. The denial of transcendence, as we might expect, is a denial of finitude. That there is, can, and must be, such things as ignorance and error, is itself a notion incompatible with such a stance.

Again, as we might expect, this amounts to a denial of the most profound meaning of finitude, for the assertion of this kind of autonomy is at one with the assertion that transcendence is the ground of all existence, that transcendence is that which grants existence, now understood as disclosedness, to that which is (disclosed), and anything which is not so disclosed simply is not. If disclosure is of something other than that, and what, something is, it fails to be disclosure, and would be occlusion; thus if something originates disclosedness, the being-disclosed which is coterminous with existence, it must originate the thing which is disclosed. Now, how can that which grants existence as such be thought of as finite, since the granting of existence is the prerogative of the Divine? The finitude of that which receives disclosure is equivalent to its openness and receptivity to that which is disclosed. But openness and receptivity are not grounds for the existence of the disclosed, but only conditions necessary to the receiver as receiver. That the autonomy of the receiver is asserted could thus only be so on condition that finitude, and therefore the Divine too, as required absolutely by finitude, be itself occluded.

Thus we say again: a true vision of the true must be to take the second region as ontologically insufficient without the first; it must be to assert the autonomy and independence of the first, and hence its hegemony, over the second for, in order for something to be disclosed it must be, though the converse is not the case unless transcendence is the ground of existence, and thereby ceases to be finite; in the third place a true vision of the true must delineate the second as dependent on the first, i.e., as having an intrinsic and necessary relation of ontological dependence on the first, in that the second is inconceivable in its being, without the first.

10, 5 Heidegger's Delineation of the Issues of Finitude and Truth

There occurs in Heidegger's Kant book, a brilliantly perspicacious passage, namely, Subsection 5, first part of section 2, A: 'The Essence of the Finitude of Knowledge', in which he treats these very issues. Although this essay is not intended to be a work of textual exegesis, we shall refer to this highly suggestive passage to get a firmer grip on the issues to hand, without, however, relating this to the development either of Heideggerian thought in general, or, in particular, to Heidegger's reading of Kant. Heidegger places the issue in the following way:

> ... finite knowledge is non-creative intuition ... Finite intuition looks to the intuitable as something on which it is dependent and which exists in its own right ... Finite intuition ... is not able by itself to give itself an object. ... But not every intuition as such is receptive – only the finite is so. Hence, the finitude of intuition lies in its receptivity. Finite intuition cannot receive anything, however, unless the latter announces itself, that is, the essence of finite intuition is such that it must be solicited by a possible object.[5]

We shall take 'intuition' here to be broadly equivalent to our 'transcendence', as capacity to allow something as such disclosed, to appear. If intuition is finite, then it is not able to give itself an object. But if this is so, then intuition as finite is dependent for appearance to occur, on that which is independently of it, and which is given by appearance, in and for intuition. Transcendence is openness of the finite as finite for appearance, an openness which is therefore receptivity to, and dependence on, that which shows itself as showing itself. The 'solicited' of the translation is *angegangen*. This is a particularly apt expression: *angehen* means 'to commence' or 'to ignite', as intransitive, and, as transitive, 'to ask', 'to concern' or even 'to attack'. That which shows itself actuates, precisely as showing itself, the possibility which is receptivity.

Heidegger further explores this finitude at a later point in the same subsection:

> If finite knowledge is receptive intuition, the knowable must show itself by itself. What finite knowledge is able to make manifest, therefore, must be an essent which shows itself, i.e., which appears, an appearance. The term 'appearance' refers to the essent itself as the object of finite knowledge. More precisely, only for finite knowledge is there such a thing as an ob-ject [*Gegenstand*]. Only such knowledge is exposed to the essent which already is. Infinite knowledge, on the other hand, cannot be confronted by any such essent to which it must conform. Such a 'conforming to…' would be a 'dependence on …' and, consequently, a form of finitude. Infinite cognition is an act of intuition which lets the essent itself come forth [*entstehen lassen*]. Absolute cognition itself reveals the essent in the act of letting it come forth and possesses it 'only' as that which arises from this very act, i.e., as e-ject [*Entstand*]. Insofar as the essent is manifest to absolute intuition, it 'is' precisely in its coming-into-Being. It is the essent as essent in itself, i.e., not as object.[6]

The finite and the non-finite are brought together here for their mutual clarification, and the dangerous word 'object' appears, which can bespeak a something only for and in a subject, that is, which alone, the subject alone, knows. But here, object is appearance, that inherently limited showing of itself which finite transcendence can, as finite, allow, but which, though limited and falling short of what is, allowing the certainty of ignorance and the possibility of error, nevertheless 'refers to the essent itself', and is not something other than that which shows itself as showing itself. Finite knowledge is finite because it must be confronted by something to which it can conform, and so is dependent on that something which itself is independently of it. This cannot be the case for infinite cognition, which is coterminous with creation, and distinct from it only notionally. As such it is not truly intuition, and if we take it to be so literally, we falsify it. It would seem that the last, apparently innocuous, sentence quoted shows the beginning of a mistake which, if left unchecked, will loom very large. Despite what he says, there appears to be a disjunction between object, appearance, and what is in itself. There is a hint here that knowing the object in itself is the prerogative of the non-finite. But if appearance is other than what is as it is, that is, in itself, then it is not appearance: the logic of appearance dictates that there be no disjunction between what appears and what is, on pain of there being no appearance *of* what is.

Yet this is precisely what Heidegger says. He tells us that '[t]he essent 'as it appears' ... is the same as the essent in itself and only this.'[7] He later adds, given that any disjunction between what appears and what is makes illusion of appearance, that '[a]ppearances are not mere illusions but the essent itself. And the essent, on its side, is nothing other than the thing "in itself".'[8] On the credit side, he tells us:

> Indeed, only insofar as it is essent can it become an object, although only to finite knowledge can it be such. It manifests itself thereby in conformity with the manner and scope of the receptive and determinative power at the disposal of finite knowledge.[9]

This is to say that appearance as finite, as necessarily inadequate because it is inexhaustive and never final, is partial presentation of what is as it appears, hence presentation nevertheless of what is, occurring in and for something which necessarily falls short of an adequate and final grasp of what is, though stretching out towards such coextensiveness as goal. That which appears to something can only do so in accordance with the way in which that something is, and to the extent of that something's resources to allow such appearance; as the Scholastic maxim has it, *quidquid recipitur ad modum recipientis recipitur*, which is virtually what is said in the last quoted sentence. Things transcend, make appearance possible, only insofar as they are, and in accordance with the resources they thereby enjoy, although the maxim can also be taken to intend the 'translation' which occurs in conceptual knowing of the real, the mechanics of which were a major preoccupation of Aristotelian theories of cognition.

But, Heidegger also maintains:

> The essent can be manifest without being known 'in itself', i.e., *qua* e-ject. The dual characterisation of the essent as thing in itself and as 'appearance' corresponds to the relation in which it stands to infinite and finite knowledge respectively, as e-ject and as ob-ject.[10]

This seems to be a clearer statement of the unfortunate alignment which we have already detected. Knowing the thing in itself is lined up with an absolutely adequate, because productive (i.e. of the thing known), knowledge of it. Thus, any knowledge which fails to be absolutely complete cannot be productive knowledge, and so is not knowledge of the thing in itself. This is fallacious. While it is true that any knowledge which fails to be absolutely complete cannot be productive knowledge, it is false that such knowledge thereby fails to be knowledge of the thing in itself. Thus we assert, in Heideggerian terms, that the essent *cannot* be manifest *unless* it is known in itself. If to know it thus is to know it as eject, then it is possible and necessary to know it as such without our knowledge's being productive of it. This is to say that it is possible to know it as eject *though eject of God's, not of our, knowledge*. The fallacy lies precisely in thinking that knowing something as eject means that it must be eject of that very knowing. This is equivalent to the belief that to know something adequately is to know it as God knows it, which is to deny that there can be any adequate finite, that is non-productive, knowing. But, conversely, to say that there can be adequate knowing is not to assert that as adequate, knowing must be Divine knowing, and, likewise, to know something as eject though not as eject of that knowing is to know it, merely, as finite and dependent on God's creativity.

The scission of eject and object appears at its sharpest in the following:

> finite knowledge as finite necessarily conceals and, indeed, from the first, conceals, in such a way that not only is the thing in itself not completely accessible to such knowledge, it is not accessible to it at all. That which is 'behind the appearance' is the same essent as the appearance, but because the appearance gives the essent only as ob-ject, it is basically impossible for it to let the essent be seen as e-ject ... in the expression 'mere appearance', the 'mere' does not signify a limitation and a diminution of the reality of the thing but serves only as the denial of the assumption that in finite knowledge the essent can be known in a manner appropriate to infinite knowledge.[11]

The final quoted sentence is the ground of what is asserted in the others. It means more than it says, for the assumption is not merely the stated and entirely correct denial that in finite knowledge the essent can be known in a manner appropriate to infinite knowledge, but also the unstated, and fallacious, assumption that there can be no real finite knowledge of the thing in itself. If this unstated assumption were granted it would follow that finite knowledge were a concealment of the thing in itself. But if that were so, then how could finite 'knowledge' be knowledge? Moreover, being a concealment of the thing in itself does indeed mean that the thing in itself is not accessible to such pseudo-'knowledge' at all. If that in its turn were so, then there could be no evidence whatever that 'that which is 'behind the appearance' is the same essent as the appearance', nor indeed that there is anything at all behind it.

To follow that reflection through would be to cut off finite transcendence from its context in reality, to turn mere appearance into its possession, which amounts to a denial that such appearance is of anything beyond itself, and to do away with the finitude of transcendence which makes it dependent on, and oriented and receptive to, a something which exists independently of it. This is to annul transcendence itself, for that which encounters only itself or its own contents cannot really be said to go beyond itself. The denial of the finitude of transcendence is at one with the occlusion both of independent being and of transcendence itself, and may be to make an idol of the finite, setting it up as not-finite.

10, 6 Transcendence-Finitude in Modern Philosophy

We do not intend to accuse Heidegger of committing the fallacy in question, nor do we mean to trace how the last-quoted incoherent paragraph relates to his, or indeed to Kant's, thinking, still less do we intend to accuse him of actually participating in its incoherence. Then why bother with the passage? Because it serves to disclose issues near the heart of modern philosophy, that is, in the period from Descartes to Kant and beyond, even to this century. That such an occlusion of finitude, with the concomitant occlusion of Being and transcendence, did occur, together, especially in the latter part of the period mentioned, with some absolutisation or idolisation of the finite, can be shown by an attentive study of the period, and will soon be obvious once we know what to look for.

Descartes is the first to set himself the hopeless task – as both Kant and Hume saw – of proving that ideas, which replace appearance in his thought, can, and need to, be validated as presentations of the real. This is at one with his tendency to absolutise the self as that which needs nothing other than itself – though slightly diluted by a reference to the Divine – both to know and to be. Even were there no external world, for Descartes, our ideas would be veracious, and represent, not just how things happen to be, but how they must be, even though they require to be vindicated as actual presentations, and to be aligned with a reality which can thus never appear in itself, and which transcendence can never reach.

Kant is the philosopher who takes the scission between object and eject as foundation of his thought; in doing away with any real finitude in favour of the synthetic activity of reason in imposing its inherent order on phenomena, he thereby also renders transcendence neither possible nor necessary. But this scission is retained by Kant precisely as scission, as polarity, which is resolved by others in favour of object, so that object comes to be coterminous with all that is, and that greater self from which it is inseparable finally attains a kind of godhood, a non-finitude, to which any transcendence is alien. All this may be contrasted with the previous epoch in which as we have noted the finitude is secured in and as the translation of the real into the conceptual, on the basis of the transcendence proper to intellect, especially as *intellectus agens*.

10, 7 Transcendence, Freedom, and Truth

Transcendence is the true meaning of Being-in-the-world, since this implies a being not merely present in the world but one for whom the world is. Transcendence can only be as finite, as open to the encounter, in disclosure, of that which is independently, on pain of the annulation of transcendence and the concomitant occlusion of finitude. This is what we have so far discovered. However, there is another element required by transcendence as necessary condition. This element is freedom. To say that there is something for which to be is to transcend is to say that there is something whose being is freedom. What are we to make of this?

That whose nature it is to transcend is a being among others as well as a being open to others. To be a being which is as open to others is to have a capacity to allow others to appear, and thereby to be as oriented to such appearance. Its being open to others shapes it as the being it is. In this way there is a subordination of its being among others to its being open to others, in that its being open to others uses its being among others to be open, and this in various ways. This subordination is use, and use bespeaks dependence, in that if something requires to use another in order to be, it cannot be unless it uses that other. Freedom is coterminous with this use both as a freedom for, and a freedom from, in such a way that freedom for is only possible as a freedom from. If that which is required in use were to obtrude itself, that is, if it were to act merely as itself, distinctly from the requirements of the user, and not in subordination to the user's activity, this would represent a breakdown of the user's proper activity. On the other hand, the actuality of the activity presupposes that such disintegration does not occur. That which acts acts *qua* that which it is, not *qua* that which it uses, even if the activity proper to that user is impossible without that proper to the used. Thus the activity of that which is used must not dictate or determine the activity of the user, and insofar as it does, the user has ceased to act. This is freedom from, in that the proper activity of the user is not determined by that proper to the used.

Applying this to the present case, those factors involved in something's mere being among others cannot determine it either as being open to others or how it is actually open in this or that particular instance: its being open is incompatible with its being determined as open by anything whose being does not include such openness, in such a way that being so determined is the disruption of being open. This argument will be applicable also to those factors proper to being with others; in any such argument as this, it is the discernment of what is the proper activity of what that is crucial in deciding what acts, and what therefore is subordinate to what, and what is therefore free from something, precisely as not being determined by it. In this way transcendence is, precisely, a transcendence of such determinations, and is incarnate as determining and formal principle whereby its hegemony is established over that of whose proper activity it makes use and unites in one.

We find this subordination well expressed in the same Heideggerian passage:

> If human intuition as finite is receptive and if the possibility of its receiving something 'given' presupposes affection, then organs capable of being affected – the organs of 'sense' – are necessary. Human intuition, therefore, is not 'sensible' because its affection takes place through 'sense' organs. Rather, the converse is true: it is because our Dasein is finite – existing in the midst of the essent which already is and to which our Dasein is abandoned – that it must of necessity receive the essent, that is, offer it the possibility of giving notice of itself. These organs are necessary in order that the notification be able to get through.[12]

Not only organs of sense but the entire entity is shaped and structured by its transcendence which stretches down to its every part.

But in what sense is freedom from also freedom for? It is important
to realise that precisely as transcending the items necessary to its
incarnation, that is, though employing their proper activity in subordination to its own distinct activity, which it, and not they in isolation, can exercise, thereby freeing itself from determination by
them, transcendence opens itself toward a Being which is itself definite and precise. In short, being free from, is possible only as being
free for, in that freedom from is not a mere blank, but is as actuality
of transcendence, capacity for all relation possible for this kind of
being, as a being for Being. In this way, the fundamental actuality
whereby this kind of being is, gives it an intrinsic and necessary orientation towards any and all revelation of which this kind of being
is capable.

But this seems a poor notion of freedom, at least at first sight, for
missing from it are those elements which make of freedom something of value, namely responsibility and choice. Are such elements
present in this fundamental notion of freedom, or is the freedom
here in question merely that of the clearing in which light has free
play?

10, 8 Freedom as Moral

The answer to this question is, yes, responsibility and choice are
and must be elements of the freedom which is inseparable from
transcendence. But, that they should be requires that transcendence
be active. We have seen that the hallmark of the finitude in which
transcendence is rooted is receptivity and hence passivity. This
receptivity is a structural feature which, as inseparable from transcendence, sculpts, as final cause, the parts of the entity whose
being is to transcend. This receptivity and passivity is present,
therefore, as determinative feature in those organs which incarnate
transcendence: if my eye is healthy and the environment appropriately disposed, I cannot but see, though I can close my eyes or look
away. Even this refusal is not an option for hearing. And so on with
the other senses and faculties in and as which transcendence is
incarnate. But, if we were to concentrate on this passivity, we
would neglect something to which transcendence equally gives
rise. The transcendence which we are is not the ability to retain
sound and colour such as is to be found in tape-recorders and cam-
eras.

This active element of transcendence, to be sure, does not annul passivity, which is inescapably part of finitude, but occurs, as it were, in the context provided by that finitude. Responsibility and choice are those very factors which constitute the activity of transcendence, and are themselves closely interwoven. To say that Mount Vesuvius was responsible for the destruction of Pompeii is quite a different assertion from that which accuses Peter of being responsible for the death of John. Of course, Peter is responsible in the way that Vesuvius was, but we usually intend more than this. When we say that Peter is responsible for the death of John we usually mean that Peter chose to bring about the death of John *and* that he might have chosen otherwise. This means, further, that Peter chose to act in a way which he knew would bring about John's death. If he either lacked or was not capable of such knowledge, or was incapable of acting in any other way, then he was not responsible in this sense. Such lack of knowledge is not simple, and must not be characterisable at least as a lack of knowledge which he should have had, and might have been expected to have. We call responsible action deliberate, though this does not exclude its being spontaneous. Vesuvius is not responsible in this sense because it is incapable of knowing what, or of doing other than, it does.

In sum, the essence of responsibility is the ability to know what one does and to be capable of choosing to do other than one does. For freedom for revelation to be more than that of the clearing, that is, for it to qualify as moral freedom, it is necessary that these features belong to it. Is this, in reality, the case?

Being able to choose to do other than one does is distinct from merely being able to do other than one does. Vesuvius might well have stayed dormant, and so was capable of behaving other than it did. That it erupted is not to be attributed to Vesuvius as such but to those efficient causes which actualised the situation of its erupting, and which we aim at when we try to explain why it erupted. Thus such an explanation removes Vesuvius from the explanatory picture except as locus in which such causal factors operated: Vesuvius is necessary for, but not sufficient to explain, its own eruption. No element of the explanation is the proper action of Vesuvius as such, except insofar as it was a set of items receptive to their influence, something they could dispose in various ways, so that their happening to coincide in Vesuvius is accidental to them.

None of this is true in the case of actions or behaviour which are chosen. When someone chooses to do or to behave in some way, that someone is a distinct and irreducible element in the explanation, otherwise the action is, like the eruption of Vesuvius, properly attributable to some other causal factors. Thus in the case of the chosen action, the action is the proper activity of the one who chooses, who is thus not a mere locus for the operation of quite other factors. This someone is therefore not only necessary but sufficient in any explanation of what they do, and any explanation of their activity must address them as necessary and sufficient source of that action. Other items may well be necessary, namely those conditions which are inseparable from their choosing and on which they rely in choosing, but none of these factors is sufficient, either alone or in concert without the agent, to explain the agent's action. It is necessary that certain social, psychological, and physical conditions be fulfilled, that a person may act, but either such fulfilment is insufficient to explain the act or it is coterminous with the occurrence of the act, otherwise it is these factors which act through the agent, much as geological factors acted through Vesuvius, and are the true agents of the act. The presence of the agent as necessary and sufficient explanation of the act means that there is something attributable of necessity to the agent as such, and to nothing else as such, and that any such something else acts in subordination to the agent, as used and relied on, by the agent.

'Why did Jane do so and so? Because she decided she wanted ... and she thought that by doing so and so she would ... ' are the irreducible terms of the explanation of any behaviour of which Jane is the proper agent; conversely, any behaviour which is properly attributable to, say, an electro-chemical event in Jane's brain is in fact a description of Jane's having an epileptic seizure, or some such event. That this is so is not contradicted by the fact that, for the story told in such an explanation to be true, Jane must rely on her brain's being capable of coming up with the appropriate electro-chemical exchanges. Any irruption of these factors into behaviour is a disruption of free agency. The same goes, *mutatis mutandis*, for any other such necessary condition.

Thus the peculiar property of free agency is that the agent be that for whom disclosure is a possibility; something for whom disclosure is not a possibility is not the sort of entity which can be said to choose. To choose is to know that a plurality of behaviours is possible for oneself, and what doing each one, and doing one rather than another, involves. It means knowing that I am not obliged to do either x or y. This in turn means knowing that it is I who can do or can refrain from doing, and that I am, minimally, the one who can act or refrain. This is what it means, at least, to be self-conscious, and such minimal self-consciousness is required if it makes sense to say that my action is free. If such awareness is missing, then either I do not know what it is for me to be able to do x or to be able to refrain from doing it.

But is such freedom necessarily implied by disclosure? Is disclosure possible without it? Disclosure is always relational: it is of something to or for someone, i.e. to or for something properly capable of receiving the disclosure. But, for something to be disclosed is for that which it is, in whatever way that it is, to be disclosed. Thus, for something, say x, to be disclosed, is for that which x is to be present to that which is capable of receiving it. But the presence of that which x is, and the presence of x itself, are distinct, and are judged according to different criteria. For x itself to be present in the way that it is, to or for y is one thing, but for that which x is to be so present is for y to know what x is, and thus to know what it is for x to be this, and that x in fact, is this. But, for y to know all that is for y to be able to say what x is: the knowledge of what it is for x to be so and so, as opposed to the presence of x itself is, or depends on, the use of language. Thus for y to be properly capable of receiving the disclosure of x is for y to be linguistic, and the fundamental meaning of language is to be a register of disclosure, namely to be the medium wherein and whereby the disclosure of what it is for something to be something comes to be and is.

As a corollary one might add that for y to know what it is for something to be something, and to know that x actually is this, are distinct. The former corresponds to a concept or predicate, the latter to its application, in and through judgemental or assertive utterance. If the two were not distinct, then to have the concept would be to know its application, and though ignorance would still be possible, error would not. Thus the distinction means that it is possible to be in error, and that if language is register of disclosure, it is, by the same token, the medium in which that which is not, can come to be. But to succeed in applying a concept – to utter true judgements – is to be capable of saying that predicates are not to be applied in a given case or area. Thus the distinction requires the possibility of denial: to be able to apply the concept means being able to judge also that and when it is *not* applicable. Of course, one can only do this if they know both what it is for a predicate to be applicable or not, and what it is for them to judge rightly and wrongly.

But if this is so, then being able to judge that predicates are applicable or not is itself a free act in the sense we have outlined, in that it involves doing something, knowing what one is doing, and knowing that one might be doing otherwise. In sum, then, if something is properly capable of receiving disclosure, then it is necessarily linguistic, and if linguistic then free in the moral sense. Thus it is the case that disclosure is only possible to that which is free in the moral sense, and openness for disclosure is not merely the freedom proper to the clearing. We might say that, in fact, the freedom of the clearing is the freedom proper to the medium and register of disclosure, namely language, but that a higher freedom, moral freedom, is proper to those who inhabit the clearing, precisely insofar as they inhabit it; or, to use the, perhaps more apt, Wittgensteinian metaphor, disclosure in the freedom proper to the game itself, but moral freedom is the necessary feature of those who make the game real by playing it.

We may add that, if this argument is correct, then there we encounter a necessary and intrinsic connection between the true and the good, in that the latter means what is worthy of choice, and our relation to the true necessarily involves choice. Let us now explore this connection.

10, 9 Value and Community

If it is necessary that moral freedom – responsibility – permeates transcendence-finitude, then this raises another important issue: that which determines such freedom is value. Freedom of whatever sort is not determined by the causality of what it uses, but encounters what determines it freely. It is Being as true which presents itself as a horizon within which and towards which transcendence emerges. The determination exercised is free correspondence to that to which one ought to correspond. Though the healthy eye must see and the healthy ear hear, a gap opens between what is disclosed and what is not yet disclosed, and can only be bridged by the engagement of freedom for and in truth, which, as value, presents itself as goal and fulfilment, that is, as what ought to be attained, but can, at the same time, be freely rejected or distorted, under the behest of other things which appear desirable. Truth can not be avoided, but it can be postponed. This primacy and ultimate ineluctability, yet postponability, of truth defines the contour of transcendence. Finite freedom is transcendence as a free stretching-out towards its completion in Being as true. This is no mere relation of one thing to another, but the realisation, free and progressive, of the illuminatedness of Being. This is the fundamental contour of transcendence within which all other transcendentals are rooted.

If all this is so, then other words of Heidegger in the same passage from the Kant book, to which we have already referred, take on added resonance.

> Now, if finite intuition is to be knowledge, it must be able to make the essent itself, insofar as it is manifest, accessible with respect to how and what it is to everyone and at any time. Finite beings capable of intuition must be able to agree in the actual intuition of the essent ... that which is intuited becomes an object of knowledge only if everyone can make it intelligible to himself and to others and in that way communicate it. So, for example, this intuited particular, this piece of chalk, must admit of being determined as chalk or as a body in order that we may be able jointly to know this essent itself as the same for each of us.[13]

There are several vital issues raised in this seemingly innocuous passage. In the first place, there is an insistence upon the agreement of intuition: the essent itself must be accessible with respect to how and what it is to everyone and at any time. It is precisely because each does not grasp his or her own object that their knowledge is finite, and that they inhabit Heraclitus's common wakeful world. Many can and must agree in one, namely, in the essent itself as common object of attention, as that which is revealed. It is not being able to offer this guarantee that plunges much modern thought into absurdity, for if there is no sense in maintaining a scission between what is and what appears, there is less sense, and as much real possibility, in maintaining that the privately owned datum can also be somehow shared. The guarantee of genuineness, that what is intuited is object of knowledge, is precisely that everyone can make 'what is' intelligible to him- or her-self, and to others: understanding is coterminous with the possibility of communication, as sharing what is thus disclosed. In this way, there is a necessary connection between the axes 'to oneself' and 'to others', of the formulation we have just posited, namely that knowledge, or better, knowing, being in the truth, is genuine insofar as one can make 'what is' intelligible to oneself and to others. Being able to 'make 'what is' intelligible to oneself and to others' is equivalent to 'being able to talk about it', and we cannot deny the necessary connection between the two axes therefore, without both doing violence to language as shared, and reintroducing the solipsistic, inwardly gazing, and therefore non-linguistic, Cartesian self.

Language is capable of disclosing the world, roughly, because of the disclosure registered in its logical and conceptual structure which actually becomes truth in propositional combination, arising out of the judgemental activities of speakers who are, equally and necessarily, moral subjects, and who are therefore morally obliged to be conscientious knowers. To be engaged in language is firstly already to inhabit a finite, and therefore temporal and historical clearing, which, as such, is beyond me, and so is the ineluctable given which I need to deploy in order to be able to understand any-thing, including myself. To be engaged in language is secondly, and consequently, to have contingently true propositions available which I did not originate, but which I, as linguistic, am capable of understanding, otherwise communication would be impossible. For language to be real there must be a community of users who can tell the truth about what is, including themselves and each other. In other words, the place of language is world, as the plurality of entit-ies, some of which transcend. One might add as a rider that if these two theses are correct, there is a priority between the two axes: one can only make what is, including oneself, intelligible to oneself, on condition that one can make it intelligible to others, in principle.

In sum: this mutual implication of understanding and communica-bility, is the guarantee of the genuineness of the disclosure, namely that what is disclosed is there and is common, inasmuch as no understanding, shared or otherwise, is possible in its absence; and for there to be any knowledge, any truth, there must be a plurality of mutually correcting, supplementing and completing knowers.

The passage thus makes visible this necessary feature of truth and of finitude, namely, the irreducible plurality of speakers who are of necessity present together in a common world. Thinking and judg-ing are not private activities to which communication and expres-sion are contingent and accidental additions. Here we discover a dialectical interlocking of the one and the many, apparent opposites which nonetheless cannot be conceived in isolation from one another. Thinking and judging are possible only within the plural context, so that the issue of language, and hence of truth and thought, is to be approached from the reality of this plural context, not by way of an autonomously conceived, sufficient individual, who, in and of itself, has all that it needs to be and to know. Nonetheless, language is instrument not agent, and the burden of the obligation imposed by truth falls on individuals who alone are free, who alone can act. There must be, if this is to be true, an orientation in each which is not yet actual utterance, but which prepares for, and makes this latter possible, an orientation, coterminous with the being of each, which opens each to all and all to each, a being-with-others which therefore cannot be either the distal pole of 'my' isolated projection, or the particularisation of some 'universal'. In short, we are moral subjects, but not mere subjects; we are many, though not as parts of a whole: to be all this is to be an inter-subject.

10, 10 Inter-subjectivity, Community, and Language

The notion of 'inter-subject' is a quasi-dialectical one, holding in one perspective, as it does, elements whose diversity would appear irreconcilable. To be a (moral) subject is to be autonomous, that is, responsible and irreducible source of action; indeed, the notion 'moral subject' is pleonastic, for to be a subject is to be moral, for the freedom which belongs to being a subject confers the responsibility for action and irreducibility to anything beyond it. But to call such a subject an inter-subject is to recognise its insufficiency, an insufficiency which is coterminous with its being, and which expresses itself in and as its need for others like itself, its need to belong to a community, its being, from its roots, an intrinsically linguistic, and hence, dialogical, entity.

It is impossible that there be any such thing as a private language, for it is impossible alone, or once only, to follow a rule. We can and indeed must, join to this Wittgensteinian insight Heidegger's new beginning in philosophy, equivalent to what he calls the *Kehre*, which is the totality of those items whose fundamental moment is the linguistic manifestation of world and inauguration of history in the clearing of an essentially plural *Dasein*. The *Kehre* is a way of thinking which offers the plurality, the community, as ultimate given, a community not of self-sufficient singulars, but of entities who are of necessity conjoined in a community, and who participate in world and history only within it. Despite the genuinely negative aspects which act as a brake on their nascent insights, both Heidegger and Wittgenstein, each in his own way, mediate this essentially pluralist view of truth. Truth is only possible in and through participation in the community, and is proper to the community as such, though the finding of truth is still the responsibility of individual moral agents.

Something which is logically private cannot function as a meaning, which is essentially shared. Predicates do not 'stand for' Aristotle's παθήματα τῆς ψυχῆς,[14] or for Cartesian ideas. I do not learn the meanings of words by private ostensive definition, and then manage to coordinate 'my' meanings with the equally private meanings of others, in virtue of some magical guarantee that the two coincide. This would be like saying that there are many solitaire players, each of whom, though cut off from all the others, can and must know that there are others, that they are all following the same rules with identical decks of cards, and that sometimes, indeed often, they make moves which correspond in mutually supportive ways.

In learning to talk, I am the client of the plurality, without which I have no access to truth. Learning to talk is learning to operate the grammar of predicates and other logical entities in the context of the language-game, their controlling instance. Meaning *is* the deployment of revealedness contained in the canons of the language-game; but we must be alive here to the contribution of the player. There can be no players without games, but neither can there be games without players. We must, in any such account, beware of turning the game into a kind of ritual, a prescribed and unvarying set of antiphons and responses, both verbal and behavioural. The rules are deployed by the player, on whom the burden of creativity rests: it is not possible to predict, say, the Sonnets of Shakespeare from the grammatical facts of Elizabethan English, though it remains true that each line and sentence can be analysed fully and adequately, in terms of that grammar. The game empowers the player, but the player's moves are his or her own.

Continuing this line of thought, it is apparent that being-linguistic and being-ethical dovetail. I cannot be truly moral alone; I can be ethical only in the face of a real other, who makes genuine claims on me and to whom I respond in word and action. Likewise, I cannot be linguistic alone; I can only be linguistic in the presence of a real other, who addresses me and to whom I respond in word and action. This structural analogy of the two moments is determined by and as my being with others in the world. There is no being in the world without being with others, or I am sufficient unto myself to know and to be; but if this is so, then, there is no being with others which is not coevally ethical and linguistic. Thus, truth appears only in and for ethico-linguistic being, which is the proper meaning, I suggest, of *Dasein*, and of the triad, freedom, finitude, and transcendence.

Finitude makes itself felt too, and in more than one way. 'Others' may appear, though not as my projections, nevertheless as a kind of average presence alongside me. My ineluctably ethico-linguistic being is that very orientation we referred to above, which is present in each, which is not yet actual utterance, but which prepares for, and makes it possible, my being-with-others, or the being-with-one-another which underlies the essential plurality of those who are capable of truth. But the real other is as other, part of the world too, and is independently of me and of all those structures which I require in order to be. As such the other is undisclosed. Yet, as real inter-subject, this other is capable of becoming a co-subject. I can come face-to-face with this other, in the mutuality of a 'we', with him or her. In such a mutuality I can offer or withhold disclosure and receive whatever disclosure is offered, as it is offered, or with-held, insofar as it is withheld. This is possible only if each recognises, accepts and respects the sovereignty of the other as free, as undis-closed though capable of self- and receptive of other-disclosure, as well as the uniqueness which underlies being undisclosed: in the encounter with the other, there is always something new, which previous disclosure may prepare us for but never predict. This is the way of being towards one another which is carried by, and car-ries, the 'thou', and its process and occurrence is friendship.

As Heidegger pointed out, everything is either a who or a what, so that there can be 'I-' or better, 'we-it' relations, where that which is disclosed is disclosed to us or to me as it. But, present in the 'we' of community to which alone revelation can occur, is the possibility of the mutuality of 'I-thou', and growing out of that, the creative occurrence, celebratory of difference and union, of friendship, and all that accompanies it, such as respect, the recognition of worth, loyalty, fidelity, and tolerance. A poignancy is also granted in that this is a possibility contingent on chance and the good will of the partners, who can, as ethical, refuse it, and is not at all the automatic culmination of an ineluctable train of factors. However, knowledge, whether of whom or of what, is made possible only by a letting be, by a respect for what is as it is on the part of the knower. It is pre-cisely this which makes another structural analogy, namely between friendship and knowledge, such that friendship is a know-ing, and knowledge, it is not too far-fetched to say, is a kind of friendship.

Another moment in which finitude makes itself felt is in the diversity of language games. Just as most others will not enter the intimacy of friendship with me, and remain known only as, as it were, abstracts or generalisations, even so, for the same reason I do not participate in language or meaning or the whole οἰκουμένη of speakers directly, but proximally only to *this* finite meaning, with *these* definite others in *this* particular group, that is, in this particular language-game. Truth is always refracted through the prism of the many language-games. This makes it necessary to make a very un-Wittgensteinian point, namely, that just as there must be a plurality of mutually correcting, supplementing and completing knowers, the plurality of finite games must stand in the same relation to one another, otherwise we will be forced to maintain that there is some game which is sacrosanct, and therefore, because it is incapable of correction and supplement, complete and perfect in itself. It could be argued that this is precisely what Wittgenstein does say. But, if our analysis here is correct, the business of the game, as of all language, is to mediate meaning and hence truth, and no finite mediation of these is complete or free from error. Thus, not only will the opportunity and necessity of the interplay of games in relation to one another be offered, but in a viable and veridical game, the various possibilities of overcoming its limitations will also be offered, variously in the many games, in and by an understanding of the rules which govern it, an understanding inseparable from that which allows us to use them in playing it. Otherwise, we could never come to know that or how a given game is deficient, or we would be forced to say that games are not truth-bearing, mediating an understanding of *the* world, as opposed to being blind fictions, meaningless rituals. One might add that games are, in fact, such rituals, thereby recognising that the term 'game' is analogical and misleading if taken literally.

In sum, we might say that finitude always imposes temporality; not simply in the sense that finite things are temporal, but also in the sense that our transcending finitude is a process which can only occur in time, and the process as communal, wrought proximally as the overcoming of extant language-games as the exploration of possible meaning, is history.

We come now to the final citation we shall make from the Heideggerian passage:

> The understanding, in turn, is not only involved in the finitude of intuition, it is itself even more finite inasmuch as it lacks the immediacy of finite intuition. Its mode of representation is indirect; it requires a reference to something general by means of which, and according to which, the several particulars become

capable of being represented conceptually. This detour (discursiveness), which is essential to the understanding, is the clearest index of its finitude.[15]

Divine intuition is coterminous with creativity. The notion of 'intuition' bespeaks the immediate grasp of something. I can intuit green, though knowing that the grass is green, and even the concept 'what it is to be green', i.e., the grammar of the predicate 'x is green', presents more difficulties. We require language in order that that which something is be manifest, but language does not work intuitionally but discursively. I can point out a green object to one capable of colour vision, and who understands the language-game 'pointing', but, who does not know, for some reason, what to call the grass's colour. To get the concept he must be capable of understanding its use. But the predicate itself is neither a name nor an index. As predicate, it must be capable of application to many. Thus its mode of representation is indirect. More precisely, as something applicable to many, it is therefore perfectly adequate to none, but it is still that whereby and according to which, the several particulars become capable of being represented as what they are, that is, conceptually. The mystery of each thing resides not in any vagueness, for anything which is is definite, but in its particularity and uniqueness. No predicate, as universal, can exactly fit what it reveals. Revelation is therefore incomplete and partial. Descriptions, ever tighter tailorings wrought in ever longer and more nuanced predicate-strings, are required.

In this way, we encounter the finitude proper to language as register of disclosure. Finitude shapes the falling-short which is transcendence. We have seen that I am not a subject but an inter-subject, and what this in detail means: that I am not sufficient for myself to be or to know; that I thus cannot be or know alone, except contingently; that I variously require others as individuals and in community, and the linguistic web which binds the community in order to know; that my participation in community is mediate, via the actual games we play; that these are, proportionally, finite, partial and mutually correcting. All of this is the falling-short which belongs to transcendence as finite. But this finitude is emblematically present *as* language. Language is as falling-short of the real, as finite, and this finitude is the moment intended by all other moments of finitude which belong to transcendence, and contains them virtually. The essence of finitude which transcends is language, the partial and conceptual presentation of the real.

10, 11 Divinity, Intelligibility, and Human Vocation

This, then, is our discussion of truth and its regions, a discussion which has led us to discover the foundation of truth in transcendence which is coevally finitude and freedom. As we have grasped it, transcendence is at once outward movement towards Being, which, as disclosed, is truth, and, inseparably, finitude, which ineluctably requires the inward movement of what is disclosed to that which can only transcend as being-affected. In short, transcendence is simultaneously movement out and in. Our perspective so far has been from the inner towards the outer, though with Heidegger's help we have not simply ignored being-affected. But on this basis it is both possible and necessary to accomplish a kind of *Gestalt*-switch. This is not to introduce new lines into our drawing, but to change our interpretation of the whole, and to see this whole in a new way, so that a new dimension of significance is revealed. To do this is to take the *inward* movement as dominant, and so not to see transcendence simply as one area superimposed on another, certainly larger, and perhaps unlimited, never wholly covered by the smaller, however this may stretch itself outward to cover ever more; this would be to see the movement from the perspective of that which is outside, as moving in.

This leads at once to a whole nexus of problems which most modern philosophers, and even Heidegger himself, seem unwilling to discuss. The picture thus arrived at is not that there is a progressive and inevitable absorption by transcendence of all Being, but that all that is, insofar as it is, is capable of being disclosed in and for transcendence, unless there is a necessary limit to the extent of transcendence. To say this is to take the principle of the coextensiveness of Being and truth seriously. Thus, all that is stands at least potentially in the light of actual disclosure. That something is capable of being disclosed is the case either necessarily or contingently. If things are so contingently, then they are so on some other basis than their existence. But if things are disclosed on some other basis than their existence, they are not disclosed insofar as they are, and so are not disclosed: the disclosure of something means the disclosure of it as and how it is, insofar as it is disclosed. This, then is the final and fundamental meaning of the equiparation of Being and truth, which emerges as a necessary truth. Things cannot be disclosed contingently, and so are disclosed necessarily. But this means that existence as such is the principle of being-disclosed: existence is not just a necessary feature for something's disclosure, but also a sufficient one, a conclusion we have anticipated many times here and in other parts of our study. This is to say that things are intelligible insofar as they are, that, insofar as they are, they are intrinsically oriented to disclosure, and are, insofar as they are, transparent for the light of transcendence. Thus all failure of disclosure is either merely contingent or a not-yet disclosure. Things, insofar as they are, yield themselves to transcendence, much as things in darkness are seeable without being actually seen. It is sufficient for light to fall on them, other things being equal, for this to come about, and were this not the case, the light which shines on them could not render them actually visible.

But this, in turn, would mean that all that is, insofar as it is, looks towards transcendence for disclosure, in virtue of *esse*. The inward movement towards transcendence genuinely belongs to what is, as well as to transcendence, otherwise transcendence gives itself its own object and is able to create intelligibility insofar as it knows, and since intelligibility is inseparable from Being, it would follow that transcendence originates Being. Though transcendence cannot give itself its own object, the inward movement towards it is an ontological feature of everything, as open for disclosure.

This is perhaps a surprising conclusion, for then there is something in what is which goes unactualised without transcendence. All that is requires transcendence in order to be as true, an actuality prepared for and anticipated in the ontological structure of all that is. Thus, the seemingly tiny area of light which is transcendence is no stranger to the vast darkness which surrounds it, which thereby turns out to be a friendly darkness. In some sense, all that is anticipates transcendence as the phase of what is in which what is gains actual (finite) disclosure, disclosure, that is, of, in and by, finitude. But how is any such thing possible?

Transcendence is that phase of finite being by virtue of whose existence all finite existence is lit up from within, and is thereby anticipated in the ontological structure of all that is. Are we reduced to saying that the being of transcendence is not merely contingent, or that evolution is guided, or that a version of the argument from design to the existence of – what, a demiurge? – is after all warranted, like the argument to the effect that, because the factors in the beginning of the universe which allow the emergence of observers like us are so unlikely, and because the slightest deviation from what they actually are would so easily have produced another result, those factors are evidence of deliberation in the production of such observers? Is there a kind of 'anthropic principle'[16] at work here?

It is precisely of this question – how is such an intrinsic orientation of Being to knowing to be explained? – that modern thinkers fight shy. One could interpret the transcendental philosophy as an attempt to work out the implications of this not being so, yet without sacrificing our commonsense belief that we live in a world, an ordered whole of objects and events, while Hume's philosophy seems to be a flat denial of it. Something like this denial seems to lurk at the heart of Heidegger's interpretation of understanding in terms of projection.[17]

We shall not attempt to discuss here any such anthropic principle nor to rehabilitate a version of the argument from design. Yet, the assertion that there is such an inherent ontological orientation is equivalent to realism, and we suggest that the choices here are limited: either realism or scepticism is correct, and scepticism cannot be stated coherently. So, astounding as it may seem, and though it may be disheartening to the kind of thinker who likes to confine the scope of principles within certain well-defined parameters, we are forced to accept this strange and risky idea: Being as such is intelligible, and stands potentially open in all its vastness before us. This is not to deny finitude; intelligibility is not the same as being actually understood, and ignorance and error are unavoidable. But it does mean that the necessary and intrinsic limit to the extent of transcendence is the real itself. Finitude and transcendence are thus dialectically linked: the real is what is ever more nearly approached in knowing: its endless approachability is its intelligibility to our finitude, the finitude which is inseparable from transcendence as approach.

Two final points emerge from these considerations, themselves inextricably linked, namely, the effect of all this on our articulation of the human vocation, and the relation of transcendence, especially towards truth, and the Divine. Probably the second is 'easier' than the first, because it would seem that any attempt to articulate the specifically human vocation in general must take in far more areas of human knowledge and activity than the merely philosophical. From one point of view, religion is nothing other than just such an articulation. Moreover, in speaking of any such vocation, we must accept that it is realised in as many diverse ways as there are individual persons, even though what is common to all is their vocation's dovetailing with their being created; to be called is ultimately to be called into Being. And even were we able to know the details of each human life, we might still remain in ignorance of its vocation, coterminous with its creation, since it does not follow that, though creation is a vocation, it is one which is disclosed in the slightest, even to the one who is called. But that there is such a personal vocation for each is as true as that each, insofar as he or she is, is created.

In regard to Divinity, then: hiddenness and unhiddenness belong to it. Some apophatic theologians opine that what is darkness to us is so only because of our finitude, and that such darkness is truly an unapproachable light. This certainly must be the case in and for the Godhead, which from this perspective must be the uninterrupted, unsurpassable self-presence of Being with and for Being, whose finite analogy is the intelligibility of all in and for transcendence. For it would be absurd to suppose that Divine self-knowledge could be in any way capable of improvement: imperfection or 'getting to know' are ruled out. Likewise, an unconscious God seems absurd in the face of the reality of freedom, of which Divinity must be the unsurpassable instantiation. The connectedness of being, awareness and bliss is not contingent in and for Divinity.

From this vantage-point alone, the explanation of the intrinsic openness of Being in and for transcendence is to be found. If God is *ipsum Esse per se subsistens*, then the finite cannot but instantiate in its contingent way those features – the transcendentals – which belong to Being as such: in this way the finite cannot but be a contingent analogy of the necessary. Thus, if luminous self-presence is in God, and there can be no contingent truths about Divinity, it follows that the self-presence of Being for Being must characterise *analogice* created reality. But God still might have created nothing, or a world which lacked beings like us. A world which must be intelligible to finite knowers though there are actually none in it may appear odder than one in which they exist; but in the world we actually have there are many things and events which, though intelligible, never happen to be known. Thus, in looking up we find some justification for what we know, namely that there is a phase of finite being in which all Being becomes luminous. Looking down, however, can give no clear and unambiguous final explanation of what we know. Evolution, like any other scientific theory, explains in giving patterns how, not reasons why, nor does it make what it explains necessary: what is contingently comes to be, and perishes contingently. Nor is this to say that evolution is guided, or guided from within. It is not that God plays or does not play dice, nor does Divinity require contrivance – even the 'laws' of evolution – in order to create. All the scientist can tell us is that the pattern whereby things happen, whereby what is contingently comes contingently to be, is such that it is capable of producing such (contingent) entities as we are.

This does not get us very far. The world is closed and independent along the line of essence, and nothing other than finite factors need be encoded in our articulation of the essential pattern; it is only through existence, as really distinct from essence, that the relation to the Divine is manifest. The pattern does not explain existence as such but rather how it is that all things in the world are mutually related. There is a gap between what is below and what is above, but this gap is not to be bridged by positing a 'god' who rigs the game, or needs to. The pattern is capable of producing us – we come contingently to be from that which is contingently – but why does it actually produce us? The answer is neither because it had to nor because 'God' interfered with it, but it does seem to lie in that upper air where God dwells, sharing by creation traits which belong of necessity to (Divine) Being. This could count as an explanation of why the pattern of relation is capable of producing us. But why does it actually do so? Because of the way in which contingent entities instantiate it. Then, that this result is desirable – as making the world more perfect – is explicable in terms of what we can know of the Divine.

But the Divine as such is and remains hidden from us, and that it does exist is knowable only from the contingency of the world. God is truth, disclosedness, but only properly for God. Yet, that God is is the ultimate context of all other truth and meaning, the pole at which all other truth points, precisely as vindication and fulfilment of that meaning, which for us, and as finite, is interrupted and postponed, for meaning is merely the way in which the transcendentals are instantiated in human thought and practice. It is at this point that we may speak of the meaning of the human vocation in general. Transcendence mediates between finitude and Divinity. Transcendence is for Being in more than one sense: 'for' as 'towards' and as 'on behalf of'. As open to Being, transcendence is open to Divinity as Being, and to Being as 'Thou'; but transcendence is the phase of Being in which finitude becomes limitedly self-present and lit from within. Transcendence thus has a sacerdotal role, but the precise nature of this priestliness escapes us. That this is so is an issue present in the heart of the three great monotheistic faiths. In Christianity we are told that we are to become partakers of the Divine nature,[18] which is the ultimate realisation of the relation whereby God is 'Thou' for us, and, at the same time, that this adoption of us by God has resonations throughout all creation,[19] which awaits the coming of the children of God with eager longing, for without them it is, of itself, subjected to futility. This, however, is a religious vision which goes far beyond the mere mediation we have suggested, towards a Παρουσία in which the world is once again made whole.

Notes to Chapter Ten

1. LT Part 2, subsections 21 and 24 - 25.

2. LT Part 1, chapter 5.

3. The passage is the myth of Prometheus, the identification is to be found at *Protagoras* 320 d. See also LT Part 1, subsection 2.

4. See Gadamer, *Wahrheit und Methode*, (Tübingen: Mohr, 1972), Zweiter Teil, II, 3, c, beta: 'Die Logik von Frage und Antwort.'

5. *Kant and the Problem of Metaphysics*, translated by James S. Churchill. Foreword by Thomas Langan, (Bloomington: Indiana University Press, 1972), pp. 30-31.

6. *ibid.*, pp. 35-36.

7. *ibid.*, p. 36.

8. *ibid.*, p. 37.

9. *ibid.*, p. 36.

10. *ibid.*, p. 37.

11. *ibid.*, p. 38.

12. *ibid.*, p. 31.

13. *ibid.*, p. 32.

14. *De Interpretatione* 16 a 3.

15. Heidegger, *op. cit.*, p. 34.

16. See Roger Penrose, *The Emperor's New Mind*, (Oxford: OUP, 1989), pp. 433 -434, for the anthropic principle. But, see also, Daniel C. Dennett's treatment of it in *Darwin's Dangerous Idea. Evolution and the Meanings of Life*, (London: Penguin, 1995), pp. 165-166, and chapter 15 of the same work for a general criticism of Penrose.

17. For the latter, see LT Part 1, subsection 23.

18. II Peter, 1, 4.

19. Romans, 8, 19-23.

CHAPTER ELEVEN

The Good

11, 1 Introduction

We come in this chapter to discuss that transcendental property of
Being called the good. The explicit emergence of the good takes
place within the area occupied by truth, and we have already
remarked the internal relatedness of truth and goodness, in such a
way that there can be no truth without the good. Clearly and explicitly here, then, the good emerges, as we have anticipated, as foundation of truth. Truth may well be the 'nearest' transcendental in the
context of ontological discussion, but it is to be located as subordinate to the good, as a kind of good; yet the good, for its part, would
be inconceivable without the disclosure which is truth. This means
that while the transcendentals are convertible with Being, they are
also convertible with each other. Yet, each transcendental adds its
own note to the definition of transcendence which is onto-anthropology.

Each transcendental deploys itself in a distinct way, and our apprehension of each relies in each case on a slightly different model. The
model which most readily suggests itself in the discussion of truth
is sight. We tend to equate understanding with seeing: we speak of
insight, we see the model even in the origin of the word 'theory',
and so on. However there is more than just seeing in the model we
require of the good. Transcendence is moral freedom, and in this
way the good dovetails with the deployment of freedom which is
action. One sees the truth but one does the good. Seeing and doing
are the icons of these two transcendentals. But the doing of the good
is essentially a mediation, and if it lacked this character it would be
merely random. The metaphor which seems most naturally to suggest itself to us in thinking through this issue is the free yet disci-
plined action of the musician. The good, as we suggest, is a kind of
libretto to be performed. Its appeal to freedom is never constraint,
but is that quasi-necessity or ineluctability which only transcendence knows, and is captured by the verb 'ought'.

The position of the good relative to transcendence underlies much if not all talk about the good, and is vital to an adequate understanding of it. There can be no transcendence without the good, precisely as presupposed by, as *a priori* to, not as created by, the exercise of freedom. To deny this is to do away with the good altogether, to make it invisible and intractable, or to mask it with a caricature of itself. Again, therefore, as in the case of truth, transcendence does not create its towards-which: transcendence is participation. It is here that the bivalence of the transcendentals is probably most manifest. It is also here that our treatment of the transcendentals is at its most anthropological, because in order to understand the good, we must understand the dynamisms it sets up in transcendence. The good is 'of Being', but it is also to be done and lived.

The rest of our treatment therefore, is built around this core, and we discuss those items and theses which are present in the dynamism set up by the good, such as tolerance, good will, autonomy, and the relation between wrongdoing and ignorance. These in turn necessitate some discussion of the notion of sacrifice, without which we cannot understand choice, and sacrifice itself involves some ontological account of suffering, which presents itself as the opposite of the good, as the disruption of the good as such, the flaying of particular entities of their worth. The notion of sacrifice is itself a heuristic one for an understanding of wrongdoing, for sacrifice is integral to worship, and idolatry is wrongly directed worship. In this, we find a model which makes culpable wrong-doing intelligible. The relation of the good and the Divine is also an issue treated at different points in this chapter, for perhaps more urgent to any worthwhile theology than the identification of the Divine with the truth is the surpassing of the good by the Divine as the good and more than good.

11, 2 The Emergence of the Good from Truth

Transcendence (towards truth) is the finite and free, progressive and unending, saying of Being, and thus of Being as true, by and in a real community of essentially linguistic, and therefore themselves necessarily free, and consequently ethical, entities, ultimately in dependence on, and as united in, language as register and mediator of meaning, and proximally as engaged in particular language-games. This structure uncovers the orientation of the real to and in truth: *ens et verum convertuntur*. This, in its turn, is so insofar as, and because, what is is manifest to and for such a community, insofar as it is, and only because what is, and what is manifest, are one. The former is what there is as sayable, the latter, what is as what is said. These, then, are the two regions of truth, and their interlocking and interrelation is, read from the side of what is, based on what is, insofar as it is, and, read from the side of the speaker, based on the being-linguistic of that which speaks: to be is to be definite, and language works by allowing for progressive approximation towards that horizon as end for freedom and therefore as value. We do not add anything to Being in allowing the emergence of Being as true, no more than does daylight confer anything on the visible world in making the seeable seen. In this sense, we are the 'there of Being', and our position, relative to that of all other finite entities and kinds of entities, is a privileged one, in that other kinds of relation are ontic rather than transcendental, not to Being as such, nor as true.

The discovery of Being as good is a more profound truth which emerges in this context. We may express it thus: truth is the culmination of good: there is no truth without the good. Conversely, the good is the more profound of the two, though equally, there is no good without truth. This is the ontological analogue of the biblical equiparation of knowing and loving: to know is to love, to love is to know, and the one can be without the other only by virtue of concealment, and not really as disjoined in a radical way.

11, 3 Knowing and Loving: There is no Truth Without the Good

The fundamental direction of transcendence is towards Being as true, and we have discovered that such a being-towards is only possible for something which is morally free, though this being-ethical is so far delineated as a kind of limiting case. But if something appears as true, it to that extent appears as valuable, that is, as something which attracts, but does not compel, freedom, in the way that an efficient cause would, otherwise we do away with truth, and with it, transcendence, altogether. The peculiar attraction exercised by the true is expressed in and as 'ought'. The soul of good and value is this ought: to say something is valuable is to say that, as valuable, it shapes our action, in that it both pre- and pro-scribes our comportment towards it.

In this way the modalities of the ought are to be sharply distinguished from those of 'must' and 'can', although there are analogies in it to both. If something must be, then it is, and there is no choice relative to its being. If something can be, on the other hand, that alone does not require that it be. Ought is both similar to these and different. It can only emerge in and for something which is like that which we have described. Its emergence is coterminous with our apprehension of something as valuable. Because A is x, one ought, or ought not, to act thus. This is the general structure of ought sentences, and several points immediately become apparent.

11, 4 The Dimensions of 'ought'

The ought is clearly practical, pre- or pro-scribing to or for someone, some way of behaving, some manner of doing. The necessary and sufficient motive for this is given in the phrase 'because A is x'. The motive is necessary because it explains why one ought to act in a given way, or to abstain from so acting. The motive is sufficient because no other motive than just knowing A's being x is necessary in order to act. The notion of motive is interesting. A motive is something which stirs to action, and it will be necessary for us to say something regarding what it is. For now, it is sufficient to point out that motive can only be relevant to someone who is able to apprehend A's being x. Their apprehension that A is x, therefore, if this is sufficient for them to act, is, precisely, their motive. We shall need to raise the question as to what, precisely, such an apprehension is.

It is, however, vital to note that the description of A as x is special, in the sense that it is intrinsically evaluative: it reveals A as valuable, which of course is coterminous with this 'fact's' giving rise to prescriptions. The point here is that the evaluative element in language is irreducible to any non-evaluative talk. If someone were to ask 'why should I do, or not do, so-and-so?', the only answer can be the assertion 'because A is x'. If the next question is 'so?', the answer must take the form of an explanation that A is truly x, which is to say that A is valuable, and that we must use evaluative predicates like 'x' of it, which say more than 'merely' what A is, or what it is to be A, although A's being x(evaluative) must be coterminous with what it is to be A: to say that A is valuable per accidens is to deny that it is valuable in itself, as the thing it is, and so to assert that is is valuable relative to something else, which is therefore the true bearer of value. If our putative questioner persists, then he either does not see why A's being x makes A valuable, or what it means to say that 'x' is a value. If the former is the case, the discussion must proceed by asking what he considers valuable. If the latter, the discussion can proceed only by asking or eliciting what he considers value to be. (We shall pretend that his interrogator is a philosopher.) If this question elicits only silence, or if he in fact does not know what it is for something to be valuable, information which is probably more easily arrived at by observing what he does, then the discussion ends, presumably with the advice that he seek the help of a psychiatrist. The reason for this is that value as principle is not logically deducible from other features, and, equivalently, that deontic language is independent of other linguistic forms and registers.

As a corollary of this, we also note that someone who has no understanding of the grammar of deontic language will find it impossible adequately to describe at least some human actions and activities, which will therefore remain strictly unintelligible to him. To understand someone's behaviour is to know what their motives are, which explain what they are trying to do, and why. But if the motive is, at least in some cases, that A is x(evaluative), our putative value-blind observer can have no access to the motive. In the case of all actions which are free, the kind of motive we suggest is always present, that is, the motive, or the necessary and sufficient reason for action in the case of every free act, is the apprehension that 'A is x'. If this is not the case, then the action has a necessary and sufficient explanation which is not a motive, and therefore is not free.

We also note that our formula of value and its necessary relation to action 'because A is x, one ought, or ought not, to act thus' is addressed to something which is free, i.e. to someone. This is precisely what differentiates deontic talk from the modalities of necessity and possibility. Doing something, say y, may be obligatory precisely because A is x, but this does not make it necessary that y be done. We cannot admonish animals and natural phenomena for doing, or not doing, what they ought, because their behaviour is not free, and will be what it is anyway. Likewise to say we ought to do y is not to say that y is merely something one could do.

As Kant rightly recognised, it is as though y, precisely as something which ought to be done, were being commanded by a legitimate authority – in Kant's case, by rationality. Kantian autonomy consists in obeying the commands that we, for no other reason than that we are rational, address to ourselves.[1] Thus our formula reads 'since A is x, do/do not do y'. Formulating it this way is not absolutely necessary, but doing so does bring out certain properties of the phenomenon, the most important of which is that a command, even that of legitimate authority, can be disobeyed. This is the core of it. That a given comportment or course of action is commanded does not guarantee that the one to whom the command is addressed, though free to do so, that is, capable of doing so, will obey it. The question then becomes: how and under what circumstances, is such disobedience possible?

Before tackling this question, it is necessary to make another remark. As we have seen, it is the singular whose mode of being is freedom, and a command, though perhaps addressed to all at all times and all places, is still addressed to each. Being ethical in general is about how a singular 'who' responds, I, you, he or she, to the commands addressed by the 'fact' that A is x, and, further, to be a who rather than a what consists in being capable of responding to, by obeying or disobeying, such commands. A what, is, precisely, that for which such commands are meaningless. To be a who is to be responsible – one might almost create a pseudo etymology here – to be able to respond, so that one's response is attributable to oneself and to no other, otherwise of course, it is really the response of that other. It is in such response that the highest manifestation of individuality – inalienable responsibility – is to be found, and in its full flowering it is called conscience.[2]

If so, what, then, becomes of the community, and its relation to the acting inter-subject? Clearly, from what we have already said, the who on whom the responsibility for action devolves is necessarily dependent on language and community, and, proximally, on given language-games, in order to be able to exercise their free choice. The reason for this, we recall, is that being ethical, being an inter-subject, involves being in a real community and thus being linguistic. The how of all this must be further explored by us. But the important point here is that the ethical capacity, the capacity for the good, is actualised in and through such necessary engagement, in such a way, indeed, that the proximal language-game mediates an understanding of the language, of the very grammar, of ethics. However it is essential to be aware that a group or community as such is not what is addressed by the command, nor is responsibility proper to a group as such.

Groups as distinct from individuals do not act, are not responsible, although we sometimes use a kind of shorthand which makes it seem as if they do or were. The action of the group is reducible without residue to those of its members, even though we are frequently embarrassed when it comes to delineating the actions of individuals in certain situations, where praise or, more often, blame come into question. Though the work of individuals may be sub-merged in the actions of the many, those actions remain his or her responsibility. This embarrassment is perniciously useful, in that it allows individuals to hide within groups – crowds – which thereby take the blame, and so provide an alibi, giving the illusion of being free from responsibility. Both Heidegger and, perhaps more accur-ately, Kierkegaard, deal with the group as excuse. But we must also remark that this principle is the very one which is violated in indis-criminate attack or reprisal, which thereby represents at least as wicked an abuse as hiding within the crowd; its horror consists pre-cisely in the fact that those who are injured are either completely innocent, or at least of the particular action attributed to them. The maxim of justice must surely be not only that it is necessary to be guilty of wrongdoing to be a candidate for punishment, but also that if one is to be punished the punishment must be for, and pro-portionate to, the very act of wrongdoing of which one is actually guilty. In accordance with our formula, the expression of this fun-damental principle would be 'S is innocent: do not punish S'; 'S is guilty of y: punish S for, and proportionally to, y'.

Thus, when someone maintains that society, say, is to blame for something, what they mean is that the harshness and indifference of certain individuals, for which those individuals are responsible, and which they therefore might not have exhibited, as expressed in those individuals' actions (even though it may not, and most likely, will not, now be possible to trace those acts to their agents), is the reason why so-and-so is the case. This brings out another, related point, nicely. We speak here about harshness and indifference. Comportment must be considered harsh and indifferent in the light of what someone has a right to expect. Praise or blame is to be apportioned, in general, in the light of ethical norms of behaviour. Where such canons are missing, there cannot be said to be crime or virtue, and praise or blame cannot be apportioned. These norms are the prescriptive canons contained in ethical language-games. In this way, the ineluctable dependence of the free individual proximally on actual language games, and more ultimately on community and language, is very clear. The decisive question here is: what is the source and significance of such norms or canons? In particular, are they arbitrary, or is there some overriding and compelling reason which shapes them? Are they utterly and finally incommensurate with each other, or can they be reconciled?

Our brief phenomenology of the ought has provided us with a nice

budget of questions. But before we tackle them, there is a final point
to be made with regard to the accidental and the proper in respect
of value. Things' being accidentally valuable means that their value
is not proper to them. But if they are nonetheless valuable, this can
only mean that they are valuable in relation to another, that their
value is subordinate to, and participant in, that of another. To say
this is to say that they are a means and not an end, and that consequently to be an end means being valuable absolutely, which is
only possible if and when the value is coterminous with what the
thing in question is, insofar as it is. Thus, such things are not valuable in relation to any other, and they are not valuable as participant in the value of another. This raises another question: is this to
say that their value cannot be eclipsed by another? If not, then, that
there is a good, does not rule out that there be a better, and if there is
a better, then there must be a best, otherwise we would have an
infinite regress, and nothing in that connection would be valuable.

Thus, there is a distinction between 'being good' and 'being good
for'. This is a crucial distinction. 'Being useful for' means, more
fully, that someone can use what is to that extent useful to attain
something: x is useful for A in A's becoming y, or more simply, A
can use x to become y. In such a case, being y must be valuable to A
in some respect, and x valuable only insofar as it offers a passage to
y. One and the same thing can be at different moments or to different As, an x or a y, but to say something is always a y is to say it is
incapable of being an x. This is to say that it is always valuable for
what it is in itself. Since it is always only one thing, this in turn
means that it is good, unless it is eclipsed by another. To say that C
is better than D is to say that both C and D are good, but the claims
of C are to be preferred to those of D, and carried out before them:
though a dog and a child are both valuable, you ought to try first to
save the child from the blazing building, and afterwards, if possible, the dog. The value of the dog means that you may not, say, tor-
ture it, but its lesser value in relation to that of the child means that
one ought to tolerate or even cause the dog's suffering if this is the
only means of saving the child. (If someone were to object to this as
speciesism, or the like, that only means that it is right to be a
speciesist.) This seems to mean that to attribute greater value to C
over D means that D can become a means relative to C. Thus if
something is good unconditionally, it cannot become a means, and
so cannot be eclipsed: there can be no E which is better than C. In
this way, being unqualifiedly good means being literally an end,
not just a goal but a stopping-place in such a chain.

11, 5 The Ineluctability of the Good

This allows us now to attempt an answer to the question we posed above, namely how and under what circumstances, is disobedience to the commands imposed by value, possible? Let us examine what such disobedience entails. The command is, because A is x, that is, valuable, then do/do not do, y. To act contrary to this command is to deny the value of A: i.e., either A is not really valuable, or despite its being x, its value is not absolute. But, to lack unconditional value is not to lack value, but to be eclipsed by another, and perhaps to be capable of being a means to that other. This raises a crucial principle, namely that the value of something is not eclipsed except by something better. Value can only be eclipsed in this way by value, and this, precisely, is what 'better' means, namely that the virtual commands emanating from one source are overridden by those from another. This then, is the meaning of the disobedience we spoke of, precisely, that the commands imposed by one value are superimposed over those imposed by another, and take priority over the commands imposed by that other. This brings us to another central principle or axiom of the moral life: no one decides save in favour of what presents itself as valuable, as good.

The axiomatic or tautological quality of this principle will be obvious. It answers to Plato's principle that no-one does ill willingly, and thus that all wrong-doing is ignorance. But before discussing this, let us vindicate the tautologous nature of the principle that no one decides save in favour of the good. To be good or valuable means to be a worthy object of choice, and the opposite, to fail to be such a worthy object. Thus, if someone chooses something, that which they have chosen is for them a worthy object of choice. The opposite of this is: to choose something because it does not appear to be an object worthy of choice; under such circumstances there is no ground for the choice, which, if it is to be explicable at all, must be explained in other terms, that is in terms other than those of the intentions of the agent, and thereby fails to be a free choice, in the meaning which we have discerned in freedom. Freedom is not the capacity to choose values as opposed to something else, or, reciprocally, the something else, whatever that may be, over values, but to be able to choose among a host of possible alternatives each of which presents itself as worthy of choice, that is, as value. In this way, choice is the discernment of the best among values, or, which is equivalent, of *the* thing worth choosing.

Thus, what may appear as the most outlandish and perverse choices are always chosen because they in some sense present themselves as the thing worth choosing. Even Milton's Satan who seems deliberately to choose evil because it is evil, does so, precisely because it seems good. He says 'evil, be thou my good',[3] and not the unintelligible 'good, be thou my evil'. This is a commitment to what is evil, understood as inimical to the purposes of his Enemy, precisely because such enmity seems good to him; it is a commitment which is intelligible in the context of his discernment that it is better to rule in hell than to serve in heaven. It is possible, and only possible, to choose something which is evil in the light of some principle which makes it seem good, but it is impossible to reject good as such, and treat it as evil, for this would be to destroy all possibility of having a motive or of choice. It is possible, however, to choose something because it is forbidden; under such circumstances the choice will represent a revolt against the authority which forbids, and consequently the affirmation of one's independence from that authority as good.

11, 6 Does Choice Create the Good?

This apparently innocuous point is, in fact, decisive for our whole understanding of choice, because it allows us to attempt an answer to the question, does decision create value or reflect it? An answer to this question is vital to any determination of the essence of choice. For if what we have argued is so, then all wrong-doing is indeed ignorance. Someone's choosing what they choose, on the one hand, and its seeming to be for them the best or the only choice on the other, are mutually implicative, and therefore equivalent items. To choose wrongly is not to choose what one knows to be ill over what one knows to be valuable, but to choose something because it seems good, and to be wrong in one's judging that it is so. If this is correct, then the decisive point arises: it is possible to be wrong in one's judgement of what is valuable. This is decisive because choice is therefore not that which confers value; choice occurs on the basis of a value which is independent of choice and offered it, so that the central metaphor in the ethical life is provided by its analogy with seeing. Good is to our freedom as colour is to our eye, and just as, under certain circumstances, it is possible to judge wrongly concerning colour, it is possible to judge wrongly concerning the good. Likewise, and perhaps more alarmingly, just as, once one perceives that 'this' is red, it is impossible without pretence to judge that it is not red, so it is impossible to choose something other than this, once 'this' is discerned to be preferable. One might make use of another neat metaphor here: the agent is a magnet oriented by an already given magnetic field or object, and does not, by its mere swinging into alignment, magnetise something which exercises no attraction of itself.

This point is well worth dwelling on, as it differentiates the understanding of ethics explored here from many recent interpretations, and hearkens back to a more traditional, perhaps ultimately Platonic, view. However, there are two objections to it, whose solution will develop it further. In what follows, these will be referred to as 'Issue 1' and 'Issue 2', to make navigating easier.

11, 7 Culpable Wrongdoing and Tolerance (Issue 1)

Firstly: suppose that all wrongdoing is indeed ignorance. The necessary and sufficient reason for choosing anything is that it seems good to us, or equivalently, that it seems the best possible choice. Each chooses what seems to be *the* good, or the best, and for that reason alone. To choose wrongly is to be wrong in this apparent discernment. But this is only possible if the truth of what is truly preferable is concealed from the one who chooses, and is unavailable to them, otherwise, he or she could not have failed to choose it. We recall that someone is responsible for something only if they know that that something results from their action, and they know that they can do other than produce it, and therefore actually can do other than produce it. But if someone is mistaken as to what is good, or to be chosen, they *ipso facto* cannot choose it. Moreover, neither do they know they can choose it, since to know this involves knowing its status as the true best, for one cannot choose anything except it is to-be-chosen. Although they know what result their action will have, they are not in possession of an ethically sufficient description of that result. But if this is so, is culpable wrongdoing not impossible?

The answer to this would appear to be negative, because ignorance itself can be culpable: if I make a wrong choice in virtue of being culpably ignorant of the true good, then my choice is a culpable one. It is no excuse for a surgeon who kills her patient because of incompetence to plead ignorance of correct surgical procedure; far from extenuating her guilt, such an admission compounds it. Likewise, in law, ignorance of the law is no defence. Is such culpability possible, and if so, how?

To be culpable is to be morally responsible for ill. As we saw, an element of responsibility is being able to do something other than one does. Ignorance is culpable only if one is capable of being other than ignorant. This, then, is a necessary element of culpability, but it is not sufficient, for, in order to be culpable, one must not only be able to do other than one does, but also be aware that one ought to do so. Is the ignorant person so ignorant that knowledge of his or her ignorant state is denied them? In the case of culpable ignorance, moreover, this would seem to mean that one knows one is ignorant, that one can be other than ignorant, and that one refuses to be so. But, if what we have said above is correct, namely that it is impossible to choose evil for the reason of its being evil alone, and that all things chosen are so *sub specie boni*, how is it possible to choose ignorance knowingly? Can one ever prefer to be ignorant? If so, is this a refutation of the principle that what is chosen is so *sub specie boni*?

The resolution of this seemingly circular, paradoxical situation is a manifestation at once of the finitude and of the nobility of our grasp on the good. To be finite is always to be ignorant; to face our finitude is to recognise that this is true. No one can, and no one does, prefer error and ignorance to truth and enlightenment; but to be able to discern the true as good means facing the truth of finitude. This, in its turn, means realising that there is a shadow side to all our decisions, namely that we might have chosen otherwise, and that it is possible to be in error in one's choice. Knowing this means embracing a kind of existential humility, an expression of which we find coming from a, perhaps unexpected, source: 'I beseech you, in the bowels of Christ, think it possible you may be mistaken.'[4] Existential humility is the posture of thinking that in choosing what I choose, I may be mistaken. This involves knowing that, since I am responsible for what I do, I must entertain all reasonable claims against what I have chosen, both the actual ones *de facto* urged against it, and genuine potential objections, insofar as I can formulate them, alone and in dialogue, where more than one perspective comes into play. It follows from this that the decisions reached are reached in and by such a deliberative process alone, otherwise they are arbitrary and without foundation from the perspective of the one who chooses. In turn, knowing what constitutes reasonable claims against our position means developing, or trying to, a kind of ethico-logical connoisseurship, a discerning eye for argument, a virtue much in the style of Newman's Illative Sense. But knowing and accepting that one may be mistaken is without effect unless it influences how we decide. What is the necessary effect on our conduct of such an influence?

To allow the knowledge that one may be mistaken to influence conduct is in effect to embrace a principle of toleration, a letting-be of things, which allows them to be uncurtailed unless it is absolutely necessary to interfere with them. This principle of tolerance therefore recognises in things a validity in proportion to their capacity for sustaining damage, an insight inseparable from the quality of such damage. Commitment to good is inseparable from a hostility to evil, and in particular the evil of suffering. The insight without which this principle of toleration is impossible is precisely the insight that all that is falls into one of two distinct camps, namely, of those things which are capable of suffering, and of those which are not.

11, 8 Suffering and Sacrifice

Suffering is a condition of an entity which goes beyond mere pain. Pain itself is a specific sensory experience without which life as such would not be possible. Pain warns and safeguards by making destructible living things flee from those situations which are harmful, or incompatible with the continued existence of the living entity. It seems doubtful that life could continue in the absence of just such a sensory arrangement as in fact obtains in living things. Pain is an experience, but suffering is a state. Suffering is that state in which the continued existence of that which suffers is difficult or intolerable to it. As such, suffering is a state of being in which the very existence of the entity which suffers is put in question, in such a manner that it is perceived or experienced by the sufferer as to-be-negated, or as negation. Suffering, then, is a kind of lived negation of existence. There is a kind of horrible *cogito* which is essential to this state; not that the sufferer finds in each experience of suffering an evidence of his or her own existence, but that the sufferer experiences existing itself as pain. Not 'I think, therefore I am, therefore I am a thinking thing', but simply, all experience is an 'I-am-suffering'. At its worst, suffering is the experience of this identity between 'I am' and 'I suffer': the 'am' is a version of the 'is of identity'. The circle closes about the sufferer in that, since suffering grows to fill all that he or she is, and covers it perfectly, his suffering is his alone, unique and incommunicable. In this way, suffering has a metaphysical essence; it is a phase of Being in which Being itself is as negated.

This essence is well expressed by Milton:

> Which way I flie is Hell; *my self am Hell*;
> And in the lowest deep a lower deep
> Still threatning to devour me opens wide,
> To which the Hell I suffer seems a Heav'n.[5]

It is impossible to rationalise or quantify suffering, but it is possible to see that the capacity to suffer grows in proportion to the extent of certain other capacities. My suffering is all the greater the more I have a capacity to rise above the here and now, to perceive this as happening to me, and on that basis to be unable to see an escape, or to be so consumed by it that the only escape seems to be to cease to be: the nadir of suffering is to be without escape. But although this proportionality is genuine, it is intolerable to maintain that it is only humans who suffer, or by extension, that it is only human suffering which is to be reckoned with.

The two opposed dangers which face thinkers here are indifference and sentimentality. To be indifferent is to be blind to suffering, or at least to animal suffering, or to see it and to discount it. To be sentimental is to anthropomorphise the animal, and thereby to fail to see animals as they are. Both poles are failures to see what is there to be seen. Much animal suffering lies outside the pale of human concern. Nature is 'red in tooth and claw', and what are to us examples of the most appalling cruelty are the things of every day in non-human life: the wasp whose young hatch to devour the paralysed but still conscious spider walled in with them as food; the young tiger, still a hunting tyro, which slowly mutilates and eviscerates its victim; the games of cats with mice. Yet these very examples themselves draw the line of demarcation between the human and the non-human, in that none of these perpetrators are morally responsible for what they do, for they cannot do other than they do, being what they are, and also in that the only animals which appear to care about animal suffering are human animals. This latter point is not flippant: animals can suffer, but they cannot, it seems, see suffering for what it is, nor consequently be either willing or unwilling to be responsible for it. This, then, is the human essential: to have the capacity to see what suffering is, and to be willing or otherwise to be responsible for it.

Responsibility for suffering is sacrifice, which itself is always 'for the sake of', but the ethical quality of sacrifice very much depends on its terms. To sacrifice is to be responsible for something's or someone's suffering, for some sake or other. I can, of course, sacrifice something incapable of suffering, but this amounts simply to giving it up or doing without it, while sacrifice in the full sense is the bite of being responsible for suffering. I may sacrifice an animal or even a human being for the sake either of the common good, or of my own pleasure. I may be a Caiaphas or a Marquis de Sade, or I may be a scientist who experiments on animals to secure the healing of human disease. Or, I may submit myself to suffering to secure the good of another: Caiaphas did not sacrifice one who was unwilling to sacrifice himself. Though the cases are ethically diverse, the ontology of sacrifice permeates them all; the possibility of responsibility for suffering is the possibility of sacrifice. A genuine good is one which validates the sacrifice made to obtain it, and although not all that is good requires sacrifice for its attainment, it is the hallmark of the good to validate sacrifice. In this way our principle of tolerance turns out to be a question of the tolerability of sacrifice: if I may be mistaken, what sacrifices are tolerable for me to make? This not a question which allows a final answer, but is rather one which is coextensive with all choice and freedom, for to be open to the good is to ask what sacrifices, if any, are necessary and legitimate to obtain it.

11, 9 Good Will and Ill-doing

Now let us locate ourselves again relative to our academic-sounding question as to how and whether all sin is ignorance. To do this we must bring into play the notion of conscience or good will. Genuine good can only be manifest to one of good will, where this means living responsibly within the dynamisms, especially in the existential humility and careful contemplation of sacrifice, which we have just delineated. To be culpably ignorant is not so much to choose wrongly and knowingly, but to fail of good will. If the good is obligatory, then so are all those elements which facilitate our making the right choice. Thus, good will is obligatory, for only in and through it is the manifestation of genuine good possible. In short, good will is a duty in the Kantian sense. It is possible to choose wrongly precisely because one has neglected the primary and primal duty of good will, upon which all other obligations depend - one cannot know what these are unless and until one is of good will. One chooses wrongly and culpably precisely when one does this, and might have done otherwise, and this is so even in the case where one chooses the genuine good by accident:

The last temptation is the greatest treason:
To do the right deed for the wrong reason.[6]

But this reflection requires that we differentiate the relative positions of good will and the good. Good will is the station-point which alone offers a perspective on the good, and therefore is *a priori* relative to the good, not in the sense that it is, as it were, wired in, like an instinct, to our perceptions, but in the sense that it is a necessary condition for the manifestation of the good. To continue the analogy with visual perspective, that which is viewed from the station-point is given in virtue of the station-point, but not the station point itself; the givenness or otherwise of good will is different in kind from that of the good which it mediates. The focus of attention is the mediated good, not the mediating good, though both participate in what it is to be good.

It therefore follows that any choice we make of the mediated good is flawed insofar as we ignore or reject the mediating good. Culpability accrues to our action because we ignore the mediating good and discount any and all things which would lead us to consider it. We become fixated on the apparent mediated good so that it looms and conceals all other issues, issues which, if we attended to them, would explode the myth we have thereby constructed for ourselves. The rooted attention on the mediated apparent good becomes an alibi we construct for not embracing the mediating good. The sacrifice we therefore make is of the good for the sake of what we take and wish to take as the good. Thus, although we do not repudiate the good and choose evil for evil's sake, we ignore the true good firstly, in that we discount good will (this is what constitutes the sin) and secondly, in that this first event itself never becomes an issue for us (this constitutes culpable ignorance). We are, as finite, unable to see the immediate implications of what we discount, and the vicious circle is completed by virtue of the empire we thereby allow to the mediated good. We thus transform our transcendence toward the good into a self-deceiving and self-defeating sacrifice of the good, of the real for the bogus. No one could prefer this to the attainment of genuine good, but no one is offered the bald choice. The temptation begins in a genuine concern for good and in an entrancement with an apparent good which is offered, and which is loved inordinately. To sin against the light is inordinate love of *a* good, which, however valuable it may be, is thereby always the merely apparent good. One can only love something insofar as it appears good, and to love it inordinately in this way is to make the conditional final and absolute, and thereby to falsify it.

Is there no such thing, then, as demonic evil? By this we do not mean evil as described in myths and horror-stories, but the all-too-real evils which were and are rampant in places like Auschwitz. There is, and it is produced by the very dynamism we have been considering. There is no better definition of demonic evil than the words Milton gives to Satan: 'evil, be thou my good'. A demonic evil is an evil pursued as though it were an absolute good. But we can find a love of perversity, an apparently systematic cultivation of the worst, growing out of an inordinate love of the necessarily apparent good, at many points in human history, but probably at its clearest in the Holocaust.

This is an enormously complicated topic, but to understand the ethical dynamisms which made and make such demonic evil possible, it is necessary to perceive the culpable entrancement of the perpetrators by an apparent good which, as good, was meant to be the justification of sacrifice, but as merely apparent, required considerable emendations of reality. Such disabling might take discursive or political form, like the proliferation of courses in *Rassenkunde* in educational curricula, or the removal, in one way or another, of possible objectors from positions of effectiveness. What the apparent good actually is, is, in a sense, of little or no importance: it might be power, self-preservation at the individual or communal level, or the like. It need not be particularly valuable in itself, only that it appear somehow good. But it becomes the Moloch to which all else is sacrificed, whose nature as idol is that it illegitimately demands sacrifice. Vital here for its continued reign is the disablement of all opposition, a fundamental unwillingness to discern the ever-more pressing untruthfulness in which it is then necessary to exist. No-one can be convinced of the truth of racism unless certain questions and forms of logical evaluation are banned in principle. No one can really believe that an individual's goodness and value are dictated by the shape of their nose or the colour of their skin, unless any possibility of evidence contrary to such a belief be in principle disallowed, unless, that is, I sacrifice the good to 'my' good, and unavoidably therefore, the truth to 'my' truth.

The essence of wrongdoing then, is to prefer 'the good which I prefer' to the good, to prefer 'the truth which I prefer' to the truth, and to incarnate these preferences in our actions. Indeed one might say that the action is the preference, which can and does become sacrifice. As we saw, serving the idol good is inseparable from serving the idol truth. The false good can only be present to the extent that it pretends to be genuine, and so cannot exist without this lie. On the other hand, since truth is a good, to set up an idol truth is thereby to set up an idol good. It does not matter which comes first, since the one idolatry always brings its sibling worship with it. Does this mean that all wrongdoing is ultimately irrational? The answer is yes. To serve an idol is to fail to serve God, and to worship instead that whose eyes cannot see and whose ears cannot hear, and on whose lips is never a breath, an inanimate counterfeit of a living reality. In the same way, to serve an idol truth and an idol good is to have given submission and loyalty to a fantasy. Darkness is not another kind of light, nonsense not another kind of sense. Though such idolatry has its roots in finite directedness towards good and truth, its effect is to waste and frustrate those very factors. Like the idols themselves, those who worship them are put to silence, not through iconoclasts' actions, but in the very worship itself.

If we are correct in saying that these dynamisms are indeed the essence of wrongdoing, then wrongdoing must be impossible without them. All activity which is free and non-random is directed towards some good, and no-one can act except as towards the good, and under its behest; such are the 'axioms' of our treatment. If that good were truly coterminous with my projection, then to serve it could never be wrong, and so wrongdoing would indeed be impossible. Since this is not the case, we are led to the conclusion that notions like 'my' truth and 'my' good, are bogus. It is of the essence of the good therefore to be shared. But the same is true, *mutatis mutandis*, for 'our' good, and 'our' truth. Idols of the cave are almost always idols of the tribe. The tribe has its totem (though its members may have their household gods) whose function as totem is to be a talisman of victory over those of others. The language-games played by groups can only be played under the behest of some good, otherwise they are utterly self-involved rituals, such as we spoke of before, incomprehensible either from within or without, since for them to be comprehensible, there must be an explanation of the point of the actions available at least potentially to the players, one which they employ analogically in creating genuinely new moves which, though applications of the rules or principles of the game, transform the players' situation in new and unforeseeable ways. Here the tribal equivalent of the cave presents itself. There is a perfect analogy between the two levels, and both are usually found together, and all we need to do is to pluralise – for 'I', write 'we' – and we have the idol of the tribe.

11, 10 The Universality of the Good: *ens et bonum convertuntur*

But if this, in turn, is so, then we have made a valuable discovery: there is no genuine good which is not universal, where 'universal' means capable of commanding the loyalty of all everywhere, and any partial or sectional good must be submitted to it. This gives us what is, in effect, the Kantian principle that nothing is good unless all are, in principle, capable of being unfailingly loyal to it.[7] Allowing this good to appear as good is the truth, and hence the good, at which all moral discourse aims. It must be both possible and necessary, therefore, for all inter-subjective intention to submit to such universalist scrutiny, on pain of being meaningless and evil. If we cannot do this then the actual intentions of groups and individuals must remain at that level, and therefore must be the good; if that were so, then there is no wrongdoing.

Could we not say that wrongdoing is merely the breaking of conventional rules of conduct, necessarily enshrined in language-games, whatever these rules may happen to be? To make such a claim would be to claim that the good is itself merely conventional, constituted by the *de facto* rules of conduct enshrined in those language-games. If this were so, then what happens to be is right, and is right insofar as, and because, it is. Thus there is no space for criticism, no station-point from which it can examine its object. So, if slavery is the *de facto* game, it is thereby legitimate. Consequently, any attempt to change it is unconventional and hence both evil and nonsensical, since the rules for making sense, ethically and epistemically, are the actually obtaining rules. Further, there is no justification possible for the creation of a new game in the old one's stead, but once the new game has been established, it enjoys the same privilege of legitimation which the ousted game enjoyed before it. Moreover, in that they both disregard the conventions, there can be no difference between the reformer and the pervert, and their actions are, as unconventional, irrational.[8] Though it may sound like the beginning of a bad joke to ask what the difference is between Ghandi and Jack the Ripper, the punch-line is considerably worse, for in this perspective, their actions are in principle equally unintelligible, unless and until they actually become language-game paradigms. Surely one must argue that what makes a reformer a reformer is that his or her actions, though unconventional, are capable of becoming paradigmatic for whole forms of life, and that this is what differentiates him from the pervert, whose actions are doomed to unintelligibility for themselves and for all others, no matter what the context in which they are placed?

But, if this is so, then the good, which is mediated by the reformer, and therefore the good as such, is intended but not created, by any *de facto* rules of conduct, which must therefore be scrutinised by the communal good will, enshrined, that is, in the community which thereby identifies itself in principle with the universal οἰκουμένη to whom the good is truly and finally manifest. Every human life, every language-game, every community, is an experiment in value and freedom. Although it may do no good to tell Hitler he is a bad man, in that it will bring about no change in him, to know it is of the greatest utility to one who is able to profit from the knowledge that Hitler's is no worthwhile life for a human being.

Jack the Ripper's activity is ultimately not explicable to himself or to anyone else, and can never count as a meaningful move in any possible language-game. This, of course, is not to say that he is necessarily free of culpability, insofar as he might have done other than he did, but it does mean that his actions are examples of wrongdoing and are therefore ultimately irrational and without any possible justification. The final inexplicability of his actions is their ultimate surdic nature, and their incapacity to be interpreted as examples or instantiations of any real value. Though they may begin in the space of rationality, the questions, 'what genuine value do they serve?', or more simply, 'what is the point of them?', receive the answers, 'nothing' and 'none'. For anything to stand as a genuine value, it must be capable of receiving the loyalty of all. A self-defeating 'value' is incapable of this, because embracing it frustrates even self-gratification. The activities of a Jack the Ripper, if elevated into a paradigm of the good, would turn life into a war of each against each and all against all, in which there would be little chance for the continued existence of any. The activity of a Ghandi, on the other hand, if elevated into a paradigm, would not only allow for the good, already *de facto* present, to be continued, but would allow for its extension and completion in ways now neither possible nor, perhaps, even conceivable.

The principle which shapes this space is well captured by Kant in the various formulations of the Categorical Imperative. The only

good which can command the allegiance of all moral agents is one
in which they themselves partake of the value, precisely by being
the value. I can only affirm those values according to which I am
not to be sacrificed by another, and so I must be affirmed as unconditionally valuable by all. Since this is true for each, the value of
persons is absolute, and no persons are to be sacrificed for the sake
of the arbitrary desires of another.[9] But since personhood as such is
therefore valuable, it follows that it is to be valued in me by all,
including me. I owe the person I am as much as I owe the persons
others are: I owe the persons others are as much as I owe the person
I am; as much as, neither more nor less. Even if I am deprived of a
sense of my own worth, and view myself and others nihilistically,
this does not vitiate the principle in me or for me, by me or by others, because the good is, as that which commands the loyalty of all,
manifest to many and not merely to one, and therefore is incumbent
on me as member of the οἰκουμένη, the essentially communal plurality of inter-subjects, not as isolated subject, because such a subject
is a mere construct. It is on the basis of this that *de facto* arrange-
ments can and must be vetted and criticised, and be either rejected,
reformed or affirmed, in full consciousness that any other course or
principle is irrational.

Does this, in turn, mean that the good extends only as far as the bor-
ders of the οἰκουμένη, and no further? If all persons as persons are
valuable, are only persons valuable? The answer is no, though persons are the first value in the sense that sacrifices of non-personal
entities are and can be justified, but only as sacrifices for persons,
even though, one must add, not every need or want that a person or
persons may have warrants any sacrifice of the non-personal; moreover, the preservation of the non-personal does not justify all sacrifices on the part of persons, even where such sacrifice is a mere
doing without, and does not involve the actual death of persons.

Suffering is the experienced cancellation of the value of Being, as
we saw; the sufferer experiences existence as burden. Suffering as
such is a disvalue, and it is a disvalue because it is the cancellation
of value; it is the appearance of existence positively stripped of
value. This need not mean it is stripped of value for us, but it means
that it is stripped of value for that which exists. This means that
non-suffering existence is valuable for that whose existence it is,
and which is capable of suffering but does not suffer. If this is so,
then to be for such an entity is valuable for it, and therefore is valuable. Thus the existence of such an entity is valuable, or sets up the

entity as valuable, not merely as being. But in discovering this, in turn, we have ousted ourselves as sole centres of value. To be valuable therefore does not necessarily mean being useful for us; the notion of value is not always reducible to what is valuable to us. But if this is so, then things are valuable as such, unless it can be shown that that value is restricted to its value for us, and this does not cancel the value which belongs properly to them, though this value is subordinate to the greater and better value. Thus, to be valuable is based on being as such. Entities, even entities incapable of suffering, are thus valuable, and are to be treated as valuable, unless such treatment cuts across our loyalty to higher values, namely to those proper to non-human entities capable of suffering, and, in the first place, to persons. *Ens et bonum convertuntur.*

Two important points follow from this. Our principle of toleration is to be extended to all that is, insofar as it is, under the behest of the threefold division of nature which we have just outlined. It is again identical to a principle of humility, whereby we are evicted as sole occupants of value in the universe. We are not the only value in the universe. We do not confer value on things, we recognise it. Thus our role, as regards the rest of the universe is a quasi-aesthetic one: we are that entity in which good appears as truth. Much may be learned here from Stoic philosophy in which nature was clearly perceived as valuable. The best summation of this position was well expressed by Plutarch in his life of Cato:

> However, for my part, I regard his [Cato's] treatment of his slaves like beasts of burden, using them to the uttermost, and then, when they were old, driving them off and selling them, as the mark of a very mean nature, which recognises no tie between man and man but that of necessity. And yet we know that kindness has a wider scope than justice. Law and justice we naturally apply to men alone; but when it comes to beneficence and charity, these <often> flow in streams from the gentle heart, like water in a copious spring, even down to dumb beasts. A kindly man will take good care of his horses even when they are worn out with age, and of his dogs, too, not only in their puppyhood, but when their old age needs nursing.[10]

The moral principle here enjoined is respect for all that is, insofar as it is, and is the meaning of the principle *ens et bonum convertuntur*. The Greek name for this universal respect is ἀγάπη. This is to recognise ourselves in all humility, not as the centre of creation, not, as

Descartes would have it, as over and against creation, but rather as part of creation, with our own unique vocation as human within it, and to recognise that the same is true of all other entities after their kind. Though, as finite, we are not in a position to articulate a meaning for the existence of things other than ourselves, we manifest the value of all that is by conducting ourselves in accordance with it, that is, by loving, respecting and cooperating with non-human nature. The name of this way of being is compassion. To love the good is to love all that is good, that is, all that is. To love the good is to love to be as good as possible, which means avoiding all cruelty and vandalism; he is an unlovely person whom these faults contaminate, and he is a wrongdoer who makes his sectional interests, even if they seem to be those of our species, into an idol before which other species, in whole or in part, are to be sacrificed.

11, 11 *Bonum est diffusivum sui* (Issue 2)

The second issue we were to explore touches the relation of the good and the Divine. From the foregoing considerations it has become clear that the good is that which deserves unconditional loyalty; it is tautologous to say that the good is that which is always and ever worth striving for. But if this is so, then the Divine and unconditional good must be identical, for if the two were distinct, then the Divine would be inferior to unconditional good, and so would not be Divine, that than which no greater, and hence no better, can be thought. Likewise, that Divinity exists is the guarantee that an unconditional good exists. Such good, clearly, as Divine, is neither a good among others, nor the combination of all finite goods, but original goodness, goodness itself. God as good is not the instantiation of one or all kinds of good, but is beyond the essence of the good, present in all good, infinitely in the direction pointed to by that essence. Thus it is contradictory to deny the goodness of God, the supreme goodness of God or the necessary nature of the Divine goodness, that is, its necessary inseparability from the Divine, or therefore, positively, to hold that God is either contingently good, or good only in some respect or other. This, then, is the chief meaning of the Divine more-than-excellence: that God is not only the exemplar of all that the good is, but that the highest and best we can think of is the lower limit of the goodness proper to the Divine. This is what makes of Divinity the ethico-religious principle, namely, its deserving of that unconditional loyalty, trust and love which is worship.

This conclusion is clearly the most important we have arrived at in this series of considerations. It means that the heart and life of existence is neither neutral nor evil but ethical: Divinity is self-subsistent, and as creative, self-communicative goodness. This, it seems, is precisely the meaning of another old Scholastic 'axiom', *bonum est diffusivum sui*. Just as (finite) existence, and not destruction, is the proper work of Divinity, and the possibility of non-being which is finitude, being coterminous with, and inseparable from, being created, even so, goodness must be diffused by the Good identically with the creative granting of existence, so that evil, finally as capacity for suffering, must be inherent in finitude as such. Such reasoning may explain the possibility of evil, but does not explain its actuality, though it does allow us to understand evil as imperfection and distortion, which thereby presupposes the primal positivity and goodness of existence of which it is the distortion, and to which it is therefore secondary, and on which it is parasitic. If this reasoning is correct, it follows that it is not the good which is to be explained, but evil. The good is the heart and meaning of Being, the very positivity of Being, and evil is the anomaly, the distortion and scandal, the slur on Divinity which it is necessary to face.

It also follows that, analogously to the participatory nature of the finite in existence and coterminous with it, there is participation in the Divine goodness. Goodness Itself is the creative cause of all existence and of the good which is coterminous with it. Since things are created by Goodness they are, insofar as they are, good: they are (good), only because God is. How, then, are we to understand this particpation in the good?

A value is like a libretto, which comes alive only in performance, and the performance is the being of value, much as it is the being of music. Like a libretto, value can be seen as a set of instructions which require art and interpretation in its realisation. Freedom is this performance for, like the musician who is only really a musician when she performs, our freedom, in its turn, is only realised in our performing the good. Performance allows the music to become incarnate in sound, so that the performer stands between the two, transforming each into the other, as does the moral agent, who sees and who translates, and by and in whose action, the value comes actually to be, and is. This is another aspect of what we have discerned as the priestly character of the human vocation: the consecration of the finite by the finite, the blessing of creation by our mediation, our actualisation, of the good in and to it.

In both art and freedom there is an acquiescence in the reality of that which is performed. Interpretation does not give itself its own object, but seeks in its interpretation to do justice to what it interprets by disclosing all it is in and through performance. A paradigmatic performance lets us see what that which it interprets is and can be. The player depends upon the libretto and, in her acquiescence, in a way becomes it. The agent depends upon the good, and in performing it becomes it. But freedom is the capacity to create a space which can either include or exclude the good; idolatry is the futility and counterfeit of true worship, cacophony the caricature of music. This is the drama of freedom, but it is not true that freedom is only real if it is denial, where denial is thus the assertion of autonomy.

11, 12 Autonomy and the Vector of Freedom

But is this truly so? If I must choose what I discern to be the good, I cannot do other than I do, and so how can I be said to be free? Is the compass free if it must always point to the North? This question takes us into the heart of the finitude of freedom: freedom is finite as freedom-for. Freedom is capacity for the good, not arbitrary choice or indifference. Capacity for the good is being able to discern value and perform it. Choice which is finally indifferent is arbitrary, fortuitous and hence surdic and inexplicable. If the only explanation for my choosing A is my choosing A, then my choosing A is mere chance and coincidence, for which there can be no further explanation. That kind of choice is indifferent, precisely because it takes account of nothing but itself in choosing, and so it is not choice. This would really be to do away with freedom, for it would be to replace it by an inexplicable lottery. The only way freedom can be real is, precisely, if is not arbitrary, and therefore if choice is intelligible in terms other than itself, of its own having-chosen. Freedom is only possible as choice, itself only intelligible as positing something worthy of choice, as good. Freedom is only possible as aimed at the good.

Likewise, it is best not to forget that value is not a thing, and certainly not one thing. To choose is to commit oneself to the best and most worthy of choice among alternatives. To discern the good is to be able to see things as valuable, as commending actions to be taken at their behest. To discern the good is to make oneself able to see relative merit, to see and choose between different courses of action. To follow the good is always to choose responsibly between different alternatives, yet to stay within the territory of the good. One cannot live under water, but one may choose where to live on land.

To do away with dependence on the good is to do away with freedom, for if freedom confers the good, then freedom is anterior to the good, and so choice becomes inexplicable and arbitrary, the lottery we spoke of. Freedom as freedom requires that the good be presented to it, not for acceptance or rejection, but as a map with destinations marked on it, destinations between which we can choose, and the routes which lead to them. And the presentation of this map of Being depends upon the exercise of good will.

All this functions in relation to the question, if motives determine action, how are actions free? To ask such a question is to be in confusion. Motiveless action is random, and thus the very opposite of free action. Actions undertaken at the behest of motives are free actions, precisely because to be able to discern value and perform it requires freedom in the sense of 'freedom from' as necessary condition. Only if my act is free in this sense is it my act, and only to the extent that it is an act of good will is it free in this sense. My being motivated is my being free to put good will into practise.

The question which follows from this is: since it seems necessary to be of good will if the good is to be manifest, is it sufficient as well? Is the mere fact of being of good will sufficient to guarantee the disclosure of the good? Put another way, is what we mean by the good, that which is disclosed to good will?

The answer to this would appear to be affirmative. Acting with good will means acting in a way which is both tolerant and subject to correction. Because of this, there is in good will that which will not suffer idols, and which makes their setting-up impossible, or at least unlikely. Thus what is disclosed to conscience is not merely what is desirable, but also what is obligatory, for the structure of conscience is a being open to *the* good, and not merely to *a* good. Though this is not to say that what the good is is not betimes mysterious, or, equivalently, that there are no moral dilemmas or difficulties, it is to say that conscience is search for the best, and therefore the most worthy of choice.

11, 13 Divinity, Participation, and the Good

There is both an analogy and a disanalogy between our participation in the truth of Divinity and in the goodness of Divinity. Things

are only because God is: insofar as truth and goodness are coterminous with existence, things are revealed, and are good, therefore
only because God is goodness and truth. Divinity as such is not
revealed: Divinity is only revealed insofar as things are, and are
revealed, and the goodness which is Divinity is only revealed insofar as finite goodness is revealed. Yet Divinity as the proper and
ultimate meaning of existence, of goodness and of truth, is both
what these things finally are, and what the improper instantiations
of them intend, and fall – infinitely – short of. Yet all we have direct
access to is the imperfect and improper, not to their ultimate resolution in and as the proper and perfect. Divinity is the light which
shows colour yet which itself remains undisclosed. If this were not
so, freedom would be impossible and would be replaced by what
the later Heidegger seems to mean by freedom, namely, the clearing which is pure receptivity and passivity, something less than
ethical freedom, the freedom of the register. Freedom is the only
space where a non-Divinely originated good can come to be, precisely as a good which is the attainment of something which is not
Divine, and if this is so, then freedom becomes a kind of co-opera-
tion in creation. To call God truth and goodness is correct, but freedom is only possible if God is a *Deus Absconditus*, hidden yet
revealed by the contingent. This is the paradox of now seeing in a
glass darkly, and the hope of seeing later face-to-face. If the Divine
exists, then the partial and fragmented good and truth which we
now inhabit is to be crossed over in and into truth and goodness
itself; if the Divine does not exist, such fragments are ultimately
absurd, without other justification than that they happen to be, and
awaiting the inevitable disruption which is the fate of everything
finite. When the thin fabric of such meaning is inevitably torn, the
cold wind of the abyss blows through.

We close this chapter, then, by outlining the shape which transcendence now takes on. Transcendence is the power of sacrifice, where
this latter means not simply to destine for suffering but bespeaks
the transcendental relation freedom has with the good, which calls
forth and commands its loyalty and love. Transcendence towards
the good is only possible within, and as the necessary form of, transcendence towards the truth: openness to the truth is possible only
as openness to the good. Both good and truth represent a genuine
beyond for transcendence, so that it is not a mere encounter with
itself or its own contents. To be towards truth and goodness is what
it means to be beyond the confines of oneself. Transcendence is

thereby a being for good and truth indissolubly, and is only possible on the basis of truth and good as genuine beyond, towards
which it steps.

Notes to Chapter Eleven

1. This seems to be the point of Kant's distinction between actions done out
of a sense of duty and those which happen to conform to it but are done
from other motives. See H. J. Paton's translation of the *Grundlegung*, namely,
The Moral Law, (London: Unwin Hyman, 1989), pp. (non-marginal) 63-65.

2. Our understanding of conscience owes much to Newman, but we also
owe as much to the study by Patrick Bastable, *The Person of Conscience*,
Philosophical Studies Monograph, (Dublin: UCD, 1986).

3. *Paradise Lost*, Book IV, line 110.

4. The perhaps surprising origin of this sentiment is Oliver Cromwell.

5. *Paradise Lost*, Book IV, lines 75 - 78. My emphasis.

6. *Murder in the Cathedral*, Part 1; *The Complete Poems and Plays of T.S. Eliot*,
(London: Faber and Faber, 1969), p. 258.

7. This is essentially part of the universality disclosed in the categorical
imperative, which does not simply secure my adherence to the universal
but that of all rational beings as rational, or merely guarantee the coherence
of my behaviour alone.

8. See our treatment of proper proportionality in chapter 3 above.

9. This position is very clearly and ably defended in T. Iglesias, *IVF and
Justice*, (London: The Linacre Centre, 1990), chapter 4. See also her article
'Social and Ethical Aspects of IVF', subsection 1, which examines the principle 'no human being is property'. This article is reprinted in *Conceived in
vitro, A Question for Natural Justice*, (Dublin: UCD, 1986).

10. 'Marcus Cato', in Plutarch's *Lives*, vol. II, Loeb edition, translated by
Bernadotte Perrin, beginning of chapter V.

CHAPTER TWELVE

Beauty

12, 1 Introduction

We come now in the final chapter of our study to consider the last
transcendental, namely beauty. Once again, the internal relations of
the transcendentals act as guide for our thought. Beauty stands
between manifestation and good, and participates in both, precisely
as manifest good. That which is manifestly good is love-ly, worthy
of love, and this is the foundation of the beautiful. There are two
places in which beauty is most clearly revealed: in art and in love.
We therefore trace these manifestations of beauty and discover that
what each discloses is, precisely, transcendence as dynamism
towards the love-ly. It is as love, therefore, that transcendence has
its most essential form. It is for this reason that our treatment will
revolve around love as transcendence and love's opposite, which
we call lust. This is not meant as a puritanical denial of the sexual,
since in fact we shall suggest that lust is the very opposite of eros. In
this context we will discuss art and the artwork and shall use the
Greek tripartite distinction of love – into ἀγάπη, φιλία, and ἔρως –
as counterbalance and opposing axis. Yet these apparently diverse
wings of our amatory diptych turn out to be profoundly analogous
as incarnations of the being of the beautiful, and are made possible
and necessary as the phases of Being they are by the ontological
principle which makes beauty coterminous with Being: *ens et pul-
crum convertuntur.*

12, 2 Art and Beauty

Beauty is the neglected transcendental. Despite the content the
notion conveys, it is, and since probably the end of the Eighteenth
Century has been, less than attractive to ontologists and aestheti-
cians. One reason for this is that it can easily be confused with the
merely decorative, the pretty or the nice, qualities which, even if
they do escape the sentimental and saccharine, would seem to form
a part more of style and graciousness of living than of serious philo-

287

sophical inquiry. Critics and even artists, if and when the latter are foolish – or wise – enough to enter this arena, fight shy of it, because its use seems to deprive artistic worth of social or political relevance with the weight this latter appears to confer, and to make of art something at best unnecessary and elitist or, at worst, self-indul-gent and petty.

Art may indeed change people's beliefs regarding the world or social or political questions, but its worth is to be judged on quite another scale; if it does effect change, it does so *per accidens*, and there is no proportion between artistic worth and the ability to do so. Art is distinct from psychology, philosophy, sociology and poli-tics, nor is it, more or less disguisedly, homiletic, ideological, didac-tic, or pro- or apotreptic. It is precisely because it is none of these things that it can (though not must) occasion social awareness or even social change, but once it makes this goal an end, it thereby ceases to be art, and becomes something else: propaganda, or a kind of sociology perhaps, by and for non-sociologists. All art, as Wilde in his frivolously profound way, says, is quite useless.[1]

This is not to deny, however, that it has ontological weight: it occu-pies the same space that philosophy does, namely transcendence, with which it has an overriding – 'transcendental' – relation. Art is indeed an element of the graciousness of living, but it is more than this: it is questionable that a worthwhile life could be one from which either art or beauty were entirely absent, and no culture has ever been art-free. As such, art is not a pastime or mere entertain-ment. Art is serious, though not necessarily gloomy. Art is enlight-ening, though not necessarily informative.

12, 3 Appreciation and Lust

That is beautiful whose contemplation satisfies.[2] Beauty is value manifest as value, but to satisfy is to answer a need. The contempla-tion of beauty rests in the beautiful as end, and does not lead to any-thing beyond it: it is precisely this which is the hallmark of value as manifest. The artwork is the manifestation of the beautiful as such, though other things than artworks are beautiful and valuable, and there are many things (human beings among them) which are of greater import than the most valuable work of art, and for whose welfare, if it were necessary, even a great work of art could and should be sacrificed.

Let us explore the implications of some of these ideas. Central to an

understanding of the nature of art and the artwork is some understanding of the notion of satisfaction in the 'definition' of beauty
which we have adopted. To say that something is beautiful is to say
several things about it. It is to say that it can, and even that it
should, be appreciated, namely, as beautiful. 'Appreciated', it
would seem, is precisely the right word here, with its connotations
of respect as well as of value. To appreciate something is to recognise it as valuable and worthwhile. It is therefore to attend to it, and
heed it, to recognise it as unique and precious. Such a posture is the
very opposite of the heedless, the indifferent, the wasteful or the
destructive. It can even be to feel pain or indignation at the display
of such attitudes on the part of others. In this way, beauty is not a
'quality' among others, distinct from that which has it. Rather, it is
the shining-forth of an entity as the unique and therefore precious
entity which it is; the shining-forth of the valuable and good as
valuable and good. In this way, it is inseparable from that which the
entity is: beauty is not a something, a Platonic Idea in which things
participate, but the mode of being wherein the thing itself is
revealed as valuable. This would seem to be the meaning of the
moments of the beautiful as distinguished by Aquinas. The
shining-forth is *claritas*, the wholeness to which this is proper, as the
entity as total, is *integritas*, and internal to this is due subordination,
debita proportio, of parts to and in the whole which is the bearer of
beauty.[3]

Appreciation, therefore, is the mode of being which allows this
manifestation to take place. We use the word 'aesthetic' to describe
this appreciation, and justly, for the origin of the word is the Greek
for perception. Appreciation, as respectful, is a gazing, a hearkening, an attending. The aesthetic is analogous to, yet distinct from,
the ethical: the one is a seeing and doing of value, a seeing embodied in doing, while the other is a doing which is a seeing. In the one,
action is consequent on attending; in the other, the hearkening is
itself the action. In such attending there is repose, for its only *raison
d'être* is the attending itself, which indeed prohibits further activity.
This is the very opposite of the ethical, where the value commands
action. It is also the very opposite of that phase of ethical activity –
since wrongdoing is also ethical, however 'unethical' we may wish
to call it – which we may call the lustful. The desire for food is what
Aristotle would call ὄρεξις, right desire, if the desire is ordinate,
that is, subordinate to the total well-being, εὐδαιμονία, of the one
whose desire it is. But the appreciation of food is an enjoyment, and

therefore not aesthetic in the full sense, even though the aesthetic involves enjoyment. Food can only be fully enjoyed by eating. Thus, as an enjoyment, eating is unlike attention, for it posits the absorption of that which is enjoyed, not its preservation, its subordination to the interests of the one who enjoys, not its assertion as precious, as an end in itself, as independent of the one who appreciates. Lust is the reduction of that which is an end in itself to something which is valuable only insofar as it pleases or fulfils, with the consequent and unavoidable subordination of the thing thus enjoyed or used to the user. Lust, therefore, is not essentially something sexual, though sexuality can, regrettably, be lustful.

The essence of this mode of being is subtly disclosed by Newman in *The Dream of Gerontius*, where the demons, who are discarnate and thus beyond sexuality, are made to call themselves

> ... the great spirits,
> The powers blest,
> The lords by right,
> The primal owners,
> Of the proud dwelling
> And realm of light ...[4]

Great spirits, who proclaim themselves

> Dispossessed,
> Aside thrust,
> Chucked down,
> By the sheer might
> Of a despot's will,
> Of a tyrant's frown ...

Who is a tyrant precisely because, prefiguring a Nietzschean or even a Hitlerian rhetoric,

> The mind bold
> And independent,
> The purpose free,
> So we are told,
> Must not think
> To have the ascendant.[5]

Primal ownership, possession (and, by implication, dispossession by a jealous and vengeful tyrant), dominance, all belong to these lords-by-right precisely because of their independent mind and free purpose, which they see, in self-congratulation and -pity, as their unyielding, martyred, and thus even more ennobled, grandeur – feelings beautifully captured in Elgar's music. But we are to understand that the real order is precisely the opposite of this demonic ideology; the self-aggrandisment is not by right or nature but the willed purpose of their claim to ownership: they do not have a right to own because of their superiority, as they tell themselves, but want to prove and attain superiority by usurping ownership. Like any tyrant, they inflate themselves – or perhaps better, their selves – by subordinating, and ultimately by devouring and absorbing, others, and justify this by the lie of innate superiority. As it were: 'I must really be great if I can behave like this!'

This, then, is the ontological structure of lust: grandiosity expressed and 'vindicated' by dominance. Lust is not primarily the will to pleasure, but the will to power, a power which is expressed in appropriation (that's mine!) and the consequent 'entitlement' to exploit and enjoy heedlessly, and without respect for what is enjoyed. A necessary feature of the will to power is subordination of independence, the devaluation of the independently valuable, expressed precisely as exploitation and heedless enjoyment. Such devaluation can only be experienced as suffering in victims capable of suffering, and therefore has an intrinsic, causal orientation towards suffering, to the extent that if it fails to produce it, this is mere happy accident.

Contrary to popular, if somewhat dated, imagery, lust is not hot but cold, for it is the opposite of compassion, as the devaluation of the valuable. Don Giovanni is lustful not because he always wants a woman, but because a woman is precisely what he never wants; all he really wants is yet another name for Leporello to add to the Catalogue, to snatch up another glorious victory which confirms him as the Greatest Lover in the Whole World: 'Conquérir est notre destin; il faut le suivre.' [6] He is addicted, not to sex as such, but to the image of himself which he can craft, using sex as his raw material. He takes, by deception or violence, but never receives, and seems incapable of giving. His sexuality is one which is invaded by lust to the extent that it has long ago ceased to be genuinely sexual in any but the most mechanical sense. Warmth, joy, togetherness, or any real appreciation of the feminine, are quite foreign to his character. Women for him are not an end but an indispensable (perhaps regrettably so) means to the true end; life, we almost hear him cry, would be so much easier if only women weren't human! We find this theme of dehumanisation and the coeval desexualisation of sexuality also in Fellini's film *Casanova*, [7] where the protagonist's own sexuality is figured by a mechanical phallic bird (whose grotesque twitterings and clackings are well captured in Nino Rota's accompanying music) and whose ideal and best remembered mistress turns out to be a life-sized clockwork doll.

12, 4 Will to Power and the Idolatry of Self

The will to power is grandiosity, the idolatry of self, as individual or as group to which I am loyal. Its fundamental dishonesty consists in its being grandiose: this is to say that it is never the rightful taking of power by one entitled to it, but the more or less deliberate concealment of something, by and from oneself. This 'by' has two meanings, signifying both agent and instrument: the concealment is brought about 'by' me, as agent, but further, that which is concealed is concealed 'by' the idol I make of myself. I elaborate a grandiose fiction of myself or my group which is meant to conceal an unpalatable truth about them; what this truth is is detectable from the nature of the fiction tailor-made to conceal it. The mouse-like Raskolnikov commits murder to become Napoleon. More subtly perhaps, the truly unlovely Marquise de Merteuil in Choderlos de Laclos' novel[8] becomes a skilful puppeteer, expertly manipulating and controlling the lives of those around her – in the case of Valmont without his realising it until too late – ultimately out of a sense of resentment regarding the inferior position her society places her in as a woman.

These are masterfully drawn portraits from literature, and we could multiply examples from literature and from life. But common to all is the idea that grandiosity is meant to compensate for weakness. The will to power can only originate in the absence of power. The grandiose inflation of the self is unnecessary in an unthreatened self, and that which makes such threat possible is the experience of vulnerability. Grandiosity is lying to oneself about one's own vulnerability, covering over one's weakness by means of a fictive strength, asserting one's self in the face of, and at the expense of, the truth of finitude. No one can truly deny the fact of death, but it is possible to postpone fear of it by fantasy. It is to fantasy, the day-dream of an air-built castle of one's own existence, that being libidinous is the addiction.

Fantasy is the blockage of transcendence, since in fantasy one encounters not Being, nor even a distortion of Being, by a meontic veil of Being. There is an analogy between aesthetic and moral life in that both require the overcoming of fantasy. I can only relate rightly to others and to myself if I abandon fantasies about myself and them, and the relative values of myself and them. The virtuous person is never a Walter Mitty. Art is the realm of imagination, not of fantasy, because imagination is a play of genuine possibilities. The work of art has the power to purify perception because as the manifestation of beauty it is the focus of a self-forgetful gaze or attention, and it can be such, in turn, only because it is gratuitous, because it is not the gratification of a specific need. The effective difference between art and pornography consists in the fact that the one takes us outside ourselves and our preoccupations in the direction of value made manifest, while the other tends to imprison us there. Something that is less than art will not allow itself to be contemplated.

The contemplation of the artwork takes us beyond ourselves, outside the circle of our own needs, lets us forget for a while what obsesses us, and perhaps even allows us to see new possibilities of our situation, or of standing to what obsesses us. Thus the analogy between art and the moral life is, in strict terms, between the ability to perceive beauty and the ability to be compassionate, precisely because compassion is escape from self-obsession, and the positing of the other, particularly the suffering other, as value, as end.

12, 5 The Ontology of the Artwork

But what exactly is a work of art? In answering this, it is necessary to keep all art-forms on the same level: our remarks, therefore, must apply to all forms equally, but without the superficiality which such extreme generality often incurs. It is undeniable, however, that there are certain elements which form the milieu of artworks. Music is not just sound, but sound-figure-in-time, namely rhythm, and this is the essence, the *conditio sine qua non*, of music. Painting and sculpture are figure-in-space, whether the figure is tactile or chromatic, and there can be no atemporal space. Drama is story and history, as are all tales, with an inexorable before and after, and like music depend on time. This is so whether we consider plot or character to be primary, because character is never simultaneously present but deploys itself in action. A tale which describes character as a *fait accompli*, or atemporally, is really a treatise in psychology. Story is a structure which unfolds itself in time. Dance is movement-figure in time. Poetry, originally always a 'partner' of music, is, as is dance, as dependent on rhythm as song proper is, and to separate the word from its sensual embodiment is to destroy it as poetry, for even still, even at its most 'abstract', poetry is to be heard, a cud to be ruminated, even in isolation. But poetry is language singing, and consists of wholes of meaning, though this meaning is always to-be-uttered word-figure in time. Without these salient features the artwork in its several kinds would be unthinkable. But, if this is so, then a 'material' definition – of art in terms of its stuff – is figure-in-time.

To speak of a figure-in-time is to speak of no accidental relation, but a necessary mutual involvedness. This might be better expressed by replacing the 'in' with 'of'. There can be no figure without time, whether the figure is inherently temporal, as in music, or more obviously spatial, as in painting or sculpture. Thus all arts are in some sense musical, for the characterisation of music we have given discloses it as most essentially figure-in-time, though not all figures are sound-figures. The word 'figure' can only be used analogically, in this way. But the rhythm of music is not the pulse of a clock. The time is the artwork's time, not the world's time. This is even more essential to the artwork than any space it may take up. All artworks, of whatever kind, occupy time in this way, though not necessarily space. To frame a painting is not primarily a cosmetic or protective device, but a recognition of a more profound framing, a separation – which is not a genuine separation – intrinsic to the artwork.

This 'time' occurs in the world's time, but separates itself from that time as being given over to the figure. This time of the artwork exists actually in our perception of it, a perception filled with the figure which fills the time, and makes it its own, stealing it from the world, in which the artwork as thing or event, lives, in a kind of discontinuous continuity with all else. The figure is what presents itself as filling the artwork's time, which is not save as so filled. It is this time which is articulated in figure, which, in turn, therefore claims the time and sets the work apart from the continuity of experience, stealing a time, not as 'before this' and 'after that', but as discontinuous with all else.

To experience an artwork is to be in time and, for a while, not of it. This itself is paradoxical, and the essence of art is just this paradox of 'atemporalised' time. A great painter once remarked that the creation of a work of art demands as much guile as the committing of a crime. If this is so, then the crime is always a species of confidence trick, of fraud. Art is benevolent pretence.

The value of art consists in its ability to draw us in, to steal a piece of time. Art is only valuable insofar as it works, and works only insofar as it is valuable. Thus its value and its working are identical. This is why 'art' which sends us beyond itself is worthless as art. An artwork is not an available surrogate for an absent reality. For art to work, the work itself must be irreplaceable – not the same as being unrepeatable, for one can hear the same symphony, read the same novel, again and again – by anything else. One can want to look at another picture, but looking at this picture must not of itself make me want something other than to look at this picture. The picture must be able to flow in such a way that it makes me want to follow it. It must be able so to change that its changes make me want to see how they change, and into what they change, and each change must come as fulfilment, as well as promise. This is what beauty is, and what the artwork as such manifests. Beauty is self-disclosure which draws us into itself, not by force, but by making us want to enter it, and be drawn in. Beauty is welcome, is greeting. The essence of the beautiful is invitation.

12, 6 Beauty and the Real

Human beauty, as opposed to that of the artwork, is richer, for it is revealed in its fullness only in dialogue, which in turn bespeaks equality and mutuality of partners. This is the true meaning of I and thou. The dialogue need not be in actual words, but it occurs when each knows the other, but in lived, rather than in what it would be a caricature to call 'theoretical' (I - it) knowledge. What reveals beauty is the dialogue we call love, and in which a mutual self-disclosure, which is at once invitation and acceptance, occurs. The invitation, though it may appear to take an outward-directed form, is always inwards, towards oneself. The acceptance is always of this invitation. Knowledge here is the coming together of giving and receiving, rather than of mere knowing and known, though like knowing and known, they are inseparable. The open nature of this dialogue consists in that each antiphon of such a dialogue is promise which is fulfilment, and fulfilment which is yet promise.

Wilde's parable of the nature of beauty, which was his only novel, *Dorian Gray*, is the story of one who is overthrown by his own beauty. Dorian is at once an ageless beauty and a permanently and progressively decaying ugliness. He is the tension between these two opposites. Trapped at the peak of an unwonted physical perfection, he is unable to age and thereby unable to mark his own life with the stamp of his integral identity which we call maturity. He is only ever in love, like Narcissus, with his own reflection, which he is cursed to become, while his image takes on the role that should be played by the person he really is. It is precisely this exchange which makes him incapable of love and compassion, for he is the adored narcissistic image, which, realised and externalised, is object of adoration. His beauty becomes a trap, a promise which as promise draws in, but without hope of any fulfilment, any possibility of gift. But receiving without giving is mere taking, stealing, of which he is his own first victim, since that to which he, like all who meet him, cannot but sacrifice, is his own reflection, which he himself is. The tragedy and horror of Dorian is not that he is beautiful, or even that his is a beauty so perfect as to be inhuman and monstrous, but that he is not, and is incapable of becoming, beautiful, and it is this contradiction which eventually destroys him. The story thereby subverts the very notion of beauty which it seems to posit, a purely 'aesthetic' notion of beauty, a beauty which merely is, rather than lived, a beauty which is to be grasped entirely in being gazed at, for it needs no self-disclosure other than its very visibility, to reveal it.

If this 'radiant' notion of beauty is thereby subverted, what, within or outside Wilde's parable, can replace it? After all, it is precisely this notion of beauty as (sometimes harmful) radiance which dominates in the West, with, at least until recently, hardly any attempt being made to dislodge it – Shakespeare's sonnet 'My Mistress Eyes Are Nothing Like the Sun'[9] is, however playful and brief, just such a setting in question. The answer is revealed in an unworking of the exchange which is the basis of Wilde's parable. Precisely what Dorian becomes is the narcissistic trap-image proper to extreme immaturity or certain forms of delusion, magically made visible to all beholders. His portrait is the hidden essence of what he really is or was, doomed to corruption because of the fly-trap he has now become. The opposite and negation of all this is what is revealed by the suggested reversal. The opposite of the destructive image tied to the corrupted self is the wholesome self, expressed in and through a nurturing, in the sense of sustaining, presence. This makes of beauty an effectively sustaining presence, a notion which nicely dovetails with that of value as manifest: the value which is as manifest is sustaining presence.

12, 7 Beauty as Manifest Sustaining Presence : *ens et pulcrum convertuntur*

Nurture and sustenance are therefore the leading qualities of the manifest value which is beauty. To experience what is beautiful is to be nurtured and sustained, and conversely. More precisely, beauty is the disclosure of the sustaining and nutritive in and as effective presence. To contemplate something which pleases is only one form the beautiful can take, therefore, and is not necessarily paradigmatic for it. Opposed to the stasis of mere gazing is the dynamism of ongoing receptivity, to and of the effective presence which is disclosed as sustaining and therefore as valuable. Contemplation is never mere gazing, but active attention, actualised receptivity, outbound exploration. Clearly this structure is an analogical one, and can be applied beyond the sphere of art, to describe the mutual nurturing of a loving relationship, or the relation between Divinity and creatures; it is in this sense analogical and applicable across various categorial frontiers.

It is interesting to note that the nurturing, the sustaining, thus the fecund and prolific, is what the Greeks saw as the essence of τὸ θῆλυ, the feminine. The adjective θῆλυς had these resonances when applied to females, but when applied to males was an insult, directed at men but thereby indirectly insulting women, meaning, more or less, useless, soft and 'unmanly'. Plato, however, in the *Symposium*, uses a term, coordinate with prolific and fecund, of men which is far from insulting either to men or women, and indeed, is meant to express the essence of the intellectual and spiritual life.[10] It may also be worth noting that Wilde's having made Dorian a male may be a vehicle for more than the author's own preferences. Dorian's very maleness may represent his unfittedness for the fecundity of sustainment. The fecundity inherent in this notion of beauty bespeaks both the plurality of modes and manners in which the effective presence finds realisation, and also the range of many individuals and circumstances to and in which this occurs. Fecundity involves a bringing to birth. The German word *gebürfähig*, 'capable of bearing offspring', captures the idea well. The 'offspring' of the work of art is the gratuitous and free offering of an extended meaning-horizon to the existing one occupied by those who participate in it, and sustains them by so doing. This, indeed, is the effective presence characteristic of the artwork.

It is precisely the gratuitous nature of the artwork which defines its effective and sustaining presence. All art is indeed quite useless. It is not good for this or that, answers no specific physiological or practical need, yet a life without it is impoverished. How are such apparent inconsistencies to be reconciled? The answer would seem to lie in what we may call the iconic nature of the artwork.

12, 8 The Icon

In orthodox theology, as we saw, the icon is more than a mere representation of a sacred person or event, as are the images of the West. For the orthodox, the sacred is rendered effectively present in and through the icon; the icon is a window, not merely through which we look at the sacred, but through which the sacred reaches us. The artwork as icon shares or imitates some of these characteristics. Though the word 'icon' refers to painting in a very definite form and style, every artwork, of all forms and varieties, is iconic in our meaning of the term. The essence of the icon is what we might call its dimensionality: it mediates a depth which is discontinuous with the everyday, and which transcends the everyday in the direction of the eternal and foundational. In short, it adds to 'what is' or what just happens to be, a depth which is not its own. To understand this depth, in its discontinuity and independence, is to grasp at once the iconic nature of art, that is, the manifest value which the artwork can mediate as, and only as, icon, the effective and sustaining presence which is the essence of the artwork.

A clue to the nature of this depth is gained in the consideration that it is independent of any concrete 'content' a work may have. It is not because this play or novel is 'about' this or that that it has depth; this piece of music does not have depth as a mere function of some melodic, harmonic or rhythmical feature; this picture as artwork has depth even though it may be part of its function to proclaim itself a flat piece of coloured material and not an illusory 'window'. Depth belongs to the artwork as art-work, for its function is to mediate depth, and nothing to which depth does not belong can be considered an artwork. Thus, depth is the defining, as identically formal and functional, property of the artwork as such.

But, at the same time, the artwork manifests. It can only function as presenting itself to someone: music and drama only exist as artworks in performance, stories in being told, visual and tactile works in being looked at or touched, and although there is in each a 'text', varying systematically in kind and with context, this text stands to performance as *langue* does to *parole*, where the word 'performance' bespeaks the encounter of and with the text. The transition from the one to the other depends upon the presence of a *réalisateur* of the text, who is always, ultimately, the someone who encounters the text, and who is the necessary condition for there being a performance, as such, at all. Although songs require singers and plays actors, while paintings and novels seem to need only their authors, the *réalisateur* is there in all as the end and location of the performance, as the one who ultimately encounters the artwork, the 'someone' for whom the artwork as artwork manifests itself, the one who actively attends, interprets, listens, sees.

Such a *réalisateur* is always someone in a particular situation, engaged in this or that involvement or range of involvements with these actual others. Art, as iconic and discontinuous, manifests possibilities of hearing, seeing, feeling and being which are not those of his or her actual situation. Yet, such manifestation is not merely pastime, opiate, or escape. Although I may not be analysing my situation when I encounter the performance which is art, this situation is not merely concealed, to be replaced by mere fantasy. Art is the free and unconstrained presentation afresh of the possibilities of being, of feeling, as concretely incarnate in what is heard, seen and touched, and that not as analysis but as sensuous whole. Every artwork embodies and discloses a possibility or possibilities of what it is to be. But meaning is the disclosure of the possibilities of Being. Thus art as iconic is the manifestation of meaning not simply identical to the possibilities I am concretely offered in the everyday. The artwork is as 'musical' icon, as manifestation, as sensuous incarnation in its own time, of some such meaning.

In this way, art is ontological without being ontology. Art is not primarily analysis or judgement, but presentation. Art simply says 'here it is' and leaves 'it' without comment or analysis. Ontology can be the raw material of poetry as it was for, say, Dante, but art as art is epiphanic, never abstract or analytical, because the icon as icon is not the representation as such of what actually is, or of the logic whereby what is can be. The icon as icon is an 'entity', with an 'identity', which is, according to this logic, as are other entities. It nevertheless manifests something of these others, without 'theorising' about them or making their 'description' as such its purpose. Art, as concrete presentation of some possibility of being, is not psychology or sociology, though these may be used in constructing the body which is the icon. But art is ontological in that it occupies a privileged place, since the icon is not *just* another entity, but a

quasi-entity whose non-abstract being consists in the sensuous presentation of the possibilities of what it is to be.[11]

We must, however, refine this notion 'sensuous presentation of the
possibilities of what it is to be', for the interest of art – and we may
take this as both subjective and objective genitive – is not Being *tout
court*, but Being as revealed to transcendence. As we have seen,
there is a necessary relation between Being as true and as good, for
Being is actualised as true and as good only in and for transcendence. It is this dynamic vector of Being-for-transcendence or,
equivalently, transcendence-towards-Being, which is the existence
thematised by art. The value of art is, finally, the manifestation of
transcendence – again, subjective and objective genitive. It is in art
that we encounter the concrete embodiment of transcendence, discontinuous with, as distinct from, my actual possibilities, yet continuous with my possibilities as possibilities of transcendence, that
is, as (musical) icon. In sum, art is the revelation of revelation, by
way of one or more of revelation's necessary elements. The truth of
art is the art of truth. Drama presents what it is to be free, and to be
faced with choice, and this is what constitutes the particular and
concrete musical icon of the drama. Painting presents what it is to
reveal, and revelation is what constitutes the particular and concrete musical icon of painting. Temporality as such founds music
and dance. Story is temporality and choice. And so on. All the arts,
however, emerge as it were fanwise from the one origin, each
according to its kind, and points to and discloses that one origin,
namely 'transcendence-towards-Being: Being-for-transcendence'; it
is the coordinate movement, the rhythm, of these coeval moments
which makes the icon a musical icon.

Art is the play of beauty in finitude. In this way, the neglected transcendental, beauty, emerges as the foundational transcendental, for
its being is the very analogy, the icon, of that transcendence wherein
and whereby truth and goodness alone are finitely revealed. The
ontological structure of beauty is the ontological structure of
truth-and-goodness, of the revelation of Being as at once true and
good. Once the artwork is seen in this originative relation, it
becomes necessary and possible to see it as analogy and icon of the
Divine and the Divine's creation, which is the offering of finite
goodness and truth to transcendence and of infinite goodness and
truth for transcendence.

12, 9 The Three Kinds of Love

If we take the relation between transcendence and the beautiful as the very essence of what transcendence is, then we are afforded another name for transcendence, or at least for transcendence in this, its most proper and excellent state: this name is love. Admittedly, this is a somewhat overworked word, and, like coins too long in circulation, it has, perhaps, lost some of its lustre. Its charms and miseries are blared at us in pop-songs, and are the subject of much, some less than first rate, versification. It is cliché, and the stuff of the agony aunt's column. It is everywhere sentimentalised and trivialised, yet it remains the preoccupation of every human being, at least at some time: all human life could be seen as an attempt to find it, and candidates for it include not only human beings but even abstractions.

Let us move away from these usages and overusages, and try to see it with new eyes. The essence of love is the 'I - thou', a relation which bespeaks reciprocity, for I can only address as 'thou' someone who is essentially open to me, both as who they are and as freely self-disclosing, and this, in turn, can only be the case if I am 'thou' to them. The relation to the art-work is only 'I - thou' by analogy, for the artwork's ability to respond to our attention is a function of our ability to attend in a selective fashion, in the context which predisposes us to take certain lines in such selection. Thus, love is essentially reciprocal, and is intelligible as unrequited only in terms of an absent reciprocity.

The reciprocity which is love is caught well by Augustine, the Doctor of Love, who offers us an emblematic statement for our understanding of it: *cognoscam te, cognitor meus, cognoscam sicut et cognitus sum.*[12] This profoundly musical and poetic statement is paradigmatic in many ways. It states the kind of reciprocity which belongs to love in the full sense: to know as one is known. It states it as something yet to be, as yet imperfect, yet as willing the perfect: *cognoscam*, not *cognosco* or *cognovi*. It states it as an address, as integral within an existing 'I - thou' relation, as expressing it, so that this expression is a part of the relation, as invitation, as celebration, and as desire. It states it at the highest pitch, since the One addressed is God. To know that God exists is to know that love is the structure of ultimate reality and the ultimate structure of reality. Reality is relational and relational as love. Finally, it implies a nobility of knowledge, a fullness which reintegrates knowledge into love as the lat-

ter's essential mode, thereby making knowledge affective and evaluative: a transcendence towards beauty which discloses coevally
the mutual embrace of truth and goodness.

Traditionally, love is seen as incarnated in three different ways:
Greek distinguishes between ἀγάπη, φιλία, and ἔρως. We shall not
here attempt any historico-critical analysis of these three, but shall
invoke their help in our brief elucidation of love. These three loves
differ both in character and in extent, but there is a connection
between them. *Agape*, the widest, contains the others and is presupposed by them; though different in quality from eros, *philia* is wider
than it, which makes of eros the most exclusive and particular. That
this is so may strike us as strange, for it makes nonsense of that saying, attributed to Louis XVI, which might count as the emblem and
charter of the libertine: 'Any woman will do, any woman at all; just
give her a bath and send her to the dentist'. As we have pointed out
above, any 'love' which is indifferent to its object save as necessary
equipment, or, equivalently, which makes its objects interchangeable, is not love. Thus any reduction of eros to such an abstraction
deprives it of its character as love. An element which is removed
from eros in such abstraction is *philia*, friendship, and if eros is to
keep its erotic character, it must be a special form of friendship,
which itself is particularised and defined *agape*. Friendship, of
course, need not be erotic, but the number of friends one has is comparatively small, and friends are valued for who they are, and so
are not interchangeable. With the removal of reference to the particular, friendship disappears altogether, though eros thereby
becomes a caricature of itself, one which is, unfortunately, all too
familiar.

Agape is, then, the love of widest range, and takes in all beings. It is
the respect due to things as good, and so is identical with transcendence as transcendence towards good, namely, as coterminous with
all that is insofar as it is. At the heart of it is truth also, for it relies on
the disclosure of what is in the full sense, that is, as including the
good and as good, and therefore beautiful. (We might parenthetic-
ally recall here the root of the word 'respect' in the metaphor of seeing.) When it has finite being as its target, it cannot be other than as
benevolence. Such benevolence falls together with the knowing and
seeing which is such a feature of Augustine's saying of the essence
of love; precisely as love, as benevolence, *agape* is a seeing and
respect of the value of what is seen: benevolence takes the form of a
reluctance to do harm or cause suffering, and a positive willingness

to repair harm and remove suffering. To be benevolent is to act for the good of someone or something. From this angle, love always posits the continued existence and independence of what is loved as valuable; love wills the other's good.

In sum, the performance of value which the good enjoins takes the form of this respectful benevolence which is *agape*. *Agape* is nuanced in accordance with the value proportionate to each thing, and is therefore never disproportionate or inappropriate, though of the three it has greatest tolerance of interchangeability in respect of its object. It tends to become different in different contexts, therefore, so that it is one analogically. Benevolence to human communities, or to persons interchangeable as persons, is expressed as justice, indifferent love of particular people as courtesy if they need no help, as kindness if they do. There is really no word for the form of *agape* which honours the value of the non-human, the animal or other such entities found in the world, though perhaps gentleness, humanity or forbearance might qualify. *Agape* cannot, of course, take the form of benevolence when it comes to Divinity, but it becomes something very close to eros, which is individual love, love of one for one, or, as Plotinus might have put it, of the alone for the alone. We find such erotic particularity clearly in the saying of Augustine, for the language of eros can express the love of God. It is no accident that some of the greatest love-poetry was written as expression of the love of God, or lends itself to be interpreted as such, as, for example, the poetry of St. John of the Cross[13] or *The Song of Songs*.

It might seem that this treatment of *agape* is a little too gentlemanly. Where is the heroic self-sacrifice, the redemptive love which is the *agape* of the Gospels? Our answer is the perhaps somewhat lame one that, although such heroic and redemptive love is *agape*, it is not immediately what philosophy can treat; although *agape* is most itself in redemption, and although this is therefore not excluded from the conception we have formed of it, it also has an ordinary unheroic dimension, quotidian and workaday. More profoundly, perhaps, one might say that God's love for us is as erotic as our love for God may seem, precisely as creative and redemptive, and therefore wholly individualised and particular.

In what sense is *agape* reciprocal? It is reciprocal in the human community in that to be just, kind, and courteous is obligatory on all people as people of good will, and without these no human or humane society is possible. It is hard to see how the *agape* which targets the non-human world is reciprocal, yet it is in that the love of beauty for its own sake is a kind of self-giving of the world as beautiful. Moreover, it may also be reflexive, and this in two ways. To respect the beautiful is itself good, and whoever does so is good, while all those who fail to do so damage themselves precisely as hampering their own transcendental capacity for beauty, which is equally goodness and truth. Nevertheless, *agape* is peculiar in that it expects no return; there is more of mutuality in *philia* and eros, both of which therefore cannot but be as 'I - thou' relations, while *agape* towards non-personal entities, in a quasi-'I - thou' relation, is possible. This expecting no return, characteristic of *agape*, is most explicit in that love which may not be *agape* as such at all, but which certainly is most properly 'for' the well-being of the loved person, and which posits that person as being and becoming ever more independent and separate: this, of course, is parental love, which loves without hope of return, or at least of return of the same kind of love. Yet all love, as positing its objects as to be loved for themselves, and thus as valuable in themselves, is in some manner 'parental'.

An obvious question to ask at this point would be, what is the relation between *agape* and those structures which we have discerned in our treatment of the good, such as good will, and the like? In treating *agape*, are we merely covering the same ground again? The answer to this latter question is 'no'. The structures which we have delineated at earlier points in our study were presented only partially. Although *agape* is clearly what was meant when we dealt with them, it is only in dealing with it as a distinct and special topic that its coordinate parts, the other forms of love, are explicitly revealed. The same goes *mutatis mutandis* for *philia* and eros. Both eros and *philia* are forms of 'I - thou' relation, and we frequently refer to this kind of relation in the course of our study, but, the internal connectedness of each to the other two is revealed only at this point in our analysis. All three are forms of *love*, the shape which transcendence takes in relation to beauty, which is yet more defined, as *philia* and eros, according as beauty is itself narrowed down to how persons are disclosed. All of this reinforces the analogical nature of talk in relation to the transcendentals: the diverse forms taken by transcendence are not different 'things', but analogous proportions and relations, precisely because, and insofar as, there are not as many 'Beings', as unity, goodness, and the rest, but merely Being, as one, as good, and the like.

Philia is friendship, and although friendship is particular, it is not exclusive. It is however intrinsically non-total, for it positively ignores certain aspects of the friend, namely the sexual. It is indifferent to friendship as such what sex or gender my friend has, but the quality of my friendship is defined by our being together, by who we are, together. Aristotle famously distinguished friendship into three kinds: of pleasure, of utility, of virtue.[14] To the modern reader, perhaps, the first two appear intelligible, while the third may be exalted but looks rather dull. We chose our friends because we like them, and like them for who (rather than what) they are; we continue to be friends with them also because we know them to be good friends.

A friend, as Aristotle has it, is another self, and friends have everything in common. We are drawn to people in the first place because we have something in common with them, be this attitude, quality or interest, and this is something about them we enjoy. But our enjoyment must be of the person as sharing this something, the gratification must be in being with him or her as such, otherwise, if the person is extrinsic to the interest, we are dealing with some alliance other than friendship. A friendship of utility is really a business arrangement, not a friendship, however 'friendly' such a partnership may be. Likewise, every friendship is one based on pleasure as liking: joy in someone's company. Friends like to be together, to talk together, to do things together, to enjoy things together, to go places together, to spend time together.

Someone who harms me in any way, whatever else he may be, is not my friend, and is not made so even by long association. Likewise, he or she is not my friend if they fail to be reliable, if, as we say graphically in contemporary talk, they're not there for me. Being there means being present for me. The presence in question means, therefore, being present *for* me. This most basically means accepting my disclosure of myself. Though I disclose myself in many ways, when I choose to reveal myself, I do so by talking. A friend is one who listens. What distinguishes *philia* from *agape* is intimacy. Friendship is intimate, and intimacy bespeaks selective disclosure: I know I can safely reveal to my friend things that I would not wish to be commonly known, and he or she will allow this disclosure, which means, in turn, that they will not condemn me, unless there is some compelling reason to do so. My friend tolerates me – sometimes with wry amusement – lets me be the person I am, and likes me for it. Such tolerance is also never manipulative, for manipulation is the failure to let be, the failure to tolerate. To manipulate is a libidinous activity, for it attempts to place someone under its hegemony. To tolerate in this way is not to adopt an unconcerned *laissez-faire* attitude or to be apathetic; it is to celebrate the other as other, to appreciate independent difference as well as similarity.

Condemnation is close to abandonment, and there can be no friendship insofar as I cannot be confident it will go on. A friendship which I discover to be in danger of being over, is over. Moreover, this presence, though it respects confidence of disclosure, is not a mere matter of words. Listening is the paradigm of acceptance, and acceptance is activity. I must be ready to act as friend, and refrain from acting in a way inimical to our friendship. My presence for my friend must therefore be trustworthy, which is not something I merely assert or have to prove, but which I continuously show in my every act. Friendship therefore bespeaks the endurance of trustworthy presence for the friend, being reliable both as confidant and support, and it is in these that the truth of friendship chiefly consists. To qualify as my friend, then, in sum, my friend must accept me, hear me, find me likeable for myself, and must, as true friend, intend my good in action. The same must hold reciprocally of me. These elements constitute our mutual recognition of each other as valuable, for they are a recognition of someone's value as relative and absolute, respectively.

Eros is the third member of this triad. The caricature of eros occurs when the very thing proper to it, which it has above and beyond *philia*, is turned into its only constituent. But this is to deprive it of its properly amatory character, for thereby one's partner (usually, though wrongly in these circumstances called one's lover) becomes interchangeable with any other. To be erotic, therefore, eros must always also be friendship. But it is exclusive and total, exclusive because total. To love someone in this way is to love them wholly, as the person they are, as the man or woman they are, and with the totality of myself, as the person I am, as the man or woman I am. Precisely as total, eros is properly 'erotic' in the usual sense of that term, and is therefore sexual. To love Jane is to know, or to long to know, her in her totality, with and through the totality of myself. Thus, it is Jane I love, and, in that I love her, no-one else will do; she is in and as herself, utterly unique and irreplaceable, and she stands to me as the missing half of my own self, without whom I am incomplete: to love and be loved in this way involves becoming more than one is, namely, in the other person. This is caught by Plato, the erotic philosopher *par excellence*, in the myth of the divided hermaphrodite, sundered from its original wholeness, and condemned to seek its missing half.[15]

It is clear that Augustine's emblematic saying, though actually addressed to God, is erotic as total, though only metaphorically sexual. Eros, as love, cannot exclude *philia*; one can and must be both lover and friend, as we said. This means that erotic love seeks total *knowledge*, of all of my love, as all she is, with all of myself, and thus allows and seeks – yearns for – the most intimate, because in principle incommunicable, knowledge of the beloved. It is this context which transforms the sharing, the *philia*, which eros must also contain. To know erotically is to know immediately and experientially. Eros does not exclude talk, but what it seeks is a knowledge to which talk is never adequate, a knowledge which only a lover as such can have, a knowledge not to be 'passed on'. In this way, eros is the earthiest of loves, the least linguistic, yet most fully human. It is no accident that the language of beauty is erotic, because in eros the value of one alone, for one alone, is most clearly disclosed. We talk easily of beauty in eros, though not in friendship, even though the disclosure of my friend as true and good takes place there too, and this is because of the radiantly total nature the disclosure the beloved has in eros.

It is only in this context that the true meaning of sexuality is disclosed, for in eros it attains its character as knowledge and as gift. In all love, there is gift, but most clearly and poignantly, in eros. Sexual identity consists of both sexuality and gender, the former equivalent to being male or female, the latter to being masculine or feminine. Sexuality has to do with bodily functioning, gender with how one discloses oneself for others and receives such disclosure; gender is thus a fundamental form of self- and other-interpretation. The masculine is for the feminine, and the feminine for the masculine, and each is celebration of the other. Both sexuality and gender have in common that they bear an intrinsic relation to, are a dynamism towards, other persons, but they are only fully themselves in their actual connection with the unique other.

In erotic sexuality one makes gift of oneself without reserve, and in giving, receives the gift of the other, which is the other, with equal unreserve. Giving and receiving thereby become irrefrangibly one and the same, and each person is giver and gift, to such an extent that, in a sense, loving is a be-ing as giving. Sexuality thus becomes erotic transcendence, within and of oneself, and the beauty, which is the other as disclosed, becomes most clearly revealed; one loses oneself in the other, but one also finds oneself. Eros is the least disinterested love, but it is also the most respectful and appreciative of the other as total and thus as other. As such, eros is most distant from self-assertion and possessiveness, and is least tolerant of the will to power, and although none of these are compatible with any kind of love or friendship, eros repels them as positively painful and injurious. It is perhaps, a sad verification of the principle *corruptio optimi pessima* that the caricature of eros is notable for and as those very things that real eros so vehemently disowns. It is no doubt because eros is so easily killed and replaced by its caricature that the caricature goes so easily unchallenged. Perhaps it is for such reasons that Plato sees it as integral to moral formation; certainly, to be able to love one in this way is to become more appreciative of individuality in general. Plato does find eros indispensable in the soul's progress towards truth, forming, in its various grades, a ladder which ascends to the highest reality.

This, then, is the dialectic of erotic love, in which each loses and gains him or herself in the other, as remaining themselves and yet becoming one with the other. Again – and we believe that Plato would be of similar mind – it would appear that, for this reason more than any other, perhaps, religious language is close to the erotic.

These are at least three of the forms which transcendence takes as love. Each one is a way of making real transcendence as openness towards Being as beautiful, as love-ly, as worthy of love, as coevally true and good. Beauty takes in all other transcendentals, so that love, as 'for' beauty, is transcendence most perfectly and fundamentally. Love is a knowing which is never a mere 'knowing that'; it is a transitive knowing, without qualification, without conjunction; yet it is not merely transitive, but, in each case is variously reflexive and reciprocal. This is not to translate transcendence into mere knowing, but rather to understand knowing as transcendence, and as synonym for transcendence, much as loving is. Thus, a fundamental truth of onto-anthropology emerges: there is no being-in-the-world or -with-others which is not love as *agape*, *philia* or *eros*, and any attempt to delineate transcendence without love is to deprive it of its genuinely transcendental character. In particular, really to be in the world is to respect the world, to be so that one cannot but see its beauty, while really to be with others is to experience them as real others, that is, as worthy in all cases of *agape*, but in some also, of its progressively denser incarnations as friendship and erotic love. To come to know all this is to know the old world newly, and, perhaps, to exclaim with Miranda,

How beauteous mankind is!
O brave new world,
That has such people in't.

Notes to Chapter Twelve

1. The Preface to *The Picture of Dorian Gray*, in *The Complete Works of Oscar Wilde*, J. B. Foreman (ed.), (London: Collins, 1973), p. 17.

2. *Summa Theologiae*, 1, q.5, a.4 ad 1.

3. For *proportio* and *claritas*, see *Summa Theologiae*, 1, q. 39, a. 8; for *integritas* and *perfectio*, S. T. 2-2, q. 145, a. 2.

4. Newman, *The Dream of Gerontius*. (London: Burns Oates, 1951), pp. 26-27.

5. *ibid*, p. 28.

6. Choderlos de Laclos, *Les liaisons dangereuses*, Béatrice Didier (ed.), Livre de poche, 1987; Letter IV, p. 16.

7. *Casanova*, a film by Frederico Fellini, starring Donald Sutherland, Universal Pictures, 1977, CBS Fox Video.

8. See Laclos, *op. cit.*, Letter CXIII, where Mme. de Merteuil gives her 'typology' of women; the remarkable 'self-portrait', Letter LXXXI, where she recounts her history and the formation of her opinions; Letter CLII, where she gives her reasons for not remarrying; Letter CXLV, where we find her most herself, enjoying her proven superiority and the fruits of the ethic she has created for herself.

9. Sonnet 130.

10. *Symposium*, 208 - 209.

11. Iris Murdoch quotes some quite extraordinary passages from the letters of Rilke, relevant to all we have to say about art, which would more than repay study, in *Metaphysics as a Guide to Morals*, (London: Chatto and Windus, 1992), pp. 246 - 247.

12. This is the very first sentence of Book X of the *Confessions*.

13. Roy Campbell's English translations, or better, recreations, of these poems display well their erotic quality: *Poems of St. John of the Cross*, (Glasgow: Collins, 1979).

14. *Ethics*, book VIII, chapter 3. 1156a 6, and following.

15. *Symposium* 189 c, and following.

ANSCOMBE, G. E. M., and GEACH P. T., *Three Philosophers*, Oxford: Blackwell, 1961

AQUINAS, *Summa Theologiae*, 60 vols., Latin text, English translation, and critical apparatus, edited by Fathers of the English Province of the Dominicans, London: Blackfriars, Eyre and Spottiswoode, various dates

AQUINAS, *Summa Contra Gentiles*, vols., 1- 5, translated, with an introduction and notes by Anton C. Pegis, Notre Dame: University of Notre Dame Press, 1975

AQUINAS, *S. Thomae Aquinatis Questiones Disputatae et Questiones Duodecim Quodlibetales*, 5 vols., Taurini, Romae: Marietti, 1942

AQUINAS, *Le 'De Ente et Essentia' de S. Thomas d'Aquin*, M.-D. Roland-Gosslin, (ed.), Bibliotheque Thomiste VIII, Paris: Vrin, 1948

AQUINAS, *Selected Philosophical Writings*, selected and translated by Timothy McDermott, O.U.P., The World's Classics, 1993

ARISTOTLE, *The Basic Works of Aristotle*, edited by Richard McKeon, New York: Random House, 1941

ARISTOTLE, *Metaphysics*, 2 vols., Loeb Edition, translated by Hugh Tredennick

ARISTOTLE, *Categories and De Interpretatione*, Translated with Notes and Glossary by J. L. Ackrill, O.U.P., 1963

AUBENQUE, Pierre, *Le problème de l'être chez Aristote*, Paris: Presses Universitaires de France, 1962

AUGUSTINE, *Confessions*, volume I, Introduction and Text, edited by James J. O'Donnell, Oxford, Clarendon Press, 1992

AUGUSTINE, *An Augustine Synthesis*, arranged by Erich Przywara, London: Sheed and Ward, 1936

BASTABLE, Patrick K., *Logic: Depth Grammar of Rationality*, Dublin: Gill and Macmillan, 1975

BASTABLE, Patrick K., *The Person of Conscience*, Philosophical Studies Monograph, University College, Dublin, 1986

BENSON, Hugh H., (ed.), *Essays on the Philosophy of Socrates*, O.U.P., 1992

BERGSON, Henri, *L'Évolution créatrice*, Paris: Quadrige, Presses

Universitaires de France, 1991

BLACKBURN, Simon, (ed.), *Meaning, Reference, and Necessity: New Studies in Semantics*, C.U.P., 1975

BOBIK, Joseph, 'Matter and Individuation', in McMullin, 1965, below

BOETHIUS, *Tractates* and *The Consolation of Philosophy*, Loeb Edition, translated by Stewart, Rand, and Tester

BRODY, Baruch A., *Identity and Essence*, Princeton: Princeton University Press, 1980

BUBER, Martin, *I and Thou*, translated by R. G. Smith, Edinburgh: T & T Clark, 1994

BURRELL, David B., *Knowing the Unknowable God, Ibn-Sina, Maimonides, Aquinas*, Notre Dame: University of Notre Dame Press, 1986

BURRELL, David B., *Freedom and Creation in Three Traditions*, Notre Dame: University of Notre Dame Press, 1993

CAJETAN, Thomas De Vio, Cardinal, *The Analogy of Names and the Concept of Being*, literally translated and annotated by Edward A. Bushinski, in collaboration with Henry J. Koren, second edition, Pittsburgh: Duquesne University, Duquesne Studies, Philosophical Series, 4, 1959

CHAVANNES, Henry, *The Analogy between God and the World in Saint Thomas Aquinas and Karl Barth*, translated by William Lumley, New York: Vantage Press, 1992

CORETH, Emerich, *Metaphysics*, English edition by Joseph Donceel, with a critique by Bernard Lonergan, New York: Herder and Herder, 1968

CRITTENDEN, Charles, *Unreality. The Metaphysics of Fictional Objects*, Ithaca and London: Cornell University Press, 1991

DeCORTE, Marcel, *La doctrine de l'intelligence chez Aristote*, Paris: Vrin, 1934

DENNETT, Daniel C., *Darwin's Dangerous Idea. Evolution and the Meanings of Life*, London: The Penguin Press, 1995

DENYER, Nicholas, *Language, Thought, and Falsehood in Ancient Greek Philosophy*, London and New York: Routledge, 1993

De RAEYMAEKER, Louis, *The Philosophy of Being*, translated by Edmund H. Siegelmeyer, London: Herder Book Company, 1966

ECO, Umberto, *The Aesthetics of Thomas Aquinas*, translated by Hugh Bredin, London: Radius, 1988

FABRO, Cornelio, *Paticipation et causalité selon Saint Thomas d'Aquin*, Louvain: Publications Universitaires de Louvain, Béatrice-Nauwalaerts, 1954

FOLLON, Jacques, 'Réflexions sur la théorie aristotélicienne des quatre causes', in *Révue Philosophique de Louvain*, tome 86, no. 71, Août, 1988

GADAMER, Hans-Georg, *Wahrheit und Methode*, 3. Auflage, Tübingen: Mohr, 1972

GALE, Richard M., (ed.), *The Philosophy of Time: A Collection of Essays*, New

Jersey: Humanities Press, 1978

GARFIELD, Jay L., and KITELEY, Murray, *Meaning and Truth*, New York: Paragon House, 1991

GEACH, P. T., *Logic Matters*, Oxford: Blackwell, 1981

GEIGER, L. B., *La participation dans la philosophie de S. Thomas d'Aquin*, Paris: Vrin, 1953

GILSON, Etienne, *Le thomisme, introduction à la philosophie de Saint Thomas d'Aquin*, Paris: Vrin, 1989

GILSON, Etienne, *L'Être et l'essence*, Paris: Vrin, 1972

GILSON, Etienne, *Being and Some Philosophers*, Toronto: Pontifical Institute of Mediaeval Studies, 1952

GILSON, Etienne, *History of Christian Philosophy in the Middle Ages*, London: Sheed and Ward, 1955

GRAYLING, A. C., *An Introduction to Philosophical Logic*, Brighton: Harvester Press, 1982

GRENIER, Henri, *Thomistic Philosophy*, vol. II, *Metaphysics*, translated by J. P. E. O'Hanlley, Charlottestown, Canada: St. Dunstan's University, 1948

HAMLYN, D. W., *Metaphysics*, London: Cambridge University Press, 1984

HARTSHORNE, Charles, *The Logic of Perfection*, La Salle, Ill.: Open Court, 1991

HARTSHORNE, Charles, *Anselm's Discovery*, La Salle, Ill.: Open Court, 1991

HEIDEGGER, *Kant and the Problem of Metaphysics*, translated by James S. Churchill, foreword by Thomas Langan, Bloomington: Indiana University Press, 1972

HELLER, Mark, *The Ontology of Physical Objects: Four-dimensional Hunks of Matter*, C.U.P., 1990.

HERACLITUS, *Fragments*, text, translation and commentary by T. M. Robinson, Toronto: University of Toronto press, 1987

HUME, David, *The Philosophical Works*, edited by Green, T. H., and Grose, T. H., Aalen: Scientia Verlag, 1964

JOHN OF THE CROSS, *The Poems of St. John of the Cross*, translated by Roy Campbell, Glasgow: Fount, 1979

JONES, Gregory L., and FOWL, Stephen E., *Rethinking Metaphysics*, Oxford: Blackwell, 1995.

JULIAN OF NORWICH, *Revelations of Divine Love*, translated and with an introduction by Clifton Wolters, Penguin Classics, 1966

KANT, *Immanuel Kant's Critique of Pure Reason*, edited by Norman Kemp Smith, London: Macmillan, 1973

KANT, *The Moral Law: Kant's Groundwork of the Metaphysic of Morals*, translated and analysed by H. J. Paton, London: Unwin Hyman, 1989

KANT, *Selected Pre-Critical Writings*, translated and introduced by G. B. Kerferd and D. E. Walford, Manchester: Manchester University Press, 1968

KELLY, Thomas A. F., *Language and Transcendence: A Study in the Philosophy of Martin Heidegger and Karl-Otto Apel*, Berne: Lang, 1994

KELLY, Thomas A. F., 'Ex possibili et necessario: A Re-examination of Aquinas's Third Way', *The Thomist*, (forthcoming)

KENNY, Anthony, *Aquinas: A Collection of Critical Essays*, Garden City, NY: Doubleday-Anchor Books, 1969

KENNY, Anthony, *Aquinas on Mind*, London: Routledge, 1993

KENNY, Anthony, *Frege*, Harmondsworth: Penguin, 1995

KIM, Jaegwon, and SOSA, Ernest, *A Companion to Metaphysics*, Oxford: Blackwell, 1995

KLUBERTANZ, George, *St. Thomas Aquinas on Analogy*, Chicago: Loyola University Press, 1960

KLUBERTANZ, George, *Introduction to the Philosophy of Being*, New York: Appleton-Century-Crofts, 1963

KNOWLES, David, *The Evolution of Medieval Thought*, London: Longmans, Green, 1962

KRETZMANN, Norman, and STUMP, Eleonore, (eds.), *The Cambridge Companion to Aquinas*, Cambridge University Press, 1993

KRIPKE, Saul, *Naming and Necessity*, Oxford: Blackwell, 1984

KUHN, Thomas S., *The Structure of Scientific Revolutions*, Second Edition, enlarged, Chicago: University of Chicago Press, 1970

LACEY, A. R., *Bergson, The Arguments of the Philosophers Series*, London: Routledge, 1993

LEGRAND, Joseph, *L'Univers et l'homme dans la philosophie de Saint Thomas*, 2 vols., Bruxelles and Paris: Desclée de Brouwer, 1946

LEIBNIZ, *The Monadology and Other Philosophical Writings*, translated and with an introduction and notes by Robert Latta, O.U.P., 1971

LePOIDEVIN, Robin, and MacBEATH, Murray, (eds.), *The Philosophy of Time*, Oxford Readings In Philosophy, O.U.P., 1993

LOCKE, *An Essay Concerning Human Understanding*, edited by P. H. Nidditch, O.U.P., 1975

LONERGAN, Bernard J. F., *Verbum: Word and Idea in Aquinas*, edited by David Burrell, Notre Dame: University of Notre Dame Press, 1967

LYTTKENS, Hampus, *The Analogy between God and the World*, Uppsala: Almqvist and Wiksells Boktryckeri AB, 1952

MACKEY, James P., (ed.), *An Introduction to Celtic Christianity*, Edinburgh: T & T Clark, no date

MARITAIN, Jacques, *A Preface to Metaphysics. Seven Lessons on Being*,

London: Sheed and Ward, 1948

MATES, Benson, *The Philosophy of Leibniz. Metaphysics and Language*, O.U.P., 1986

McINERNEY, Ralph, *The Logic of Analogy. An Interpretation of St. Thomas*, The Hague: Nijhoff, 1961

McINERNEY, Ralph, *Studies in Analogy*, The Hague: Nijhoff, 1968

McMULLIN, Ernan, (ed.), *The Concept of Matter in Greek and Medieval Philosophy*, Notre Dame: University of Notre Dame Press, 1965

MELLOR, D. H., *Real Time*, London: Cambridge University Press, 1985

MOORE, G. E., 'Is Existence a Predicate', in *Proceedings of the Aristotelian Society*, Supplementary Volume XV, 1936

MURDOCH, Iris, *Metaphysics as a Guide to Morals*, London: Chatto and Windus, 1992

MURDOCH, Iris, *The Sovereignty of Good*, London: Routledge and Kegan Paul, 1974

MURDOCH, Iris, *The Fire and the Sun*, O.U.P., 1977

NEWMAN, John Henry, *An Essay in Aid of a Grammar of Assent*, London: Longmans, Green, 1895

OUSPENSKY, Leonid, *Theology of the Icon*, 2 vols., translated by Anthony Gythiel, Crestwood, NY: St. Vladimir's Seminary Press, 1992

OWENS, Joseph, *The Doctrine of Being in the Aristotelian Metaphysics*, Toronto: Pontifical Institute of Mediaeval Studies, 1978

PANNENBERG, Wolfhart, *Metaphysics and the Idea of God*, Edinburgh: T & T Clark,1990

PENROSE, Roger, *The Emperor's New Mind*, O.U.P., 1989

PHILLIPS, D. Z., *Wittgenstein and Religion*, London: The Macmillan Press, 1993

PHILLIPS, R. P., *Modern Thomistic Philosophy*, 2 vols., Westminster, Maryland: Newman Press, 1962 (vol. I) and 1964 (vol. II)

PLANTINGA, Alvin, (ed.), *The Ontological Argument*, London: Macmillan, 1968

PLATO, *The Collected Dialogues*, edited by Edith Hamilton and Huntington Cairns, Princeton: Princeton University Press, 1982

POPPER, Karl R., *The Logic of Scientific Discovery*, London: Unwin Hyman, 1990.

PRIOR, A. N., *Formal Logic*, Second Edition, O.U.P., 1962

ROSS, Sir David, *Aristotle*, London: Routledge, 1995

RUSSELL, Bertrand, *Logic and Knowledge*, edited by Robert C. Marsh, London: George Allen and Unwin, 1977

RYLE, Gilbert, *The Concept of Mind*, Harmondsworth: Penguin, 1973

SAINSBURY, Mark, *Logical Forms. An Introduction to Philosophical Logic*,

Oxford: Blackwell, 1991

SMITH, Quentin, and OAKLANDER, L. Nathan, *Time, Change and Freedom, An Introduction to Metaphysics*, London: Routledge, 1995

SOSA, Ernest, and TOOLEY, Michael, (eds.), *Causation*, Oxford Readings in Philosophy, O.U.P., 1993

STEINER, George, *Real Presences*, London: Faber and Faber, 1990

STRAWSON, P. F., *An Introduction to Logical Theory*, London: Methuen, 1977

TAYLOR, A. E., *Elements of Metaphysics*, London: Methuen, 1961

VanSTEENBERGHEN, Fernand, *Ontology*, translated by Martin J. Flynn, London: Herder, 1963

VanSTEENBERGHEN, Fernand, *Epistemology*, translated by Martin J. Flynn, London: Herder, 1949

WEISEIPL, J., *Friar Thomas D'Aquino. His Life, Thought, and Works*, Washington: Catholic University of America Press, 1983

WHITE, Alan R., *Methods of Metaphysics*, London: Croom Helm, 1987

WHITE, Alan R., *Modal Thinking*, Oxford: Blackwell, 1975

WHITEHEAD, Alfred North, *Process and Reality*, Corrected Edition, London: The Free Press, 1978

WIGGINS, David, 'Pourquoi la notion de substance paraît-elle si difficile?' in *Philosophie*, no. 30, printemps, 1991

WITTGENSTEIN, *Tractatus Logico-Philosophicus*, translated by D. F. Pears and B. F. McGuinness, London: Routledge and Kegan Paul, 1981

WITTGENSTEIN, *Philosophical Investigations*, translated by G. E. M. Anscombe, Oxford: Blackwell, 1953.

ZEMAN, J. Jay, *Modal Logic. The Lewis Modal Systems*, O.U.P., 1973